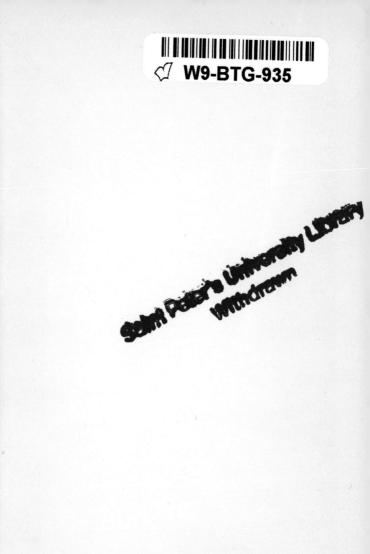

SIDONIUS

I

SUETONIUS

I

SIDONIUS

POEMS AND LETTERS

WITH AN ENGLISH TRANSLATION,
INTRODUCTION, AND NOTES BY

W. B. ANDERSON

HULME PROFESSOR OF LATIN IN THE UNIVERSITY
OF MANCHESTER

IN TWO VOLUMES

I

POEMS
LETTERS, BOOKS I–II

CAMBRIDGE, MASSACHUSETTS
HARVARD UNIVERSITY PRESS
LONDON
WILLIAM HEINEMANN LTD
MCMLXIII

First printed 1936
Reprinted 1956, 1963

Printed in Great Britain

PA
694
.7
936
.1

CONTENTS

PREFACE

THE present volume contains the first English translation of the poems of Sidonius. The task of translating the letters was originally assigned to the late Dr. E. V. Arnold. He had drafted a rough rendering, to which I have been repeatedly indebted for an apt word or phrase, but as he had not had time to consider fully the many problems presented by the Latin text, it seemed advisable to rewrite the translation. I would fain hope that its present form is such as would have met with his approval.

An attempt has been made, no doubt with indifferent success, to discover and express the whole meaning of every sentence. There is a comfortable doctrine, which has actually been propounded with reference to Sidonius, that when a writer is very hard to understand there is no need to translate him accurately. It is scarcely necessary to expose this fallacy, but one may remark that the many serious mistakes made by historians and biographers through failure to grasp the meaning of Sidonius show that no one can afford to despise conscientious verbal scholarship.

The translation, especially in the case of the poems, is accompanied by numerous explanatory notes; it would not have been intelligible without them. They have involved a good deal of pioneer work and many excursions into paths outside the

PREFACE

regular beat of a mere Latinist. I cannot expect that they will completely satisfy either the specialist or the non-specialist reader; I do, however, cherish the hope that they will clear up some obscurities and that a few of them will be of some interest to students of history and to some other scholars.

Shortly before his death Professor L. C. Purser, who had once thought of publishing a commentary on the poems of Sidonius, most kindly put at my disposal the materials which he had collected. It is a melancholy pleasure to express my deep gratitude for a thoroughly characteristic act of generosity. Dr. W. H. Semple was good enough to read the proofs of the translation and of a large part of the notes. I am indebted to him for many acute and valuable observations; my obligations to him are by no means confined to the places where I have expressly acknowledged them.

W. B. A.

INTRODUCTION

I. HISTORICAL SKETCH:

FROM A.D. 406 TO THE " FALL OF THE WESTERN EMPIRE "

THE sources available for our knowledge of the fifth century are meagre and often obscure, and the attempts of modern historians to reconstruct the facts show marked divergences. Even if the facts were certain, it would not be easy to present in short compass the history of a period so confused, so full of intrigues and struggles in so many countries.

Gaul holds a position of special prominence not only in the career of Sidonius but in the story of the decline and fall of the western Empire. It is reasonable, therefore, to start our narrative at the end of the year 406, when four German peoples [1] (Asding and Siling Vandals, Alans, and Suevians) made an incursion across the Rhine, sacking Mainz, burning Trier, and spreading their depredations far and wide. The invasion of Gaul by the usurper Constantine from Britain in 407 may have checked them for a short time, but he soon allowed them to pursue their activities without serious opposition. In 409 they crossed the Pyrenees and occupied a large part of Spain. Meanwhile the Burgundians

[1] On the geographical situation of the various German peoples see Bury, *Later Roman Empire* I., pp. 99 f.

had likewise moved across the Rhine from their territory on the upper Main, and in the end the Emperor Honorius, making a virtue of necessity, allowed them to remain in occupation of the province of Upper Germany (Germania Prima) [1] as *foederati* [2] (413).

We must now turn to the Visigoths, who were destined to play a leading part in the dissolution of the Empire. In 410 Alaric, their king, died, a few months after his capture of Rome. Athaulf, his successor, left Italy for Gaul early in the year 412, carrying off with him Placidia, sister of Honorius. After bringing about the fall of the new usurper Jovinus, who had started an insurrection in 411 and found many adherents, he made overtures to the Emperor, but as he refused to give up Placidia, nothing came of them. He then occupied Narbonne, where he married Placidia (414). Vigorous measures by the general Constantius made his situation in Gaul precarious; he therefore proceeded to Spain early in the following year, probably intending to found a Visigothic kingdom in the province of Tarraconensis, which had not been occupied by the previous German invaders. He was, however, assassinated at Barcelona; seven days

---

[1] Its capital was Worms (Borbetomagus).

[2] The *foederati* were the successors of the old client-peoples who had acted as buffer-states to protect the Roman frontiers. The ruler of a " federate " people received an annual subsidy, which in theory represented the pay of the soldiers at his disposal. When necessity compelled the Romans to admit foreign peoples into Roman territory with the status of *foederati*, the Roman land-owners had to surrender a certain proportion (generally one third) of their property to the new settlers.

INTRODUCTION

later the same fate befel his successor, and Wallia became king. Debarred from food-supplies by the Romans and foiled in an attempt to cross to Africa, Wallia came to terms, agreeing, in return for large supplies of corn, to restore Placidia and to make war upon the German invaders of Spain (416). On the first day of the following year Constantius married Placidia.

Wallia vigorously set about his task of conquering his " barbarian " neighbours. In their alarm they sought to make terms with Rome. The Asding Vandals and the Suevians seem to have gained recognition as " federates " of the Empire, but Wallia was left to work his will with the other two peoples. In a campaign of two years (416–418) he almost wiped out the Silings, and inflicted such grievous losses on the Alans that the survivors at last sought refuge with the Asdings in Gallaecia. The Vandal king Gunderic thus became " King of the Vandals *and Alans*," and handed down the title to his successors.

Then followed a momentous event. It was decided to allow the Goths to settle in Gaul as *foederati*. The lands assigned to them were the province of Aquitanica Secunda (extending from the Loire to the Garonne) and adjacent portions of Narbonensis (including Toulouse) and of Novempopulana (west of Narbonensis). Thus began the Visigothic kingdom in Gaul. Wallia died soon after leading his people to their new abode, and Theodoric I reigned in his stead.[1] The same period saw the quelling of a

---

[1] The arrangements for the new settlers were completed under Theodoric. The Goths received remarkably favourable terms, as the Roman land-owners had to surrender two-thirds of their property to them.

serious revolution among the Aremoricans of Brittany.[1] In Spain, soon after the departure of the Goths, Gunderic, king of the Vandals and Alans, attacked and defeated the Suevians, and, although more than once defeated by Roman forces, ultimately triumphed and established himself in the southern province of Baetica, from which his successor Geiseric was soon to aim a blow at the very heart of Rome.

National feeling in Gaul, which boded ill for the future of the Empire, had been accentuated in the time of the usurpers Constantine and Jovinus, who had found many adherents in that country, and it was further heightened by the severe measures which Constantius took against the ringleaders of the insurgents. It was more than ever necessary to consolidate the loyalty of the Gallo–Romans. From this time dates the regular custom of appointing natives to the office of Praetorian Prefect of Gaul and to the other important official posts in the country. Another significant measure was the organisation in the year 418 of the Council of the Seven Provinces (*Concilium Septem Provinciarum*), in which leading men of the southern provinces met every year to discuss matters affecting the public interest and to make recommendations to the authorities. Among the provinces which sent representatives were

---

[1] The Aremorici inhabited the coast-land between the Seine and the Loire. The troubles in Britain in the later years of the Roman occupation caused many of its inhabitants to emigrate to Aremorica, which owes its modern name to them. In the fifth century *Britannus* is not infrequently used to denote a native or inhabitant of Aremorica (cf. Sidonius, *Epist.* III. 9. 2; more explicitly *Britannos supra Ligerim sitos,* I. 7. 5), and it is not always easy to determine the meaning of the word.

Aquitanica Secunda and Novempopulana;[1] thus the
Roman inhabitants of the occupied lands were
stimulated to retain their Roman feelings in their
" barbarian " environment. The council met at
Arles, which had now become the residence of the
Praetorian Prefect, after Trier had been sacked
not only by the Vandals but on two occasions by the
Ripuarian Franks from the lower Rhine. Arles
became a proud capital, and everything possible was
done to make it a centre of Roman influence.

On the 2nd of July, 419, Flavius Placidus Valen-
tinianus, the future Emperor, was born. His father,
Constantius, was made a colleague in the Empire
by Honorius on 8th February, 421, but died in the
same year. He had worked hard, and with considerable success, to maintain the cohesion of the
Empire in the West. On the 15th of August,
423, Honorius died. After two years of the usurper
John, the boy Valentinian came to the throne as
Valentinian III. For the first twelve years of his
reign his mother Placidia acted as regent. From this
time the disintegration of the Empire proceeds
apace, despite the emergence of a great military
leader in the person of Aëtius. The Goths, under
Theodoric I, had turned longing eyes on the Mediterranean shores of Narbonensis. Early in the new
reign they were hurled back by Aëtius from the walls
of Arles to their own territory, where they remained
comparatively quiet, but always a potential source
of danger, for a few years. The " barbarian "
peoples on the Rhine-frontier could not be trusted
to keep the peace for long, and the Aremorici might

---

[1] For an enumeration of the Septem Provinciae see note on
Sidonius, *Epist.* I. 3. 2.

cause trouble again. Gaul thus made constant demands upon the vigilance of Aëtius. This fact, together with the enmity of Placidia and her partiality for less able supporters, prevented him from intervening in another sphere where his tried troops and his generalship were sorely wanted.

In the year 427 Count Boniface, governor of the diocese of Africa, on being summoned home to give an account of his actions, disobeyed and was proclaimed a rebel. Unable to cope with the forces sent against him, he took the fatal step of inviting the Vandals to come to his help from Spain.[1] King Gunderic lent a willing ear to this proposal, but died before he could carry it into effect (428). His successor Geiseric was only too glad to complete the preparations. In May, A.D. 429, the combined host of Vandals and Alans crossed the Straits of Gibraltar. The Imperial government came to terms with Boniface, but this reconciliation made no difference to the greedy schemes of the Vandals. Boniface, now entrusted with the defence of Africa, was no match for the enemy, and was eventually compelled, in the spring of 430, to shut himself up in Hippo Regius, which underwent a long siege.[2] Meanwhile the Vandals made themselves masters of the valuable corn-lands of Tunisia. In this critical situation Placidia appealed to the eastern Emperor, Theodosius II, for help. His trusted general, Aspar, entered Africa with a combined force drawn from east and west, which perhaps succeeded in raising the siege of Hippo, but soon sustained a severe

[1] For a different account see *Cambridge Medieval History*, I., p. 409.

[2] It was in the course of this siege that St. Augustine, Bishop of Hippo, died.

INTRODUCTION

defeat (431 or 432) and was unable to prevent the capture of town after town by Geiseric. Soon almost every important place, with the exception of Cirta (the capital of Numidia) and Carthage, was in the hands of the Vandals. Not until the year 435 did relief come. Aëtius, with his formidable army, composed largely of Huns, seemed now in a position to turn his attention to Africa. Geiseric dared not challenge him. On the 11th of February, 435, a treaty was concluded, whereby the Vandals were allowed to retain, as *foederati* of the Empire, a part of the African diocese (probably the provinces of Mauretania Sitifensis and Numidia and the north-western corner of the old proconsular province). With a man like Geiseric such an arrangement could not be permanent. An unrestricted African dominion was his first and chief object. His covetous eyes were already fixed upon Carthage.

We must now return to Aëtius. In 428 he had driven the Ripuarian Franks back from the left bank of the Rhine. Another successful contest with the Franks seems to have taken place about three years later. In the interval he had conducted decisive operations against the Iuthungi and other troublesome peoples in Noricum and Rhaetia,[1] and he had been made generalissimo of the western forces of the Empire. In 432, the year of his first consulship, he was deposed from his command to make way for Placidia's favourite, Boniface, who was recalled from Africa. Thereupon he concluded a treaty with the Franks and marched against Boniface, but was defeated near Ariminum. Boniface died two months later, and was succeeded by his son-in-

[1] See Sidonius, *Carm.* 7. 233 f.

law Sebastian. Aëtius betook himself to his old
friends, the Huns, and returned to Italy with a large
force. Placidia was compelled to reinstate him.
The treaty with Geiseric in 435 enabled him to
concentrate his attention once more upon Gaul.
In that year the Burgundians, who seem to have been
joined by Alani from Mainz, invaded the province
of Belgica Prima (the district round Trier and Metz).
About the same time the Ripuarian Franks descended
upon the same province from the north, after taking
Cologne, and Trier was captured for the fourth
time in a quarter of a century. Matters were further
complicated by a revolt of the oppressed classes
(peasants and slaves) under one Tibatto. With the
aid of a large force of Huns from Germany, Aëtius
utterly routed the Burgundians and laid their lands
waste (436). The Frankish invasion seems to have
evaporated, and the capture of Tibatto quelled the
insurrection of the Bagaudae, as they were called
(437). But the Goths were quick to avail themselves
of these disturbances, and once more invaded the
Mediterranean fringe of Narbonensis. Litorius, the
chief lieutenant of Aëtius, had had to subdue a
revolt in Aremorica;[1] he now hastened southward
and relieved the siege of Narbonne (437). After a
short-lived peace, negotiated by Avitus (the future
emperor), the Goths renewed their attacks on
Roman territory, but Litorius in a series of battles
drove them back. Near Toulouse, their capital,
they turned at bay. Litorius was defeated and
fatally wounded in a bloody battle. The Goths,

[1] Sidonius, *Carm.* 7. 246 f. For the subsequent events
mentioned in this paragraph see *vv.* 295–315 and 475–480 of
the same poem.

though victorious, had suffered heavily, and were in a mood to listen to Avitus, who had just become Praetorian Prefect, when he proposed terms of peace. It is probable that the Goths were now recognised as a sovereign people (no longer *foederati*), and that their domains were increased by the cession to them of the whole of Novempopulana.[1]

This treaty was far from being the only blow which the Roman power and prestige sustained in that momentous year (439). Geiseric perfidiously seized Carthage and made himself complete master of the proconsular province. His ruthless expropriation of the land-owners, his drastic proceedings against the orthodox Church, and the other features of his conquest are related in all histories of the period and need not be dwelt upon here. Both Valentinian, who had now taken the reins of government into his own hands, and Theodosius, the eastern Emperor, were seized with consternation. Theodosius sent a powerful naval expedition to bring the Vandals to their senses, but it never got beyond Sicily, where it was delayed by Geiseric's diplomacy until trouble nearer home necessitated its recall. A treaty was then made (442), in which the best provinces of Africa were surrendered to the Vandals, though Geiseric undertook to supply Rome with corn and gave his son Huneric as a hostage. He was soon compelled by disturbances in his own realm, caused by his despotic conduct, to seek a further *rapprochement* with the western Emperor. He brought about the betrothal of Huneric to Valentinian's daughter,

---

[1] See Stein, *Gesch. d. spätröm. Reiches*, I. 482, n. 3. Most authorities assign this improvement in the Gothic status to an earlier date; see note on Sidonius, *Carm.* 7. 215 sqq.

Eudocia, who was then six years old (445). Huneric (who was restored to his father at this time) was already married to a daughter of the Visigothic king, Theodoric I, but a charge of attempted poisoning was made a pretext for discarding her, and she was sent back to her father with her ears and nose cut off. From 442 to the death of Valentinian in 455 Geiseric kept the peace with the Empire, though this did not prevent him from encouraging the designs of the Huns on Gaul.

Meanwhile Aëtius had been active in Gaul, but the details of his operations are not very clear.[1] We learn that the Alani and the Burgundians, who had suffered grievously in the disaster of 436, at last had lands assigned them, in which they settled as *foederati*. One body of Alans found a home in the neighbourhood of Valence (440 or earlier), another, under King Goar, the old supporter of the usurper Jovinus, was settled near Orléans (442). In the following year the Burgundians received a permanent abode in Sapaudia (Savoy). It was apparently about this time that Roman troops were finally withdrawn from Britain. In 446 Aëtius obtained the signal honour of a third consulship. We have scanty details of another rising in Aremorica, occasioned by the exactions of the Roman treasury. It began perhaps in 446, and lasted for some years; in the end the Aremoricans gained a position of complete independence, nominally as *foederati*, and some other Celtic peoples who had joined them seem to have won the same privilege. Some time before 446 the Ripuarian Franks were once more flung back across the Rhine by Aëtius. Probably after this came the

---

[1] The account in this paragraph follows Stein.

attempt of the Salian Franks under Chlogio to extend their territory to the Somme, and their defeat near Vicus Helenae.[1] In Spain the Suevians, under their king Rechiar, who had recently married a daughter of Theodoric, crowned their long-standing hostility by devastating the province of Tarraconensis, the great stronghold of the Roman Empire in Spain.

The approach of the half-century was darkened by the growing menace of the Huns under Attila. It was fortunate for Aëtius and for the Roman cause that the specious overtures of Attila were regarded with suspicion by Theodoric and that the mission of Avitus secured the support of the Goths. The bloody battle of the Mauriac (or Catalaunian) Plains, near Troyes, in which Theodoric lost his life, saved Gaul from the invaders (451). Aëtius, however, did not follow up his success. He persuaded the new Gothic king, Thorismund, to lead his warriors home, and Attila was enabled to withdraw with comparative ease, to ravage northern Italy and to threaten the existence of Rome until his death in 453. Before the end of this year Thorismund, who had renewed the old policy of Gothic expansion, was murdered by his brothers Theodoric and Frederic, and the former ascended the throne as Theodoric II. The new king had a tincture of Latin civilisation, gained partly through the teaching of Avitus,[2] and at the beginning of his reign he gave signal proofs of friendship. He resumed the " federate " status which his father had discarded, then he proceeded to Spain, where he quelled an anti-Roman peasant rising and induced his Suevian brother-in-law, Rechiar, to restore the

---

[1] Sidonius, *Carm.* 5. 212 sqq.
[2] Sidonius, *Carm.* 7. 495–498.

province of Carthaginiensis to the Empire (454). The western Roman world was beginning to breathe more freely, when it was suddenly convulsed by the news that Aëtius had been murdered by his Emperor.

Whatever one may think of Valentinian's motives, the results of this deed were serious. The Goths became restless, the Salian Franks under Chlogio took Cambrai and extended their conquests to the Somme, the Ripuarian Franks and the Alamanni once more crossed the Rhine, and Count Marcellinus, who commanded in Dalmatia, declared himself independent of the western Empire. A conspiracy was formed, in which Petronius Maximus, a prominent noble who had filled the highest offices of state, joined forces with old followers of Aëtius, and on the 15th of March, 455, Valentinian met the fate which he had brought upon Aëtius in the previous year. With him died that loyalty to the dynastic principle which had protected his family for nearly a century. The Empire of the West now begins to fade away in a miserable succession of brief reigns. The first in this series of ill-fated princes was the Petronius Maximus who has just been mentioned. Little more than two months after his accession he was seeking flight before the approach of Geiseric, whom he had wantonly provoked. The furious crowd fell upon him, stoned him to death, and tore him limb from limb. The Vandals entered Rome three days later and plundered it for two weeks, returning at last to Carthage with immense booty and some very important captives, including Eudoxia, the widow of Valentinian, her two daughters, and Gaudentius, the younger son of Aëtius.

Petronius Maximus had made Avitus a *magister*

militum,[1] and had sent him to secure the favour of
Theodoric for the new régime. Avitus was at the
court of Toulouse when news came of the Emperor's
assassination and of the sack of Rome. Theodoric
urged him to seize the throne, and offered his support.
Avitus allowed himself to be persuaded. A hastily
summoned gathering of Gallo–Roman senators met
at Viernum, or Ugernum (Beaucaire, near Arles),[2]
and enthusiastically hailed him as the future champion
of Gaul and saviour of the Empire. On the 9th of
July, 455, he was proclaimed Emperor by the soldiers.
He reached Rome in September, and assumed the
consulship at the beginning of the following year.
The Vandals claimed his immediate attention.
Geiseric had seized the lands which had been left to
Rome by the treaty of 442, and had declared his
independence of the Roman suzerainty. Avitus
tried both threats and armed force against him. An
armament which he sent to Sicily under Ricimer
foiled a Vandal attempt on Agrigentum and afterwards won a naval victory near Corsica (456). But
the Gallic Emperor was looked on askance by the
Italian senators, and the people began to murmur
when a failure of the corn-supply threatened them
with famine. Avitus agreed to lessen the number
of mouths to be fed by dismissing the force of federate
troops which had accompanied him from Gaul. But
these had first to be paid; he therefore melted down
and sold a number of bronze statues which had
escaped the ravages of the Vandals. An open revolt
broke out. At the head of it were Ricimer, the
ambitious Suevian whom Avitus had raised to the

---

[1] See n. on Sidonius, *Carm*. 7. 377 f.
[2] Sidonius, *Carm*. 7. 572.

INTRODUCTION

second military command of the West, and Majorian, friend and old companion-in-arms of Ricimer, who had been made *comes domesticorum* by Valentinian after the murder of Aëtius.[1] Avitus, deprived of his loyal troops, was helpless, and fled to Arles. After a vain appeal to Theodoric, who had gone to Spain and was engaged in a merciless war with the Suevian king, he mustered a force as best he could and marched into Italy. Near Placentia he was defeated and captured. He was spared for the moment and allowed to become Bishop of Placentia (October 17th or 18th, 456);[2] but he could not feel safe, and soon attempted to return to his home in Auvergne. He died on the way; possibly he was murdered.

The fall of Avitus aroused consternation and indignation in Gaul. Both the national feeling of the Gallo-Romans and their loyalty to the Empire had received a rude shock. The central government had shown its weakness in many ways; Africa was lost to the Empire, and the Roman name, of which they were proud, was sadly tarnished. In order to repair the distresses of the time the resources of Gaul had been raided with special severity. To Avitus the Empire had owed much in time of peril. Both as Gauls and as Romans they had looked to him to inaugurate a brighter era. And now these hopes had gone for ever; the Italian senators, it seemed, would rather let the Empire go to ruin than allow the supreme power to be held by one outside their own charmed circle. It is no wonder if this sudden

[1] See n. on Sidonius, *Carm.* 5. 308.
[2] For this merciful method of making a fallen potentate harmless we may compare the case of Glycerius, below, p. xxx.

xxii

INTRODUCTION

revulsion of feeling led to desperate measures.
Lyons was the centre of the revolt. The rebellious
Gallo-Roman nobles allied themselves with the
Burgundians and admitted a Burgundian garrison
into the town. The insurgents, or a section of them,
seem to have invited Count Marcellinus to lead them
and to assume the Imperial diadem.[1] He had held
a command under Aëtius, and after the murder of
his old chief he had shown vigour and decision and the
courage of his convictions;[2] he would be an in-
spiring leader, and he would make short work of
an Italian clique if it stood in his way. Theodoric,
who had seen in his compact with Avitus a satisfactory accommodation of Gothic and Imperial
interests, was now in no mood to keep the peace.
On his return from Spain he renewed the old attacks
on Narbonensis.

The coalition of Ricimer and Majorian resulted in
the elevation of the latter to the throne (457).[3]
Whatever one may think of his part in the fall of
Avitus, Majorian was certainly a man of ability
and character. Apart from internal affairs, his most
urgent task was the crushing of Geiseric. He
enlisted a great army, composed mostly of foreign
contingents, and prepared a large fleet, which was
to assemble off the coast of Spain. His plan was to
march through Gaul and Spain, gathering contingents from the federate peoples as he went, and
then to cross the strait for a decisive struggle. He

[1] See n. on Sidonius, *Epist.* I. 11. 6.
[2] See above, p. xx.
[3] There is a controversy about the exact date of Majorian's
formal accession. See nn. on Sidonius, *Carm.* 5. 9 ff. and
384 ff.

set out late in the year 458. On his way he had to subdue the rebellious Gallo–Romans.[1] Lyons capitulated, apparently a little before the Emperor arrived in person, on favourable terms which seem to have been arranged by the quaestor Petrus.[2] Majorian showed a wise leniency. Even the severe taxation which he at first imposed upon the insurgents seems to have been remitted, and danger from the Burgundians was removed by allowing them to occupy the province of Lugdunensis Prima, with the exception of Lyons itself. The Goths had next to be mastered; this was accomplished by Aegidius, who, with the aid of reinforcements sent by the Emperor, drove them back from Arles. In their case also Majorian was conciliatory, and Theodoric agreed to a continuation of the old federate status.[3]

Majorian's expedition came to grief in the following year (460). An act of treachery enabled Geiseric to surprise the Roman fleet off the coast of Spain between Cartagena and Alicante and to capture a great number of the ships. Majorian had to conclude a humiliating treaty by which Geiseric probably obtained legal possession of the African provinces which he had recently seized; he may also have received at the same time Corsica, Sardinia, and the Balearic Islands, which were certainly in his possession a few years later. After spending some time in

[1] It seems probable that Marcellinus dissociated himself from the revolt when he heard that his old comrade-in-arms Majorian had been proclaimed Emperor.

[2] Sidonius, *Carm.* 5. 568–573.

[3] In this and in the preceding paragraph I have for the most part followed the orthodox version. Stein's ingenious account, though valuable, seems at times to strain the evidence, including the evidence of Sidonius.

Gaul, Majorian returned to Italy with a small follow-ing, having disbanded the " barbarian " contingents enlisted for the Vandal campaign. On the 2nd of August, 461, he was attacked and captured near Tortona by a large body of Ricimer's armed retainers, and five days later he was beheaded.

Ricimer, the Patrician (a title which he had held since 457),[1] was now the real ruler of the West, though as a " barbarian " and an Arian he could not aspire to the throne.   In November, 461, he set up a puppet-Emperor in the person of Libius Severus. But he soon found himself in difficulties. Geiseric, who hated him, made piratical attacks on the coasts of Italy and Sicily. Marcellinus, who probably held the rank of *magister militum* in Dalmatia, and Aegidius, the *magister militum* in Gaul, threw off their allegiance, and Theodoric renounced the compact which he had made with Majorian. The eastern Emperor was induced to hold Marcellinus in check, but the troubles in the Gallic provinces were not so easily ended. The threatened invasion of Italy by Aegidius was kept off by purchasing Gothic and Burgundian friendship at a heavy price. The Burgundians, under King Gundioc, were allowed to occupy Lyons, and their territory was further en-larged, so that they barred the land-route to Italy ; the sea-route was barred by allowing the Goths to seize Narbonne and the greater part of Narbonensis Prima, which extended from the Pyrenees to the Rhone (462). The Goths were also encouraged to extend their conquests in Spain, but when Theodoric's brother Frederic tried to push the Gothic power

[1] On this title as applied to Ricimer see **n.** on Sidonius, *Carm.* 2. 90.

beyond the Loire he was signally defeated near Orléans by Aegidius (463), who had found a valuable ally in Childeric, king of the Salian Franks. Fortunately for Ricimer and his allies, Aegidius died in the following year. But the wily Vandal had still to be dealt with. Geiseric thought it politic to listen at last to the representations of Leo, the eastern Emperor, so far as to give up Eudoxia and her daughter Placidia, whom he sent to Constantinople; Eudocia, the other daughter, who had married Huneric, was retained. In return for this concession he is said to have received as much of Eudocia's inheritance as was situated in the East and also a promise from Leo to abstain from hostilities against him. Soon he addressed further demands to the West, claiming a large share of the property of Valentinian III, and making the capture of Gaudentius a pretext for claiming the property of Aëtius. In addition he demanded that Olybrius, an accommodating senator who had married Placidia either in Africa or in Constantinople, should receive the sceptre of the West. Annual raids on Italy and Sicily reinforced his demands. Nothing short of a great effort of East and West in common had any prospect of crushing him.

On the 14th of November, 465, Libius Severus died. He had really been a usurper, as Leo, who had never acknowledged him, had legally been the sole Roman Emperor since the death of Majorian.[1] There followed seventeen months in which Leo had no colleague in the West. Geiseric continued to press the claims of Olybrius and to attack Italy and Sicily. At last he had the temerity to raid the Peloponnese.

[1] So Iordanes, *Rom.* 335; but his statement has been questioned.

INTRODUCTION

Leo was stung to action. He now acceded to in-
sistent requests from Italy, and appointed a colleague
to rule in the West and to collaborate in a great
offensive against the Vandals. The man of his
choice was Anthemius, who besides being a son-in-
law of the late Emperor Marcian had a distinguished
record of public service to his credit. Anthemius
was created Augustus on the 12th of April, 467.
In the same year his daughter Alypia was given in
marriage to Ricimer. Next year the great offensive
was launched. Basiliscus, the commander-in-chief,
sailed with an enormous force to take Carthage;
an army began to march from Egypt through
Tripolitana to co-operate in the conquest of Africa;
Marcellinus, who held the chief command of the
western forces, was sent to capture Sardinia. Basiliscus, after defeating a Vandal fleet sent against him,
anchored near Carthage, and had Geiseric at his
mercy, but the resourceful Vandal persuaded him
(probably with the aid of a large bribe) to grant a
truce of five days. Thereupon the Vandals brought
up fire-ships and launched an unexpected attack,
inflicting such serious losses that Basiliscus retreated
to Sicily. The final blow came with the assassination
of Marcellinus, who had crossed over to Sicily after
recovering Sardinia. This dastardly deed was almost
certainly brought about by Ricimer, whose position
in Italy would have been very insecure if Marcellinus
had come back covered with glory. Geiseric
promptly regained Sardinia, and a little later Sicily.
The eastern forces were withdrawn, and those of the
West were required for the defence of Italy and for
operations against the Goths in Gaul.

In 466 Euric had murdered his brother Theodoric

and become king of the Visigoths. It soon became clear that he meant to throw off his nominal dependence on Rome and to extend his dominions over all the Gallic lands. The union of East and West for the war against Geiseric, with whom he had meditated an alliance, deterred him for a time, but the disastrous failure of the great expedition gave him his opportunity. He seems to have counted on a large measure of support from the Gallo-Romans. His success in this direction was probably less than he had expected, owing to the antagonism of the Catholic Church and the traditional loyalty of the upper classes; but Arvandus, the Praetorian Prefect, and many others went over to his side. Arvandus was summoned to Rome, impeached for High Treason, and condemned to death, though the sentence was afterwards commuted to one of banishment. Matters now came to a crisis. Anthemius prepared an expedition, and the Bretons of Aremorica, under King Riothamus, marched to defend the territory north of the Loire. Riothamus was completely defeated near Vicus Dolensis (Déols, dép. Indre), and fled with the remnant of his army to the Burgundians. Euric thus became master of Tours and Bourges and of a large part of the province of Aquitanica Prima (east of Aquitanica Secunda, which had been occupied by the Goths for more than fifty years); he was, however, prevented from extending his conquests north of the Loire by Count Paulus and, after the death of Paulus in 470, by Syagrius, son of Aegidius, with the aid of the Franks under King Childeric. But there were prizes to be won in other parts. In Aquitanica Prima Auvergne, whose inhabitants prided themselves on their Latin blood [1] and on their connexion with Rome, still remained unconquered; more important still were those cities of Narbonensis which still remained Roman, especially Arles, the headquarters of the Roman administration. But before these could be subdued the army which Anthemius had organised had to be met and defeated. It crossed the Alps in 471, under the leadership of Anthemiolus, son of the Emperor, and three other generals, but on its way to Arles it was totally defeated on the left bank of the Rhone, all its generals being slain. Euric overran and plundered the lower Rhone-valley from Valence to the sea, but as he had impinged on Burgundian territory he thought it prudent to abandon for the present his conquests in that region and to transfer his attention to two centres of opposition farther west. A fierce war had been waged with the Suevians in Spain for some years. Euric himself took command, and ultimately (about 473) made himself master of practically the whole of the peninsula except the old home of the Suevians in the north-west. This diversion of large Gothic forces made it easier for the Arvernians to defend their capital (modern Clermont-Ferrand). The exploits of Ecdicius,[2] the youngest son of the late Emperor Avitus, the courageous helpfulness of his brother-in-law Apollinaris Sidonius, now Bishop of Auvergne, and the garrison provided by the Burgundians, who had no desire to see a further extension of Gothic power, enabled the townsmen to hold out for some years. But their resistance could not go on for ever, and the Empire was

[1] See n. on Sidonius, *Carm.* 7. 139.
[2] See especially Sidonius, *Epist.* III. 3.

too weak to defend its last strongholds in the west.

In 472 Ricimer, whom no Emperor could satisfy in the long run, brought about the fall and assassination of Anthemius. A few weeks later he himself died, and before the end of the year the Emperor whom he had set up, Olybrius (who, as we have seen, had been Geiseric's nominee) was also no more. Four months later (March, 473) the Burgundian Gundobad, Ricimer's successor as Patrician, caused the *comes domesticorum* Glycerius to be proclaimed Emperor by the troops in Ravenna. This election, however, was not recognised by the eastern Emperor, Leo I, who nominated Julius Nepos, a nephew of Marcellinus. Glycerius could offer no resistance, and was put out of harm's way by being consecrated Bishop of Salona, in Dalmatia. Nepos seems at first to have planned vigorous measures against the Goths, and he made the heroic Ecdicius *magister militum praesentalis* and Patrician. But a change soon occurred, the details of which are not entirely clear. Whatever the reason, Ecdicius soon lost his new dignities and was replaced by Orestes, a Roman from Pannonia, who had once been Attila's secretary. Nepos, in agreement with the Burgundian king, sought to arrange terms of peace with Euric (475). The negotiations were entrusted to a delegation of bishops. They arranged that Auvergne should be surrendered, while the Empire should still rule in southern Provence, including Arles and Marseilles. It was a bitter blow to the Arvernians to be thus sacrificed by an Empire for which they had fought and suffered so long. The rule of Rome in the west was now crumbling to pieces. The Danubian provinces had actually, if not nominally, thrown off their allegiance, and Spain was lost.

The rest of the miserable tale may be told in a few words. Orestes rose against Nepos, compelling him to take refuge in Dalmatia. Preferring to remain Patrician, he elevated to the Imperial throne, on 31st October, 475, his son Romulus, who is generally designated by the nickname given him in pity or contempt for his youth, Augustulus. Less than a year sufficed to end this usurping reign. The " barbarian " mercenaries quartered in Italy, unable to obtain pay from a depleted exchequer, demanded that one third of the land should be made over to them. When their demand was refused they rose in rebellion and proclaimed their leader, the Scirian Odovacar, King of Italy. Augustulus was mercifully allowed to retire into private life. In this situation Euric found an opportunity of winning the coveted strip of Provence for which the Romans had recently sacrificed Auvergne (476 or 477).

Nepos was still legally Emperor, and thus the eastern Emperor had a colleague until the death of Nepos in 480. Even apart from this, as modern historians do not fail to point out, it is incorrect to speak of the year 476 as marking the fall of the Roman Empire in the West.[1] Nevertheless, the events of that year were of immense significance. Italy, the ancient home of the Empire, now saw one third of her land in possession of " barbarians," and began to suffer the fate which had already overtaken the proud lands of Gaul and Africa. She had a foreign ruler in her midst, unhampered by the presence even of a puppet-Emperor such as Ricimer

[1] See, for example, Bury, *op. cit.*, I., p. 408.

had liked to set up. It is true that the Roman Empire continued to exist in the West even after the death of Nepos. Legally the lack of a western Emperor did not matter; the Emperor who ruled in Constantinople ruled also in Italy, and even " barbarian " rulers such as Odovacar and Theodoric the Ostrogoth found it expedient to acknowledge his sovereignty. But such legal technicalities and such ostentatious deference cannot hide the fact that the substance of power was in other hands and that a momentous change had taken place.

II. LIFE AND WORKS OF SIDONIUS

GAIUS SOLLIUS MODESTUS(?) APOLLINARIS SIDONIUS[1] was born at Lyons (Lugdunum) on the 5th of November;[2] the year is uncertain, but it must have been about A.D. 430.[3] His family was one of considerable distinction. His great-grandfather had held an official position of some importance, his grandfather, the first of his family to adopt the Christian religion,

[1] In his works he is usually called simply Sollius or Sidonius. The latter is not strictly a surname (*cognomen*) but a *signum*. These *signa*, which properly denoted membership of some association, were often adopted by persons of good birth. *Modestus* has strong MS. authority in the *incipit* of *Carm.* 4, less strong in the *subscriptiones* of most books of the *Letters*. It may be authentic, but it ought perhaps to be regarded with as much suspicion as *Sophronius* in the name of Jerome. The notion that it is due to a wrong inference from *Epist.* IX. 12. 3 is scarcely credible.

[2] *Carm.* 20. 1.

[3] This is inferred from *Epist.* VIII. 6. 5, which tells us that in the year 449 he was *adulescens atque adhuc nuper ex puero.* On the whole, 331 or 332 seems the most likely date.

xxxii

INTRODUCTION

had been Praetorian Prefect of Gaul, and his father held the same exalted position when Sidonius was little more than a boy.[1] His mother was connected with the distinguished house of the Aviti. We do not know where he received his education; some think it was partly at Lyons and partly at Arles. The great institutions of higher learning in Gaul, which had flourished so long under Imperial patronage, seem by this time to have fallen on evil days,[2] but the upper classes still retained their predilection for the traditional training of pagan Rome as represented in the schools of grammar and rhetoric. Sidonius went through the usual courses in grammar, literature, rhetoric, philosophy (with its satellites arithmetic, geometry, astronomy, and music)[3] and law. He has recorded the names of two of his teachers, Hoënius,[4] who taught him poetry, and Eusebius,[5] who taught him philosophy. He mentions Claudianus Mamertus, the famous author of the *De Statu Animae*, as having conducted edifying philosophical disputations with him and other ardent students;[6] but it is not certain

---

[1] See *Epist.* I. 3. 1, with note; cf. III. 12. 5, V. 9. 1 (grandfather), V. 9. 2, VIII. 6. 5 (father).

[2] It is a frequent mistake to attribute to the age of Sidonius the conditions enjoyed a little earlier by Ausonius as a professor at Bordeaux. The disturbed state of the country and the growing financial stringency had in all probability caused the withdrawal of active Imperial patronage from the schools of "grammar" and rhetoric. See Roger, *L'enseignement des lettres classiques d'Ausone à Alcuin*, Paris, 1905, pp. 48–88. This excellent book has not received the attention which it deserves.

[3] See *Carm.* 14 *epist.* § 2, *Carm.* 22 *epist.* §§ 2 sq.

[4] *Carm.* 9. 313.

[5] *Epist.* IV. 1. 3.

[6] *Epist.* IV. 11. 2.

that Claudianus held any official post as a teacher, or
that this seminar, as one might call it, formed part of
Sidonius's regular course of higher education; it
may have taken place later and in a different place.
Certainly these teachers never made Sidonius a
philosopher. He seems to have learnt enough Greek
to construe Menander [1] without much difficulty.

A good deal of the learning acquired in the schools
at this time was somewhat superficial, and much of it
was in " tabloid " form. Historical examples were
a regular part of the educational course; Sidonius
was always ready to produce one or a dozen at the
shortest notice (though not always accurately) to
embellish his writings. The way in which he repeats
the same stock illustrations time after time casts some
light on the nature of the instruction received. The
case was somewhat similar with myths and legends,
which sprout up everywhere in his poetry, and with
literary criticism, in which lists of past authors with
brief ready-made descriptions were served up to the
student. Nevertheless a great deal of literature was
read, with comments on diction, style, and subject-
matter, great emphasis being placed on antiquarian
details, especially those dealing with mythology.
Sidonius shows an intimate acquaintance with many
writers, especially poets, and he must have acquired
much of it in his student days. Among the poets,
Virgil, Horace, Lucan, Juvenal, Martial, Statius,
Ausonius, Claudian and others were known to him at
first hand, most of them intimately.[2] Among the

[1] *Epist.* IV. 12. 1.
[2] It is interesting to note that he shows even in his early
works some knowledge of the Christian poet Prudentius. He
had also some acquaintance with Plautus, and he seems to
have been fond of Terence.

INTRODUCTION

prose authors whom he knew well were Pliny the
Younger, Apuleius, and Symmachus.[1] But the letter
counted for more than the spirit. The authors of
the past were treasures from which to steal subject-
matter, learned allusions, and tricks of diction. The
highest compliment which could be paid by one fifth-
century writer to another was that he recalled one or
more of the ancients. Creative work in the true
sense was not fostered in the schools. The training
in rhetoric had the same tendency as that given by
the *grammaticus*. The study of rhetoric, though not
without good points, had for centuries emphasized the
importance of form rather than of matter. A straining after effect, an ostentatious and often unnatural
use of words, forced antithesis, far-fetched conceits,
silly paradoxes, over-elaboration and a constant
sacrifice of clearness to cleverness—these were some
of the features which this training too often produced.
They are all found abundantly in Sidonius, and,
strange to say, his contemporaries admired them,
even if they did not always understand what he
meant.

Amid the almost complete silence of Sidonius about
his formative years we read of one trivial incident
which gave him much pleasure.[2] At the beginning
of the year 449 the new consul Astyrius inaugurated
his office in an imposing ceremony at Arles, and the
young Sidonius, whose father was Praetorian Prefect
of Gaul at the time, occupied a place of great honour,

[1] Perhaps Fronto should be added to this list. Cicero is
often mentioned, and some acquaintance with his works
(especially the letters *Ad Familiares*) is shown. There are
also indications that the works of Sallust, Livy, Seneca,
and Tacitus were to some extent known to Sidonius.

[2] *Epist.* VIII. 6. 5.

being allowed to stand beside the curule chair. There
is no doubt that the young man was already planning
to follow the family tradition by entering the government service and attaining to high office, perhaps even
to the consulship itself, which none of his family had
reached. His prospects, already bright, were soon
greatly enhanced when he married Papianilla,
daughter of Avitus. The marriage, which was
obviously a happy one, brought him the delightful
estate of Avitacum, near Clermont-Ferrand.
Auvergne, in which it was situated, thus became " a
second fatherland " [1] to this young Lyonese, who
was destined to have a pathetic opportunity of showing his devotion to it. There seem to have been four
children of the marriage, a son and three daughters.[2]

Avitus was proclaimed Emperor in July, A.D. 455,

[1] *Carm.* 17. 20.
[2] The son is the Apollinaris to whom *Epist.* III. 13 is addressed; cf. V. 9. 4, V. 11. 3, VIII. 6. 12, IX. 1. 5. When
Count Victorius, the governor, was driven out of Auvergne
about the year 480 owing to his outrageous conduct, Apollinaris accompanied him in his flight to Rome. There Victorius, continuing his misbehaviour, was put to death, and
Apollinaris was imprisoned at Milan. He succeeded in escaping and returned to Auvergne. In 507 he fought along
with other Arvernians in the disastrous battle against Clovis
at Vouillé (Campus Vogladensis). About eight years later,
when his father's old see of Clermont fell vacant, he obtained
it, not, it seems, without a good deal of intrigue (in which his
wife and a sister named Alcima joined) and bribery (Greg.
Tur. *Hist. Fr.* III. 2). He died a few months after his installation. Sidonius makes no mention of Alcima, but he
mentions as daughters Severiana (*Epist.* II. 12. 2) and Roscia
(V. 16. 5). Mommsen, perhaps unnecessarily, doubts whether
these three names all belong to separate persons. He also
credits Sidonius with twins. This amusing error, which has
become an article of faith with subsequent writers on Sidonius,
is due to a very unscholarly misunderstanding of *Carm.* 17. 3.

and his proud son-in-law accompanied him to
Rome. On the first of January in the following year
the new Emperor assumed the consulship, and
Sidonius delivered to an applauding throng a long
panegyric in verse (*Carmen* 7). The honour of a
bronze statue in the Forum of Trajan was decreed to
the young poet, whose fortune now seemed to be
made.[1] But his elation was short-lived. The fall
of Avitus and the subsequent rebellion in Gaul have
already been described.[2] Sidonius might well be
excused for joining in the insurrection. Petrus, the
Imperial secretary, who seems to have arranged the
terms of capitulation, would no doubt recognise this;
moreover he was a literary man himself,[3] and he probably admired the young poet who had so recently
won the plaudits of the Romans. It seems certain
that he secured pardon for Sidonius at the earliest
opportunity. When Majorian arrived in Lyons late
in the year 458 Sidonius, already pardoned (see *Carm.*
4), delivered a panegyric in his honour (*Carm.* 5).
The concluding lines of the poem show that Majorian
had not yet fully decided the fate of Lyons and of the
insurgent Gallo-Romans. The poet seeks to arouse
his pity, and professes to detect in the Imperial
countenance a look of compassion. Whether the
poet's pleading worked on Majorian or not, it is
certain that he was merciful, though he imposed a
heavy tax as a punishment. In *Carmen* 13, which
was in all probability composed very soon after the
panegyric, Sidonius pleads for a remission of this
burden, and it seems safe to conclude that his plea

[1] *Carm.* 8. 7–10, *Epist.* IX. 16. 3 *vv.* 25–28.
[2] See pp. xxi–xxiv.
[3] See *Carm.* 3, with note on *v.* 5.

INTRODUCTION

was successful. Although it must have been very hard to forgive the man who had conspired with Ricimer to bring about the downfall of Avitus, the generosity of Majorian, his innate nobility of character and his attractive personality won the heart of Sidonius, and Majorian did what he could to cement their friendship. In the following year or in the year 460 we find Sidonius occupying a government post at Rome,[1] and in the year 461 we find that he has the title of Count (*Comes*),[2] which, if not given in virtue of a definite office of state, betokened at least that he was an accepted member of the court circle. In that year he travelled from Auvergne to Arles, where Majorian was sojourning after the disastrous failure of his expedition against Geiseric,[3] and he has left us a long and interesting account of an Imperial dinner-party at which he was a guest.[4] But the end of Majorian was at hand, and in August of that year Sidonius was once more bereft of an Imperial patron.[5]

---

[1] See note on *commilitio recenti, Epist.* I. 11. 3, also n. on § 1 of the same letter. So far as is known, Sidonius had not previously held any appointment in the Imperial civil service. It has been conjectured that he was *tribunus et notarius* under Avitus. He may have been, but there is absolutely no evidence of it.

[2] *Epist.* I. 11. 13.

[3] See p. xxiv.

[4] *Epist.* I. 11. By an unfortunate inadvertence M. A. Loyen attributes to Mr. Stevens and personally approves the view that this party took place in A.D. 459; see *Journ. Rom. Stud.* XXIV. (1934), p. 85. This date is quite impossible, as the letter itself shows (§ 10); the date 459 is suggested by Mr. Stevens not for this dinner-party but for the one mentioned in *Epist.* IX. 13. 4 (Stevens, *Sidonius Apollinaris*, p. 51).

[5] For the fall of Majorian see p. xxv.

INTRODUCTION

How he spent his time in the ensuing six years may be partially inferred from his own writings, several of which, both poems and letters, must have been written in this period, although anything like an accurate dating is generally impossible.[1] It seems certain that he lived partly in the old family home at Lyons and partly at Avitacum, and that from time to time he visited numerous friends in different parts of the country, passing many a happy day like those which he spent with Tonantius Ferreolus and Apollinaris (*Epist.* II. 9). His visit to Bishop Faustus at Riez (*Carm.* 16. 78–88) almost certainly took place in the same period. It is quite possible that the visit to the court of Theodoric II at Toulouse (*Epist.* I. 2) occurred in one of these years, and he may well have combined it with a series of visits to friends in Bordeaux and its neighbourhood, including a stay with Pontius Leontius at Burgus, which he celebrates in *Carm.* 22. We learn from *Carm.* 22 *epist.* § 1 that he spent a considerable time at Narbonne, where Consentius and many other friends lived, in A.D. 462 or a very little later. In all probability this was the occasion on which he enjoyed the hospitality which he celebrates in *Carm.* 23. 434–506.

The murder of Theodoric, the accession of Euric

---

[1] It is commonly said that Sidonius at some time held the Praetorian Prefectship of Gaul. This idea arises from a misinterpretation of *Epist.* IV. 14. 2 and 4 and from the expression *fori iudex* in the so-called *Epitaphium Sidonii* found in the Codex Matritensis (10th or 11th century). I cordially agree with those who impugn the authority of this " epitaph " (see especially Stevens, p. 166, n. 2, and p. 211); but even if it were an authentic document one could not say that its vague language proves that Sidonius was Praetorian Prefect. *Fori iudex* was possibly suggested by *Epist.* IX. 3 *v.* 32, *iura gubernat*, which refers to the Prefecture of the City.

(466), and the elevation of Anthemius to the Imperial
throne (April 12, 467) have been related elsewhere.[1]
Early in the new reign Sidonius was commissioned
by the Arvernians to present to the Emperor a
petition, the subject of which he does not disclose.
He has described his journey in a long and interesting
letter (I. 5), which was supplemented early in the
following year by another (I. 9). He arrived in
Rome at a time when the whole city was joyfully
celebrating the marriage of Ricimer to Alypia, the
daughter of Anthemius. To further the business
with which he was entrusted, Sidonius attached
himself to two powerful senators, Gennadius Avienus
and Caecina Basilius. As the 1st of January, 468,
approached, on which date Anthemius was going to
assume the consulship, Basilius suggested to Sidonius
that it would be profitable for him to " bring out the
old Muse " and compose a panegyric. This he did,
and once more he stood before a Roman throng to
sing the praises of an emperor-consul. He must
surely have spoken with a lump in his throat as he
thought of that other New Year's Day, twelve years
before, when he had stood before a similar gathering
and prophesied a glorious reign for Avitus. But his
facile Muse did all that was necessary, and his reward
came promptly in his appointment as Prefect of the
City. This preferment may have been designed to
please the Gallo–Roman nobles as well as to recognise
the virtues of the panegyric, but it obviously gave him
great delight.[2] The office of Prefect of the City was
still one of the most exalted in the Empire. The
Prefect was President of the Senate and also head
of the judicature and of the police both in Rome and

---

[1] See pp. xxvii f.   [2] See *Epist.* I. 9. 8.

for a hundred miles around it. Besides this he was controller of the food-supply. This was a worrying responsibility in a period when the hostility of Geiseric might at any time cause a shortage, and we read of one occasion when Sidonius feared an outcry from the populace and anxiously awaited the arrival of five ship-loads of wheat and honey.[1]

He tells us no more of his prefectship, which he held for a year. We may imagine that he was glad to be freed from a rather thankless office and to leave Rome with the prestige of an ex-prefect and the honourable title of Patrician. He had another reason for preferring Gaul to Rome in the year 469, for it was then that his friend Arvandus was brought to Rome for trial on a serious charge and so conducted himself that it was impossible to save him.[2] Arvandus had become Praetorian Prefect of Gaul in A.D. 464, and had given such satisfaction at first that his term of office was increased to five years. But his conduct had undergone a change, and his oppression and malversation could no longer be borne. He was arrested by order of the Council of the Seven Provinces and sent to Rome for trial. Meanwhile the three delegates sent from Gaul to prosecute him were furnished with evidence which made the charge against him infinitely more serious. A letter from him to Euric had been intercepted, in which he advised the Gothic king to abandon his pacific attitude toward the " Greek Emperor " (Anthemius), to attack the Bretons, and to arrange a division of Gaul between the Goths and the Burgundians.

[1] *Epist.* I. 10. 2.
[2] On the case of Arvandus see *Epist.* I. 7; also p. xxviii above.

INTRODUCTION

Sidonius was in an embarrassing position. The three accusers sent from Gaul were old friends of his, but he had also been on friendly terms with Arvandus. Along with some others he did all that was possible to help the prisoner by advising him to make no admissions and to be wary of any traps that might be set for him. Their advice was received with scorn by Arvandus, whose arrogance and self-confidence almost passed belief. Sidonius left Rome before the trial came on. Arvandus was condemned on a charge of High Treason and sentenced to death, but the sentence was commuted to one of exile.

We next find Sidonius (apparently in A.D. 469 or 470) enthroned at Clermont as Bishop of the Arverni. We do not know what immediately led to this change, but he was not the first or the last noble who abandoned the honours of state for the responsibilities of a see. There were various reasons which made such a translation desirable. The weakening power of the Empire was bitter to all who loved the Roman name. As the Imperial power declined, it was the Church above all that upheld the standard of Roman civilisation and maintained and diffused the Roman spirit amid " barbarian " surroundings. To Sidonius this must have meant much. Again, the bishop was a great refuge in time of trouble. He could aid the distressed in a very special way and stand up to the oppressor, whether Roman official or barbarian potentate. It had long been the custom to vest certain judicial powers in him. He also administered large funds, which might be used both for the relief of distresses and for the furtherance of the Catholic religion, but which too often tempted greedy intriguers to possess themselves of a diocese. In Gaul,

xlii

INTRODUCTION

Euric, a fanatical Arian, was hostile to the orthodox church, seeing in it not only the promoter of a hated creed but the fosterer of the Roman, " anti-barbarian " spirit. There was, therefore, plenty of work to challenge the zeal of a patriot who cared also for religion. In countries like Gaul it was not merely the man of piety that was required for this task. It was often not only a great advantage but a necessity to have as bishop a man of rank and wealth, a man who could face even Euric himself and command respect, and who could, through his experience as an administrator backed by his own generosity, provide the means to resist aggression and to help the ruined and homeless outcasts whose numbers were being multiplied by the excesses of friend and foe alike. Sidonius must have felt all this. At the same time he felt how ill-fitted he was for the task. A sense of his own unworthiness to be a spiritual guide oppressed him not only now but to the end. The worldly ambitions which were characteristic of his class might often be patriotic, but they were not set upon the " City of God." Moreover he was now asked to become a bishop so suddenly that any adequate preparation for his ecclesiastical duties was out of the question. In entering the Church he would be entering a world which was strange to him, and in which he would have much both to learn and to unlearn. And he was no theologian. His poem to Faustus (*Carm.* 16) shows not only an imperfect knowledge of the Scriptures but a naïve unorthodoxy which would have drawn from a less tolerant ecclesiastic a horrified rebuke. He remained a close friend both of the heretical Faustus and of Claudianus Mamertus, who dedicated to Sidonius the *De Statu*

Animae, in which the views of Faustus are vigorously assailed. This impartiality does credit to his heart; at the same time it cannot be said with certainty that he really understood what the controversy was all about. Nevertheless, the poem to Faustus shows Sidonius as a devout Christian with a profound admiration for the saintly character, and there is plenty of other evidence that along with all his enthusiasm for the pomp and pageantry of power and amid all his literary preoccupation with the products of heathen mythology he retained a sense of humble dependence on a divine Providence. It is easy to be cynical and point out that the position of a bishop gave both dignity and (what offices of state did not always give) comparative safety. It must, however, be remembered that he felt both then and even later the glamour of the government service, and as far as we know he might have looked forward to further distinctions, perhaps even to the most coveted honour of all, that of the consulship. Be that as it may, we cannot deny that he was renouncing much; his domestic and social life could not be quite the same as before, his liberty was curtailed, his wealth might have to be sacrificed, and there were dangerous times ahead in Auvergne, which he cannot have failed in some measure to foresee and to fear. The insinuation of some historians that Sidonius sought the episcopal throne, and that he did so from motives of worldly prudence, is not justified either by his own words [1] or by intrinsic probability.

It is sometimes held that Sidonius spent some time in the lower ranks of the clergy before being installed as bishop; [2] but the evidence for this is not conclusive.

---

[1] See Stevens, *Sidonius Apollinaris,* p. 130, n. 2.
[2] See Mommsen in Luetjohann's edition, p. xlviii.

Sometimes a layman was rushed through the lower degrees,[1] but in some cases even this formality was dispensed with. Sidonius took his new status very seriously. He resolved to write no more worldly verses.[2] This was a great renunciation for a man who had for so many years found delight in thrumming on the antique lyre. On the whole, his austere vow was kept as well as could reasonably be expected. There was indeed sterner work to be done, even apart from the ordinary duties of spiritual oversight. Auvergne, with all its ancient pride in the Roman name, was in imminent danger of going the way of other parts of Gaul and falling into the clutches of the barbarian. Romans, even members of the old governing class, were more and more inclined to acquiesce in the new order of things, and even to accept official positions under the sovereign Goth or the nominally federate Burgundian. In the parts of the country which still remained to the Empire there were traitors to the Roman name. Seronatus,[3] undeterred by the fate of Arvandus, freely encouraged Gothic encroachment, and did what he could to curry favour with Euric and to further his designs. He was indeed, thanks to Arvernian loyalty,

---

[1] Ambrose "passed from baptism to the episcopate in the course of a week" (C. H. Turner in *Cambridge Medieval History*, p. 152). Sidonius himself, when entrusted with the task of choosing a bishop for the see of Bourges, chose a layman : see *Epist.* VII. 9, where he reproduces the address which he delivered on the occasion. In the circumstances his choice was not an unreasonable one.

[2] *Epist.* IX. 12. 1. He speaks of verses in general, but he obviously did not mean to debar himself from writing poems with a Christian content. See also IX. 16. *vv.* 41–64, especially 55 f.

[3] *Epist.* II. 1, V. 13, VII. 7. 2.

brought to justice and executed, but this was only a slight set-back to the sinister schemes of Euric. Sidonius soon found that the see of Clermont called for all the qualities of a man and a patriot. Unfortunately it is impossible to follow with any certainty the course of the struggle, which began probably in A.D. 471 and ended four years later with the sacrifice of Auvergne by the Empire for a transitory gain. The Goths besieged the city every year, retiring on the approach of winter after wasting the land. There were sallies and some fierce fighting, but the pressure went on relentlessly. The Burgundians had sent a garrison to help the besieged, Ecdicius, brother-in-law of Sidonius, raised a force mostly at his own expense and himself performed prodigies of valour,[1] and the good bishop did all that he could to animate the defenders and to relieve the distressed. That they were distressed there is no doubt. In all probability the citizens who resided outside the walls, when they had not fled to safer regions, had taken refuge within, and these, along with the Burgundians and other troops, were difficult to house as well as to feed. The Burgundians seem to have been troublesome,[2] and the Goths had seen to it that supplies were scarce. As things grew worse, Sidonius could not help feeling that the troubles must be a divine judgment for some unknown sin;[3] and indeed the people had grown slack in their public prayers.[4] He therefore instituted at Clermont the special prayers, or " Rogations," which Bishop Mamertus was said to have used with miraculous

---

[1] See *Epist.* III. 3. 3–8.   [2] *Epist.* III. 4. 1.
[3] *Epist.* III. 4. 2; VII. 10 (11). 2.
[4] *Epist.* V. 14. 2.

effect at Vienne. But although these, as he tells us, had a good effect, circumstances were too strong; as their privations increased and no help came, the people murmured more and more, and all the efforts of their bishop could not quell the talk of surrender. At this juncture Sidonius besought the saintly priest Constantius to come from Lyons to his aid. Aged though he was, Constantius braved the rigours of a severe winter and a difficult journey to encourage the waverers, and succeeded in nerving them to further resistance.[1] Ecdicius seems to have been absent for a considerable time at the Burgundian court.[2] Perhaps he was trying to persuade the king to launch a great offensive against the Goths. The language of Sidonius is vague (he does not even say what court Ecdicius was visiting); but we must remember that his letters were revised and modified before publication and that the original wording may have been much more explicit.

In the year 474 the Quaestor Licinianus arrived in Gaul, carrying with him the patent of the patriciate, which, with the Mastership of the Forces, was now conferred upon Ecdicius. Sidonius was delighted at this,[3] and he reposed great hopes in the coming mission of Licinianus to the Gothic court.[4] We know nothing of that mission except that it gained no concession from Euric, at least as far as Auvergne was concerned. If the appointment conferred on Ecdicius was meant to convince the Goth that the Emperor Nepos was organising a formidable resistance, it failed dismally. It seems safe to say that the speedy supersession of Ecdicius, the declared enemy

---

[1] *Epist.* III. 2.   [2] *Epist.* III. 3. 9.
[3] *Epist.* V. 16.   [4] *Epist.* III. 7. 2 sqq.

of the Goths, by a more innocuous *magister militum*
betokened a change of policy in the direction of
conciliation with Euric. But the history of all these
doings is so obscure that we need not dwell longer
upon them. The end came in the following year
(475), when Rome ceded Auvergne to the Goths in
order to retain or regain [1] a small strip of Provence.
At this betrayal of the most loyal part of Gaul after
years of suffering for the Roman cause Sidonius was
filled with consternation. A moving letter written
to Bishop Graecus of Marseilles, who had had a hand
in the drafting of the treaty,[2] voices his indignation
and scorn. " Our slavery," he says, " is the price that
has been paid for the security of others." [3]

Clermont was occupied by Victorius, a Roman in
the Gothic service, now created Count of Auvergne.
He spared the town, no doubt by order of Euric, and
probably pardoned all but the most prominent of the
resisters. It was impossible to ignore the uncom-
promising hostility of the bishop. Sidonius was
confined in the fortress of Livia, near Carcassonne.[4]
He seems to have been given some titular duties to
alleviate the indignity of his imprisonment,[5] and

[1] It is just possible that the Goths had been in possession of
the whole of Provence for two years and that the corner of
it which included Arles was regained by the bargain of A.D.
475; see Stevens, pp. 209 sqq.
[2] The part played by Epiphanius and the four other
bishops (Basilius of Aix, Leontius of Arles, Faustus of Riez,
Graecus of Marseilles) in the making of the treaty is a vexed
question. See Stevens, pp. 207–209.
[3] *Epist.* VII. 7.
[4] Liviana, according to the Peutiger Table; Sidonius
speaks only of *moenia Liviana.* It has been identified with
the modern Capendu.
[5] *Epist.* IX. 3. 3 *per officii imaginem solo patrio exactus.*

although he complained bitterly of his lot, he does not seem to have been badly treated. He had a friend at the Gothic court, Leo of Narbonne,[1] who was now a trusted minister of Euric, discharging duties similar to those discharged for the Roman Emperor by the *quaestor sacri palatii*.[2] Leo asked him to transcribe the life of Apollonius of Tyana by Philostratus, probably wishing to give him a task which would take his mind off his troubles. When this was completed and sent to Leo Sidonius had already won his freedom through the good offices of his friend (possibly before the end of the year 476). His movements after his release are not entirely clear. It seems certain that he was not allowed to return to Clermont immediately.[3] Sooner or later he went to Bordeaux, and eventually he appeared as a suppliant at the court of Euric.[4] Two months passed without an answer to his suit.[5] At this point he sent to his friend Lampridius,[6] who enjoyed the favour of the Gothic king, a letter containing a poem of 59 hendecasyllabic lines, in which he not only makes reference to his own plight but draws an impressive picture of the Gothic court, crowded with embassies from near and far—even from distant Persia—all anxious to win the gracious favour of the

[1] See note on *Carm.* 9. 314.

[2] On this office see note on *Carm.* 1. 25. In *Epist.* VIII. 3. 3 Leo is described as the king's mouthpiece.

[3] *Epist.* VIII. 9. 3, *ago adhuc exulem.*

[4] *Epist.* VIII. 9. Sidonius does not say definitely that the court was then at Bordeaux. It is possible that he had gone on from Bordeaux to Toulouse, the Gothic capital.

[5] Perhaps he had already had one audience; *semel visos, Epist.* VIII. 9. 5. *v.* 17, is obscure, but may mean this.

[6] See note on *Carm.* 9. 314.

mighty Euric.[1] It is almost certain that he wished
this poem to be brought to the notice of the king.[2]
Whatever its effect may have been, it is certain that
Sidonius was eventually allowed to return to Clermont
and to resume his duties as bishop.

The events of the past few years had left their mark
upon him. Truer to the traditions of his class than
most of his friends had been, he had clung wistfully,
hoping against hope, to his faith in the Empire.
Even as late as the year 474 he regarded the consulship as a dazzling prize.[3] He had indeed come to see
that worldly ambition is not everything, and he maintained in his later years that the humblest of God's
ministers held a rank more exalted than the highest
dignities of state.[4] But in his eyes the two views
were not inconsistent. Church and State were
merged in the great unity of Romanism. To maintain the Catholic faith against Arianism and to
maintain the Roman civilisation against barbarism—
these were sacred duties bound up with the heritage
into which he had been born. The sense of that
heritage was strong in Sidonius. As a Gallo–Roman
noble he had been cradled and nurtured in the traditions of the past, and it was a matter of pride as well
as of conviction to uphold them. The whole ten-

---

[1] Mommsen has some interesting pages on this poem:
Reden u. Aufsätze, pp. 136 sqq.

[2] It is absurd to suppose that Euric was ignorant of Latin.
It is true that he used an interpreter when dealing with
Epiphanius (Ennod., *Vit. Epiph.* 90); but that need not mean
more than that he did not feel quite capable of dealing with
the highly polished language of the Roman envoy; see Roger,
op. cit., p. 58. We need not, of course, assume that he
personally read the poem of Sidonius, but if he did, he
probably understood its general drift.

[3] *Epist.* V. 16. 4.   [4] *Epist.* VII. 12. 4.

dency of his education had been to turn his gaze backward. The literature and the history of bygone days were his inspiration, and he could not imagine any culture worth having which was not drawn from that all-sufficient source. Deep down in his heart was the vision of the Empire, a spiritual as well as a material force, appointed from of old to guard all that was most precious. In that last struggle of the Arvernians the heroic bishop was fighting for this idealised Rome, majestic even in her day of humiliation. Amid all the despair of those times there had lurked a hope that somehow the Empire might arise from its ashes and assert itself. But such self-deception could continue no longer. He had to realise that now, for better or worse, the " barbarian " kings were the inheritors of the Empire in the West. Perhaps, as he surveyed the scene at Euric's court, even he dimly perceived that the change now going on was " not so much the Germanisation of the Romans as the Romanisation of the Germans." [1] Rome was not a spent force, even in the West. But for Sidonius the revulsion was too violent. Although the pictures sometimes drawn of his despair after his return to Clermont have been exaggerated through misunderstanding of his Latin combined with arbitrary dating of his letters, there can be little doubt that the shattering of his hopes and ideals told heavily upon him. But he did not break down utterly. He had many friends who did what they could to cheer him. The preparation of his letters for publication helped to divert him, though it must have given him many a pang by calling up memories of other days. Above all there were his episcopal

---

[1] Mommsen, *Reden u. Aufsätze*, p. 139.

duties. All the evidence goes to show that he was loved and trusted by his flock, that he took a helpful interest in their various concerns, and that he was assiduous in the performance of his ecclesiastical functions.[1] The governor, Count Victorius, who was a Catholic, showed himself helpful and sympathetic— but alas! only for a time. One would like to think that Sidonius did not live to see the change which happened. It is just possible that he was spared the distress which his son brought upon his house.[2] We do not know the year of his death ; A.D. 479 seems the earliest date to which it can be assigned, but a somewhat later date seems probable.[3] He was canonised, and in Clermont his feast is still celebrated on the 21st of August.

Sidonius is one of the many writers who " lisped in numbers, for the numbers came." He wrote poetry from early years,[4] and some of it was circulated among his friends, but there is no evidence that any of it was published before the collection still extant appeared. That collection falls into two parts, which were probably published separately but subsequently combined. The first part consists of the

[1] For the conduct of Sidonius as bishop see Chaix, Vol. II, Stevens, c. VII. The present volume does not contain any of the letters written by Sidonius as bishop; these begin in Book III.

[2] See p. xxxvi, n. 2.

[3] Mommsen supports 479, and is followed by Duchesne and Stein. This dating, however, depends too much on an arbitrary handling of the worthless " epitaph " (see p. xxxix, n. 1). Aprunculus, the successor of Sidonius in the see, died in A.D. 490, but the date of his installation is unknown. The last letter of Sidonius is assigned to A.D. 479 or 480; see, however, p. lix, n. 2.

[4] *Carm.* 9. 9 sq.; *Epist.* V. 21, IX. 16. 3 *vv.* 41 sqq.

panegyrics mentioned above, which occur in reverse order,[1] together with prefaces and dedications. The second professedly consists of youthful poems. The panegyrics are constructed on the formal lines laid down by the rhetoricians and hitherto carried out most thoroughly in poetry by Claudian. Sidonius observes all the pitiable conventions of the *genre*, and succeeds in writing three " poems " which for prolonged insipidity, absurdity, and futility would be hard to beat. It is often very difficult to see what he means—all the more difficult because he so frequently means very little. It is true that he occasionally brings forth a striking epigram—all the Latin poets could do that,—but these are by no means always as new as some of their admirers seem to think. A tenacious memory has given him plenty of material to steal from his predecessors. If imitation is the sincerest flattery, never—not even by Silius Italicus —were previous writers honoured with a more thorough-going adulation. But the imitation does not go beneath the surface. Some of it is merely mechanical. The old mythological machinery is made to work overtime; its figures are now rusty, creaking puppets, but he dresses them up in garish tinsel and spangles and makes them present a ludicrous caricature of their old-time splendour. It is pathetic to think that such mouldy antiquarianism was considered a worthy tribute to the master of the

---

[1] If this order is due to Sidonius himself, he may have desired to put the recently delivered panegyric on Anthemius in the place of honour as a compliment to the Emperor: but this is doubtful. Klotz points out that the order of the prose *Panegyrici Latini* is similarly reversed, except that Pliny, the model of them all, is naturally put first.

Roman world. The thought, when there is any worth speaking of, is thin, or at least unoriginal. The great object is not to think noble thoughts but to coin clever phrases. The ancients are ransacked for suggestions of all kinds, but their features are disguised by all the virtuosity of the schools, verbal jingles and bad puns, forced contrasts, unnatural use of words, straining after " point " in season and out of season. It cannot be said that any one of these faults was new; but in Sidonius they occur with such devastating frequency and with such grotesque exaggeration that the reader is often driven to distraction. The English language is quite incapable of reproducing all the oddities of these poems. The consequence is that, however feeble the translator, they must needs seem more tolerable in his version than in the original. Having said all this—and one could easily say a great deal more to the same effect—one feels bound to admit that there are a few places where the author deviates into sense, and even into real feeling not ineptly expressed, as when he exposes the sorrows of Lyons in the panegyric on Majorian or the character and prowess of the Arvenians in the panegyric on Avitus. There are also some descriptive touches and sentimental outbursts which suggest that the poet might have been more worthy of his calling if he had lived in an age of less depraved taste. But even these better morsels are soon spoilt by some bizarre absurdity. The chief value of the panegyrics—apart from the light which they incidentally throw on the literary training and ideals of the fifth century—lies in their historical information, which is of considerable importance.

The second part of the poems (*Carm.* 9–24) was

dedicated to Felix.[1] The dedicatory poem is a most extraordinary production. It is 346 lines long and consists mostly of a list (with various embellishments) of the subjects (mostly mythological) which he is not going to treat and the writers whose themes or style he is not going to reproduce. The other poems are of various kinds. Some are in hexameters, the others are in elegiacs or hendecasyllabics. There are a few epigrams, not unpleasing, especially nos. 12 and 17. No. 13 is the poem already mentioned in which he beseeches Majorian to remit the tax. Of the two *epithalamia* (nos. 11 and 15), each of considerable length, the best that can be said is that they are not the only absurd experiments in that conventional form to be found in European literature. The first one, with its tortuous conceits, is a nerve-racking problem for the would-be interpreter; in the second one Sidonius, after parading unblushingly his

---

[1] Sidonius tells us that Felix had asked him to gather together in a book the "trifles" which he had written and circulated in his younger days (*Carm.* 9. 9–11). In *vv.* 318 ff. he says that he rarely commits such efforts to the permanent medium of a papyrus-sheet, and when he does so the sheet is always a short one (not a roll); in other words, those "measures of his barren Muse" (*v.* 318) are not, as a rule, carefully preserved, and they are always short. This passage has often been misunderstood. Some authorities, ignoring *rarae*, take the passage to mean "I am entrusting these poems (for publication) to a short roll," and infer that the long poems 22 and 23 cannot have been included in the original collection, but were added in a second edition. The fact is, in all probability, that 22 and 23 were specially written for inclusion in the published collection, and when Sidonius speaks about his *brevis charta* he is thinking of the more youthful poems which form the main body of the book : indeed the two longer poems may possibly not have been written at the time when he wrote the prefatory poem to Felix.

ignorance of philosophy and astronomy, shows one or two genial traits which the jaded reader will scarcely appreciate. It is rather inappropriately followed by a very pious poem to Bishop Faustus. The description of Jonah in the whale's belly (*vv.* 25–30) is a striking instance of the poet's uncanny powers. It is, unfortunately, quite possible that Faustus and some other contemporaries admired its ingenuity. But the poem is not all as bad as that part. Although Sidonius can never wholly rid himself of his mannerisms, the second half (and indeed some of the earlier parts also) does at least suggest some sincere feeling, and the parts dealing with Lérins and Riez have an interest of their own. No. 22 is a very showy and obscure description of the " Burgus " of Pontius Leontius. Sidonius has no idea that the reader of what purports to be a description of a house might desire to learn what the house was really like rather than what the author could achieve as a verbal trickster. There is also the inevitable parade of gods and other mythological figures. *Hic multus tu, frater, eris* (*v.* 220; see note *ad loc.*) is, unfortunately, the best thing in this poem of 235 lines. No. 23 is a *tour de force*, 512 hendecasyllabics addressed to his friend Consentius of Narbonne. Though it has a fair share of the usual faults, it shows some skill and is probably the most interesting of all the longer poems. The description of the battered city, recently occupied by Theodoric, has a certain effectiveness. The praise of Theodoric may profitably be compared with *Epist.* I. 2. Pantomimic performances, which obviously enjoyed a considerable vogue even in those Christian times, are described in a notable passage. The picture of the chariot-race is a wonderfully vigorous effort, based on Statius ; unfortunately it is marred by some obscurity in the climax. The last part of the poem gives an interesting and valuable picture of the social life enjoyed by the Gallo–Roman nobles. The collection ends with an epilogue speeding the book on its way from the author to friends in different parts of the country.

Poem 22 (see the prefatory letter, § 1) was written not long after the occupation of Narbonne by Theodoric in A.D. 462. Probably the visit to Narbonne there mentioned is the same as the one mentioned in no. 23, which must in any case have been written not earlier than the year 462 and not later than 466 (the date of Theodoric's death). If these two poems were specially written for inclusion in the published edition (see p. lv, n. 1), we may plausibly assign the publication of poems 9–24 approximately to A.D. 463. The panegyrics must, of course, have been published after the delivery of the panegyric to Anthemius in the year 468. It is customary to assign them to 469 The letters also contain a number of poems. Several of them, in accordance with the stern resolution which Sidonius took on obtaining his bishopric, are of a religious cast, but these, with the exception of the poem in IX. 16. 3, are all very short. It may be of some interest, as the statements made on the subject are generally rather vague, to examine the letters with the object of discovering how seriously Sidonius took his vow to keep the old pagan Muse in check. Book II contains an inscription for the church built by Bishop Patiens at Lyons (II. 10. 4) and also an epitaph (II. 8. 3), which has no Christian content ; but as the letters in this book seem all to have been written before his episcopate, they are not relevant to our enquiry. Apart from these, there are five poems in the first seven books. Three of these, all with a Christian tone (IV. 11. 6, a lament for Claudianus Mamertus, IV. 18. 5, an inscription for the rebuilt church of St. Martin at Tours, and VII. 17. 2, an epitaph on the monk Abraham), may be assigned to the period of his bishopric, but the other two (III. 12. 5, a Christian epitaph on his grandfather, and IV. 8. 5, a trivial inscription for a drinking-cup) cannot be assigned to the same time with any probability. Thus the complete collection of his letters as originally planned contains no evidence of "pagan" poetry written by Sidonius after becoming bishop. The first of the two supplementary books contains the poem already mentioned describing Euric's court (VIII. 9. 5);[1] it has no trace of Christian influence. In the same book (VIII. 11. 3) Sidonius quotes a poem written in his old style which certainly belongs to his pre-episcopal days. So far he has only once broken his vow, and that one breach is so venial that it can scarcely be counted against him. Book IX is interesting. In the 12th letter, written "three Olympiads," *i.e.* 12 years, after his entry into holy orders (§ 2), he tells Oresius of the vow he had made on entering the ranks of the clergy to give up his old habit of versifying. This letter is placed, surely of set purpose, immediately before one written several years later, which contains a breach of his rule. Then, after a kindly letter to a young man with literary ambitions, there comes another in which his rule is broken. Next there comes, in the

---

[1] See pp. xlix sq.

last letter of all, a sort of palinode in verse, in which, after sketching his secular career and mentioning the honorary statue which his poetry had brought him, he speaks in penitent tones of his early verses and registers a vow no more to indulge in verse-writing, unless it be to celebrate the holy martyrs.[1] The way in which these last few letters expose his lapse from grace is as good as a sermon. Oresius had asked him for a poem (*Epist.* 12). After explaining that he had renounced such frivolities Sidonius promises to see if he can find any old compositions to satisfy his friend. Nothing of the kind is given in the letter. In the next letter (IX. 13) we find that Tonantius has asked him for a poem in Asclepiads which he might recite at a dinner-party. Sidonius with some show of diffidence sends him 28 Asclepiad verses in which he protests that he cannot now fitly satisfy such a request. This is a small lapse, but the mischief has been done; the memory of his happy days in the Muses' company comes upon him and he goes on to quote a poem of 120 lines which he had composed at a dinner-party in the reign of Majorian.[2] In letter 15 he relapses more completely into the bad old ways. Gelasius has heard of the verses written to Tonantius and wants some for himself. Sidonius

---

[1] No doubt in imitation of Prudentius. So far as is known he never carried out this ambition.

[2] In § 6 Sidonius says that this poem has been lying in a book-box for about 20 years. Most authorities think that the dinner-party must have occurred at Arles in 461, like the one described in *Epist.* I. 11. In that case 481 is an approximate date for the letter to Tonantius; even if we make allowance for the vagueness of " about 20 " we can scarcely make it earlier than 479, the year in which many persons would place the death of Sidonius. Mr. Stevens, however (p. 51), would assign the dinner party to the year 459.

composes a poem specially for him, 55 lines praising
contemporary writers, and at the end he hints that
he might be induced to write some more poetry for
his friend.   Then comes the great renunciation in the
last letter of the book.   Thus we find that the poem
to Euric, which is scarcely to be counted, the very
short poem in *Epist.* IX. 13, and the longer one in no.
15 are the only breaches of his self-denying rule, as
far as one can gather from his correspondence.   It
is a very creditable record.

It is not known in what year Sidonius began to
prepare his letters for publication; A.D. 469 is as
likely a date as any.[1]   The idea was suggested by his
friend Constantius of Lyons, to whom the work was
dedicated in the introductory letter.   It is certain
that the collection was published in instalments,
and not improbable that each book was published

---

[1] This date was suggested by Mommsen.   At first sight
it conflicts with *Epist.* I. 1. 4, in which Sidonius says that he
has a long-established reputation as a poet.   But in the first
place there can be no doubt that copies of the panegyrics
were circulated very soon after these poems were recited
(*Carm.* VIII, which accompanied a copy of the panegyric
on Avitus sent to Priscus Valerianus, says, of course with some
exaggeration, that the applause which greeted the poem is
still echoing through Rome); in the second place, it is quite
likely that *Carmina* 9–24 were first published about A.D. 463;
see p. lvii.   Again, those who would put the publication of
the first book of the letters after the restoration of Sidonius
to the see of Clermont (*i.e.* about A.D. 477) forget that his
attitude to his secular poetry had then changed, and he
would scarcely have spoken of it with the self-satisfaction
which he betrays in *Epist.* I. 1. 4.   But the question cannot
be definitely settled.   As it is incredible that any book of
the letters was published during the siege of Clermont, Book
III, which mentions the siege, must be assigned to a subsequent date.

INTRODUCTION

separately.[1] The last letter of Book VII is an epilogue addressed to Constantius. There the work was meant to end. But the letters had aroused much interest; there was a demand for a supplement, and more and more friends wished to be represented in the collection by letters addressed to them. At the instance of Petronius he added an eighth book.[2] In the last letter of this book, which is, like the epilogue of Book VII, addressed to Constantius, he says that he has now no letters left which are worth publication, but he gives a broad hint that with a little more time he might work up a few, and that a ninth book is not an impossibility. Firminus urged him to produce another book, pleading that Pliny had written nine books.[3] Sidonius complied, and added a book of sixteen letters which are by no means the least interesting in the collection. With that volume the published correspondence closes.

Sidonius revised his old letters for publication and added several specially written for inclusion in the collection. His chief model is Pliny,[4] though Symmachus also had a great influence on him, especially

---

[1] The evidence on this head, which is rather complicated, will be best considered in the commentary as the passages bearing upon it occur; it may, however, be pointed out here that it is wrong to cite *Epist.* I. 1. 1 as evidence that Book I was published separately. There Sidonius agrees to a request to include in one "volumen" *all* his letters that merit publication. *Volumen* must therefore mean "book" in the sense of a complete work (a meaning for which there is excellent authority). Those who take it as "book" in the sense of a division of a larger work ignore the word *omnes*.

[2] See VIII. 1. For Petronius see note on I. 7. 4.

[3] IX. 1. 1.

[4] *Epist.* IV. 22. 2; *ego Plinio ut discipulus assurgo.*

in the later books.[1] The mere fact that nearly every
letter has only a single theme is, as in the case of
Pliny, a sure sign that they were considerably
modified; real letters to friends are not generally so
limited.[2] Much that we should have liked to know
about the age and its personalities must have been
pruned away. Many of the letters are simply
miniature panegyrics; derogatory remarks are much
rarer than one would expect them to be in the
genuine familiar correspondence of an average human
being. The many letters to bishops assume a very
humble, sometimes abject, tone. Nearly every
letter is assiduously worked up according to the
principles of contemporary rhetorical teaching. It is
impossible here to give any adequate idea of the
ostentatious combination of stylistic elaboration
with sesquipedalian verbiage, Frontonian archaisms,
weird neologisms, and verbal jingles which makes
the correspondence such a nerve-wracking conglomeration. But it would be a mistake to regard the
style and diction of Sidonius as something new and
without precedent. He was in the main only carrying out with misguided zeal and a conspicuous lack
of taste the principles which had been taught in the
schools of rhetoric for centuries. These principles
were often sound enough, and might be helpful to
people who really had something to say, but even as
the young men in Quintilian's time had seized on

[1] There are some signs of the influence of Cicero, *Ad Fam.*
The more homely and informal style of the letters to Atticus
can scarcely have appealed to him.
[2] An interesting exception is the reference to the unstudious
habits of his son Apollinaris in *Epist.* IX. 1. 5; but we may
be sure that this is inserted in imitation of Cicero's words
about young Marcus.

INTRODUCTION

Seneca's *dulcia vitia*[1] for imitation and ignored the
qualities which made him a great writer, so also
after his time the young students and, too often,
their professors as well, were inclined to regard composition as a field for the exploitation of specious
" tricks of the trade," which became ends in themselves and were developed in the most fantastic
manner. This tendency increased as time went on.
Sidonius was not an original genius : he was a conscious artist working with traditional materials and
seeking only to exploit to the uttermost limit all the
" tips " which he had derived from the mechanical
teaching of the schools and from his reading of earlier
writers. The result is a *reductio ad absurdum* of all the
resources of rhetoric and a travesty of the Latin
language. But although he had detractors, most of
his educated contemporaries seem to have admired
him. So many recherché effects had never before
been found concentrated in such small space. If he
took liberties with the meaning of words, that only
increased the dazzling glamour of it all. If he was
obscure—well, anyhow it was great art, great art,
my masters ! It is pathetic to find Ruricius humbly
trying to imitate him though compelled to admit
that he did not understand him.[2] One may be sure
that in preparing the letters for publication Sidonius
elaborated and multiplied their mystifying artifices ;
but most of them must have been rather terrible even
in their original form. There are some cases where
he writes more simply, but his manner never completely leaves him.

Sidonius, imitating Pliny, arranges his letters with-

[1] Quintilian X. 1. 129.
[2] Ruric. *Epist.* II. 26. 3.

out regard to chronological order, though all the letters contained in Books I and II seem to have been originally written before his election to the bishopric. There are some signs of intentional grouping. The whole of Book VI and the first eleven letters of Book VII are addressed to bishops; the same is true of letters 13–15 in Book VIII and 2–4 in Book IX. In the latter part of Book IX, as we have seen, the letters seem to be arranged according to a set plan. The collection includes a letter from Claudianus Mamertus (IV. 2), which is followed by the reply of Sidonius. There is one letter to Papianilla; all the other recipients are men. Not many people are honoured by more than one letter, as the number of persons anxious to have their names perpetuated by inclusion in the correspondence was very large and Sidonius was anxious to oblige them.

Whatever one may think about their style and diction, the letters of Sidonius are an invaluable source of information on many aspects of the life of his time. It is true that one is often tempted to sigh for information which he withholds and to upbraid him for telling us so little when he might have told so much. The appetising lists sometimes drawn up of subjects on which he might well have thrown light make one's mouth water.[1] But he did not set out to write a history, and he was unfitted for such a task.[2] His views were limited. It is doubtful if he really thought or cared much about the social evils and distresses of his day until he was brought into contact

[1] See, for example, Hodgkin, *Italy and her Invaders*, II. pp. 372 f.
[2] On his conscious unfitness for historical writing, see below, p. lxvi.

with them as a bishop; and even then perhaps he only partially realised them. For a good part of his life his horizon was bounded by the pride and pre-judices of his class; indeed his aristocratic pride some-times breaks out rather ludicrously even in his later years. He was not a deep thinker, but he was a keen observer of external details. Many of his descriptions, in spite of their pretentious language, are both vivid and picturesque. From his pages we gather much knowledge of the lives led by the Gallo-Roman nobility as the Empire in the West tottered to its fall. Its pleasures, its good-fellowship, its ambitions, and sometimes its lack of ambition, its often narrow and pedantic but not unwholesome interests, its apparent indifference to many of the most terrible things going on around it, all pass before our eyes. We find also some valuable pictures of the " barbar-ians " who were taking over the Roman heritage. Here and there we get pleasing sidelights on the lives of great clerics, and we are helped to realise the power, mostly beneficent, wielded by the great Gallic bishops and priests in those troubled times. For these and many other glimpses we may well be grateful. As for Sidonius himself, when one has recovered from the exhaustion caused by wrestling with his showy pedantry one cannot repress a liking for him. Amid all his prejudices, his time-serving pliability at certain junctures, his excessive pride in his lineage and his ill-disguised literary vanity, one can discern a sympathetic nature and a simple goodness of heart. He accepted great responsibilities at a testing time and rose nobly to the occasion. He walked humbly before God, and all his pride fell from him as he contemplated his unfitness for his high

lxv

calling. Though strictly orthodox he is untouched
by the bitterness which so often showed itself in the
religious controversies of the day. He abhors the
religion of the Jews, but he can admire a Jew as a
man, and he dares to say so.[1] No one without
goodness and charm could have had such a circle of
devoted friends as he had. He could write in all
sincerity to Bishop Faustus: "Thanks be to God, not
even my enemies can charge me with half-hearted
friendship" (*Epist.* IX. 9. 5).

Besides his poems and letters Sidonius wrote a
number of short speeches or addresses (called by him
contestatiunculae), a copy of which he sent to Bishop
Megethius (*Epist.* VIII. 3). It is not certain that he
published them. Gregory of Tours (*Hist. Fr.* II.
22) refers to masses (*missae*) composed by him. He
was urged to write on the war with Attila and especially on the siege of Orléans and the wonderful
achievements of its bishop, Anianus. He found such
a large task too exacting, but promised to celebrate
the glories of Anianus (*Epist.* VIII. 15). There is
no evidence that this projected work was ever written.
He declined to write a historical work which Leo had
suggested to him (*Epist.* IV. 22). He did not translate the life of Apollonius of Tyana, as is often said,
but merely transcribed it (see p. xlix). He wrote
many poems besides those which have come down
to us, but it is not certain that he published any
collection of them.[2]

---

[1] *Epist.* III. 4. 1; cf. VI. 11. 1.

[2] In *Epist.* II. 8. 2, before quoting the epitaph on Philomathia, he says to Desideratus: *quam* (sc. *neniam*) *si non
satis improbas, ceteris epigrammatum meorum voluminibus applicandam mercennarius bybliopola suscipiet. Ceteris* is loosely

INTRODUCTION

The numerous manuscripts of Sidonius seem all to be derived from a single archetype of no great antiquity. They suffer from extensive dislocations, interpolations, corruptions, " corrections " and lacunae, but as they can very often be successfully used to check one another a text in the main satisfactory can be evolved from them. It is difficult to construct a convincing *stemma codicum*,[1] but we may divide the MSS. into four classes on the basis of certain dislocations and of differences in their contents. I have added to the MSS. most used by Luet-

---

used : he means " the existing books (or perhaps ' rolls ') of my epigrams." It is probably a case of " transferred epithet "; *ceterorum* would have been more logical : " the books containing my other epigrams."

Klotz (in Pauly-Wissowa, *R.-E.*, s.v. *Sidonius*) understands *epigrammata* to mean " small poems," hence " trifling verses " (*nugae*). He takes the reference to be to the extant *Carmina*. This view may well be correct, although there does not seem to be any passage in Sidonius where the word *epigramma* must necessarily have such an extended meaning. It generally means a short poem; see especially *Carm.* 22 *epist.* § 6, where *paucitas* is mentioned as characteristic of an *epigramma*; cf. *Epist.* IV. 8. 4, IX. 13. 2 *v.* 16, IX. 14. 6. The extended meaning may be present in *Epist.* IX. 12. 3, IX. 13. 5 (where there is a competition in the production of *epigrammata* and Sidonius composes a poem of 120 lines), and IX. 16 *v.* 56. It is certainly found in Alcimus Avitus, who humbly speaks of a quite lengthy poem as an *epigramma*; see especially *Poem.* VI. prol. (p. 274 *v.* 7, Peiper). The source of this use is probably Pliny, *Epist.* IV. 14. 9.

[1] The *stemma* of Leo (in Luetjohann's edition, p. xli) perhaps comes as near to the truth as it is possible to get. It is repeated with the addition of the codices N and R by M. C. Burke, *De Apollinaris Sidonii codice nondum tractato*, Munich, 1911.

johann and Mohr the codex R.[1] It is impossible
to mention all the codices.

Class I. (containing all the writings in the proper
order, except that in *Epist.* IX letters 6 and
7 are put after 9).
C. *Matritensis* Ee 102 (formerly at Cluni),
Madrid. X–XI cent. Much interpolated.
Akin to this MS. is Vaticanus 3421. X cent.

Class II. (All with disturbance in the order of the
letters in Books VI and VII; some contain
all the works, some *Epist.* alone, some *Epist.*
and some poems).
F. *Parisinus* 9551. XII cent.

Class III. Intermediate between I and II.
P. *Parisinus* 2781. X–XI cent.

Class IV. (a superior class, but with large lacunae.
Some contain only *Epist.*)
T. *Laurentianus* plut. XLV. 23, Florence.
XI–XII cent.
M. *Marcianus* 554, Florence. X cent. (*Epist.*
and *Carm.* I–VIII.)
L. *Laudianus* lat. 104, Oxford. *Epist.* only.
IX cent. The best MS.
N. *Parisinus* 18584. *Epist.* only. X cent.
Closely akin to L, but with more lacunae
and numerous " corrections."
V. *Vaticanus* 1783. *Epist.* only. X cent. Muti-
lated at the beginning and in the middle.

---

[1] See note 1, p. lxvii. Dr. M. Tyson has kindly ascertained
for me that this Rheims codex has safely survived the Great
War. My knowledge of its readings is derived entirely from
Burke's pamphlet.

R. *Remensis* 413, Rheims. *Epist.* only. IX–X
    cent. Closely akin to V. V and R. are
    less closely related to L than N is.

The fullest account of variant readings is given in
Luetjohann's edition. Mohr gives a shorter but
very useful *apparatus criticus*.

The following is a short list of works useful to
the student of Sidonius. An excellent and, on
the historical side, much more comprehensive
bibliography will be found in the work of Stevens
mentioned below, pp. 216–220.

TEXT: CRITICAL EDITIONS.

Gai Sollii Apollinaris Sidonii epistulae et carmina.
    Recens. et emend. C. Luetjohann. (*Monu-*
    menta Germaniae Historica Auct. Antiquiss.,
    VIII). Berolini, MDCCCLXXXVII. On the
    death of Luetjohann the editing was com-
    pleted by Mommsen and Leo, with the assist-
    ance of U. von Wilamowitz-Moellendorff
    and Buecheler. Mommsen added a life of
    Sidonius and very useful indices of persons
    and places. An index of words and linguistic
    usages, helpful as far as it goes, was compiled
    by E. Grupe, and a list of parallel passages by
    E. Geisler. Interesting information about
    this edition will be found in *Mommsen und*
    Wilamowitz: *Briefwechsel*, Berlin, 1935 (nu-
    merous letters: see the index to the vol.
    s.v. Sidonius).
C. Sollius Apollinaris Sidonius. Recens. P. Mohr.
    Lipsiae, MDCCCLXXXXV.

INTRODUCTION

A masterpiece, invaluable for its notes on subject-
matter: the only pity is that they are not more
numerous. The commentary is reprinted in Migne's
Patrologia Latina, LVIII.

There are some useful notes in the edition with
French translation by Grégoire and Collombet, 3 vols.,
Lyon–Paris, 1836, but as the text is antiquated and
the translation contemptible, the work is of no
great value.

Translations.

Sidonius has very seldom been translated into any
language. The only rendering worth mention is a
translation into English of the letters alone by O. M.
Dalton, 2 vols., Oxford, 1915. This translation,
though it does not profess to follow the Latin closely,
has been justly welcomed by students of Sidonius.
It is accompanied by a valuable introduction and
some helpful notes. Besides the effort of Grégoire
and Collombet, mentioned above, there is another
French translation (not markedly superior) by Baret
in Nisard's *Collection des auteurs latins* (with text:

INTRODUCTION

along with Ausonius and Venantius Fortunatus),
Paris, 1887.

LIFE AND WORKS OF SIDONIUS.

Chaix, L. -A. *Saint Sidoine Apollinaire et son siècle.*
2 vols. Clermont-Ferrand, 1866.
Uncritical, but of considerable value.

Fertig, M. *Cajus Sollius Apollinaris Sidonius u.
seine Zeit, nach seinen Werken dargestellt.* 3
parts. Würzburg, 1845–6, Passau, 1848.

Germain, A. *Essai littéraire et historique sur
Apollinaris Sidonius.* Paris, 1840.

Kaufmann, G. *Die Werke des Cajus Sollius
Apollinaris Sidonius als eine Quelle für die
Geschichte seiner Zeit.* Göttingen, 1864.

Mommsen, T. *Apollinaris Sidonius u. seine Zeit.*
In *Reden u. Aufsätze,* Berlin, 1905 etc.
Also in Luetjohann's edition; see above.

Stevens, C. E. *Sidonius Apollinaris and his Age.*
Oxford, 1933.
A stimulating and valuable work, to which
every reader must feel much indebted, even if
he cannot everywhere agree with the author.

There are useful articles on Sidonius in the Herzog–
Hauck *Realencyclopädie für protestantische Theologie
und Kirche* (by Arnold), the Pauly-Wissowa *Real-
encycl. d. klass. Altertumswissenschaft* (by Klotz), the
histories of Latin Literature by Teuffel (vol. 3, 6th
ed. by Kroll and Skutsch) and Schanz-Hosius-
Krüger (IV. 2); also in Ebert's *Allgemeine Gesch. d.
Litteratur d. Mittelalters im Abendlande,* 2nd ed., vol.
I, pp. 419–448.

INTRODUCTION

HISTORY AND CIVILISATION OF THE FIFTH CENTURY.

Bury, J. B. *History of the later Roman Empire.*
Vol. I, London, 1923.

Cambridge Medieval History. Vol. I. 2nd ed.,
Cambridge, 1924.

Dill, S. *Roman Society in the last Century of the
Western Empire.* 2nd ed., Lond., 1899, etc.
   A very readable and illuminating work, with
   some excellent pages on Sidonius and his
   times.

Duchesne, L. *Early History of the Christian Church*,
Vol. III. Translated by C. Jenkins. London,
1924.

Fauriel, C. *Histoire de la Gaule méridionale sous
les conquérants germains.* Vol. I, Paris,
1836.

Gibbon. *Decline and Fall of the Roman Empire*,
cc. 35 and 36 (in vols. III and IV of Bury's
edition, Lond., 1909).
   This part scarcely shows Gibbon at his best.

Hodgkin, T. *Italy and her Invaders.* Vols. I and
(especially) II. 2nd ed., Lond., 1892.
   Marked by good sense and an absence of the
   vagueness and evasiveness too often found
   in historical works on the fifth century.

Roger, M. *L'enseignement des lettres classiques
d'Ausone à Alcuin.* Paris, 1910.

Seeck, O. *Geschichte d. Untergangs d. Antiken Welt.*
Vol. VI. Stuttgart, 1920. Also articles in
Pauly-Wissowa, *R.-E.*, on various personages,
e.g. Avitus, Anthemius, Euric.
   Seeck's work is valuable, but prejudiced and
   often unreliable.

Stein,. E. *Geschichte d. spätrömischen Reiches.*
I Band. Vienna, 1928.
A very able and important work, though one may
not always agree with it.

Sundwall, J. *Weströmische Studien.* Berlin, 1915.
With a valuable prosopography of the fifth century.

THE LANGUAGE OF SIDONIUS.

No comprehensive treatment of this subject exists.
Besides Grupe's contribution to Luetjohann's edition
the following pamphlets may be mentioned:

Engelbrecht, A. *Untersuchungen über die Sprache
des Claudianus Mamertus.* Vienna, 1885.

Grupe, E. *Zur Sprache d. Apoll. Sidonius.* Zabern,
1892.
Stresses the influence of legal language on the
vocabulary of Sidonius.

Kretschmann, H. *De latinitate C. Sollii Apoll.
Sidonii.* 2 parts. Memel, 1870, 1872.

Mohr, P. *Zu Apoll. Sidonius.* Bremerhaven, 1886.

Müller, M. *De Apoll. Sidonii latinitate.* Halle,
1888.

MISCELLANEOUS.

Bitschofsky, R. *De C. Sollii Apoll. Sidonii studiis
Statianis.* Vienna, 1881.

Brakman, G. *Sidoniana et Boethiana.* Utrecht,
1904.

Geisler, E. *De Apoll. Sidonii studiis.* Breslau,
1885.

INTRODUCTION

Holland, R. *Studia Sidoniana.* Leipzig, 1905.

Kraemer, M. *Res libraria cadentis antiquitatis Ausonii et Apoll. Sidonii exemplis illustrata.* Marburg, 1909.

Schuster, M. *De C. Sollii Apoll. Sidonii imitationibus studiisque Horatianis.* Vienna etc., 1908.

Semple, W. H. *Quaestiones exegeticae Sidonianae.* Cambridge, 1930.
   Discusses the interpretation of various passages. A very helpful work.

ABBREVIATIONS USED IN THE TEXTUAL AND EXPLANATORY NOTES

add. = *addidi(t).*
C.M.H. = *Cambridge Medieval History.*
Class. Quart. loc. cit. = *Classical Quarterly* xxviii. (January, 1934).
codd. = *codices,* i.e. all the MSS. (or all the other MSS.) whose readings seem worth recording.[1]
def. = *defendit.*
dist. = *distinxi(t)* (" punctuated ").
edit. = *editio.*

Other abbreviations, when not self-evident, refer to authorities mentioned in the bibliographical part of the Introduction.

---

[1] When a reading stands alone after a colon (*e.g.* sat es *Mohr*: satis), *codd.* is to be supplied.

THE POEMS OF GAIUS SOLLIUS APOLLINARIS SIDONIUS

GAI SOLLII APOLLINARIS
SIDONII CARMINA

I

PRAEFATIO PANEGYRICI DICTI ANTHEMIO
AVGVSTO BIS CONSVLI

Cum iuvenem super astra Iovem natura locaret
    susciperetque novus regna vetusta deus,
certavere suum venerari numina numen
    disparibusque modis par cecinere sophos.
Mars clangente tuba patris praeconia dixit   5
    laudavitque sono fulmina fulmineo ;
Arcas et Arcitenens fidibus strepuere sonoris,
    doctior hic citharae pulsibus, ille lyrae ;
Castalidumque chorus vario modulamine plausit,
    carminibus, cannis, pollice, voce, pede.   10
sed post caelicolas etiam mediocria fertur
    cantica semideum sustinuisse deus.
tunc Faunis Dryades Satyrisque Mimallones aptae
    fuderunt lepidum, rustica turba, melos.
alta cicuticines liquerunt Maenala Panes   15
    postque chelyn placuit fistula rauca Iovi.

---

    [1] Mercury (Hermes), who was born in a cave of M. Cyllene,
in Arcadia.
    [2] Apollo; cf. 23. 266.

2

THE POEMS OF GAIUS SOLLIUS APOLLINARIS SIDONIUS

I

PREFACE TO THE PANEGYRIC IN HONOUR OF THE EMPEROR ANTHEMIUS, CONSUL FOR THE SECOND TIME

WHEN nature established the young Jupiter above the stars and the new god was entering upon an ancient sovereignty, all the deities vied in paying worship to their deity, and uttered in diverse measures the same " bravo." Mars with trumpet's blare acclaimed his sire and with thunderous din praised the thunderbolts. The Arcadian[1] and the Archer God[2] sounded the clanging strings, the one more skilled to strike the zither, the other the lyre. Castalia's maiden band gave forth their plaudits in varied strains with songs, reeds, thumb, voice and foot. But after the denizens of heaven, 'tis said, the god brooked even the inferior chants of demigods; then Dryads in union with Fauns, Mimallones[3] with Satyrs, a rustic multitude, poured forth a sprightly song. The Pans that sound the hemlock-reed left high Maenalus, and after the lyre the hoarse pipe

[3] Nymph-attendants of Bacchus.

hos inter Chiron, ad plectra sonantia saltans,
    flexit inepta sui membra facetus equi;
semivir audiri meruit meruitque placere,
    quamvis hinnitum, dum canit, ille daret.   20
ergo sacrum dives et pauper lingua litabat
    summaque tunc voti victima cantus erat.
sic nos, o Caesar, nostri spes maxima saecli,
    post magnos proceres parvula tura damus,
audacter docto coram Victore canentes,   25
    aut Phoebi aut vestro qui solet ore loqui;
qui licet aeterna sit vobis quaestor in aula,
    aeternum nobis ille magister erit.
ergo colat variae te, princeps, hostia linguae;
    nam nova templa tibi pectora nostra facis.   30

II

PANEGYRICVS

Auspicio et numero fasces, Auguste, secundos
erige et effulgens trabealis mole metalli
annum pande novum consul vetus ac sine fastu

---

¹ This idea recurs in 14. 27–30.

² Victor, *quaestor sacri palatii* under Anthemius. The
holder of this office acted as the Emperor's mouthpiece in the
Consistory, the Senate, and elsewhere. He was responsible
for the drafting of laws and of Imperial answers to petitions.
Rutilius Namatianus (1. 172) likewise describes the quaestor
as "speaking with the mouth of the Emperor." Cf. Claudian,
Fl. Mall. Cons. 35, and below, *C.* 5. 569; also *Epist.* viii. 3. 3.
Phoebi ore refers to Victor's poetry.

³ *vestro = tuo*; so in the next line *vobis = tibi*. There
seems to be no certain instance of this use before the third
century. It is quite common in Sidonius.

4

pleased Jove's ears. Amid this throng Chiron, dancing to the sounding quill, moved his ungainly horse-limbs elegantly, and that beast-man earned a hearing and found grace even though he neighed in the midst of his singing.[1]

So tongues rich and poor made an acceptable offering, and the greatest tribute in that day's sacrifice was song. In like manner, O Caesar, chiefest hope of our time, I come after great lords and offer thee humble incense, boldly singing my lay in presence of the learned Victor,[2] who is wont to speak either with the voice of Phoebus or with thine,[3] and who, though he is quaestor in thine everlasting court, shall everlastingly be my master.[4] So, my prince, let offering of diverse utterance pay worship to thee; for thou makest our hearts new temples for thy habitation.

II

PANEGYRIC[5]

RAISE up, Augustus, thy second[6] fasces, seconded by Fortune; gleaming with mass of gold upon thy robe do thou, an old consul, begin the new year, and deem it no disgrace to grace[7] the roll of office

[4] *i.e.* although he is your subordinate, he shall always be my master. *Magister* implies "teacher," but there is a play on the use of the word in the titles of various Imperial officials. Victor may have been one of Sidonius' teachers at Lyons or elsewhere, but the present passage does not prove it.

[5] Recited to the Senate on Jan. 1, A.D. 468. See Introd., p. xl, and *Epist.* 1. 9.

[6] A play (as old as Ovid) on the two meanings of *secundus*, "second" and "propitious." Anthemius had been consul for the first time in A.D. 455.

[7] The translator has done his poor best to reproduce one part of the verbal jingle *fastu, fastis, fastigatus*.

scribere bis fastis; quamquam diademate crinem
fastigatus eas umerosque ex more priorum   5
includat Sarrana chlamys, te picta togarum
purpura plus capiat, quia res est semper ab aevo
rara frequens consul. tuque o cui laurea, Iane,
annua debetur, religa torpore soluto
quavis fronde comas, subita nec luce pavescas   10
principis aut rerum credas elementa moveri.
nil natura novat: sol hic quoque venit ab ortu.

    Hic est, o proceres, petiit quem Romula virtus
et quem vester amor; cui se ceu victa procellis
atque carens rectore ratis respublica fractam   15
intulit, ut digno melius flectenda magistro,
ne tempestates, ne te, pirata, timeret.
te prece ruricola expetiit, te foedere iunctus
adsensu, te castra tubis, te curia plausu,
te punctis scripsere tribus collegaque misit   20
te nobis regnumque tibi; suffragia tot sunt
quanta legit mundus. fateor, trepidavimus omnes,
ne vellet collega pius permittere voto
publica vota tuo. credet ventura propago?
in nos ut possint, princeps, sic cuncta licere,   25

    24–26. *dist. ego.* Cf. 7. 310, 421 sq.

---

   [1] *i.e.* of Tyrian purple. Gallienus was the first emperor to
wear the *chlamys* at Rome (*Hist. Aug., Gallien,* 16. 4).

   [2] *i.e.* the *toga picta* (purple with gold embroidery), which,
with the *tunica palmata,* had become the official garb of the
consuls, and is here contrasted with the Imperial garb.

   [3] *pirata* : with special reference to Geiseric. Cf. *v.* 354.

   [4] *foed. iunct., i.e.,* the " barbarian" *foederati* (Introd.,
p. x, n. 2). Their assent was important.

6

twice with thy name. Although thou walkest with
a diadem surmounting thy hair and thy shoulders
are covered by a Tyrian[1] mantle after the fashion
of thy predecessors, yet may the bright purple
of the consul's gown[2] charm thee more; for repeated
consulships have from all time been rare. And
thou, Janus, to whom a laurel wreath is due every
year, dispel thy lethargy, bind thy locks with any
foliage; and be not affrighted by the sudden radiance
of our prince, nor deem that the elements are in upheaval. Nature is making no change; this day's
Sun also has come from the East.

This, my Lords, is the man for whom Rome's
brave spirit and your love did yearn, the man to
whom our commonwealth, like a ship overcome by
tempests and without a pilot, hath committed her
broken frame, to be more deftly guided by a worthy
steersman, that she may no more fear storm or
pirate.[3] The country-dweller's prayer, the good-
will of the leagued peoples,[4] the trumpet in the camp,
the plaudits in the senate-house all called for thee;
for thee have the tribes recorded their suffrages,[5]
and thy colleague hath consigned thee to us and the
sovereignty to thee: all the votes that the whole
world can muster are for thee. I confess we were all
sore disquieted lest thine honest colleague should
commit to thine own decision what all the people
had decided. Will future generations believe it?—
to ensure, O Prince, that this complete power over

[5] A mere rhetorical flourish. The mention of the army,
the Senate, and the eastern Emperor is quite correct, as
they all played some part in the election of a western
Emperor, but the people might merely "acclaim" him
after his election. Cf. 5. 386–388.

de te non totum licuit tibi.   facta priorum
exsuperas, Auguste Leo ; nam regna superstat
qui regnare iubet : melius respublica vestra
nunc erit una magis, quae sic est facta duorum.

    Salve, sceptrorum columen, regina Orientis,   30
orbis Roma tui, rerum mihi principe misso
iam non Eoo solum veneranda Quiriti,
imperii sedes, sed plus pretiosa quod exstas
imperii   genetrix.   Rhodopen   quae   portat   et
    Haemum,
Thracum terra tua est, heroum fertilis ora.   35
excipit hic natos glacies et matris ab alvo
artus infantum molles nix civica durat.
pectore vix alitur quisquam, sed ab ubere tractus
plus potat per vulnus equum ; sic lacte relicto
virtutem gens tota bibit.   crevere parumper :   40
mox pugnam ludunt iaculis ; hos suggerit illis
nutrix plaga iocos.   pueri venatibus apti
lustra feris vacuant, rapto ditata iuventus
iura colit gladii, consummatamque senectam
non ferro finire pudet : tali ordine vitae   45
cives Martis agunt.   at tu circumflua ponto
Europae atque Asiae commissam carpis utrimque

---

[1] Leo, the eastern Emperor, who nominated Anthemius
as Emperor of the West.
[2] Constantinople was called New Rome in a law of Constantine.   Other titles were " Eastern Rome " and " Second
Rome."
[3] *Plus* often usurped the functions of *magis*, as *magis*
usurped those of *potius*.   *Sed magis* is used for " but rather "
even in the poetry of the classical period.   Here *sed plus* has
the same meaning.   *Plus quam* is sometimes found in the
8

II. PANEGYRIC ON ANTHEMIUS

us should be thine, full power over thyself was denied thee. Augustus Leo,[1] thou dost surpass the deeds of thy forerunners; for he who can command a man to reign towers above regal power. Now your government shall be more perfectly one, having thus become a government of two.

All hail to thee, pillar of sceptred power, Queen of the East, Rome of thy hemisphere,[2] no longer to be worshipped by the eastern citizen alone, now that thou hast sent me a sovereign prince—O home of Empire, and more precious in that thou appearest before the world as Empire's mother! The land of the Thracians, whereon Rhodope and Haemus rest, is thine, a region fruitful of heroes. Here children are born into a world of ice, and their native snow hardens the soft limbs of infants even from the mother's womb. Scarce anyone is reared at the breast; rather[3] is he dragged from the maternal bosom to suck from a horse through a wound; thus deserting milk the whole race drinks in courage. They have grown but a short time, and anon they play at battle with javelins; this sport is prompted by the wounds that suckled them. The boys, gifted hunters, clear the dens of their beasts; the young men, enriched with plunder, honour the laws of the sword; and when their old age has reached its fullness not to end it with steel is a disgrace. Thus do these countrymen of Mars order their lives. But thou, surrounded by the sea, dost imbibe a tempered blend of Europe's and Asia's air, commingled from two sides;

sense of *potius quam*. Another use of *plus = magis* is to form comparatives (*e.g. v.* 33 above). This is common in Sidonius: see Schmalz-Hofmann, *Syntax*, pp. 463 f.

9

temperiem; nam Bistonios Aquilonis hiatus
proxima Calchidici sensim tuba temperat Euri.
interea te Susa tremunt ac supplice cultu   50
flectit Achaemenius lunatum Persa tiaram.
Indus odorifero crinem madefactus amomo
in tua lucra feris exarmat guttur alumnis,
ut pandum dependat ebur; sic trunca reportat
Bosphoreis elephas inglorius ora tributis.   55
porrigis ingentem spatiosis moenibus urbem,
quam tamen angustam populus facit; itur in aequor
molibus et veteres tellus nova contrahit undas;
namque Dicarcheae translatus pulvis harenae
intratis solidatur aquis durataque massa   60
sustinet advectos peregrino in gurgite campos.
sic te dispositam spectantemque undique portus,
vallatam pelago terrarum commoda cingunt.
fortunata sat es Romae partita triumphos,
et iam non querimur: valeat divisio regni.   65
concordant lancis partes; dum pondera nostra
suscipis, aequasti.
        Tali tu civis ab urbe
Procopio genitore micas, cui prisca propago
Augustis venit a proavis; quem dicere digno

64. sat es *Mohr* : satis.

---

[1] Sidonius means *Calchedonius* or *Chalcedonius*, from Chal-
cedon, which faced Constantinople on the Asiatic side of the
strait.

[2] *Lunatus* may mean "moon-shaped" or "crescent-
shaped," but among the many forms of the tiara I have not
found one really entitled to such a description. The epithet
may refer to the ornamentation. Martial uses *lunatus* for
"decorated with crescents."

[3] Dicarchus, or Dicaearchus, was the founder of Puteoli.
The reference is to *pulvis Puteolanus (pozzolana)*, a volcanic
earth found near Puteoli. The cement made from it sets
hard when submerged in water. The "invasion" of the sea

for the Thracian blasts of Aquilo are gradually softened by the breath of Eurus' trumpet, wafted from Calchis[1] hard by. Meanwhile Susa trembles before thee, and the Persian of Achaemenes' race in suppliant guise inclines his crescent-tiara.[2] The Indian, with hair steeped in fragrant balm, disarms for thy profit the throat of his land's wild denizens, that he may make payment of curved ivory; thus the elephant takes home ingloriously a mouth shorn of the tribute yielded to the Bosphorus. Thou dost spread out a great city of spacious walls, yet doth the multitude therein make its bounds too narrow; so the sea is invaded with massive masonry and new land cramps the old waters; for the dusty sand of Puteoli[3] is brought thither and made solid by entering the water, and the hardened mass bears upon it imported plains amid an alien flood. Thus art thou ordered; on all sides thou beholdest harbours, and, walled in as thou art by the sea, thou art surrounded by all the blessings of earth. Right fortunate art thou in having shared Rome's triumphs, and now we regret it no longer; farewell to the division of the empire! The two sides of the balance are poised; by taking over our weights thou hast made all even.

A citizen from such a city, thou shinest also with the lustre of thy father Procopius,[4] whose ancient lineage springs from imperial ancestors, a man

here described took place at various points of the shore when the walls of Constantine were no longer able to contain the whole population. For subsequent extensions and for the harbours see Bury, *Later Rom. Emp.* I. pp. 70–73.

[4] Procopius, a Galatian who rose to be *magister militum per Orientem* and patrician. He obviously claimed descent from the Procopius who was a so-called Emperor for a few months (365–6), and who seems to have been related to the house of Constantine.

non datur eloquio, nec si modo surgat Averno   70
qui cantu flexit scopulos digitisque canoris
compulit auritas ad plectrum currere silvas,
cum starent Hebri latices cursuque ligato
fluminis attoniti carmen magis unda sitiret.

    Huic quondam iuveni reparatio credita pacis   75
Assyriae; stupuit primis se Parthus in annis
consilium non ferre senis; conterritus haesit
quisque sedet sub rege satraps : ita vinxerat omnes
legati genius. tremuerunt Medica rura,
quaeque draconigenae portas non clauserat hosti, 80
tum demum Babylon nimis est sibi visa patere.
partibus at postquam statuit nova formula foedus
Procopio dictante magis, iuratur ab illis
ignis et unda deus, nec non rata pacta futura
hic divos testatur avos. Chaldaeus in extis   85
pontificum de more senex arcana peregit
murmura; gemmantem pateram rex ipse retentans
fudit turicremis carchesia cernuus aris.
suscipit hinc reducem duplicati culmen honoris :

---

[1] Orpheus. There is a similar passage in 23. 178–94.
[2] Sidonius likes elliptical uses of *magis* and *plus*. The point
here seems to be " the river was thirsty rather than thirst-
quenching." Cf. 23. 194.
[3] *i.e.* to Procopius.

12

whom no eloquence could worthily celebrate—not even if from Avernus that bard[1] should arise who once with his song swayed rocks and with his tuneful fingers impelled the woods to hasten, all ears, to the sounding quill, while the waters of Hebrus stood still and, its flow held fast, the waves of the entranced river were strangely athirst[2] for song.

To him[3] once in his youth was committed the restoring of peace with Assyria.[4] The Parthian was amazed that he had no power to withstand the aged wisdom of those youthful years. Every satrap that sat below the king faltered in terror, so strongly had the envoy's genius gripped them. The Median realms trembled, and Babylon, that had not closed her gates against the serpent-born foe,[5] now at last thought herself too widely opened. Then when a treaty had been established between them on new terms, recited by Procopius to the Magi, they took oath by their gods, fire and water, and he called his divine ancestors to witness that the bargain should be upheld. An aged Chaldaean over a victim's entrails, in the manner of the pontiffs, muttered the mystic words, and the king himself, holding a jewelled bowl, stooped and poured out cups over the incense-burning altar. When the envoy returned, the eminence of a twofold honour welcomed him;

[4] *Assyriae, Parthus, Medica.* All these refer to the Persian empire. This embassy negotiated terms of peace with Varahran V in A.D. 422 after a war caused by the persecutions of Christians in Persia. Bury, II. pp. 4 f.

[5] Alexander the Great; see *vv.* 121–3. Babylon admitted Alexander without a struggle. Sidonius absurdly implies that she showed contempt for his impending attack by keeping her gates open. A similar idea occurs in *v.* 449 (unless we read *strident*).

13

patricius nec non peditumque equitumque magister
praeficitur castris, ubi Tauri claustra cohercens   91
Aethiopasque vagos belli terrore relegans
gurgite pacato famulum spectaret Orontem.

Huic socer Anthemius, praefectus, consul et idem,
iudiciis populos atque annum nomine rexit.   95
purpureos Fortuna viros cum murice semper
prosequitur ; solum hoc tantum mutatur in illis,
ut regnet qui consul erat. sed omittimus omnes :
iam tu ad plectra veni, tritus cui casside crinis
ad diadema venit, rutilum cui Caesaris ostrum   100
deposito thorace datur sceptroque replenda
mucrone est vacuata manus. cunabula vestra
imperii fulsere notis et praescia tellus
aurea converso promisit saecula fetu.
te nascente ferunt exorto flumina melle   105
dulcatis cunctata vadis oleique liquores
isse per attonitas baca pendente trapetas.

---

[1] He became *magister utriusque militiae* (or *m. peditum et
equitum* or *m. peditum equitumque*), receiving the eastern command. In the eastern Empire there were five such officers,
two "in the Presence" and three with special districts assigned
to them. They all received the patriciate sooner or later. In
the west there were originally only two such *magistri militum*
(this, or *mag. militiae*, is a handy abbreviation which may be
used of all such officers). These were called *magister peditum*
and *mag. equitum* respectively, but as the *magister peditum* held
a superior command over both infantry and cavalry he came
to be called *magister peditum equitumque* or *magister utriusque
militiae*. By and by this title was extended to the *magister
equitum*, and his all-powerful superior is specially designated
as *Patricius*; he was "The Patrician" *par excellence*, not only
commander-in-chief but leading adviser and right-hand man
of the Emperor. In this sense the title was borne by Aëtius,
Ricimer, and others. [This seems to be the prevalent view;
see, however, Professor Norman Baynes in *Journ. Rom.
Stud.* XII. (1922), pp. 224–229.]

II. PANEGYRIC ON ANTHEMIUS

Patrician now and Master of Horse and Foot,[1] he was set in command of camps where he must needs hold the barriers of Taurus and force the roaming Ethiopians over the border by the terror of war and behold Orontes with calmed flood subservient to his will.

His wife's father was Anthemius,[2] who, as prefect and likewise consul, ordered peoples by his judgments and the year by his name. Men of the purple [3] are ever attended by Fortune with purple ready to bestow; the only change that happens to them is that he who was consul becomes sovereign. But I pass over all the others: come thou to my lyre, thou whose hair frayed by the warrior's helmet came [4] to wear the diadem, thou who hast laid aside the breastplate to receive the glowing purple of a Caesar, and whose hand hath been emptied of the sword to be filled with the sceptre. Thy cradle gleamed with tokens of imperial power, and the prophetic earth, altering her progeny, gave promise of a golden age. They tell how, at thy birth, honey appeared, making rivers flow tardily with sweetened waters, and oil ran through the amazed mills while the olive-berry still

[2] Anthemius, a leading figure in the early part of the fifth century; *comes sacrarum largitionum* 400, *magister officiorum* 404, *praefectus praetorio orientis* 404–415, consul 405, *patricius* not later than 406; regent for the young Theodosius II on the death of Arcadius (408). He built the new walls of Constantinople (413).

[3] *i.e.* of Imperial or consular family: for the association of purple with the consulship see *v.* 7 n., also 24. 98. The meaning is that consulships and the Imperial throne are the natural destiny of such persons.

[4] *venit* is Historic Present, which Sidonius uses very freely. The rather frigid iteration *veni—venit* is no doubt intentional.

protulit undantem segetem sine semine campus
et sine se natis invidit pampinus uvis.
hibernae rubuere rosae spretoque rigore   110
lilia permixtis insultavere pruinis.
tale puerperium quotiens Lucina resolvit,
mos elementorum cedit regnique futuri
fit rerum novitate fides. venisse beatos
sic loquitur natura deos : constantis Iuli   115
lambebant teneros incendia blanda capillos ;
Astyages Cyro pellendus forte nepoti
inguinis expavit diffusum vite racemum ;
praebuit intrepido mammas lupa feta Quirino ;
Iulius in lucem venit dum laurea flagrat ;   120
magnus Alexander nec non Augustus habentur
concepti serpente deo Phoebumque Iovemque
divisere sibi : namque horum quaesiit unus
Cinyphia sub Syrte patrem ; maculis genetricis
alter Phoebigenam sese gaudebat haberi,   125
Paeonii iactans Epidauria signa draconis.
multos cinxerunt aquilae subitumque per orbem
lusit venturas famulatrix penna coronas.
ast hunc, egregii proceres, ad sceptra vocari
iam tum nosse datum est, laribus cum forte paternis
protulit excisus iam non sua germina palmes.   131

---

[1] Verg. *Aen.* II. 682.

[2] Herodotus I. 108. He dreamed that a vine issued from
his daughter's womb and spread over all Asia.

[3] This story does not seem to occur in any previous writer.
Possibly it was in the early part (now lost) of Suetonius'
Iulius.

[4] Alexander the Great claimed to be the son of Zeus Ammon,
Augustus was rumoured to be the son of Apollo ; these gods
were said to have visited the mothers in the form of serpents.
For accounts of Alexander's miraculous birth see, for example,

II. PANEGYRIC ON ANTHEMIUS

hung upon the bough. The plain brought forth without seed a waving crop and the vine-branch looked grudgingly on the grapes brought into being without her. Roses blushed red in winter and lilies scorning the cold mocked the surrounding frosts. When Lucina is bringing such a birth to fulfilment the order of the elements gives way and a changed world gives assurance of coming sovereignty. Thus does nature declare that blessed gods have arrived. Flames played lovingly round the childish locks of the staunch Iulus[1]; Astyages,[2] fated to be dethroned by his grandson Cyrus, shuddered to see the grape-clusters spreading from the vine that grew from the womb; the mother-wolf gave suck to the untroubled Quirinus; Julius came into the world whilst a laurel blazed[3]; Alexander the Great and Augustus are deemed to have been conceived of a serpent god,[4] and they claimed between them Phoebus and Jupiter as their progenitors; for one of them sought his sire near the Cinyphian Syrtes, the other rejoiced that from his mother's marks he was deemed the offspring of Phoebus, and he vaunted the imprints of the healing serpent of Epidaurus. Many have been encircled by eagles, and a quick-formed ring of cringing plumage has playfully figured the crown that was to come. But as for this prince of ours, illustrious Lords, right early might it be known that he was destined for the sceptre, when it came to pass that in his father's house a severed vine-branch brought forth shoots no longer its own. That was the

Justin. xi. 11 and Plutarch *Alex.* cc. 2 sq.; for Augustus see Suet. *Aug.* 94. From *v.* 126 it seems clear that Sidonius represents Augustus as claiming to be the son of Aesculapius, and therefore the *grandson* of Apollo.

imperii ver illud erat ; sub imagine frondis
dextra per arentem florebant omina virgam.
at postquam primos infans exegerat annos,
reptabat super arma patris, quamque arta terebat 135
lammina cervicem gemina complexus ab ulna
livida laxatis intrabat ad oscula cristis.
ludus erat puero raptas ex hoste sagittas
festina tractare manu captosque per arcus
flexa reluctantes in cornua trudere nervos,   140
nunc tremulum tenero iaculum torquere lacerto
inque frementis equi dorsum cum pondere conti
indutas Chalybum saltu transferre catenas,
inventas agitare feras et fronde latentes
quaerere, deprensas modo claudere cassibus artis,
nunc torto penetrare veru : tum saepe fragore   146
laudari comitum, frendens cum belua ferrum
ferret et intratos exirent arma per armos.
conde Pelethronios, alacer puer et venator,
Aeacida, titulos, quamquam subiecta magistri   150
terga premens et ob hoc securus lustra pererrans
tu potius regereris equo. non principe nostro
spicula direxit melius Pythona superstans
Paean, cum vacua turbatus paene pharetra
figeret innumeris numerosa volumina telis.   155

---

140. tendere *Buecheler.*

---

¹ As the boy's hands seem to be otherwise engaged (*v.* 136),
the idea may be that he eagerly pushes the visor up with his
face until it is sufficiently open for his purpose. In any case
the metal bruises him as he tries to snatch a kiss—this seems
to be the meaning of *livida oscula*; but the same adjective is
used in 7. 742 to denote the discoloration of the skin through
wearing a helmet, and Dr. Semple (*Quaest. Ex.,* p. 69) may be
right in finding the same reference here. *Cristis* means

spring-time of his sovereignty; in the guise of leafage happy omens burgeoned along that withered branch. But when the early years of infancy were past he would clamber over his father's armour, and gripping with his two forearms the neck pressed by the close-fitting metal he would loosen the helmet and find an entrance for his livid kisses.[1] In boyhood it was his sport to handle eagerly arrows that had been seized from the foe, and on captive bows to force the resisting strings on to the curving horn, or to hurl with boyish arm the quivering javelin, or with a leap to throw upon the back of a chafing steed all his weight of steel chain-armour and heavy lance; or at other times to find and chase the wild beasts, to seek them in their leafy lurking-places and, when he espied them, sometimes to enclose them in a tight net, sometimes to pierce them with cast of spear. Then would he oft be cheered with great noise by his comrades, as with gnashing teeth the beast received the steel and the weapon entered and passed clean through the shoulders. Now hide thy Thessalian honours, scion of Aeacus,[2] high-mettled boy and hunter—though, as thou didst bestride thy master's compliant back, and so traverse the haunts of beasts in safety, it was rather thou that wert controlled by thy steed. Even Paean Apollo did not aim his shafts better than our prince, as the god stood over Python and, sore distressed, with quiver well-nigh emptied, pierced those numerous coils with innumerable weapons.

"helmet," as in 7. 242. This rare use occurs first in Silius IV. 156, but Sidonius probably borrowed it from Claudian, *Rufin.* I. 346.

[2] *Aeacida,* Achilles: *magistri,* Chiron the centaur.

THE POEMS OF SIDONIUS

Nec minus haec inter veteres audire sophistas :
Mileto quod crete Thales vadimonia culpas ;
Lindie quod Cleobule canis " modus optimus esto ";
ex Ephyra totum meditaris quod Periander.;
Attice quodve Solon finem bene respicis aevi ;   160
Prienaee Bia, quod plus tibi turba malorum est ;
noscere quod tempus, Lesbo sate Pittace, suades ;
quod se nosse omnes vis, ex Lacedaemone Chilon.
praeterea didicit varias, nova dogmata, sectas :
quidquid laudavit Scythicis Anacharsis in arvis ;
quidquid legifero profecit Sparta Lycurgo ;   166
quidquid Erechtheis Cynicorum turba volutat
gymnasiis, imitata tuos, Epicure, sodales ;
quidquid nil verum statuens Academia duplex
personat ; arroso quidquid sapit ungue Cleanthes ;
quidquid Pythagoras, Democritus, Heraclitus   171
deflevit, risit, tacuit ; quodcumque Platonis
ingenium, quod in arce fuit, docet ordine terno,

165. laudatum est *codd.*

---

[1] Cf. 15. 44 sqq., where the maxims of the Seven Sages are
the same as here, except in the case of Solon. The saying
attributed to Periander seems to have been originally μελέτη
(Doric μελέτα) τὸ πᾶν, " practice is everything," "practice
makes perfect"; but Sidonius, like several other ancient
authors, takes μελέτα as the imperative of the verb μελετᾶν,
" to practise."

[2] The Cynics were more allied in doctrine to the Stoics than
to the Epicureans, and Sidonius may really be thinking of the
Cyrenaics; but Augustine, *C.D.* xix. 1 ad fin., asserts
that philosophers with very different views of the *summum
bonum* (in some cases " virtue," in others " pleasure ") adopted
the dress and customs of the Cynic school and were called
Cynici. Origen, *In Exod. Hom.* iv. § 6 (p. 178, ll. 21 ff.,
Baehrens), alleges that the Cynics make " pleasure and lust "
their *summum bonum*; cf. Augustine, *Contra Acad.* III. 19. 42.

[3] The doctrine that certain truth is unattainable belongs
especially to the New Academy, but Cicero, as Mr. Semple

20

II. PANEGYRIC ON ANTHEMIUS

And amid all these doings he busied himself no
less in hearkening to the lore of ancient sages[1]; how
Thales, that son of Miletus, condemned all lawsuits,
how Cleobulus of Lindus sings " Let moderation be
our ideal," how Periander of Corinth practises
everything, how Athenian Solon keeps his eye wisely
fixed on life's end, how Bias of Priene deems the
wicked to be the majority, how Pittacus, native of
Lesbos, advises to mark well the opportune time,
and how Chilon of Lacedaemon would have all men
know themselves. Moreover, he learned new doctrines of divers schools—whatsoever in the Scythian
land Anacharsis praised, all the gain that Sparta
got with Lycurgus for her law-giver, all that the
company of Cynics debates in the Erechthean
gymnasium, copying the disciples of Epicurus[2]; all
that the two Academies[3] loudly proclaim, affirming
naught to be true; all the wisdom that Cleanthes
has won with much biting of nails[4]; the tears of
Heraclitus, the laughter of Democritus, or the
silence of Pythagoras; whatsoever teaching Plato's
intellect, which dwelt in the citadel,[5] sets forth in

points out (p. 71), claims that the attitude of the Old Academy,
even of Plato himself, was similar (*Ac.* I. 46).

[4] The biting of the nails seems to have been traditionally
associated with Cleanthes. Cf. *Epist.* IX. 9. 14. Probably he
was so represented in some well-known work of art.

[5] *in arce.* Plato taught that the rational part of the soul
resides in the head, which is, as it were, the citadel which
commands the non-rational parts (the passionate and the
appetitive), situated respectively in the breast and under the
midriff. The doctrine is briefly stated in Cic. *Tusc.* I. 20.
In arce fuit could also mean " was pre-eminent" (cf. 23. 142),
and there may be a *double entente* here. *Ordine terno* probably
refers, not to the tripartite division of the soul, but to the
division of Philosophy into Physics, Logic, and Ethics. See
15. 100 f. and note.

quae vel Aristoteles, partitus membra loquendi,
argumentosis dat retia syllogismis;   175
quidquid Anaximenes, Euclides, Archyta, Zenon,
Arcesilas, Chrysippus Anaxagorasque dederunt,
Socraticusque animus post fatum in Phaedone vivus,
despiciens vastas tenuato in crure catenas,
cum tremeret mors ipsa reum ferretque venenum
pallida securo lictoris dextra magistro.   181
praeterea quidquid Latialibus indere libris
prisca aetas studuit, totum percurrere suetus:
Mantua quas acies pelagique pericula lusit
Zmyrnaeas imitata tubas, quamcumque loquendi 185
Arpinas dat consul opem, sine fine secutus
fabro progenitum, spreto cui patre polita
eloquiis plus lingua fuit, vel quidquid in aevum
mittunt Euganeis Patavina volumina chartis;
qua Crispus brevitate placet, quo pondere Varro,
quo genio Plautus, quo fulmine Quintilianus,   191
qua pompa Tacitus numquam sine laude loquendus.

179. in *C*, *om. codd. plerique.*
186. secutus fabro progenitum *Mohr et Luetjohann* : locutus
tabro progenitus.

---

[1] Homer.   [2] Cicero.
[3] Demosthenes, cf. 23. 143; Juvenal X. 130-32. The
father of Demosthenes was a wealthy sword-manufacturer.
Polita contains an allusion to the father's trade; Sidonius
uses *polire* in the sense of "sharpen"; cf. expolire, 23. 144.
[4] The works of Livy. The Euganei inhabited Venetia,
but were driven out by the Veneti. *Euganeus* in poetry
means "Venetian," and especially "Paduan." Padua
(Patavium) was Livy's birthplace.
[5] Sallust (C. Sallustius Crispus).
[6] Sidonius, like other late authors, uses *genius* in various
meanings, not always easy to determine. The renderings
given in this version generally follow the *Thesaurus Linguae
Latinae.*

22

II. PANEGYRIC ON ANTHEMIUS

triple array; or again, the snares that Aristotle, dividing speech into its members, sets for us with his syllogistic reasoning; and also whatever has been bestowed by Anaximenes, Euclid, Archytas, Zeno, Arcesilas, Chrysippus and Anaxagoras, and by the soul of Socrates as it lives after his death in the *Phaedo*, a soul that recked naught of the huge fetters on his wasted leg, while death's self trembled before the prisoner and the executioner's hand was pale as it proffered the poison, though the master's heart was untroubled. Besides these he was wont to range through all that antiquity strove to inscribe on Latin pages: the battles and the ocean perils that Mantua paraded, copying the trumpet-tones of Smyrna's bard[1]; whatever aid to speaking the consul of Arpinum[2] affords, he who follows without ceasing that smith's son[3] who set his father at naught, deeming more precious a tongue made keen by use of eloquence; or again whatever the volumes of the Paduan[4] deliver for all time in those Euganean pages; the brevity that wins applause in Crispus,[5] the weightiness of Varro, the wit[6] of Plautus, the lightning of Quintilian,[7] and the majesty of Tacitus,[8] a name never to be uttered without praise.

[7] This can scarcely refer to the *Institutio Oratoria*. Quintilian in early life published one of his speeches, and garbled versions of others were published without his authority. But Sidonius is almost certainly thinking not of these but of the declamations (mostly still extant) which were falsely attributed to Quintilian. Cf. 9. 317; *Epist.* V, 10. 3. *Fulmen* is applied to eloquence by Quintilian himself, VIII. 6. 7 and XII. 10. 65 (the latter passage alluding to the famous saying of Aristophanes about the "flashing and thundering" Pericles, *Acharnians* 531); also by Cicero and others.

[8] Sidonius plays on the word *Tacitus* ("silent"); cf. 23. 154, *Epist.* IV. 22. 2.

His hunc formatum studiis, natalibus ortum,
moribus imbutum princeps cui mundus ab Euro
ad Zephyrum tunc sceptra dabat, cui nubilis atque
unica purpureos debebat nata nepotes,   196
elegit generum ; sed non ut deside luxu
fortuna soceri contentus et otia captans
nil sibi deberet ; comitis sed iure recepto
Danuvii ripas et tractum limitis ampli   200
circuit, hortatur, disponit, discutit, armat.
sic sub patre Pius moderatus castra parentis,
sic Marcus vivente Pio, post iura daturi,
innumerabilibus legionibus imperitabant.
hinc reduci datur omnis honos, et utrique magister
militiae consulque micat, coniuncta potestas   206
patricii, celerique gradu privata cucurrit
culmina conscenditque senum puer ipse curulem,
sedit et emerito iuvenis veteranus in auro.

Iamque parens divos : sed vobis nulla cupido   210
imperii ; longam diademata passa repulsam

205. honos *edit. Greg. et Collomb.* : honor.

---

[1] Marcian, Emperor of the East, 450-57.
[2] Aelia Marcia Euphemia.
[3] He received the dignity of a *comes rei militaris*, a frequent stepping-stone to a *magisterium militum*, as in the present case.
[4] History does not record any military service on the part of Marcus Aurelius before the death of Antoninus Pius.
[5] A gilded curule chair was used by the Emperors on ceremonial occasions, but there is no evidence that gold ornamentation was allowed on other *sellae curules*. It was, however, at this time allowed on the *sellae gestatoriae* of consuls (see *Epist.* VIII. 8. 3), and Sidonius may be referring to this.
[6] *i.e.* his father-in-law Marcian : *divos* : cf. *v.* 318. It is odd to find the Christian Sidonius writing thus ; but literary tradition is far more potent than religion in his poetry.

II. PANEGYRIC ON ANTHEMIUS

By such studies was he moulded, from such lineage
sprung, in such habits nurtured; and the prince [1] to
whom at that time the world from east to west was
giving the sceptre, on whom an only daughter,[2] now
of age for wedlock, must needs bestow grandchildren
that should wear the purple, chose this man for her
husband. Yet he did not rest in slothful luxury,
content with her father's glory, seeking a life of
ease and owing nothing to himself; nay, receiving
a count's authority [3] he traversed the Danube bank
and the whole length of the great frontier-lines,
exhorting, arranging, examining, equipping. Even
so had Pius under his father's sway ruled his father's
camps; thus Marcus, too, while Pius still lived [4];
these two, destined later to be lawgivers, then
commanded legions innumerable. When Anthemius
returned, every office was bestowed upon him; he
shone upon the world as Master of Both Services
and as consul; to this was added the authority of
Patrician; and thus with speedy step he ran through
the highest dignities that a subject may reach;
youth though he was, he mounted the curule throne
of the elders, and sat, a young veteran, on the gold [5]
that belongs to the old campaigner.

And now thy father [6] was numbered with the gods;
but thou hadst no craving for empire; the diadem
after a long rejection chose out an illustrious man,[7]

---

[7] Leo I occupied a comparatively humble position (he was a
tribunus militum, with the rank of count) when he was suddenly
promoted to the Imperial throne at the age of nearly 60.
The words *longam passa repulsam* cannot refer to the very
short interval between the death of Marcian and the accession of Leo; they state (with what truth we cannot say) that
Anthemius had persistently declined the offer of Marcian to
designate him as his successor.

25

insignem legere virum, quem deinde legentem
spernere non posses : soli tibi contulit uni
hoc Fortuna decus, quamquam te posceret ordo,
ut lectus princeps mage quam videare relictus.   215
post socerum Augustum regnas, sed non tibi venit
purpura per thalamos, et coniunx regia regno
laus potius quam causa fuit ; nam iuris habenis
non generum legit respublica, sed generosum.
fallor, bis gemino nisi cardine rem probat orbis :   220
ambit te Zephyrus rectorem, destinat Eurus,
ad Boream pugnas et formidaris ad Austrum.

Ante tamen quam te socium collega crearet,
perstrinxisse libet quos Illyris ora triumphos
viderit, excisam quae se Valameris ab armis   225
forte ducis nostri vitio deserta gemebat.
haud aliter, caesus quondam cum Caepio robur
dedidit Ausonium, subita cogente ruina
electura ducem post guttura fracta Iugurthae
ultum Arpinatem Calpurnia foedera lixam   230
opposuit rabido respublica territa Cimbro.

---

¹ Bury (I. 314) wrongly takes *ordo* to mean the Senate.

² Illyricum ; for its extent see Hodgkin I. 295. The name
of the unworthy *dux* is unknown. Some have absurdly tried
to identify him with Arnegisclus, *magister militum per Thracias*,
who died fighting bravely against Attila in A.D. 447. After
the break-up of the Hunnish dominion in A.D. 454 the Ostro-
goths were allowed by Marcian to settle in Pannonia. Some
years later, when Leo had refused to pay the subsidy which
Marcian had granted them, they overran and devastated Illyricum. It was obviously one of these raids that Anthemius
checked, but no other writer mentions the episode. Sidonius
is likewise the sole authority for the campaign against
Hormidac (*vv.* 236 sqq.)

³ Walamir was one of the three Ostrogoth kings.

⁴ Caepio, defeated with great slaughter by the Cimbrians
at Arausio (Orange), 105 B.C.

II. PANEGYRIC ON ANTHEMIUS

one whom thou couldst not slight when he in his turn chose thee. Fortune hath given thee this unique honour, that although the order of succession demanded thee,[1] thou art looked on as a prince chosen, not as a prince by inheritance. Thou reignest after an Augustus who was thy wife's father, but the purple came not to thee by thy marriage; thy royal bride hath been rather the glory of thy royalty than its cause, for when the commonwealth chose thee to wield the reins of state it was for thy kingly soul, not for thy kin. My judgment errs if the four quarters of the earth do not approve the choice; the West seeks thee, the East sends thee, as ruler; thou fightest in the North and art feared in the South.

But I would fain touch on the triumphs that the Illyrian region[2] beheld before thy colleague made thee his partner, when that land, deserted, as it chanced, through a Roman leader's fault, was bemoaning its devastation by the arms of Walamir.[3] Even so was it in former days when Caepio's[4] slaughter had given up Ausonia's best warriors to the enemy; the terrified commonwealth, compelled by that crashing blow, essayed to choose a leader; 'twas after the strangling of Jugurtha, and they set against the frenzied Cimbrian the batman[5] from Arpinum who had avenged Calpurnius' treaty.[6]

[5] Ancient writers are fond of exaggerating the lowly origin of Gaius Marius. *Lixa* properly means " camp-sutler," but in later Latin we sometimes find *lixae* used where *calones* would be more correct. The *calones* were slave-attendants of officers or soldiers.

[6] The treaty made with Jugurtha in 111 B.C. by Calpurnius Bestia and Aemilius Scaurus, who had been bribed by the Numidian.

hic primum ut vestras aquilas provincia vidit,
desiit hostiles confestim horrere dracones.
ilicet edomiti bello praedaque carentes
mox ipsi tua praeda iacent.

                    Sed omittimus istos 235
ut populatores: belli magis acta revolvo;
quod bellum non parva manus nec carcere fracto
ad gladiaturam tu Spartace vincte parasti,
sed Scythicae vaga turba plagae, feritatis abundans,
dira, rapax, vehemens, ipsis quoque gentibus illic
barbara barbaricis, cuius dux Hormidac atque   241
civis erat. quis tale solum est moresque genusque:

  Albus Hyperboreis Tanais qua vallibus actus
Riphaea de caute cadit, iacet axe sub Vrsae
gens animis membrisque minax: ita vultibus ipsis 245
infantum suus horror inest. consurgit in artum
massa rotunda caput; geminis sub fronte cavernis
visus adest oculis absentibus; acta cerebri
in cameram vix ad refugos lux pervenit orbes,
non tamen et clausos; nam fornice non spatioso 250
magna vident spatia, et maioris luminis usum

        242. moresque *Mohr*: murique.
        246. atrum *C*.

---

[1] The typically Roman " eagle " (the traditional legionary
standard) is contrasted with the " dragons " of the " barbarians." But the use of dragon-ensigns had found its way
into the Roman army long before, and it is possible that by
this time they had entirely supplanted the ordinary standard.
For a description of them see 5. 402. It seems probable that
the " eagle " belonged only to the full legion of 6,000 men,
and not to the smaller units which were now dignified with
the title of *legio*. See Grosse, *Röm. Militärgeschichte*, pp.
229–34.
  [2] *axe sub Vrsae*. "The Huns came originally from the

28

II. PANEGYRIC ON ANTHEMIUS

Thereupon the province, beholding thine eagles,[1] ceased of a sudden to shudder at the dragons of the foe. Straightway crushed in war and reft of their spoil they in their turn were spoils for thee, lying prostrate at thy feet.

But such folk I pass by as mere raiders; rather do I now relate the exploits of a real war; which war no small band contrived, no Spartacus, bondsman destined for the gladiator's work, who had burst open his prison, but a roaming multitude from Scythian clime, teeming with savagery, frightful, ravening, violent, barbarous even in the eyes of the barbarian peoples around them, a race whose leader was Hormidac, a man of their own nation. Their land, their habits and their origin were after this manner.

Where the white Tanais, driven down through the valleys of the far north, falls from the Riphaean crags, in the region of the Bear,[2] there dwells a race with menace in heart and limbs[3]; for truly the very faces of their infants have a gruesomeness all their own. Their heads are great round masses rising to a narrow crown; in two hollows beneath the brow resides their sight, but the eyes are far to seek; the light, as it forces its way into the arched recesses in the skull,[4] can scarce reach those retreating orbs —retreating, but not shut; for from that vault of narrow space they enjoy a spacious vision, and pel-

East, but it was from the North that they drove the Goths down on the Romans." L. C. Purser.

[3] For other descriptions of the Huns see Claud. *Rufin.* I. 323–31 (imitated here), Amm. Marc. XXXI. 2. 1–11, Iordan. *Get.* 24 and (on Attila) 35.

[4] *cameram*, one of the two *cavernae* (247). *Cameras* (or *orbem* for *orbes*) would have been clearer. It seems best to make both nouns plural in the translation.

perspicua in puteis compensant puncta profundis.
tum, ne per malas excrescat fistula duplex,
obtundit teneras circumdata fascia nares,
ut galeis cedant : sic propter proelia natos   255
maternus deformat amor, quia tensa genarum
non interiecto fit latior area naso.
cetera pars est pulchra viris : stant pectora vasta,
insignes umeri, succincta sub ilibus alvus.
forma quidem pediti media est, procera sed exstat 260
si cernas equites : sic longi saepe putantur
si sedeant.   vix matre carens ut constitit infans,
mox praebet dorsum sonipes ; cognata reare
membra viris : ita semper equo ceu fixus adhaeret
rector ; cornipedum tergo gens altera fertur,   265
haec habitat.   teretes arcus et spicula cordi,
terribiles certaeque manus iaculisque ferendae
mortis fixa fides et non peccante sub ictu
edoctus peccare furor.   gens ista repente
erumpens solidumque rotis transvecta per Histrum 270
venerat et siccas inciderat orbita lymphas.
hanc tu directus per Dacica rura vagantem
contra is, aggrederis, superas, includis ; et ut te
metato spatio castrorum Serdica vidit,
obsidione premis.   quae te sic tempore multo   275

271. siccas *Mohr* : sectas *codd.* : strictas *Rossberg*, tectas
Buecheler.

---

[1] Or perhaps "a larger eye." *Perspicua* is possibly used
metri gratia for *perspicacia*, "clear-sighted"; but I have not
found any parallel for such a use.

[2] *i.e.* the nostrils.

[3] The paradoxical description of frozen rivers, etc. as "dry"
or "solid" water is common in the Latin poets : cf. 5. 512, 7.
150.   The notion of wheels traversing the water is derived
from Virgil (*Georg.* III. 360 sq.), and is worked to death by
the post-Augustans. Cf. 5. 519; similarly of riders, 7. 43.

II. PANEGYRIC ON ANTHEMIUS

lucid pin-points in those sunken wells give all the
service that an ampler light[1] could bring. Moreover,
the nostrils, while still soft, are blunted by an
encircling band, to prevent the two passages[2] from
growing outward between the cheek-bones, that
thus they may make room for the helmets; for those
children are born for battles, and a mother's love
disfigures them, because the area of the cheeks
stretches and expands when the nose does not
intervene. The rest of the men's bodies is comely;
chest large and firm, fine shoulders, compact stomach
beneath the flanks. On foot their stature is mid-
dling, but it towers aloft if you view them on horseback: thus are they often deemed long of frame
when seated. Scarce has the infant learnt to stand
without his mother's aid when a horse takes him on
his back. You would think the limbs of man and
beast were born together, so firmly does the rider
always stick to the horse, just as if he were fastened
to his place: any other folk is carried on horseback,
this folk lives there. Shapely bows and arrows are
their delight, sure and terrible are their hands;
firm is their confidence that their missiles will bring
death, and their frenzy is trained to do wrongful
deeds with blows that never go wrong. This people
had burst forth in a sudden invasion; they had come,
crossing with wheels the solid Danube, marking
the moistureless waters with ruts.[3] Straight against
them didst thou go, as they roamed through the
Dacian fields; thou didst attack and vanquish and
hem them in; and soon as Serdica[4] beheld thee with
thine encampment laid out, thou didst straitly besiege
them. The town marvelled at thee as thou didst

[4] *Serdica.* Near the modern Sofia.

in vallo positum stupuit, quod miles in agros
nec licitis nec furtivis excursibus ibat.
cui deesset cum saepe Ceres semperque Lyaeus,
disciplina tamen non defuit; inde propinquo
hoste magis timuere ducem.   sic denique factum est
ut socius tum forte tuus, mox proditor, illis   281
frustra terga daret commissae tempore pugnae.
qui iam cum fugeret flexo pede cornua nudans,
tu stabas acies solus, te sparsa fugaci
expetiit ductore manus, te Marte pedestri   285
sudantem repetebat eques, tua signa secutus
non se desertum sensit certamine miles.

I nunc et veteris profer praeconia Tulli,
aetas cana patrum, quod pulchro hortamine mendax
occuluit refugi nutantia foedera Metti!   290
nil simile est fallique tuum tibi non placet hostem.
tunc vicit miles, dum se putat esse iuvandum:
hic vicit postquam se comperit esse relictum.
dux fugit: insequeris; renovat certamina: vincis;
clauditur: expugnas; elabitur: obruis atque   295
Sarmaticae paci pretium sua funera ponis.
paretur; iussum subiit iam transfuga letum
atque peregrino cecidit tua victima ferro.
ecce iterum, si forte placet, conflige, vetustas!

---

[1] See Livy I. 27 f. *Metti* may be gen. sing. of *Mettius*
(the usual form) or of *Mettus* (Verg. *Aen.* VIII. 642).
[2] It seems clear from *v.* 297 that the *dux* here mentioned is
the deserter. *Sua* in *v.* 296 is equal to *eius*, as often in Sidonius.
[3] *Sarm.*, *i.e.* with the Hunnish forces.

tarry thus for long within the rampart, because thy
soldiers went not forth into the fields in regular or
stealthy raids. Though oft they lacked corn and
always wine, they lacked not discipline; hence
though the foe was nigh they feared their general
more. So at length it came to pass that he who
chanced to be thine ally then but straightway
played thee false gained nothing when he retreated
before the foe at the first onset; for when he had
begun to flee, turning aside and laying bare the
wings, thou didst stand thy ground, a host in thyself;
to thee did those warriors rally whom their captain's
flight had scattered, back to thee came the cavalry
as thou didst toil and sweat, fighting on foot; and
following thy standards the soldiers felt that they
were not deserted in the fray.

Go to now, ancient generation of our fathers!
Proclaim, if ye will, the praises of old Tullus, for
that he lied in a noble exhortation and concealed the
collapse of the treaty with the deserter Mettus![1]
There is nothing like that here; thou, Anthemius,
wouldst not choose to have even thine enemy
misled. Those old-time soldiers conquered in the
belief that they would be aided; but these conquered
in the knowledge that they were deserted. The
captain[2] flees; thou dost pursue; he renews the
fray; thou conquerest; he shuts himself in; thou
dost storm his entrenchment; he slips away; thou
dost overwhelm him, and dost demand his life as the
price of peace with the Sarmatians.[3] Thy will is
done, and straightway the deserter has suffered the
death decreed and has fallen—thy victim, though
slain by a foreign sword. Come now, Antiquity!
Enter the contest once more, if it please thee!

Hannibal ille ferox ad poenam forte petitus,   300
etsi non habuit ius vitae fine supremo,
certe habuit mortis : quem caecus carcer et uncus
et quem exspectabat fracturus guttura lictor,
hausit Bebrycio constantior hospite virus ;
nam te qui fugit, mandata morte peremptus,   305
non tam victoris periit quam iudicis ore.

    Nunc ades, o Paean, lauro cui grypas obuncos
docta lupata ligant quotiens per frondea lora
flectis penniferos hederis bicoloribus armos ;
huc converte chelyn : non est modo dicere tempus
Pythona exstinctum nec bis septena sonare   311
vulnera Tantalidum, quorum tibi funera servat
cantus et aeterno vivunt in carmine mortes.
vos quoque, Castalides, paucis, quo numine nobis
venerit Anthemius gemini cum foedere regni,   315
pandite : pax rerum misit qui bella gubernet.

    Auxerat Augustus naturae lege Severus
divorum numerum. quem mox Oenotria casum
vidit ut aerei de rupibus Appennini,
pergit caerulei vitreas ad Thybridis aedes,   320
non galea conclusa genas (nec sutilis illi

---

    [1] *Forte*, "as it so happened," is sometimes little more than "padding." Servius alleges that Virgil has so used it in two places; the allegation would be truer of Sidonius. I have translated it where possible.

    [2] Prusias of Bithynia. Hannibal took poison to avoid falling into the hands of the Romans, when Prusias sought to betray him.

    [3] *Nam* = "but," as in several other places. The use is common in late Latin, and its germ can be found in Cicero. See Schmalz-Hofmann, *Synt.*, p. 679.

    [4] *Modo*, "now," as often in these poems.

    [5] For the varying accounts of the number of Niobe's children see the note in Sir J. G. Frazer's trans. of Apollodorus in this series, Vol. I, p. 340.

II. PANEGYRIC ON ANTHEMIUS

When the surrender of the bold Hannibal was claimed by those that would punish him,[1] though in that last hour he had not power to live, yet had he power to determine his death; and so, when the dark dungeon awaited him, and the iron hook, and the lictor appointed to break the prisoner's neck, he swallowed the poison, a stauncher man than his Bithynian host[2]: but[3] the man that deserted thee was cut off by a death that had been commanded, and it was a judge's rather than a victor's lips that sealed his doom.

Now grant thy presence, Paean Apollo, whose hook-beaked gryphons the well-schooled curb doth constrain with its bond of laurel, whensoever thou wieldest thy leafy reins and guidest their winged shoulders with double-hued ivy! Hither direct thy lyre! It is not now[4] the time to sing of Python's destruction or to hymn the twice seven wounds of the Niobids[5]—victims whose dooms are preserved to thine honour in song, so that their deaths live in deathless poesy. Ye Muses, likewise, reveal in brief words by what divine power Anthemius came to us with a covenant made by the two realms; an empire's peace hath sent him to conduct our wars.

By nature's law Severus had been added to the ranks of the gods.[6] Oenotria,[7] when from the crags of towering Apennine she beheld this calamity, hied her to the glassy abode of blue Tiber. She had not encased her cheeks in a helmet (and she wore no

---

[6] Libius Severus was Emperor from 19th Nov., A.D. 461, to 15th Aug., 465. Some said that he was murdered by Ricimer, and *naturae lege* may be meant as an emphatic denial of this (probably unfounded) allegation. See Hodgkin, II. 432.

[7] *Oenotria*, old and poetical name for Italy, here treated as a goddess.

circulus inpactis loricam texuit hamis),
sed nudata caput; pro crine racemifer exit
plurima per frontem constringens oppida palmes,
perque umeros teretes, rutilantes perque lacertos 325
pendula gemmiferae mordebant suppara bullae.
segnior incedit senio venerandaque membra
viticomam retinens baculi vice flectit ad ulmum.
sed tamen Vbertas sequitur: quacumque propinquat,
incessu fecundat iter; comitataque gressum 330
laeta per impressas rorat Vindemia plantas.

   Ilicet ingreditur Tiberini gurgitis antrum.
currebat fluvius residens et harundinis altae
concolor in viridi fluitabat silva capillo;
dat sonitum mento unda cadens, licet hispida saetis
suppositis multum sedaret barba fragorem; 336
pectore ructabat latices lapsuque citato
sulcabat madidam iam torrens alveus alvum.
terretur veniente dea manibusque remissis
remus et urna cadunt. veniae tum verba paranti 340
illa prior: " venio viduatam praesule nostro
per te, si placeat, lacrimis inflectere Romam:
expetat Aurorae partes fastuque remoto
hoc unum praestet, iam plus dignetur amari.
instrue quas quaerat vires orbique iacenti 345

---

[1] She wore a crown of towers, representing in this case the
Italian towns. The goddess Roma also has a towered crown
(*v.* 392).

[2] The meaning "straightway" may be intended, but
it does not quite suit the previous paragraph. Sidonius has
a peculiar use of *ilicet*, found in 15. 42 and in at least nine of the
ten passages where it occurs in the *Epistles*. There it is
a particle of transition, with the force of "so," "so then,"
"well," sometimes "in short." For a discussion of the
subject see Mohr's pamphlet, *Zu Apollinaris Sidonius*, Bremerhaven 1886. The meaning "straightway" will serve in most
passages of the Poems where the word occurs.

hauberk fashioned with stitched rings of tight-driven hooks), but bared was her head. Instead of hair there overran her forehead a vine-branch with clustered grapes, binding fast her many towns,[1] and along her shapely shoulders and radiant arms jewelled brooches gripped her flowing robe. The slowness of old age was in her gait, and she held as a staff an elm covered with vine-foliage, and guided her venerable limbs thereby. Yet Abundance attended her; wherever she drew nigh, with her coming she spread fruitfulness over her path, and Vintage, accompanying her steps, joyfully made the juice rise wherever her feet trod.

So[2] she entered the cave of Tiber's stream. There sat the running river.[3] On his green hair drifted a like-hued clump of tall reeds. The water sounded as it fell from his chin, though a beard of shaggy bristles underneath did much to dull the roar. From his breast he threw out streams, and falling more rapidly the flood now furious furrowed his soaking stomach. As the goddess drew nigh fear seized him; his hands relaxed, and the urn and the oar fell from them. He was devising words of excuse when she broke in: " I come that through thee, if it please thee, I may sway by my tears Rome, now bereft of our ruler. I would have her turn to the region of Dawn; let her put her disdain aside and by granting this one thing deserve even greater love. Teach her what strength she must enlist, and tell her in what world she must crave

---

[3] A feeble paradox, somewhat toned down in the translation. The river-god is identified with the river in *currebat* and distinguished from it in *residens*.

quo poscat dic orbe caput.   quemcumque creavit
axe meo natum, confestim fregit in illo
imperii Fortuna rotas.   hinc Vandalus hostis
urget et in nostrum numerosa classe quotannis
militat excidium, conversoque ordine fati   350
torrida Caucaseos infert mihi Byrsa furores.
praeterea invictus Ricimer, quem publica fata
respiciunt, proprio solus vix Marte repellit
piratam per rura vagum, qui proelia vitans
victorem fugitivus agit.   quis sufferat hostem   355
qui pacem pugnamque negat? nam foedera nulla
cum Ricimere iacit.   quem cur nimis oderit audi.
incertum crepat ille patrem, cum serva sit illi
certa parens; nunc, ut regis sit filius, effert
matris adulterium.   tum livet quod Ricimerem   360
in regnum duo regna vocant; nam patre Suebus,
a genetrice Getes.   simul et reminiscitur illud,
quod Tartesiacis avus huius Vallia terris
Vandalicas turmas et iuncti Martis Halanos
stravit et occiduam texere cadavera Calpen.   365
quid veteres narrare fugas, quid damna priorum?

---

[1] Geiseric took Carthage in A.D. 439 and made it his capital.
Byrsa is properly the citadel of Carthage. The epithet
Caucaseos is very loose; the Vandals had not come from the
region of the Caucasus, though the Alans, who were now subjects
of the Vandal king, had done so.

[2] *piratam*: cf. *v.* 17. Geiseric was an incorrigible pirate,
even when he was not actually at war. It was an attack by
him on the Peloponnese that finally induced Leo to concert
a gigantic offensive of East and West against him and to make
Anthemius Emperor of the West. Shortly before this (461–
465) Geiseric had made a series of devastating descents upon
Italy and Sicily. The joint expedition, of which Sidonius speaks
so hopefully, came to a disastrous end in A.D. 468, owing
mainly to the incompetence of the commander-in-chief,
Basiliscus.

a head for her own stricken world. Whenever
Fortune hath chosen a man born in my clime, she
hath instantly broken the wheels of his empire. On
this side the Vandal foe presses hard; and every
year he wars with multitudinous navy to destroy us;
the natural order hath been reversed, and now parched
Byrsa launches against me the frenzy of the Caucasus.[1] Yea more, unconquerable Ricimer, to whom
the destiny of our nation looks for safety, doth
barely drive back with his own unaided force the
pirate [2] that ranges over our lands, that ever avoids
battles and plays a conqueror's part by flight. Who
could brook an enemy that refuses both concord and
combat? For never does he make a treaty with
Ricimer. Hear now why he hates our leader with
such exceeding hate.[3] His father is unknown, yet
he prates ever of him, since 'tis well known his mother
was a slave-woman.[4] So now, to make himself out
a king's son, he proclaims his mother's shame. He
is jealous also because two kingdoms call Ricimer to
kingly power, Suevian as he is on the father's side,[5]
Gothic on the mother's. He likewise remembers
this, that Wallia,[6] grandsire of Ricimer, laid low on
Spanish soil the Vandal squadrons and the Alans,
their comrades in the war, and their corpses covered
Calpe in the far west. But why tell of ancient routs,
of the losses of bygone generations? Nay, he calls

[3] Geiseric's feud with Ricimer was not due merely to the
causes mentioned here. See Hodgkin, II. 434 f.
[4] Geiseric's father was Godigiselas, a king of the Asding
Vandals.
[5] Ricimer's father was a Suevian chief.
[6] The Visigoth Wallia, father of Ricimer's mother, an-
nihilated the Siling Vandals in Spain and crushed their allies
the Alans, the remnant of whom took refuge with the Asding
Vandals in Gallaecia (A.D. 416–418). See Introd., p. xi.

THE POEMS OF SIDONIUS

Agrigentini recolit dispendia campi.
inde furit, quod se docuit satis iste nepotem
illius esse viri quo viso, Vandale, semper
terga dabas. nam non Siculis inlustrior arvis 370
tu, Marcelle, redis, per quem tellure marique
nostra Syracusios presserunt arma penates;
nec tu cui currum Curii superare, Metelle,
contigit, ostentans nobis elephanta frequentem,
grex niger albentes tegeret cum mole iugales 375
auctoremque suum celaret pompa triumphi.
Noricus Ostrogothum quod continet, iste timetur;
Gallia quod Rheni Martem ligat, iste pavori est;
quod consanguineo me Vandalus hostis Halano
diripuit radente, suis hic ultus ab armis. 380
sed tamen unus homo est nec tanta pericula solus
tollere, sed differe potest: modo principe nobis
est opus armato, veterum qui more parentum
non mandet sed bella gerat, quem signa moventem
terra vel unda tremant, ut tandem iure recepto 385
Romula desuetas moderentur classica classes."
    Audiit illa pater, simul annuit. itur in urbem.
continuo videt ipse deam, summissus adorat,
pectus et exsertam tetigerunt cornua mammam;

382. sed : si *Buecheler.*

---

[1] Ricimer with his fleet frustrated an attempted raid by
Geiseric on Agrigentum and afterwards defeated him in
Corsican waters, A.D. 456. See Introd., p. xxi; Bury, I. 327.
[2] Marcellus, the capturer of Syracuse (212 B.C.).
[3] Manius Curius Dentatus, conqueror of Pyrrhus (275 B.C.),
had four elephants at his triumph (Eutrop. II. 14); L. Caecilius

40

to mind the havoc of Agrigentum's plain.[1] Madly he rages because his adversary has amply proved himself the grandchild of that hero at sight of whom the Vandal did ever turn in flight. No whit more glorious didst thou, Marcellus,[2] return from Sicilian lands, thou through whom our arms did beset the homes of Syracuse by land and sea; or thou, Metellus, whose fortune it was to outdo the triumph of Curius,[3] when thou didst display to us a throng of elephants, and the dusky herd screened the white chariot-steeds with their mighty bulk, and the triumphal parade hid the winner of the triumph. If the Norican is restraining the Ostrogoth, it is that Ricimer is feared; if Gaul ties down the armed might of the Rhine, it is he that inspires the dread; and because the Vandal foe plundered me while the Alan, his kinsman, swept off what remained, this man took vengeance by the force of his own arms. But he is only one man; alone he cannot remove these perils, but only delay their day; we need now an armed prince who in the manner of our sires shall not order wars but wage them,[4] one before whom land and sea shall quake when he advances his standards, so that at last with power regained the Roman war-trump may direct Rome's dormant navies."

Father Tiber heard and heeded. To the city he went and straightway with his own eyes beheld the goddess, and bowed in humble adoration, so that his horns touched her breast and her uncovered bosom.

Metellus had many (authorities differ as to the number) when he triumphed after defeating the Carthaginians at Panormus (250 B.C.).

[4] This anticipation was not fulfilled. Anthemius did not personally take part in the great expedition against Geiseric.

mandatas fert inde preces; quas diva secuta   390
apparat ire viam. laxatos torva capillos
stringit et inclusae latuerunt casside turres;
infula laurus erat. bullis hostilibus asper
applicat a laeva surgentem balteus ensem.
inseritur clipeo victrix manus; illius orbem   395
Martigenae, lupa, Thybris, Amor, Mars, Ilia
   complent.
fibula mordaci refugas a pectore vestes
dente capit. micat hasta minax, quercusque tropaeis
curva tremit placitoque deam sub fasce fatigat.
perpetuo stat planta solo, sed fascia primos   400
sistitur ad digitos, retinacula bina cothurnis
mittit in adversum vincto de fomite pollex,
quae stringant crepidas et concurrentibus ansis
vinclorum pandas texant per crura catenas.
ergo sicut erat liquidam transvecta per aethram   405
nascentis petiit tepidos Hyperionis ortus.

   Est locus Oceani, longinquis proximus Indis,
axe sub Eoo, Nabataeum tensus in Eurum:
ver ibi continuum est, interpellata nec ullis

---

399. placitoque *Drakenborch*: placidoque *codd.*, *def.*
Semple.

---

[1] *fascia* (= confining band) is evidently applied here to
the sole of the sandal: cf. *Epist.* VIII. 11. 3, carm. *v.* 13,
fasceata. It cannot mean a *fascia pedulis*, which did not
come near the front of the foot. The meaning is that the
leather of the sole is not continued upwards over the toes to
form uppers. Two thongs encircle the great toe and are
passed cross-wise through large leather loops, which are
attached to the sole and form a network on both sides of the
foot when the laces have drawn them tight. After passing
through the last pair of loops these shoe-strings were passed
round the leg and fastened. The *vincla* are the laces, and

II. PANEGYRIC ON ANTHEMIUS

Then he delivered his message of entreaty, and the goddess, compliant, made ready for the journey. Stern was her look as she bound up her flowing hair; then she shut in her towers and hid them under a helmet; laurel formed her fillet. Her belt, rough with shield-studs taken from enemies, made fast a sword, which rose high on her left side. Her conquering arm was thrust into a shield, whose orb was filled with the twin sons of Mars, with the wolf and Tiber and Love and Mars and Ilia. A clasp fixes with gripping tooth the raiment that retreats back from her breast. Her threatening spear flashes, and an oak bowed down with trophies sways and tires the goddess under its welcome burden. The covering of her sole is of one piece,[1] but this strip is not carried beyond the tips of the toes; the great toe sends two strings upward from its encircled socket in opposite directions, so that they bind the sandal tight and, with the side-loops drawn together, weave a curving mesh of ties up the leg. In this guise, then, she was wafted through the clear bright air, seeking the warm rising-place of the nascent sun.

There is a region by Ocean's shore, nigh to the distant Indians, under the eastern sky, stretching towards the Nabataean[2] wind. Perpetual spring is there, the ground is not made pale by any invading

---

v. 404 seems to refer to the pattern which they and the converging loops make along the instep rather than to the whole network of thongs which, as explained above, covered both sides of the foot. It is unfortunate that Sidonius uses both *cothurnus* and *crepida* for the same thing; the latter is by far the more appropriate word.

[2] *i.e.* eastern; cf. Ovid *Met.* I. 61; Lucan IV. 63. The Nabataei were a people of Arabia Petraea. In 5. 284 the second vowel of *Nabataeus* is long.

frigoribus pallescit humus, sed flore perenni   410
picta peregrinos ignorant arva rigores;
halant rura rosis, indiscriptosque per agros
fragrat odor; violam, cytisum, serpylla, ligustrum,
lilia, narcissos, casiam, colocasia, caltas,
costum, malobathrum, myrrhas, opobalsama, tura 415
parturiunt campi; nec non pulsante senecta
hinc rediviva petit vicinus cinnama Phoenix.
hic domus Aurorae rutilo crustante metallo
bacarum praefert leves asprata lapillos.
diripiunt diversa oculos et ab arte magistra   420
hoc vincit, quodcumque vides; sed conditur omnis
sub domina praesente decor, nimioque rubore
gemmarum varios perdit quia possidet ignes.
fundebat coma pexa crocos flexoque lacerto
lutea depressus comebat tempora pecten.   425
fundebant oculi radios; color igneus illis,
non tamen ardor erat, quamvis de nocte recussa
excepti soleant sudorem fingere rores.
pectora bis cingunt zonae, parvisque papillis
invidiam facit ipse sinus; pars extima pepli   430
perfert puniceas ad crura rubentia rugas.

412. indiscriptosque *Mohr et Luetjohann*: indescriptosque.
413. fragrat *F*, flagrat *CPT*.

---

[1] The phoenix gathers all kinds of fragrant herbs to be burnt with him on his " life-giving pyre " (Lactant. *Phoen.* 90). In this connexion Sidonius never fails to mention cinnamon; see 7. 353, 9. 325, 11. 125, 22. 50; cf. Lactant. *Phoen.* 83.

[2] Here dawn and the goddess of dawn are mixed up, like the Tiber and the Tiber-god in *v.* 333. The dew of dawn looks like sweat, but is not sweat; for the rays of Dawn

seasons of cold; the fields bedizened with ever-blooming flowers know not the frosts of strange lands. The countryside is fragrant with roses, and throughout those unowned and undivided fields a sweet aroma breathes. The plains ever bring forth violets, clover, thyme, privet, lilies, narcissus, casia, culcas, marigold, costum, malobathrum, myrrh, balm, frankincense. Yea, when old age knocks at his door, the phoenix that dwells hard by seeks from hence the cinnamon that brings a new life.[1] Here the home of Aurora, overlaid with plates of flashing gold, displays withal smooth pearls on its broken surface. On all sides are things to capture the gaze, and, thanks to their masterly artistry, whatsoever meets the eye seems to surpass the rest. But all that beauty is dimmed in the presence of its mistress, who with her blushing radiance destroys the diverse fires of the gems, because she has fires of her own. Her combed hair poured forth saffron hues; her arm was bent as the comb sank in and arranged the yellow tresses on her temples. Her eyes poured forth rays; fiery their hue, but the heat of fire was not there, although when night is shaken off the dews received from it are wont to have a semblance of sweat.[2] Her bosom was girdled by a double band, and even the fold in her robe mocked the smallness of her breasts.[3] The lower part of the dress extended its crimson folds down to her rosy knees.

(Aurora), which are diffused from her eyes, have no heat in their fiery glow: morning receives its dew from the departing night, not from the dawn.

[3] The meaning is not clear. Possibly " made her small breasts envious," though *invidiam facere* regularly means "to bring reproach upon."

sic regina sedet solio; sceptri vice dextram
lampadis hasta replet; Nox adstat proxima divae,
iam refugos conversa pedes, ac pone tribunal
promit Lux summum vix intellecta cacumen.   435
hinc Romam liquido venientem tramite cernens
exsiluit propere et blandis prior orsa loquellis
" quid, caput o mundi," dixit, " mea regna revisis ?
quidve iubes ? " paulum illa silens atque aspera
        miscens
mitibus haec coepit : " venio (desiste moveri   440
nec multum trepida), non ut mihi pressus Araxes
imposito sub ponte fluat nec ut ordine prisco
Indicus Ausonia potetur casside Ganges,
aut ut tigriferi pharetrata per arva Niphatis
depopuletur ovans Artaxata Caspia consul.   445
non Pori modo regna precor nec ut hisce lacertis
frangat Hydaspeas aries inpactus Erythras.
non in Bactra feror nec committentia pugnas
nostra Semiramiae rident ad classica portae.
Arsacias non quaero domus nec tessera castris   450
in Ctesiphonta datur. totum hunc tibi cessimus
        axem:

446. Pori *Sirmondus* : phari(i).

---

[1] Rome asserts that she has not come to reclaim her old
eastern conquests.

[2] Araxes, in Armenia. Augustus is said to have built a
bridge over it. Cf. Verg. *Aen.* VIII. 728.

[3] The Romans had never conquered any part of India. But
here and in *vv.* 446 f. Rome may merely be indicating that
she does not intend to emulate Alexander the Great.

[4] *Erythraeus* is often used by poets for Indian (from the
mare Erythraeum, which, in the largest sense of the term,
extended to the coast of India). Sidonius seems to have
invented the town of Erythrae; cf. 5. 285, 11. 105, 22. 22.
In 7. 354 *Erythraeus* really means " Arabian "; the vague
geography of the poets often merges Arabia or Aethiopia with

46

II. PANEGYRIC ON ANTHEMIUS

Thus she sits, a queen on her throne, but instead of sceptre the shaft of a lamp fills her right hand. Night stands near the goddess, with her feet already turning to flee, and behind the dais Light scarce perceived is beginning to reveal the topmost peak. When from hence the goddess saw Rome drawing nigh through the cloudless air, she sprang up in haste and was the first to speak, thus beginning with kindly words: " O head of the world, why dost thou revisit my kingdom ? What are thy commands ?" The other was silent for a brief space, then thus began, mingling harsh and gentle phrase : [1] " I come (cease to be thus perturbed, and be not grievously alarmed), not that Araxes,[2] mastered by me, may have to flow beneath a bridge forced upon it, nor that in the ancient manner the Indian Ganges [3] may be drunk from an Italian helmet, nor that a consul, ranging through the fields of tiger-haunted Niphates, home of archers, may triumphantly despoil Artaxata by the Caspian Sea. I do not now beg for the realm of Porus, nor that these arms may thrust a battering-ram to shatter Erythrae [4] on the bank of the Hydaspes. I am not hurling myself against Bactra, nor are the gates of Semiramis' town [5] laughing to hear our trumpets starting the fight. I crave not the palaces of Persian kings, nor is word being passed in camp of mine to march on Ctesiphon. All this region [6] we have yielded up to thee. Do I not even

India; so in another reference to the Phoenix, 9. 325; the same bird appears among the Indian captives of Bacchus, 22. 50.

[5] *i.e.* of Babylon, which had, however, decayed after the death of Alexander the Great. For the contemptuous refusal to close the gates see n. on *v.* 80.

[6] For the boundaries of the eastern and western Empires as finally settled after the death of Theodosius (A.D. 395) see Gibbon, c. 29 init., Hodgkin, I. 677–8.

et nec sic mereor nostram ut tueare senectam?
omne quod Euphraten Tigrimque interiacet olim
sola tenes: res empta mihi est de sanguine Crassi,
ad Carrhas pretium scripsi; nec inulta remansi   455
aut periit sic emptus ager; si fallo, probasti,
Ventidio mactate Sapor. nec sufficit istud:
Armenias Pontumque dedi, quo Marte petitum
dicat Sulla tibi; forsan non creditur uni:
consule Lucullum. taceo iam Cycladas omnes: 460
adquisita meo servit tibi Creta Metello.
transcripsi Cilicas: hos Magnus fuerat olim.
adieci Syriae, quos nunc moderaris, Isauros:
hos quoque sub nostris domuit Servilius armis.
concessi Aetolos veteres Acheloiaque arva,   465
transfudi Attalicum male credula testamentum;
Epirum retines: tu scis cui debeat illam
Pyrrhus. in Illyricum specto te mittere iura
ac Macetum terras: et habes tu, Paule, nepotes.
Aegypti frumenta dedi: mihi viceret olim   470
Leucadiis Agrippa fretis. Iudaea tenetur
sub dicione tua, tamquam tu miseris illuc
insignem cum patre Titum. tibi Cypria merces
fertur: pugnaces ego pauper laudo Catones.
Dorica te tellus et Achaica rura tremiscunt,   475

---

475. rura *Mohr*: iura.

---

[1] Three Persian kings had borne the name Sapor (Shāpūr),
but Sidonius uses it to denote any Persian, or rather Parthian,
king or prince. It was Pacorus, son of Orodes I, who was
defeated and slain by P. Ventidius Bassus in 38 B.C. See
n. on 7. 99.

[2] Attalus III of Pergamum, who died in 133 B.C., bequeathed, or was said to have bequeathed, his dominions to
the Romans; hence arose the Roman province of Asia.

[3] L. Aemilius Paullus defeated Perseus of Macedon at
Pydna (168 B.C.).

48

thus deserve that thou protect mine old age? All
that lies between Euphrates and Tigris thou hast
long possessed alone; yet that possession was bought
by me with the blood of Crassus; at Carrhae I paid
down the price; nor did I remain unavenged nor
lose the land thus bought; if my word is not good,
Sapor[1] hath proved it, slain by Ventidius. Nor is
this enough. I gave up the Armenias and Pontus—
by what martial might assailed, let Sulla tell thee;
perchance one man's word is not enough, then ask
Lucullus. I keep silence now about all the Cyclades
—but Crete, which my Metellus won, is thrall to thee.
I made over to thee the Cilicians, yet Magnus had
routed them long ago. To Syria I added the Isaur-
ians, whom thou governest now, yet these likewise
Servilius subdued beneath our arms. I yielded up
to thee Aetolia's ancient race and the lands where
Achelous flows; with ill-starred trustfulness I handed
over to thee the bequest of Attalus.[2] Thou dost
hold Epirus, though thou knowest who won the title
to it from Pyrrhus. I see thee extending thy rule
to Illyricum and the land of the Macedonians, and
yet descendants of Paulus[3] still live. I gave thee the
corn of Egypt, though Agrippa had conquered the
land for me long since in the strait of Leucas.[4] Judea
is held beneath thy sway, as if it were thou that hadst
sent there the glorious Titus and his sire. To thee is
the revenue of Cyprus brought, while I in poverty
belaud my warlike Catos.[5] The Dorian land and
Achaia's fields tremble before thee, and thou stretch-

---

[4] *i.e.* at the battle of Actium.
[5] The younger Cato (" Uticensis ") was sent to Cyprus in
58 B.C. to annex the island.

tendis et in bimarem felicia regna Corinthon :
dic, Byzantinus quis rem tibi Mummius egit ?
  " Sed si forte placet veteres sopire querellas,
Anthemium concede mihi. sit partibus istis
Augustus longumque Leo ; mea iura gubernet   480
quem petii ; patrio vestiri murice natam
gaudeat Euphemiam sidus divale parentis.
adice praeterea privatum ad publica foedus :
sit socer Augustus genero Ricimere beatus ;
nobilitate micant : est vobis regia virgo,   485
regius ille mihi. si concors annuis istud,
mox Libyam sperare dabis. circumspice taedas
antiquas : par nulla tibi sic copula praesto est.
proferat hic veterum thalamos discrimine partos
Graecia, ni pudor est : reparatis Pisa quadrigis   490
suscitet Oenomaum, natae quem fraude cadentem
cerea destituit resolutis axibus obex ;
procedat Colchis prius agnita virgo marito
crimine quam sexu ; spectet de carcere circi
pallentes Atalanta procos et poma decori   495
Hippomenis iam non pro solo colligat auro ;
Deianira, tuas Achelous gymnade pinguis
inlustret taedas et ab Hercule pressus anhelo

---

¹ See 195–7.
² Alypia, daughter of Anthemius, was married to Ricimer
in 467 A.D. Sidonius reached Rome in the midst of the
celebrations (*Epist.* I. 5. 10).
³ *i.e.* by the defeat of Geiseric.
⁴ Cf. 14. 12, 23. 392.
⁵ Medea : *crimine* refers to the murder of her brother
Absyrtus (see 5. 132–7).
⁶ *i.e.* not merely on account of the gold, as on the first
occasion, but because she would fain have Hippomenes win.
⁷ Cf. 11. 87, 14. 16–20. The struggle of Achelous with
Hercules for the possession of Deianira is often mentioned in

est thy prosperous sovereignty to where Corinth lies between the two seas: pray tell me this—what Byzantine Mummius did this work for thee?

"But if haply it please thee to lay old grievances to rest, grant me Anthemius. In these lands let Leo be emperor, and long may he reign! But let my laws be in the hands of him whom I have asked of thee; and let the star of her deified father rejoice that Euphemia his daughter is robed in the purple of her ancestors![1] Add also a private compact to our public one: let a parent who is Emperor be blessed by having his daughter wedded to Ricimer.[2] Both shine with the lustre of high rank; in her ye have a royal lady, in him I have a man of royal blood. If thou dost willingly agree to this, thou shalt permit me to hope for Libya[3] anon. Survey the nuptials of olden time, and no union such as this event can offer itself to thy view. Here let Greece bring forward, unless she be ashamed, those marriages of her ancients which were won by peril. Let Pisa bring back her four-horse chariot and revive Oeno-maus,[4] who fell by a daughter's guile, when the waxen linch-pins betrayed him, unloosing the axles; let the maid of Colchis[5] come forward, who was brought to her husband's knowledge by her crime before he knew her as a woman; let Atalanta gaze on her pale suitors from the starting-place in the circus and no longer gather the apples of the comely Hippomenes for their gold alone[6]; let Achelous, with the oil of the wrestling-school upon him, glorify the nuptials of Deianira,[7] and, clasped tightly by the panting Her-

ancient literature. See Sir J. G. Frazer's n. on Apollodorus II. 7. 5 (Vol. I, p. 256 in this series). *Gymnade pinguis* is oddly used of a river-deity.

lassatum foveat rivis rivalibus hostem :
quantumvis repetam veteris conubia saecli,   500
transcendunt hic heroas, heroidas illa.
hos thalamos, Ricimer, Virtus tibi pronuba poscit
atque Dionaeam dat Martia laurea myrtum.
ergo age, trade virum non otia pigra foventem
deliciisque gravem, sed quem modo nauticus urit 505
aestus Abydenique sinus et Sestias ora
Hellespontiacis circumclamata procellis ;
quas pelagi fauces non sic tenuisse vel illum
crediderim cui ruptus Athos, cui remige Medo
turgida silvosam currebant vela per Alpem ;   510
nec Lucullanis sic haec freta cincta carinis,
segnis ad insignem sedit cum Cyzicon hostis,
qui cogente fame cognata cadavera mandens
vixit morte sua.   sed quid mea vota retardo ?
trade magis."   515
              Tum pauca refert Tithonia coniunx :
" duc age, sancta parens, quamquam mihi maximus
      usus
invicti summique ducis, dum mitior exstes
et non disiunctas melius moderemur habenas.
nam si forte placet veterum meminisse laborum,
et qui pro patria vestri pugnaret Iuli,   520
ut nil plus dicam, prior hinc ego Memnona misi."

    Finierant ; geminas iunxit Concordia partes,
electo tandem potitur quod principe Roma.

----

¹ Anthemius was in command of the fleet in the Hellespont
when called to the Imperial throne.
² Xerxes.
³ Sidonius is wrong. It was Mithridates who commanded
the sea throughout his disastrous siege of Cyzicus (74–73 B.C.),
though his ships could not save him from famine. See also
22. 163–168.

cules, refresh his wearied adversary with spiteful spate:
recall as I may the marriages of the olden time, this
man excels all the god-descended heroes, she the
heroines. Valour hath this union in her charge;
she demands it for thee, Ricimer, and thus the laurel
of Mars bestows on thee the myrtle of Venus. Come
then, deliver to me this man who neither cherishes
lazy ease nor is numbed by indulgence, but who even
now is harassed by the heaving deep,[1] by the bay of
Abydos and the shore of Sestos with the tempests of
the Hellespont roaring all around. Not so firmly,
methinks, was this narrow sea held even by him[2]
who burst through Athos and with his Median oarsmen made his swelling sails rush through wooded
mountains; nor was this strait so hemmed by
Lucullus' ships[3] when before famed Cyzicus idly
lingered that enemy who when hunger pressed him
devoured the bodies of his kin and thus lived by the
death of his own. But why do I delay the fulfilment
of my prayer? Rather deliver him now to me!"

Then answered Tithonus' spouse in these few
words: "Come, take him, reverend mother, although
I have great need of a mighty and unconquerable
leader,—provided that thou wilt now show thyself
more kindly, and so we may better wield the reins
in joint control. For if haply it please thee to
remember the toils of olden days, I was before thee—
to mention but this—in sending Memnon[4] hence to
fight for the native land of your Iulus."

They had finished, and Concord united the two
sides, for Rome at length gained the emperor of her

[4] Memnon, who appears in post-Homeric accounts as an
ally of the Trojans, was the son of Tithonus and Eos (Aurora).

nunc aliquos voto simili vel amore, vetustas,
te legisse crepa, numquam non invida summis   525
emeritisque viris. Brenni contra arma Camillum
profer ab exilio Cincinnatoque secures
expulso Caesone refer flentemque parentem
a rastris ad rostra roga, miseroque tumultu
pelle prius, quos victa petas ; si ruperit Alpes   530
Poenus, ad adflictos condemnatosque recurre ;
improbus ut rubeat Barcina clade Metaurus,
multatus tibi consul agat, qui milia fundens
Hasdrubalis, rutilum sibi cum fabricaverit ensem,
concretum gerat ipse caput. longe altera nostri   535
gratia iudicii est : scit se non laesus amari.

    Sed mea iam nimii propellunt carbasa flatus ;
siste, Camena, modos tenues, portumque petenti
iam placido sedeat mihi carminis ancora fundo.
at tamen, o princeps, quae nunc tibi classis et
      arma   540
tractentur, quam magna geras quam tempore parvo,
si mea vota deus produxerit, ordine recto
aut genero bis mox aut te ter consule dicam.

537. sed Luetjohann : et.

---

[1] Camillus was exiled on a charge of having made an unfair
division of the booty taken at Veii (Liv. V. 32. 8).

[2] Caeso, son of the great L. Quinctius Cincinnatus, was
exiled, and a heavy fine was imposed upon him, which his
father had to pay (Liv. III. 11–14). Three years later (458
B.C.), Cincinnatus was summoned from the plough to the
dictatorship in order to rescue the Romans from the Aequians
(Liv. III. 26–29).

[3] M. Livius Salinator, consul in 219 B.C., condemned on
a charge similar to that brought against Camillus (n. on v. 527),
retired from Rome to the country and took no part in public

choice. And now, Antiquity, thou who art ever jealous of the greatest men and greatest benefactors, prate if thou wilt of choices made by thee with like eagerness and affection! Bring Camillus [1] forth from his exile to confront the arms of Brennus; give Cincinnatus the fasces once more after banishing Caeso, invite the weeping parent from the rake to the rostra,[2] and in miserable discord drive men out, only to seek their help in thine hour of defeat! Should the Carthaginian have burst the Alps asunder, have recourse to men that have been broken and condemned; if the insatiate Metaurus is to be reddened by the defeat of Barca's son, let a consul thou hast fined do the work for thee, and as he routs Hasdrubal's thousands, let him who has fashioned a bloody sword for his use himself show an unkempt head.[3] Far different is the graciousness of our choice; he has never been wronged, but knows that he is loved.[4]

But now too strong are the breezes that drive my sails before them. Check, O Muse, my humble measures, and as I seek the harbour let the anchor of my song settle at last in a calm resting-place. Yet of the fleet and forces that thou, O prince, art handling and of the great deeds thou doest in little time I, if God further my prayers, shall tell in order due in the second consulship of thy daughter's

affairs until he was compelled to return in 210 B.C. He came in the guise of disgrace and mourning, with unkempt hair and matted beard and in shabby attire (Liv. XXVII. 34. 5). He was made consul for the year 207 with C. Claudius Nero, with whom he shared in the victory over Hasdrubal at the Metaurus.

[4] i.e. he has not had to suffer injury, like those old Romans, before gaining the love of the people.

nam modo nos iam festa vocant, et ad Vlpia poscunt
te fora, donabis quos libertate, Quirites,   545
quorum gaudentes exceptant verbera malae.
perge, pater patriae, felix atque omine fausto
captivos vincture novos absolve vetustos.

III

AD LIBELLVM

Quid faceret laetas segetes, quod tempus amandum
   messibus et gregibus, vitibus atque apibus,
ad Maecenatis quondam sunt edita nomen;
   hinc, Maro, post audes arma virumque loqui.
at mihi Petrus erit Maecenas temporis huius;   5
   nam famae pelagus sidere curro suo.
si probat, emittit, si damnat carmina, celat,
   nec nos ronchisono rhinocerote notat.
i, liber: hic nostrum tutatur, crede, pudorem;
   hoc censore etiam displicuisse placet.   10

---

[1] Ricimer had been consul in A.D. 459.

[2] The forum of Trajan. The public manumission of some
slaves was regularly performed by the consuls when they
entered upon their office. Cf. Claud. IV. *Cons. Hon.* 612–618.
The ceremony included the traditional blow on the cheek
(*alapa*), the significance of which is uncertain. See Mr.
R. G. Nisbet's interesting paper in *J.R.S.* VIII. 1., pp. 1–14.

[3] *i.e.* as a result of his coming victory over Geiseric.

[4] These two lines are partly a quotation, partly a paraphrase, of the opening of Virgil's *Georgics.*

III. TO HIS LITTLE BOOK

husband,[1] or in thy third; but now a festival doth call
us, and thy presence at the Ulpian Forum[2] is demanded by those citizens-to-be on whom thou wilt
bestow liberty, whose cheeks receive their buffets with
joy.   Forward, then, Father of thy country, blest of
fortune, and with happy omen release old captives,
to bind new ones anon.[3]

III

TO HIS LITTLE BOOK

What made the cornfields joyous, what season
is dear to harvest-crops and flocks, to vines and
bees,[4] was once declared in a poem addressed to
Maecenas; thereafter, Maro, thou didst dare to
sing of " arms and the man." But to me Petrus [5]
shall be the Maecenas of this time; for I glide
over the sea of fame under his guiding star. If he
approves my poems he lets them go forth, if he
condemns them, he suppresses them, but he never
censures me with the snorting snout of a rhinoceros.
Go, then, my book; for believe me, he sustains my
bashfulness; with him for censor it is a pleasure
even to have displeased.

[5] Petrus, Imperial secretary (*magister epistularum*) under
Majorian, a man of some literary ability (see *Carm.* 9. 306 sqq.,
Epist. IX. 13. 4 and the *carmen* which follows). He was evidently instrumental in reconciling the Emperor to Sidonius after
the trouble at Lugdunum (Introd., p. xxxvii), and also in negoti-
ating terms of surrender for the besieged Gallo–Romans and
their Burgundian allies: see 5. 564–573.

IV

PRAEFATIO PANEGYRICI DICTI DOMINO IMPERATORI CAESARI IVLIO VALERIO MAIORIANO AVGVSTO

Tityrus ut quondam patulae sub tegmine fagi
  volveret inflatos murmura per calamos,
praestitit adflicto ius vitae Caesar et agri,
  nec stetit ad tenuem celsior ira reum;
sed rus concessum dum largo in principe laudat,   5
  caelum pro terris rustica Musa dedit;
nec fuit inferius Phoebeia dona referre:
  fecerat hic dominum, fecit et ille deum.
et tibi, Flacce, acies Bruti Cassique secuto
  carminis est auctor qui fuit et veniae.   10
sic mihi diverso nuper sub Marte cadenti
  iussisti invicto, victor, ut essem animo.
serviat ergo tibi servati lingua poetae
  atque meae vitae laus tua sit pretium.
non ego mordaci fodiam modo dente Maronem   15
  nec civem carpam, terra Sabella, tuum.
res minor ingenio nobis, sed Caesare maior;
  vincant eloquio, dummodo nos domino.

---

12. invicto victor *Stangl*, erecto victor *Leo*: victor victor.

---

[1] Verg. *Ecl.* I. 1. Tityrus is, as usual, taken to represent Virgil.

[2] Octavian, as a Triumvir, might be spoken of as angry with Cremona, which supported Brutus and suffered severely when confiscated lands were assigned to the veterans of Philippi. The confiscations were extended to the territory around Mantua, "too near, alas! to hapless Cremona" (Verg. *Ec.* IX. 28), and Virgil was evicted. Thus the "wrath" of Octavian might be said to have extended to Virgil. There is no other authority for the statement in *v.* 4; probably Sidonius is writing from a confused recollection.

IV

PREFACE TO THE PANEGYRIC PRONOUNCED IN HONOUR OF THE LORD EMPEROR, IULIUS VALERIUS MAIORIANUS, CAESAR AUGUSTUS

That Tityrus [1] of old under the canopy of a spreading beech might pour forth his warblings breathed into the reed, Caesar vouchsafed him in his hour of distress the right to live and possess his land, and the wrath of majesty endured not against an humble offender.[2] But the rustic Muse, praising thus a bounteous prince for a farm restored, gave in return for that earthly boon a place in heaven; nor was such repayment with the gifts of Phoebus too poor a recompense, for whereas the one man had made the poet a master of lands, the poet made him a god. To Flaccus likewise, when he had followed the campaigns of Brutus and Cassius, he who was the source of his pardon was also the source of his song.[3] So it is with me; laid prostrate not long since in the ranks of thy foe, I was bidden by thee, my conqueror, to keep an unconquered spirit. So let the tongue of a poet thus preserved yield its service to thee, and let my praises be the recompense for my life. I will not now fix a malignant tooth in Maro or carp at the citizen of the Sabine country. My work must needs be less than theirs in talent, but it is greater in its Caesar. Let them surpass me in the power of utterance, so long as I surpass them in my lord and master.

---

[3] If this refers to Maecenas, the statement is incredible; Horace was first introduced to Maecenas in 38 B.C. But, as Geisler says (p. 11, n. 5), the context suggests that the reference is to Octavian.

V

PANEGYRICVS

Concipe praeteritos, respublica, mente triumphos:
imperium iam consul habet, quem purpura non plus
quam lorica operit, cuius diademata frontem
non luxu sed lege tegunt, meritisque laborum
post palmam palmata venit; decora omnia regni   5
accumulant fasces et princeps consule crescit.
personat ergo tuum caelo, rure, urbibus, undis
exsultans Europa sophos, quod rector haberis,
victor qui fueras. fateor, trepidaverat orbis
dum non vis vicisse tibi nimioque pudore   10
quod regnum mereare doles tristique repulsa
non moderanda subis quae defendenda putasti.

Sederat exserto bellatrix pectore Roma,
cristatum turrita caput, cui pone capaci
casside prolapsus perfundit terga capillus.   15

---

[1] Delivered at Lugdunum late in the year 458. See
Introd., p. xxxvii.

[2] The *tunica palmata*: n. on 2. 6 f.

[3] These words seem to be a flattering reference to the
interval between April 1 and December 28, 457. The date
of Majorian's accession is a vexed problem; see Stein, p.
554 n. and N. Baynes in *Journ. Rom. Stud.* XII (1922),
pp. 223 f. and XVIII (1928), pp. 224 f.   The scanty evidence
available seems to indicate that on April 1 he was proclaimed
by the soldiers with the connivance of Leo, the eastern
Emperor, but that his formal adoption by Senate, army and
people did not take place until December 28. Sidonius (*v.* 388,
collega) tells us that Leo gave his assent on the latter occasion.
This was strictly necessary (see n. 5 on p. 7), and there

V

PANEGYRIC [1]

Picture to your minds, O Roman people, all your
past triumphs; now a consul holds the imperial
power, one whom the hauberk clothes no less than
the purple, whose brow is wreathed with the diadem
not through vain parade but through lawful power,
and to whom as reward of his toils doth come the
palm-decked robe [2] after the victor's palm. Now the
fasces crown all the splendours of sovereignty, and
the prince is magnified in the consul. Therefore
jubilant Europe shouts a " bravo " for thee, echoing
through sky and countryside and cities and waters,
since thou who wert a conqueror art now greeted as
ruler. I confess it, the world trembled with alarm
while thou wert loth that thy victories should benefit
thee, and with overmuch modesty wert grieved that
thou didst deserve the throne, and so with a woful
refusal wouldst not undertake to rule that which
thou hadst deemed worth defending.[3]

Rome, the warrior-goddess, had taken her seat.
Her breast was uncovered, on her plumed head was
a crown of towers, and behind her, escaping from
under her spacious helmet, her hair flowed over her

seems to be no cogent reason for doubting the poet's assertion.
Stein rather arbitrarily takes the mention of Leo to refer to
April 1, while implicitly admitting that the reference in the
same sentence to " commons, Senate and army " applies
only to December 28. The attitude of Leo does seem to have
been wavering and baffling, and may well have made Majorian
hesitate, but it is very doubtful if Majorian would have committed himself irrevocably on December 28 without at least a
formal assent from the eastern Emperor.

laetitiam censura manet terrorque pudore
crescit, et invita superat virtute venustas.
ostricolor pepli textus, quem fibula torto
mordax dente forat; tum quidquid mamma refundit
tegminis, hoc patulo concludit gemma recessu.   20
hinc fulcit rutilus spatioso circite laevum
umbo latus; videas hic crasso fusa metallo
antra Rheae fetamque lupam, quam fauce retecta
blandiri quoque terror erat; quamquam illa vorare
Martigenas et picta timet; pars proxima Thybrim 25
exprimit; hic scabri fusus sub pumice tofi
proflabat madidum per guttura glauca soporem;
pectus palla tegit, quam neverat Ilia coniunx,
liquenti quae iuncta toro vult murmura lymphis
tollere et undosi somnum servare mariti.   30
ista micant clipeo; cuspis trabe surgit eburna,
ebria caede virum. propter Bellona tropaeum
exstruit et quercum captivo pondere curvat.
consurgit solium saxis quae caesa rubenti
Aethiopum de monte cadunt, ubi sole propinquo 35
nativa exustas adflavit purpura rupes.
iungitur hic Synnas, Nomadum lapis additur istic,
antiquum mentitus ebur; post caute Laconum
marmoris herbosi radians interviret ordo.

<hr>

19. forat *Wilamowitz*: vorat.

<hr>

[1] Compare the shorter description of Rome's shield, 2. 395 sq.
[2] The reference is to *lapis Syenites*, a red granite quarried
near Syene (Assouan), on the Egyptian side of the Ethiopian
border. Syene was supposed to lie on the tropic; its heat was
proverbial. See also *Epist.* II. 2. 7. For similar lists of
stones see 11. 17–19, 22. 136–141, *Epist.* II. *loc. cit.*

back. She has a sternness ready to rebuke exultation, her modest mien but makes her more terrible, and her valour is loth to see her beauty triumph. Purple-hued is her robe, which a clasp pierces with the bite of its twisted tooth; that part of her mantle which her breast throws off is gathered up by a jewel under her ample bosom. Here a glowing shield[1] of vast circumference supports her left side. Thereon can be seen, cast in thick metal, the cave of Rhea, and the mother-wolf, whose very caresses were fearsome with those open jaws—yet even in her pictured guise she is afraid to devour the sons of Mars. The near side figures Tiber, outstretched under a porous rock of scaly tuff and breathing forth his humid slumber through his grey-green throat. His breast is covered with a robe which his wife Ilia had spun, and she, close to that dripping couch, would fain stop the plashing and guard the sleep of her watery mate. Such are the pictures that sparkle on the shield. Her spear, set on an ivory shaft, towered up, drunk with the slaughter of men. Near by Bellona was building up a trophy and making an oak tree bend with the weight of captured spoils. The lofty throne was fashioned of the stones that are quarried and lowered from the ruddy Aethiopian mount, where the sun is nigh and thus a natural purple has tinged the seared crags.[2] Here Synnadian, there Numidian marble, that counterfeits old ivory,[3] was added; after these the grass-hued marble from Laconian scaur interposed a row of radiant green.

[3] Numidian marble (" giallo antico ") " varies in colour from the faintest straw tint to deep shades of rich yellow." (M. W. Porter, *What Rome was built with*, p. 37.)

THE POEMS OF SIDONIUS

Ergo ut se mediam solio dedit, advolat omnis   40
terra simul. tum quaeque suos provincia fructus
exposuit: fert Indus ebur, Chaldaeus amomum,
Assyrius gemmas, Ser vellera, tura Sabaeus,
Atthis mel, Phoenix palmas, Lacedaemon olivum,
Arcas equos, Epirus equas, pecuaria Gallus,   45
arma Chalybs, frumenta Libys, Campanus Iacchum,
aurum Lydus, Arabs guttam, Panchaia myrrham,
Pontus castorea, blattam Tyrus, aera Corinthus;
Sardinia argentum, naves Hispania defert
fulminis et lapidem; scopulos iaculabile fulgur   50
fucat et accensam silicem fecunda maritat
ira deum; quotiens caelum se commovet illic,
plus ibi terra valet.
                    Subito flens Africa nigras
procubuit lacerata genas et cernua frontem
iam male fecundas in vertice fregit aristas   55
ac sic orsa loqui: " venio pars tertia mundi,
infelix felice uno. famula satus olim
hic praedo et dominis exstinctis barbara dudum
sceptra tenet tellure mea penitusque fugata
nobilitate furens quod non est non amat hospes.   60
o Latii sopite vigor, tua moenia ridet
insidiis cessisse suis: non concutis hastam?
non pro me vel capta doles?   tua nempe putantur

56. loqui est *codd. plerique.*

---

[1] This stone was probably a kind of cat's-eye. According to one popular belief it was found only in places which had been struck by lightning (Isid. *Etym.* XVI. 13. 5. Some said this only of a rare variety of thunder-stone: Plin. *N.H.* xxxvii. 135). The stone was called *ceraunius* (sc. *lapis*), *ceraunia* (sc. *gemma*), or *ceraunium.*
[2] Or possibly "becomes more precious."
[3] Cf. 2. 358 sq.

64

V. PANEGYRIC ON MAIORIANUS

So when she had seated her on the throne in the midst, all lands flocked to her at once. The provinces display their several fruits; the Indian brings ivory, the Chaldaean nard, the Assyrian jewels, the Chinaman silk, the Sabaean frankincense; Attica brings honey, Phoenicia palms, Sparta oil, Arcadia horses, Epirus mares, Gaul flocks and herds, the Chalybian arms, the Libyan corn, the Campanian wine, the Lydian gold, the Arab amber, Panchaia myrrh, Pontus castory, Tyre purple, and Corinth bronzes; Sardinia offers silver, Spain ships and the thunderstone [1]—for there the flashing levin-bolt stains the rocks, and the fertilising wrath of the gods impregnates the heated flint: whensoever in that clime the sky stirs itself to fury, the earth there waxes stronger. [2]

Of a sudden Africa flung herself down weeping, with her swarthy cheeks all torn. Bowing her forehead she broke the corn-ears that crowned her, ears whose fruitfulness was now her bane; and thus she began: "I come, a third part of the world, unfortunate because one man is fortunate. This man, son of a slave-woman, [3] hath long been a robber; he hath blotted out our rightful lords, and for many a day hath wielded his barbarian sceptre in my land, and having driven our nobility utterly away this stranger loves nothing that is not mad. [4] O slumbering energy of Latium! He makes scornful boast that thy walls yielded to his cunning. [5] Wilt thou not then brandish the spear? Dost thou not grieve for me, even though thou too hast been captured? In sooth it is

[4] There is a double meaning in *nobilitas* (nobles and nobleness): he has driven away all that is noble and loves only what is mad.
[5] The Vandals under Geiseric sacked Rome in June, A.D. 455. *Insidiis* may contain a reference to the suspected collusion of Geiseric with the Empress Eudoxia. See Bury I. 324.

surgere fata malis et celsior esse ruina;
sed melius, quod terror abit: iam vincere restat, 65
si pugnas ut victa soles.   Porsenna superbum
Tarquinium impingens complevit milite Tusco
Ianiculum quondam; sed dum perrumpere portas
obsidione parat totam te pertulit uno
Coclitis in clipeo; presserunt milia solum 70
multa virum pendente via; nec ponte soluto
cum caderet cecidit.   rex idem denique morte
admonitus scribae didicit sibi bella moveri
non solum cum bella forent; mox pace petita
in regnum rediit, non tam feriente fugatus 75
quam flagrante viro.   steterat nam corde gelato
Scaevola et apposito dextram damnaverat igni,
plus felix peccante manu, cum forte satelles
palleret constante reo tormentaque capti
is fugeret qui tortor erat.   Brennum tremuisti, 80
post melior: quodcumque tuum est, quodcumque
     vocaris,
iam solus Tarpeius erat; sed reppulit unus
tum quoque totam aciem, Senones dum garrulus
     anser
nuntiat et vigilat vestrum sine milite fatum.
me quoque (da veniam quod bellum gessimus olim) 85
post Trebiam Cannasque domas, Romanaque tecta
Hannibal ante meus quam nostra Scipio vidit.

65. quo *codd. plerique.*

---

[1] Cf. 7. 5, Hor. *Carm.* iv. 4. 57–68, etc.
[2] *corde gelato*, which should refer to fear (Luc. VII. 339),
here means " perfectly cool."   There is a characteristically
absurd contrast between the coolness of Scaevola and the heat
of the fire.

believed that thy fortunes are exalted by ills and that a fall makes thee rise all the higher;[1] but now thy case is better, for the menace hath departed from thee; now victory awaits thee if thou but fight as thou art wont to fight after defeats. Once Porsenna, forcing Tarquin the Proud upon thee, filled Janiculum with Tuscan soldiery; but as he made ready by siege to break through thy gates, he met in the one shield of Cocles the whole of thee. Myriads bore hard upon that lone man while the passage across hung doubtful; and when the bridge was broken he fell, yet did not fall. The selfsame king at last took warning from his scribe's death and learned that he was being warred against not only when war was raging; thereupon he sought peace and returned to his kingdom, driven back less by a man's blow than by his burning. For Scaevola had stood with heart cool as ice[2] and doomed his right hand to the fire near by (happier he in that his hand struck in error), while the retainer grew pale as he saw the offender's courage, and the torturer fled from the prisoner's tortures. Thou didst quake before Brennus,[3] though later thou wast more than his match. It had come to such a pass that all the possessions and all the name thou now enjoyest were bound up in the Tarpeian mount [4] alone; but then also one man drove back a whole host, when the cackling goose announced the Senones and thy destiny kept watch without warriors. Me also (forgive me that I warred with thee aforetime) thou didst crush after the Trebia and Cannae, yet my Hannibal viewed Rome's roofs ere Scipio saw

---

[3] The Gaul who captured Rome (390 B.C.).
[4] *i.e.* the Capitol, which was not taken.

quid merui? fatis cogor tibi bella movere,
cum volo, cum nolo.   trepidus te territat hostis,
sed tutus claudente freto, velut hispidus alta   90
sus prope tesqua iacet claususque cacuminat albis
os nigrum telis gravidum; circumlatrat ingens
turba canum, si forte velit concurrere campo;
ille per obiectos vepres tumet atque superbit,
vi tenuis fortisque loco, dum proximus ' heia! '   95
venator de colle sonet: vox nota magistri
lassatam reparat rabiem; tum vulnera caecus
fastidit sentire furor.   quid proelia differs?
quid mare formidas, pro cuius saepe triumphis
et caelum pugnare solet? quid quod tibi princeps 100
est nunc eximius, quem praescia saecula clamant
venturum excidio Libyae, qui tertius ex me
accipiet nomen? debent hoc fata labori,
Maioriane, tuo.   quem cur conscendere classem
ac portus intrare meos urbemque subire,   105
si iubeas, cupiam, paucis ex ordine fabor.

   " Fertur, Pannoniae qua Martia pollet Acincus,
Illyricum rexisse solum cum tractibus Histri
huius avus; nam Theudosius, quo tempore Sirmi
Augustum sumpsit nomen, per utramque magistrum

---

101. *sic codd. Bernensis et Paris. 2782*: nunc praetura (praeterea *M*) eximius quem saecula *ceteri.*

---

[1] Probably a reference to the defeat of the Vandals off
Corsica in A.D. 456 (n. on 2. 367).
[2] Rather an unfortunate expression, coming from the
lips of Africa; but Sidonius, like his model Virgil (*Aen.* I.
22), is thinking of the conquest of Carthage. Carthage was
Geiseric's capital.
[3] *i.e.* after the two Scipios. *Nomen* refers to the honorary
surname *Africanus.*

68

ours. What is my fault? I am compelled by some
fate to stir up wars against thee, when I will it and
when I will it not. It is a frightened foe that
frights thee now,[1] but he is guarded by the enclosing
sea, as a shaggy boar lies low on the edge of the
wild and, thus shut in, sharpens the white weapons
wherewith his black jaws are loaded: around him
barks a great pack of hounds, hoping he may choose
to give them battle in the open plain, but he amid
his barrier of briers swells with insolence, poor in
dash but strong in situation, till the huntsman
coming near shouts from the hill ' Have at him ';
then the master's well-known voice revives the jaded
fury of the dogs to a blind frenzy that scorns to feel
wounds. Why dost thou delay the fight? Why
dost thou fear the sea, when even heaven is wont
so oft to battle for thy victories? And hast
thou not now a peerless prince, whom the prophetic ages proclaim as destined for Libya's destruction,[2] and who shall be the third[3] to get an
added name from me? To thy toil, Majorian, fate
owes this guerdon. And the reason why I desire,
if thou shouldst so bid, that he embark with his
fleet and sail into my harbours and enter my city—
this I will briefly declare in due order.

" 'Tis recorded that, where stands in all its might
the martial city of Acincus[4] in Pannonia, his grandfather ruled the land of Illyricum together with the
Danube-regions: for Theodosius, when he took the
name of Augustus at Sirmium,[5] before setting forth

---

[4] Acincus (more usually Aquincum, Aquinquum or Acin-
cum), a town in Pannonia Inferior on the right bank of the
Danube; mod. Alt-Ofen or O'-Buda.

[5] Sirmium, modern Mitrovitza, capital of Pannonia Inferior.

militiam ad partes regni venturus Eoas   111
Maiorianum habuit. Latiis sunt condita fastis
facta ducis quotiens Scythicis inlata colonis
classica presserunt Hypanim, Peucenque rigentem
mente salutatis inrisit lixa pruinis.   115
hunc socerum pater huius habet, vir clarus et uno
culmine militiae semper contentus, ut unum
casibus in dubiis iunctus sequeretur amicum.
non semel oblatis temptavit fascibus illum
Aetio rapere aula suo, sed perstitit ille,   120
maior honoratis : coepit pretiosior esse
sic pretio non capta fides.   erat ille quod olim
quaestor consulibus : tractabat publica iure
aera suo : tantumque modum servabat ut illum
narraret rumor iam rebus parcere nati.   125
   " Senserat hoc sed forte ducis iam livida coniunx
augeri famam pueri, suffusaque bili
coxerat internum per barbara corda venenum.
ilicet explorat caelum totamque volutis
percurrit mathesim numeris, interrogat umbras, 130
fulmina rimatur, fibras videt, undique gaudens
secretum rapuisse deo.   sic torva Pelasgum
Colchis in aplustri steterat trepidante marito

115. vid. Class. Quart. loc. cit. p. 17.

---

[1] His name was Domninus.

[2] He must have controlled the war-chest of Aëtius. His office is compared with that of the *quaestor consulis* in republican Rome. This official accompanied his chief to war and afterwards to his province; his duties were mainly financial. Hodgkin, II. 404, wrongly says that Domninus was quaestor. Apart from other considerations, the words of Sidonius himself imply that the official designation of Domninus, whatever it may have been, was certainly not *quaestor*.

to the eastern parts of the realm, had a Majorian
as his Master of Both Services. The exploits of this
leader have been inscribed in Rome's public annals
whensoever his troops were launched against the
Scythian landsmen and marched over the Hypanis,
and even the camp-followers mocked at frozen
Peuce, bidding welcome to the frosts. This leader's
daughter was married to our prince's father,[1] a
renowned man who was content to the end with a
single high office in the imperial service, that he
might follow one single friend and cling to him in
times of jeopardy. Not once but oft the court
strove with offers of the consulship to steal him from
his Aëtius, but he stood firm, a greater man than
those who received these dignities; and a loyalty
which no price could tempt came to be held more
precious. He was what of old the quaestor was to
the consuls;[2] he controlled the public funds by right
of his office; and such moderation did he maintain
that rumour declared he was thus early saving the
future possessions of his son.

"But as it chanced, the wife of the leader,[3]
already jealous, had perceived that the youth's
renown was thus waxing greater, and, filled with
spleen, she had nursed the hidden venom in her
barbarian heart. So now she searches the sky,
casting up numbers and exhausting the astrologer's
lore; she questions ghosts, explores the thunderbolts, and gazes at entrails, rejoicing to wrest God's
secret purpose from every source. Even thus
grimly had stood the Colchian woman[4] on the stern

---

[3] The young Majorian got his first taste of military service
under Aëtius. The explanation here given of his sudden
dismissal may be merely a piece of popular gossip.

[4] Cf. 2. 493.

Absyrtum sparsura patri facturaque caesi
germani plus morte nefas, dum funere pugnat   135
et fratrem sibi tela facit; vel cum obruit ignem
taurorum plus ipsa calens texitque trementem
frigida flamma virum, quem defendente veneno
inter flagrantes perhibent alsisse iuvencos.

   " Ergo animi dudum impatiens, postquam audiit isti
imperium et longum statui, laniata lacertos   141
ingreditur, qua strata viri, vocemque furentem
his rupit: ' secure iaces, oblite tuorum,
o piger: et mundo princeps (sic saecula poscunt)
Maiorianus erit; clamant hoc sidera signis,   145
hoc homines votis.   isti quid sidera quaero,
fatum aliud cui fecit amor? nil fortius illo,
et puer est cupidus numquam, sed parcus habendi;
pauper adhuc iam spargit opes, ingentia suadet
consilia et sequitur, totum quod cogitat altum est,
urget quod sperat.   ludum si forte retexam,   151
consumit quidquid iaculis fecisse putaris
istius una dies: tribus hunc tremuere sagittis
anguis, cervus, aper.   non sic libravit in hostem
spicula qui nato serpentis corpore cincto   155
plus timuit cum succurrit, dum iactibus isdem
interitum vitamque daret stabilemque teneret
corde tremente manum, totamque exiret in artem

152. consumpsit *LM*.

---

[1] Alcon. Cf. 183. The son whom he saved was Phalerus,
one of the Argonauts.

V. PANEGYRIC ON MAIORIANUS

of the Grecian ship in the presence of her terrified
husband, ready to throw Absyrtus in pieces at his
father and commit a horror worse than her brother's
murder, as she used a corpse for battle and made
missiles of her own kin: so too when, herself burning with a fiercer warmth, she quenched the fire of
the bulls, and chilled was the flame that enwrapped
her trembling lover, who, they say, through the
protection of a magic drug, felt cold amid the blazing
cattle.

" So after long chafing, when she heard that
the sovereignty was ordained even from of old
for that youth, she tore her arms and entered thus
where her lord's couch stood, and broke forth into
these frenzied cries: ' Heedless thou liest there,
sluggard, oblivious of thine own, and Majorian (for
so the ages claim) is to be the world's chief; the
stars proclaim this by signs and mankind by their
prayers. Why do I search for stars baneful to him for
whom love has created another destiny? No power is
stronger than love. And the youth is never covetous,
but is moderate in his getting; though his wealth
as yet is slender, he is already lavish with his means.
Great plans he urges and follows. All his thoughts
aspire high, and he pushes forward whatever his
hopes conceive. Were I to recount his sport—one
single day of his wipes out all that thou art reputed
to have performed as bowman: three arrows laid
trembling before him a snake, a stag and a boar.
Not so surely was the shaft launched against the
foe by him [1] who, when his son was encircled by a
serpent's body, felt a new dread in the act of succouring, as he dispensed both life and destruction with
the same shot, keeping a steady hand with a quaking
heart, and as hope drew closer his fear found relief

spe propiore metus, dans inter membra duorum
unius mortem. libeat decernere caestu: 160
cessit Eryx Siculus, simili nec floruit arte
Sparta, Therapnaea pugilem cum gymnade pinguem
stratus Bebryciis Amycus suspexit harenis.
qui vigor in pedibus! frustra sibi natus Ophelte
Sicaniam tribuit palmam, plantasque superbas   165
haud ita per siccam Nemeen citus extulit Arcas,
cuius in Aetolo volitantem pulvere matrem
horruit Hippomenes, multo qui caespite circi
contemptu praemissus erat, cum carceris antro
emicuit pernix populo trepidante virago,   170
nil toto tactura gradu, cum pallidus ille
respiceret medium post se decrescere campum
et longas ad signa vias flatuque propinquo
pressus in hostili iam curreret anxius umbra,
donec ad anfractum metae iam iamque relictus   175
concita ter sparso fregit vestigia pomo.
qui videt hunc equitem Ledaeum spernit alumnum
ac iuvenem, Sthenoboea, tuum, cui terga vetustas
pennati largitur equi Lyciamque Chimaeram
quem superasse refert, vulnus cum sustulit unum   180
tres animas. vitam tum si tibi fata dedissent,
Maioriane ferox, vetuisses Castora frenos,
Pollucem caestus, Alconem spicula nosse,

---

[1] Son of Aphrodite and Butes and founder of the town and
temple of Eryx, in Sicily, according to some accounts; but
the legends about him vary a great deal. His prowess as a
boxer is referred to by Virgil, *Aen.* V. 391 f., 401 ff.; *vv.*
410–414 mention the boxing contest in which Hercules
defeated and killed him. According to another version,
it was a wrestling-bout.

[2] Amycus, the boxing king of the Bebryces, vanquished by
Pollux in the course of the Argonautic expedition.

[3] Euryalus, son of Opheltes (Verg. *Aen.* IX. 201), the victor
in the foot-race at the games celebrated in Sicily by Aeneas
(*Aen.* V. 315–361).

74

V. PANEGYRIC ON MAIORIANUS

in the full exercise of his skill, dealing death to
one amid the entangled bodies of two. Or suppose
he chooses to try the issue in boxing—Sicilian Eryx[1]
has now yielded up his glory, nor did Sparta bloom
with such prowess when on the sand of Bebrycia the
prostrate Amycus[2] looked up at the boxer greasy
with the oil of the Laconian gymnasium. And what
power of foot is his! In vain does the son of Opheltes[3]
claim the palm won in Sicily: nor did the swift
Arcadian[4] so lift his proud feet as he sped over
thirsty Nemea, he whose mother, as she flitted over
the Aetolian dust, dismayed Hippomenes, con-
temptuously sent far ahead along the course, when
that fleet man-like maid dashed forth from the
mouth of the starting-pen before the breathless
throng, never to plant her whole foot anywhere,
while he with blanched cheeks looked back and saw
the intervening space behind him grow ever less,
and scanned the long distance to the goal; and
now he felt her breath close upon him and he was
running, sore distressed, upon his adversary's
shadow, till at the turning-point he bade fair to be
left behind; then he arrested those flying steps by
thrice throwing her an apple. Whoso sees him on
horseback scorns the child of Leda[5] and Sthenoboea's
loved one,[6] whom ancient story dowers with a
wingéd mount, telling also that he overcame the
Lycian Chimaera, destroying three lives with one
stroke. Had fate granted it to thee to live then,
gallant Majorian, thou wouldst have taken from
Castor, Pollux, and Alcon their title to mastery of

[4] Parthenopaeus, son of Atalanta; he was one of the
"Seven against Thebes" and won the foot-race at the first
celebration of the Nemean games. According to another
version, he was the winner of the archery-contest.

[5] *i.e.* Castor: cf. 182.   [6] *i.e.* Bellerophon: cf. 184.

75

Bellerophonteis insultaturus opimis.
si clipeum capiat, vincit Telamone creatum,   185
qui puppes inter Graias contra Hectoris ignem
ipsam etiam infidi classem defendit Vlixis.
missile si quanto iaculetur pondere quaeris,
segnius insertae trepidans pro fasce Camillae
excussit telum Metabus, nec turbine tanto   190
stridula Pelidae per Troilon exiit ornus;
nec sic heroum tardantem busta Creontem
Atticus Aegides rupit Marathonide quercu;
nec sic intortum violatae Phoebados ultrix
in Danaos fulmen iecit, cum Graecia Troiae   195
noctem habuit similemque facem fixusque Capherei
cautibus inter aquas flammam ructabat Oileus.

    " ' Parva loquor. quid quod, quotiens tibi bella
      geruntur,
discipulus, non miles adest ? et fingit alumnum :
aemulus econtra spectat. quod viceris odit   200
et quos vincis amat. totus dormitat ad istum
magnus Alexander, patris quem gloria torsit.
quid faciam infelix ? nato quae regna parabo
exclusa sceptris Geticis, respublica si me
praeterit et parvus super hoc Gaudentius huius   205
calcatur fatis ? istum iam Gallia laudat
quodque per Europam est. rigidis hunc abluit undis

---

[1] Ajax, son of Telamon : see Ovid, *Met.* XIII. 5 ff.

[2] The tale of Metabus is told in Verg. *Aen.* XI. 539–566.

[3] Theseus slew Creon, who had refused burial to Polynices
and the other assailants of Thebes. See Statius, *Theb.* XII.
768 ff.

[4] The " lesser Ajax," son of Oïleus, had assaulted Cassandra
in the temple of Pallas Athena. The vengeance of the
goddess is here, as often (*e.g.* Verg. *Aen.* I. 39–45), associated
with the destruction of the returning Greek ships on Cape
Caphereus. Pallas wrecks the ships, hurling many thunderbolts, one of which strikes Ajax and flings him upon a pointed
rock. *Facem* refers to the lightning.

the bridle, the boxing-glove and the arrow, and thou wouldst have made a mockery of Bellerophon's proud spoils. Should he take up his shield, he surpasses the offspring of Telamon,[1] who among the Greek ships defended against Hector's fires even the fleet of the treacherous Ulysses. If you ask with what force he hurls the javelin—more feebly did Metabus [2] fling his dart when alarmed for the bundle that held Camilla; with a less powerful swing did the ashen shaft of Peleus's son pass whirring through the body of Troilus; not with such strength did the man of Athens, son of Aegeus, crush with Marathonian oak Creon, who was hindering the burial of the heroes[3]; nor was the thunderbolt sent hurtling so violently against the Greeks by the maiden avenger of Phoebus' wronged votary, when Greece suffered a night such as Troy's with like flaring of brands, and the son of Oïleus,[4] pinned on the cliffs of Caphereus, vomited flame amid the waters.

" ' But these are trifles I speak of. There is more: whenever thou wagest war, he is near thee as a learner, not as a soldier, and while he professes himself thy pupil he looks on thee with a rival's eye. He hates the thought that thou hast conquered, and them that thou conquerest he loves. Compared with him, Alexander the Great, to whom his father's glory was torture,[5] is an arrant sluggard. Unhappy me! What shall I do? What realm shall I win for my son, debarred as I am from a Gothic sceptre,[6] if Rome ignores me and, to crown all, our little Gaudentius is trodden underfoot by this youth's destiny? Already Gaul and all Europe sound his praises. He

---

[5] See Plutarch, *Alex.* c. 5.

[6] The wife of Aëtius was, or claimed to be, of royal Gothic descent. Her father, Carpilio, was *comes domesticorum* under

Rhenus, Arar, Rhodanus, Mosa, Matrona. Sequana
    Ledus,
Clitis, Elaris, Atax, Vacalis ; Ligerimque bipenni
excisum per frusta bibit. cum bella timentes   210
defendit Turonos, aberas ; post tempore parvo
pugnastis pariter, Francus qua Cloio patentes
Atrebatum terras pervaserat. hic coeuntes
claudebant angusta vias arcuque subactum
vicum Helenam flumenque simul sub tramite longo
artus suppositis trabibus transmiserat agger.   216
illic te posito pugnabat ponte sub ipso
Maiorianus eques. fors ripae colle propinquo

    214. *fortasse* arcusque sub ictu.   *Vid. Class. Quart. loc. cit.*
p. 18.

Honorius, and her elder son was named after him. The
younger son, Gaudentius, was named after his paternal grandfather. He was born about 440 and in 455 was taken by
Geiseric as a prisoner to Africa, where he apparently died not
later than 462. The present passage seems to imply that
Carpilio, the elder brother of Gaudentius, was dead. He had
been a member of an embassy to Attila on behalf of Aëtius
(Cassiod. *Var.* I. 4. 11), perhaps in A.D. 434. It may have
been on this occasion that he was detained by the Huns as a
hostage. He seems to have regained his liberty, possibly by
flight (Priscus, fr. 8, F. H. G. IV. 81). Nothing further is
known about him.
    [1] Ledus, the Laz, near Montpellier. *Clitis* unknown. *Elaris*
= *Elaver*, the Allier, a tributary of the Loire. *Atax*, the *Aude*.
Vacalis (*Vachalis, Vacalus, Vahalis*), the Waal.
    [2] Tours may have been threatened by an invasion of the
Aremoricans. It is usual to connect these words with 7. 246,
where the subjugation of the Aremoricans by Litorius
(apparently in A.D. 437) is mentioned. But there was another

bathes in the icy waters of Rhine, Arar, Rhone,
Mosa, Matrona, Sequana, Ledus, Clitis, Elaris,
Atax, Vacalis[1]; the Liger he cleaves with an axe
and drinks piece by piece. When he defended the
Turoni,[2] who feared the conflict, thou wast not
there; but a little later ye fought together where
Cloio[3] the Frank had overrun the helpless lands of
the Atrebates. There was a narrow passage at
the junction of two ways, and a road crossed
both the village of Helena, which was within bow-
shot, and the river, where that long but narrow
path was supported by girders. Thou wert posted
at the cross-roads, while Majorian warred as a
mounted man close to the bridge itself.[4]   As chance

Aremorican rising about 446, and Tours may then also
have been threatened. On the other hand, Sidonius may be
referring to an occurrence not elsewhere recorded.

[3] Other forms are C(h)lodio, Chlogio. The incident here
related (for which Sidonius is the only authority) is usually
dated A.D. 428 ("about the year 431," C. M. H.). This dating
is quite incompatible with the mention in v. 205 of Gaudentius
(born about 440), taken in conjunction with the repeated
insistence on the extreme youth of Majorian (who was, indeed,
still *iuvens* at the time of his accession: see v. 524); needless
to say, it is also incompatible with the usual explanation of
the reference to Tours (see the last note). The date was in
all probability after 440 and may have been several years later.
Stein (p. 493, n. 2) gives 451 as the *terminus ante quem*.

[4] The above rendering is given with some diffidence, but
seems preferable to any other that has been offered. The
meaning is that a narrow road ran from the cross-roads
through the village and was continued over the bridge which
spanned the river. The two strategic points were the cross-
roads and the bridge; there Aëtius and Majorian were
respectively posted. The *agger* and the *trames* are the same
thing. *Artus* is here translated as if it agreed with *tramite*,
in order to bring out the antithesis of the juxtaposed adjectives
longo and *artus*—a feeble "point" for the sake of which Sidonius

barbaricus resonabat hymen Scythicisque choreis
nubebat flavo similis nova nupta marito.   220
hos ergo, ut perhibent, stravit; crepitabat ad ictus
cassis et oppositis hastarum verbera thorax
arcebat squamis, donec conversa fugatus
hostis terga dedit; plaustris rutilare videres
barbarici vaga festa tori coniectaque passim   225
fercula captivasque dapes cirroque madente
ferre coronatos redolentia serta lebetas.
ilicet increscit Mavors thalamique refringit
plus ardens Bellona faces; rapit esseda victor
nubentemque nurum.   non sic Pholoetica monstra
atque Pelethronios Lapithas Semeleius Euan   231
miscuit, Haemonias dum flammant orgia matres
et Venerem Martemque cient ac prima cruentos
consumunt ad bella cibos Bacchoque rotato
pocula tela putant, cum crudescente tumultu   235
polluit Emathium sanguis Centauricus Othryn.
nec plus nubigenum celebrentur iurgia fratrum:
hic quoque monstra domat, rutili quibus arce cerebri
ad frontem coma tracta iacet nudataque cervix
saetarum per damna nitet, tum lumine glauco   240
albet aquosa acies ac vultibus undique rasis
pro barba tenues perarantur pectine cristae.

---

has dislocated and complicated the sentence. For a fuller
discussion see *Class. Quart. loc. cit.* pp. 17 ff. *Pugnabat* in *v.*
217 means merely " was serving," or " was under arms ";
the fighting began later. Helena has not been identified with
certainty; most historians now seem to favour Hélesmes
(Dép. Nord); other possibilities are Vieil-Hesdin and Lens.

[1] *Scyth.*, *i.e.* Frankish. Contrast 2. 239, 7. 246, 280, 304,
where " Scythian " refers to the Huns; 5. 329 (Vandals:
see n. on 2. 351); 7. 403, 498 (Goths).

[2] The Centaurs were sons or descendants of Ixion and a
cloud.

would have it, the echoing sound of a barbarian
marriage-song rang forth from a hill near the river-
bank, for amid Scythian [1] dance and chorus a yellow-
haired bridegroom was wedding a young bride of
like colour. Well, these revellers, they say, he laid
low. Time after time his helmet rang with blows,
and his hauberk with its protecting scales kept off
the thrust of spears, until the enemy was forced to
turn and flee. Then might be seen the jumbled
adornments of the barbarian nuptials gleaming red
in the waggons, and captured salvers and viands
flung together pell-mell, and servants crowned with
perfumed garlands carrying wine-bowls on their
oily top-knots. Straightway the spirit of Mars
waxes fiercer and the nuptial torches are snapped
asunder by the more fiery goddess of war; the
victor snatches their chariots and carries off the
bride in the hour of her bridal. Not so fiercely did
Bacchus, Semele's son, embroil Pholoe's monsters
and the Thracian Lapithae, when his revels inflamed
the Thracian women, stirring up both love and war,
and they used for the struggle first of all the bloody
meats of the feast, and whirling the wine about
deemed their cups weapons; while, as the affray
grew fiercer, the blood of Centaurs defiled Emathian
Othrys. And truly the quarrel of the cloud-born
brothers [2] deserves no more renown; for this youth
likewise subdues monsters, on the crown of whose
red pates lies the hair that has been drawn towards
the front, while the neck, exposed by the loss of its
covering, shows bright. Their eyes are faint and
pale, with a glimmer of greyish blue. Their faces
are shaven all round, and instead of beards they
have thin moustaches which they run through with

strictius assutae vestes procera cohercent
membra virum, patet his altato tegmine poples,
latus et angustam suspendit balteus alvum.   245
excussisse citas vastum per inane bipennes
et plagae praescisse locum clipeosque rotare
ludus et intortas praecedere saltibus hastas
inque hostem venisse prius ; puerilibus annis
est belli maturus amor.   si forte premantur   250
seu numero seu sorte loci, mors obruit illos,
non timor ; invicti perstant animoque supersunt
iam prope post animam.   tales te teste fugavit
et laudante viros.   quisnam ferat ?   omnia tecum,
te sine multa facit.   pugnant pro principe cuncti :
quam timeo, ne iam iste sibi ! si regna tenebit,   256
huic vincis, quodcumque domas.   nil fata relinquunt
hic medium : percussor enim si respuis esse,
servus eris.   certe recto si tramite servat
sidera Chaldaeus, novit si gramina Colchus,   260
fulgura si Tuscus, si Thessalus elicit umbras,
si Lyciae sortes sapiunt, si nostra volatu
fata locuntur aves, doctis balatibus Hammon
si sanctum sub Syrte gemit, si denique verum,
Phoebe, Themis, Dodona, canis, post tempora nostra
Iulius hic Augustus erit.   coniunctus amore   266
praeterea est iuveni, grandis quem spiritus armat
regis avi.   quo te vertas ?   ad culmina mundi

---

[1] The oracle of Apollo at Patara : Verg. *Aen.* IV. 346.

[2] The god Ammon (or Hammon) was represented as a ram,
or in human form with the head (sometimes with only the
horns) of a ram.

[3] Reference to Ricimer. The " royal grandfather " is
Wallia ; see n. on 2. 362-5.

V. PANEGYRIC ON MAIORIANUS

a comb. Close-fitting garments confine the tall
limbs of the men; they are drawn up high so as
to expose the knees, and a broad belt supports their
narrow middle. It is their sport to send axes hurtling through the vast void and know beforehand
where the blow will fall, to whirl their shields, to
outstrip with leaps and bounds the spears they
have hurled and reach the enemy first. Even
in boyhood's years the love of fighting is full-
grown. Should they chance to be sore pressed by
numbers or by the luck of the ground, death may
overwhelm them, but not fear; unconquerable they
stand their ground, and their courage well-nigh out-
lives their lives. Such men did he put to flight with
thee to witness and to praise. Who could endure
it? All thine exploits he shares, many more he
performs without thee. All men fight for their
emperor; I fear, alas! he now fights for himself. If
he should win the sovereignty, then all the conquests thou makest are victories for him. Here the
fates leave no middle course; if thou refuse to be
his assassin, thou wilt be his slave. Certain is this:
if the Chaldaean goes not astray in his star-gazing,
if the Colchian has knowledge of herbs, the Tuscan
of lightning, if the Thessalian tempts forth the
ghosts of the dead, if the Lycian oracle[1] hath discernment, if the birds can tell our destiny by their
flight, if Hammon nigh to the Syrtes wails forth a
hallowed rede with prescient bleatings,[2] yes, if
Phoebus, Themis, Dodona chant forth the truth,
then when our day is over this man shall be Julius
Augustus. Moreover, there is linked with him in
bonds of affection one who is armed with the great
spirit of a royal grandfather.[3] Whither canst thou

83

hic fatum fert, ambo animum.   consurge simulque
aggredere ignaros.   neutrum mactare valebis,   270
si iubeas utrumque mori ; sed necte dolosas
blanditias uni, ferro tamen iste petatur.
quid loquor incassum ? nihil est quod tanta cavemus :
ut regnet victurus erit ! '

                " Commotus in iras
Aetius sic pauca refert : ' compesce furentis   275
impia vota animi.   mortem mandare valebo
insontis, taceam nostri ? quisquamne precatur
ut sine criminibus crimen fiat bene nasci ?
ad poenam quis fata vocet ? tua viscera ferro,
Maioriane, petam, Phoebus si nocte refulget,   280
Luna die, duplex ponto si plaustra novatur
Parrhasis, Atlantem Tanais, si Bagrada cernit
Caucason, Hercynii nemoris si stipite lintris
texta Nabataeum pro Rheno sulcat Hydaspen,
si bibit Hispanus Gangen tepidisque ab Erythris 285
ad Tartesiacum venit Indus aquator Hiberum,
si se Pollucis perfundit sanguine Castor,
Thesea Pirithoi, Pyladen si stravit Orestae
vel furibunda manus, raperet cum Taurica sacra
matricida pius.   sed ne sprevisse dolorem   290
forte tuum videar, vivat careatque parumper
militia.   heu ! potuit nobis, nisi triste putasses,
fortunam debere suam.'

---

¹ The Bears.
² *Eryth.* : n. on 2. 447.

turn? To the world's topmost pinnacle he directs his fate and both direct their thoughts. Arise and assail them at the same time unawares. Neither of them wilt thou be able to slay if thou shouldst order that both die; nay, rather weave crafty flatteries for the one, and let this man be attacked with the sword. But why do I speak vain words? 'Tis for naught that we seek to avert these fateful events. He will surely live that he may reign.'

"Aëtius, stirred to wrath, thus briefly answered: 'Curb the impious longings of thy frenzied spirit! Can I order the death of a man who is innocent, not to say our friend? Can anyone urge that where no crime is charged it be made a crime to be well-born? Who can summon the fates to judgment? I will assail thy body with the sword, Majorian,— yes, if the sun shines by night and the moon by day, if the two Arcadian constellations [1] have their wains refreshed in the sea, if Tanais looks on Atlas and Bagrada on the Caucasus, if the boat compacted of timbers from the Hercynian forest cleaves the eastern Hydaspes instead of the Rhine, if the Spaniard drinks of the Ganges and the Indian comes from warm Erythrae [2] to the Spanish Ebro to draw water, if Castor steeps himself in his brother's blood, if the hand of Pirithous laid Theseus low, or the hand of Orestes, frenzied as it was, struck Pylades down when the filial matricide was snatching the holy image from the Tauric shrine. Nevertheless, I would fain not be deemed to have slighted thy distress; so he shall live, indeed, but he shall be taken from his soldiering for a brief space. Alas! But for thy gloomy thoughts he might have owed his rise to me!'

85

" Sic fatur et illum
rure iubet patrio suetos mutare labores,
fatorum currente rota, quo disceret, agri   295
quid possessorem maneat, quos denique mores
ius civile paret, ne solam militis artem
ferret ad imperium.　suspenderat ilicet arma
emeritus iuvenis, sterilis ieiunia terrae
vomere fecundans.　sic quondam consule curvo
vertebas campos, paulum si pace sequestra   301
classica laxasses, fortis cui laeva regebat
stivam post aquilas, humili dum iuncta camino
victoris fumum biberet palmata bubulci.

" Principis interea gladio lacrimabile fatum   305
clauserat Aetius ; cuius quo tutius ille
magna Palatinis coniungeret agmina turmis,
evocat hunc precibus.　sed non se poena moratur
sanguinis effusi (numerum collegerat ergo,

295. agri Luetjohann : agro.

---

[1] Aëtius was slain by Valentinian III and the eunuch chamberlain Heraclius on Sept. 21, A.D. 454.　Petronius Maximus, who had instigated this murder in the vain hope of succeeding Aëtius as " the Patrician," soon turned upon his imperial master and caused him to be assassinated on March 16, A.D. 455.　On the following day he was proclaimed Emperor. A month and a half later he was killed as he sought flight before the Vandals' advance on Rome.　When Geiseric departed after plundering the capital, Avitus was proclaimed Emperor in Gaul, and he entered Rome before the end of the year, accompanied by our poet, his son-in-law.　Scarcely a year later he was deposed by Ricimer and Majorian, and died shortly afterwards.　After an interregnum he was succeeded, in the year 457, by Majorian, who would perhaps have been elevated two years before had not Petronius Maximus stood in his way.　It must have been very hard for Sidonius to write this part of the poem.　Avitus, of course, is not mentioned.

V. PANEGYRIC ON MAIORIANUS

" So spake he, and ordered the fighter to exchange his wonted toil for his native fields; but fate's revolving wheel was here at work, to the end that he might learn what is in store for the possessor of land and likewise what conduct the civil law creates, and so he might bring to the throne more than a soldier's skill. Straightway he had hung up his armour, this veteran young in years, and was making the leanness of a barren land fruitful with the plough. Even so in old times thou wert wont, O Rome, to upturn thy fields by the work of a stooping consul, when peace had intervened for a little and thou hadst relaxed thy campaigning; and his stout left hand would control the plough after he had ruled the legions, while near the lowly hearth a peasant-conqueror's palm-decked robe drank in the smoke.

" Meanwhile Aëtius [1] had fulfilled his melancholy fate by the sword of the emperor; who, that he might with more safety win over the great hosts of his victim to join the Palatine bands, called on Majorian with prayers to come to him.[2] But punishment for the blood that he had shed was not long in coming (so 'twas a mere mob he had rallied round

[2] After the death of Aëtius, Valentinian summoned Majorian from his retreat and made him *comes domesticorum*. The *palatini*, like the old Praetorian Guards, were stationed in various parts of Italy. They were under the command of the *magister utriusque militiae*. The *domestici*, another body of guards, usually but not always in attendance at the Court, were commanded independently by the *comes domesticorum*. *Magna agmina* refers particularly to the great body of armed retainers (*buccellarii*) which Aëtius had enlisted in his service, and which almost certainly outnumbered the regular troops available in Italy.

non animum populi): ferri mala crimina ferro   310
solvit et in vestram plus concidit ille ruinam.
iam tunc imperium praesentis principis aurea
volvebant bona fata colu; sed publica damna
invidiam fugere viri. quicumque fuerunt
nomen in Augustum lecti, tenuere relictum   315
Caesaribus solium: postquam tu capta laboras,
hic quod habet fecit. Traianum Nerva vocavit,
cum pignus iam victor erat: Germanicus esset
ut titulis, meritis fuerat. res ordine currit;
hanc ambit famam quisquis sic incipit. olim   320
post Capreas Tiberi, post turpia numina Gai,
censuram Claudi, citharam thalamosque Neronis,
post speculi immanis pompam, quo se ille videbat
hinc turpis, quod pulcher, Otho, post quina Vitelli
milia famosi ventris damnata barathro,   325
his titulis princeps lectus similique labore
Vespasianus erat.

          " Sed ne fortasse latronis
me clausam virtute putes, consumpsit in illo
vim gentis vitae vitium; Scythicam feritatem
non vires, sed vota tenent, spoliisque potitus   330
immensis robur luxu iam perdidit omne
quo valuit dum pauper erat. mea viscera pro se
in me nunc armat; laceror tot capta per annos

326. labori *CPTF.*

---

[1] At this point it is perhaps necessary to remind the reader
that Africa is addressing all these words to the goddess Roma.

[2] See Suet. *Claud.* 16 for the eccentric conduct of Claudius
as censor.

[3] See Juvenal II. 99.

[4] This was not true of Geiseric, though it may have been
true of many of his followers.

V. PANEGYRIC ON MAIORIANUS

him, not the hearts of the people); the sword's
crime he expiated by the sword, and so he fell, O
Rome, bringing thee lower than he himself was
brought. Yet even then the kindly fates with their
golden distaff were evolving the reign of our present
chief; but the calamities of the people shrank from
bringing enmity on such a man. All who had been
chosen to bear the name of Augustus had held a
throne left for them by the Caesars; but he, when
thou[1] wert captured and in sore trouble, created that
which he now holds. Nerva called Trajan to power
when his son was already a conqueror; in official
title he was styled Germanicus, but his deeds had
made him so already. The one thing leads to the
other: whoever begins thus aims at the same glory.
In olden days after Tiberius in Capri, after Gaius'
base assumption of divinity, after the censorship of
Claudius,[2] after Nero with his lyre and his lechery,
after the parade of that horrible mirror[3] in which
Otho, foul because he was fair, was wont to behold
himself, after Vitellius' five millions of money condemned to the bottomless pit of his scandalous belly,
Vespasian had been chosen emperor with the same
titles won by the same toil as Trajan's and Majorian's.

"But lest haply thou think that I am securely
hemmed in by the valour of the Robber, know that
in him the vileness of his vices has sapped the vigour
of his race.[4] His Scythian[5] savagery is governed not
by his strength but by his desires; spoils immense
he has won, but already by his profligacy he has
lost all that made him strong when he was poor.
Now he arms mine own flesh against me for his own
ends, and after all these years of captivity I am being

[5] See nn. on 219 above and on 2. 351.

89

ure suo, virtute mea, fecundaque poenis
quos patiar pario.   propriis nil conficit armis :   335
Gaetulis, Nomadis, Garamantibus Autololisque,
Arzuge, Marmarida, Psyllo, Nasamone timetur
segnis, et ingenti ferrum iam nescit ab auro.
ipsi autem color exsanguis, quem crapula vexat
et pallens pinguedo tenet, ganeaque perenni   340
pressus acescentem stomachus non explicat auram.
par est vita suis ; non sic Barcaeus opimam
Hannibal ad Capuam periit, cum fortia bello
inter delicias mollirent corpora Baiae
et, se Lucrinas qua vergit Gaurus in undas,   345
bracchia Massylus iactaret nigra natator.
atque ideo hunc dominum saltem post saecula tanta
ultorem mihi redde, precor, ne dimicet ultra
Carthago Italiam contra."

                                 Sic fata dolore
ingemuit lacrimisque preces adiuvit obortis.   350
his haec Roma refert : " longas succinge querellas,
o devota mihi : vindex tibi nomine divum
Maiorianus erit.   sed paucis pauca retexam.
ex quo Theudosius communia iura fugato
reddidit auctoris fratri, cui guttura fregit   355

---

¹ This is related by Livy, XXIII. 18. 11–16, and is a favourite
topic with later writers.
² In this answer of the goddess Roma the poet takes the
opportunity of indicating the hardships suffered by Gaul
during the past 75 years, with the object of enlisting Majorian's
sympathy and of excusing the recent rebellion

cruelly torn under his authority by the prowess of mine own; fertile in afflictions I bring forth sons to bring me suffering. Naught doth he perform with his own arms; Gaetulians, Numidians, Garamantians, Autololi, Arzuges, Marmaridae, Psylli, Nasamones—it is these that make him feared, but he is sunk in indolence and, thanks to untold gold, no longer knows aught of steel. His cheeks are bloodless; a drunkard's heaviness afflicts him, pallid flabbiness possesses him, and his stomach, loaded with continual gluttony, cannot rid itself of the sour wind. His followers live like him: Hannibal of Barca's race was not so utterly undone in affluent Capua's land,[1] when Baiae enfeebled amid all its allurements bodies that were strong for war, and the Massylian took to swimming and flourished his swarthy arms about where Gaurus stoops down to the Lucrine waters. So do thou, I pray thee, give me but this one lord after these many ages to be my avenger, that so Carthage may cease to war against Italy."

So speaking, she groaned in her distress, and the starting tears gave support to her prayers. Rome answered[2]: " Curb thy long plaint, my faithful one; Majorian shall be thine avenger commissioned by heaven.[3] But a few things in few words I will recall. Ever since Theodosius restored a joint authority to his patron's exiled brother, whose neck was broken by a hand destined to be turned against

[3] Mr. Stevens (p. 46, n. 5) inadvertently accuses the poet of inconsistency here : " In v. 352 Rome tells Africa who her saviour is to be, but in v. 104 Africa is represented as already knowing his name." But in the earlier passage Africa says " Majorian is the deliverer I want," and here Rome says " Majorian you shall have "; there is no inconsistency.

post in se vertenda manus, mea Gallia rerum
ignoratur adhuc dominis ignaraque servit.
ex illo multum periit, quia principe clauso,
quisquis erat, miseri diversis partibus orbis
vastari sollemne fuit. quae vita placeret,   360
cum rector moderandus erat? contempta tot annos
nobilitas iacuit : pretium respublica forti
rettulit invidiam.   princeps haec omnia noster
corrigit atque tuum vires ex gentibus addens   364
ad bellum per bella venit ; nam maximus isse est,
non pugnasse labor.   terimus cur tempora verbis?
pervenit et vincit."   tali sermone peractum
concilium, verbisque deae famulante metallo
aurea concordes traxerunt fila sorores.

Hos me quos cecini Romae Libyaeque labores 370
vota hominum docuere loqui ; iam tempus ad illa
ferre pedem quae fanda mihi vel Apolline muto :
pro Musis Mars vester erit.   conscenderat Alpes
Raetorumque iugo per longa silentia ductus
Romano exierat populato trux Alamannus   375

---

¹ Gratian, who had raised Theodosius to Imperial power
(hence *auctor*), was assassinated by his soldiers when the
pretender Magnus Clemens Maximus invaded Gaul (A.D. 383).
Maximus invaded Italy in 387 in order to attack Valentinian II
(half-brother of Gratian), who fled to the East.   Maximus was
beheaded in the following year, whereupon Theodosius not
only restored Valentinian to his former sway but gave him
in addition the share of the Empire which Gratian had held.
The death of Valentinian (A.D. 392) seems to have been brought
about by Arbogastes, though the story of the strangling is
doubtful.   Arbogastes killed himself after the battle of the
Frigidus (Sept. 6, 394).

² *principe clauso*, referring to Honorius and Valentinian III
in Ravenna.   These emperors were helpless, or worse, without
the control of stronger hands (Stilicho, Constantius, Placidia,
Aëtius) : hence *rector moderandus erat* (*v.* 361).

V. PANEGYRIC ON MAIORIANUS

itself,[1] my land of Gaul hath even till now been ignored by the lords of the world, and hath languished in slavery unheeded. Since that time much hath been destroyed, for with the emperor, whoe'er he might be, closely confined,[2] it has been the constant lot of the distant parts of a wretched world to be laid waste. What manner of life could satisfy when the ruler required a controlling hand? For many a year the nobility have lain prostrate and despised, and enmity has been the state's reward for the valiant. Now our prince is amending all this,[3] and he advances to your wars by way of other wars, adding fresh forces from divers peoples[4]; for 'tis the going, not the fighting, that is hardest. But why do we waste time in words? He comes, he conquers." With such speech the assembly was ended, and the fateful sisters harmoniously spun golden threads, whose metal humbly obeyed the words of the goddess.

These afflictions of Rome and Africa that I have sung the yearnings of mankind did teach me to proclaim; now it is time to advance to deeds which must needs be told, even were Apollo dumb. Thy Mars shall take the Muses' place. The savage Alaman had scaled the Alps, and, led down by way of the Rhaetian ridge over its long silences, had emerged, plundering the Roman land; he had sent

---

[3] This is perhaps as much a prayer as a statement of fact.

[4] Allusion to the Emperor's design of securing the loyalty and co-operation of the various foreign peoples in Gaul and Spain as a preliminary to the expedition against Geiseric. He had made a beginning with the conquered Burgundians, and the submission of the Visigoths came in the following year. See also n. on vv. 470–549.

perque Cani quondam dictos de nomine campos
in praedam centum noviens dimiserat hostes.
iamque magister eras: Burconem dirigis illo
exigua comitante manu, sed sufficit istud
cum pugnare iubes; certa est victoria nostris   380
te mandasse acies; peragit fortuna triumphum
non populo, sed amore tuo; nolo agmina campo
quo mittis paucos. felix te respicit iste
eventus belli; certatum est iure magistri,
Augusti fato. nuper ferus hostis aperto   385
errabat lentus pelago, postquam ordine vobis
ordo omnis regnum dederat, plebs, curia, miles,
et collega simul. Campanam flantibus Austris
ingrediens terram securum milite Mauro
agricolam aggreditur; pinguis per transtra sedebat
Vandalus opperiens praedam, quam iusserat illuc 391
captivo capiente trahi. sed vestra repente
inter utrumque hostem dedcrant sese agmina planis
quae pelagus collemque secant portumque reducto
efficiunt flexu fluvii. perterrita primum   395

385. ferus hostis *ego.* (*Class. Quart. loc. cit. p.* 19); *cf.* 7. 285:
post hostis *codd.*
386. postquam : simul *C.*

---

[1] Campi Canini, a north-Italian region, near Bilitio
(Bellinzona), in the upper part of the Ticinus valley.
[2] Majorian became *magister militum* on Feb. 27, 457.
[3] I have discussed the following passage in *Class. Quart.*
XXVIII (1934), pp. 18 sqq.
[4] See n. 5, p. 7 and n. on *vv.* 9–12 of this poem. It
seems clear that the reference here is to the formal accession
on December 28, 457. The fight with the Vandals must have
taken place in the following year, probably not many months

nine hundred foemen to scour for booty the plains named long ago after Canius.[1] By this time thou wert Master of the Forces[2]; and thou didst send thither Burco with a band of followers, small indeed, but that suffices when *thou* bidst them fight; 'tis certain victory for our troops when they go under thine orders; Fortune brings about a triumph not through their numbers but through their love for thee. I crave no armies in a field to which thou sendest but a few men! [3] The happy issue of that campaign is due to thee, for thou didst fight with the authority of a Master, but with the destiny of an Emperor. Lately, when the throne had been bestowed on thee in due order by all orders— commons, senate, army, and thy colleague too [4]— a savage foe was roaming at his ease over the unguarded sea. Under southerly breezes he invaded the Campanian soil and with his Moorish soldiery attacked the husbandmen when they dreamed not of danger; the fleshy Vandal sat on the thwarts waiting for the spoil, which he had bidden his captives [5] to capture and bring thither. But of a sudden thy bands had thrown themselves between the two enemy hosts into the plains which sunder the sea from the hills and fashion a harbour where the river makes a backward curve. First the multitude

before the Panegyric was delivered (see also *v.* 489 n.). The fight with the Alamanni related in the previous lines must have happened before December 28, 457, but not necessarily before April 1, as there is good ground for believing that Majorian remained technically a Magister Militum until his formal accession in December. The two latest editors have caused great confusion by punctuating after instead of before *nuper* in *v.* 385.

[5] The Moors (*v.* 389), who had been subjugated by Geiseric.

montes turba petit, trabibus quae clausa relictis
praedae praeda fuit; tum concitus agmine toto
in pugnam pirata coit: pars lintre cavata
iam dociles exponit equos, pars ferrea texta
concolor induitur, teretes pars explicat arcus   400
spiculaque infusum ferro latura venenum,
quae feriant bis missa semel. iam textilis anguis
discurrit per utramque aciem, cui guttur adactis
turgescit zephyris; patulo mentitur hiatu
iratam pictura famem, pannoque furorem   405
aura facit quotiens crassatur vertile tergum
flatibus et nimium iam non capit alvus inane.
at tuba terrisono strepuit grave rauca fragore,
responsat clamor lituis, virtusque repente
ignavis vel parva furit. cadit undique ferrum,   410
hinc tamen in iugulos: hunc torta falarica iactu
proterit, ad mortem vix cessatura secundam;
hunc conti rotat ictus; equo ruit aclyde fossus
ille veruque alius; iacet hic simul alite telo,
absentem passus dextram; pars poplite secto   415
mortis ad invidiam vivit, partemque cerebri
hic galeae cum parte rapit, fortique lacerto

412. proterit *Luetjohann*: pr(a)eterit.

---

[1] See n. on 2. 232. These standards in the form of dragons
or serpents were made of cloth or of flexible skins, hollow inside,
and with a silver mouth. When the wind blew in at the mouth
they contorted themselves in a manner which suggested real
serpents. The last line of the description is hard. I have
followed an ingenious suggestion of Dr. Semple that *inane*
means "air"; the use is much bolder than in an expression
like *vastum per inane* (v. 246), but probably pleased Sidonius,
as it enabled him to introduce one of his innumerable paradoxes ("cannot hold the emptiness"). Literally the words

of plunderers flees in terror towards the mountains, and so, cut off from the ships they had left, they become the prey of their prey; then the pirates are aroused and mass their whole forces for the battle. Some land their well-trained steeds in hollow skiffs, some don the meshed mail of like hue to themselves, some get ready their shapely bows and the arrows made to carry poison on the iron point and to wound doubly with a single shot. Now the broidered dragon [1] speeds hither and thither in both armies, his throat swelling as the zephyrs dash against it; that pictured form with wide-open jaw counterfeits a wrathful hunger, and the breeze puts a frenzy into the cloth as often as the lithe back is thickened by the blasts and the air is now too abundant for the belly to hold. Now the trumpet's deep note sounds with terrific blast; a responsive shout greets the clarions, and even the puny spirit of cowards suddenly bursts into frenzy. From everywhere a shower of steel comes down, but from our side it comes down on the throats of the foe; a hurtling javelin lays one man in the dust, scarce to exhaust its force with a second victim; another man is sent spinning by the thrust of a pike; one gashed by a harpoon, another by a lance, falls headlong from his horse; yet another, flung down by a flying shaft, lies there, the prey of a hand beyond his ken; some of them, with the thigh-sinews severed, live on to envy death; again, a warrior sweeps off part of a foeman's brain and part of his helmet together, cleaving the hapless skull with two-edged

mean " and the belly no longer has room for the excessive air," *i.e.* more air than the dragon's belly can hold blows in at the mouth.

disicit ancipiti miserabile sinciput ense.
ut primum versis dat tergum Vandalus armis,
succedit caedes pugnae: discrimine nullo   420
sternuntur passim campis, et fortia quaeque
fecit iners.   trepidante fuga mare pallidus intrat
et naves pertransit eques, turpique natatu
de pelago ad cymbam rediit.   sic tertia Pyrrhi
quondam pugna fuit: caesis cum milibus illum   425
Dentatus premeret, lacerae vix fragmina classis
traxit in Epirum qui Chaonas atque Molossos,
qui Thracum Macetumque manus per litora vestra
sparserat et cuius vires Oenotria pallens
ipsaque, quae petiit, trepidaverat uncta Tarentus. 430
hostibus expulsis campum, qui maximus exstat,
iam lustrare vacat; videas hic strage sub illa
utrorumque animos: nullus non pectore caesus,
quisquis vester erat; nullus non terga foratus,
illorum quisquis.   clamant hoc vulnera primi   435
praedonum tum forte ducis, cui regis avari
narratur nupsisse soror, qui pulvere caeco
clausus et elisus pilis vestigia turpis
gestat adhuc probrosa fugae.   sic agmina vestra
cum spoliis campum retinent et Marte fruuntur. 440
    Interea duplici texis dum litore classem
inferno superoque mari, cadit omnis in aequor
silva tibi nimiumque diu per utrumque recisus,
Appennine, latus, navali qui arbore dives
non minus in pelagus nemorum quam mittis aquarum.

444. navali qui *Mohr*: navalique.

---

[1] The blackamoor turns pale again in *v.* 602.
[2] *i.e.* it is no longer a flat plain but a hill of corpses.
[3] The Adriatic and the Tuscan Sea.

sword wielded by a strong arm. Soon as the Vandal
began to turn and flee, carnage took the place of
battle; all were laid low promiscuously throughout
the plain, and even the coward did the most doughty
deeds. In their panic flight the horsemen plunged
pallid [1] into the water and passed beyond the ships,
then swam back in disgrace to their boats from the
open sea. Like to this in olden days was the third
fight of Pyrrhus: when Dentatus had slain thousands
and pressed him sore, he scarce dragged some fragments of his shattered fleet to Epirus—he who had
spread over thy shores bands of Chaonians and
Molossians, Thracians and Macedonians, he at whose
might Oenotria grew pale and luxurious Tarentum,
that invited him, was herself dismayed. With the
foe driven out there was freedom to survey the
plain, which now stood up high.[2] Here in that
slaughtered pile could be discerned the spirit of each
host: no man of thine but had been stricken in the
breast, none of the foe who was not stabbed in the
back. This truth is loudly proclaimed by the
wounds of him who chanced on that day to be com-
mander of the robbers, a man whom it is said the
daughter of the greedy king had wedded; enveloped
by the blindly flying dust and crushed under a mass
of pikes he still carried the infamous marks of a
shameful flight. Thus thy battalions hold the field
with all its spoils and reap the reward of their prowess.

Meanwhile thou buildest on the two shores fleets for
the Upper and the Lower Sea.[3] Down into the water
falls every forest of the Apennines; for many a long
day there is hewing on both slopes of those mountains
so rich in ships' timber, mountains that send down
to the sea as great an abundance of wood as of

THE POEMS OF SIDONIUS

Gallia continuis quamquam sit lassa tributis,   446
hoc censu placuisse cupit nec pondera sentit
quae prodesse probat. non tantis maior Atrides
Carpathium texit ratibus cum Doricus hostis
Sigeas rapturus opes Rhoeteia clausit   450
Pergama; nec tantae Seston iuncturus Abydo
Xerxes classis erat tumidas cum sterneret undas
et pontum sub ponte daret, cum stagna superbo
irrupit temerata gradu turmaeque frequentes
Hellespontiaco persultavere profundo;   455
nec sic Leucadio classis Mareotica portu
Actiacas abscondit aquas, in bella mariti
dum venit a Phario dotalis turba Canopo,
cum patrio Cleopatra ferox circumdata sistro
milite vel piceo fulvas onerata carinas   460
Dorida diffusam premeret Ptolomaide gaza.
hoc tu non cultu pugnas, sed more priorum
dite magis ferro, merito cui subiacet aurum
divitis ignavi. tales ne sperne rebelles:
etsi non acies, decorant tamen ista triumphos.   465
nec me Lageam stirpem memorasse pigebit
hostis ad exemplum vestri; namque auguror hisdem
regnis fortunam similem, cum luxus in illa
parte sit aequalis nec peior Caesar in ista.
  Ilicet aggrederis quod nullus tempore nostro   470

467. isdem *CTP.*

---

[1] A timely hint to Majorian !
[2] *pontum sub ponte*: cf. 23. 44.
[3] These lines describe the muster of Majorian's forces and the march over the Alps into Gaul. Modern historians (*e.g.* Hodgkin and Bury) absurdly imagine that the reference is to an expedition into Pannonia. The list of peoples in *vv.* 474–477 is a lurid commentary on Rome's dependence upon foreign contingents to do her fighting, although Sidonius ingeniously turns a lamentable fact into a compliment to Majorian. The poet makes it abundantly clear that Majorian

waters.   Gaul, though wearied by unceasing tribute,[1]
is now eager to gain approval by a new levy for this
end, and feels not a burden wherein she beholds a
benefit.   The elder son of Atreus did not cover the
Carpathian Sea with so many ships when the Dorian
foe, bent on seizing the wealth of Sigeum, beleaguered
Rhoeteian Pergamum; not so vast was the fleet
that Xerxes had when he sought to link Sestos with
Abydos and paved the swelling waters, setting a
bridge over the breakers,[2] and with haughty step
burst in upon the outraged flood, and his multitudinous squadrons pranced over the Hellespontine
deep.   Not so fully did the Mareotic fleet in Leucas'
harbour hide the waters of Actium, when a multitude
that was a woman's dower came from Egyptian
Canopus to fight her husband's battles, and proud
Cleopatra, with her country's sistrum girded upon
her and her yellow boats loaded with pitch-black
warriors, weighted the wide sea with the treasure
of the Ptolemies.   Thou dost not fight in this array,
but rather as our forerunners did, with wealth of
steel, whereto the wealthy coward's gold submits.
Yet scorn not such troublers of the peace, for these
splendours, though they grace not the ranks of battle,
grace the pageantry of a triumph.   And truly I shall
never grieve to have mentioned the house of Lagos
as prototype of thy foe; for I forecast a like fate
for these two kingdoms, since on their side the
luxuriousness is equal, and on our side is a Caesar
as good as there was then.

[3] Straightway thou dost attempt what no emperor

began early in his reign to organise an army and a navy for
an attack on Geiseric in Africa.   The muster here described
has that ultimate end in view, though the troubles in Gaul
had first to be settled.   See also n. on 364 sq.

Augustus potuit: rigidum septemplicis Histri
agmen in arma rapis. nam quidquid languidus axis
cardine Sithonio sub Parrhase parturit Vrsa,
hoc totum tua signa pavet; Bastarna, Suebus,
Pannonius, Neurus, Chunus, Geta, Dacus, Halanus,
Bellonotus, Rugus, Burgundio, Vesus, Alites,   476
Bisalta, Ostrogothus, Procrustes, Sarmata, Moschus
post aquilas venere tuas; tibi militat omnis
Caucasus et Scythicae potor Tanaiticus undae.
quid faciat fortuna viri? quascumque minatur,   480
has tremuit iam Roma manus; modo principe sub te
ne metuat prope parva putat, nisi serviat illi
quod timuit regnante alio.
                              Iam castra movebas
et te diversis stipabant milia signis;
obsequium gens una negat, quae nuper ab Histro 485
rettulit indomitum solito truculentior agmen
quod dominis per bella caret, populoque superbo
Tuldila plectendas in proelia suggerit iras.
hic tu vix armis positis iterum arma retractas:
Bistonides veluti Ciconum cum forte pruinas   490
Ogygiis complent thiasis, seu Strymonos arvis
seu se per Rhodopen seu qua nimbosus in aequor
volvit Hyperboreis in cautibus Hismarus Hebrum
dat somno vaga turba, simul lassata quiescunt

---

[1] The reference is almost certainly to the Huns. Tuldila is
not mentioned elsewhere.

[2] i.e. soon after the battle described in vv. 385–440. The
mutiny obviously occurred in Italy, before the passage of the
Alps. Presumably it affected only a part of the Hun
contingent.

[3] " Thracian . . . Theban," a silly paradox; " Theban "
here means little more than " Bacchanalian."

in our time has availed to do: thou dost carry off to
war the frozen army of the seven-mouthed Danube.
All the multitude that the sluggish quarter of the
earth doth produce in the Sithonian region beneath
the Arcadian bear fears thy standards; Bastarnian,
Suebian, Pannonian, Neuran, Hun, Getan, Dacian,
Alan, Bellonotan, Rugian, Burgundian, Visigoth,
Alites, Bisalta, Ostrogoth, Procrustian, Sarmatian,
Moschan have ranged themselves behind thine
eagles; in thy service are the whole Caucasus and
the drinker of the Don's Scythian waters. What
shall such a hero's fortune accomplish? Every band
wherewith he now threatens others has at some
time caused Rome to tremble; but now under thy
sovereignty she counts it almost a small thing to
be free from fear, unless she also sees humbly at
her service that which she feared when another
reigned.

Now thou wert moving thy camp, and around
thee thronged thousands under divers standards.
Only one race[1] denied thee obedience, a race
who had lately, in a mood even more savage than
their wont, withdrawn their untamed host from
the Danube because they had lost their lords in
warfare, and Tuldila stirred in that unruly multitude a mad lust of fighting for which they must
needs pay dear. Hereupon, having scarce laid
down thine arms,[2] thou takest them up again; as
when the Thracian women fill the frosty land of the
Ciconians with Theban[3] troops of revellers, and on
the fields by the Strymon or over the slopes of
Rhodope, or where cloudy Hismarus rolls Hebrus
down amid the Hyperborean rocks to the sea, the
roaming band give themselves up to sleep, and

orgia et ad biforem reboat nec tibia flatum;   495
vix requies, iam †ponte ligant† rotat enthea
   thyrsum
Bassaris et maculis Erythraeae nebridos horrens
excitat Odrysios ad marcida tympana mystas.
tu tamen hanc differs poenam, sed sanguinis auctor
maioris, dum parcis, eras. non pertulit ultra   500
hoc pro te plus cauta manus vestrumque pudorem
sprevit pro vobis; primi cadit hostia belli
quisque rebellis erat. praedam quoque dividis illis,
mens devota quibus fuerat: quae territa servit
exemplo, gaudet pretio. Pharsalica Caesar   505
arva petens subitas ferro compescuit iras;
sed sua membra secans, ut causae mole coactus,
flevit quos perimit; vestris haec proficit armis
seditio: quodcumque iubes, nisi barbarus audit,
hic cadit, ut miles timeat.   510
               Iam tempore brumae
Alpes marmoreas atque occurrentia iuncto
saxa polo rupesque vitri siccamque minantes
per scopulos pluviam primus pede carpis et idem
lubrica praemisso firmas vestigia conto.
coeperat ad rupis medium quae maxima turba est
interno squalere gelu, quod colle supino   516
artatis conclusa viis reptare rigenti
non poterat revoluta solo: fors unus ab illo

     496. sponte *T* : iam sponte vigens *R. M. Henry.*
     507. ut *ego (Class. Quart. loc. cit.* p. 19): et.

---

  [1] See n. on 2. 447. Things connected with Bacchus are,
like the god himself, often associated with India.
  [2] The famous mutiny of the Ninth Legion at Placentia,
49 B.C.
  [3] *i.e.* ice. See n. on 2. 271.

straightway the rout falls into wearied repose, and no longer does the breath awake a resounding note in the double pipe; but scarce has rest begun, when . . . an inspired Bassarid once more whirls the thyrsus, and, bristling in her dappled garb of Erythraean [1] fawn-skin, rouses the Odrysian votaries to beat the languid tabors. Yet thou didst put off the punishment of this offence; but in sparing thou didst cause greater bloodshed; for a band of thy men, more careful of thy weal, could bear this crime no longer, and for thy sake spurned thy mildness, and the rebels fell one and all, victims offered at the war's beginning. Thou didst divide the spoil among those whose hearts had been true; and these hearts, that trembled when they aided in the punishment, were cheered by their reward. Caesar, bound for the field of Pharsalia, stayed a mutinous outburst with the sword [2]; yet as he thus cut off his own limbs, driven thereto by the compelling need of his cause, he wept for those he destroyed. But this rising was a benefit to thine arms; henceforth whatever thine orders might be, if a barbarian hearkened not he fell, that the soldiers might fear.

And now in winter thou didst thyself lead the way over the marble slopes of the Alps, over crags that rise to meet the sky, over rocks like glass and dry rain [3] resting amid threatening scaurs; and with a lance thrust out before thee thou didst steady thy slipping feet. Half-way up the mountain the main part of thy force felt a chilling frost encrusting their very hearts, for confined in narrow paths on a hill-slope they could not clamber up the frozen face, but ever rolled back; then it came to pass that one of the column, a man whose wheels had in

agmine, canentem cuius rota triverat Histrum,
exclamat: " gladios malo et sollemne quieta   520
quod frigus de morte venit; mea torpor inerti
membra rigore ligat, quodam mihi corpus adustum
frigoris igne perit.   sequimur sine fine labori
instantem iuvenem; quisquis fortissimus ille est
aut rex aut populus, castris modo clausus aprica   525
vel sub pelle iacet; nos anni vertimus usum.
quod iubet hic lex rebus erit; non flectitur umquam
a coeptis damnumque putat si temporis iras
vel per damna timet.   qua dicam gente creatum
quem Scytha non patior?   cuius lac tigridis infans
Hyrcana sub rupe bibit?   quae sustulit istum   531
axe meo gravior tellus?   en vertice summo
algentes cogit turmas ac frigora ridet,
dum solus plus mente calet.   cum classica regis
Arctoi sequerer, Romani principis arma   535
Caesareumque larem luxu torpere perenni
audieram: dominos nil prodest isse priores
si rex hic quoque fortis erat."   maiora parantem
dicere de scopulo verbis accendis amaris:
" quisquis es, oppositi metuis qui lubrica clivi,   540
frange cutem pendentis aquae scalptoque fluento
sit tibi lympha gradus.   turpes depone querelas;
otia frigus habent.   numquid mihi membra biformis
Hylaei natura dedit?   num Pegasus alis

537. isse] desse M.

---

[1] Cf. 2. 270.
[2] The word-play is made possible by the fact that damnum may mean " fault," " vice," as well as " loss."

their time scoured the whitened Danube,[1] ex-
claimed: " I would rather have a sword-thrust and
that common coldness that comes from a quiet
death: numbness ties my limbs with cramping stiff-
ness, and my body is seared and consumed by the
burning cold. We follow a young general that per-
sists in toil without ceasing; but even the bravest,
whether king or people, is now enclosed in camp
or fort or lies down under tents of skin in sunny
places, while we pervert the uses of the year.
What he orders will be a law to all creation. He is
never turned from his enterprises, and he thinks his
character is lost if even his losses make him fear the
violence of the season.[2] Of what race must I pronounce him born, with whom I, a Scythian, cannot
cope? What tigress gave suck to him in infancy
under some Hyrcanian height? What land more
severe than mine own clime reared him? Lo! on
the very summit he musters his chilled squadrons,
and laughs at the cold, for he alone has in his soul a
warmth that is stronger. When I followed the
standards of a northern king I heard that the emperor's arms and the house of the Caesars were
sunk in unending luxury. It is no gain to me that
my former lords are gone if, after all, there is here
too a valiant king." He was ready to utter more
violent words when thou, speaking from the crest,
didst stir him with bitter taunts: " Whosoe'er thou
art that fearest the slippery rise that confronts thee,
break the skin of the hanging water, then dig into
the flow and make the pool thy stepping-stone. Have
done with thy base complaints; idleness is the cause
of cold. Did nature give *me* the limbs of double-
bodied Hylaeus? Did Pegasus help me with wings

adiuvit, quidquid gradior, pennasque volanti   545
dat Calais Zetusque mihi, quem ninguida cernis
calcantem iam dorsa iugi? vos frigora frangunt,
vos Alpes? iam iam studeam pensare pruinas;
aestatem sub Syrte dabo." sic agmina voce
erigis exemploque levas primusque labores   550
aggrederis, quoscumque iubes; tum cetera paret
turba libens, servit propriis cum legibus auctor.

Qui tibi praeterea comites quantusque magister
militiae, vestrum post vos qui compulit agmen,
sed non invitum! dignus cui cederet uni   555
Sulla acie, genio Fabius, pietate Metellus,
Appius eloquio, vi Fulvius, arte Camillus.
si praefecturae quantus moderetur honorem
vir quaeras, tendit patulos qua Gallia fines,
vix habuit mores similes cui teste senatu   560
in se etiam tractum commiserat Vlpius ensem.
qui dictat modo iura Getis, sub iudice vestro

---

[1] *i.e.* in Africa, fighting against the Vandals.

[2] This "Master of the Forces" cannot be the Patrician
Ricimer. He may be either Nepotianus (father of the future
emperor Julius Nepos), who seems to have obtained the rank
of second *magister* under Avitus, or (less probably) Aegidius,
who was *mag. militum per Gallias* from 458 to 463 (according
to the usual account: Stein, p. 560, thinks otherwise). The
holder of this district-command had for some years been
dignified with the title *magister utriusque militiae*; the original
title was *mag. equitum per Gallias*. See also n. on 7. 359 sqq.

[3] Q. Caecilius Metellus Pius (consul, 80 B.C.) received his
extra surname owing to the strenuous efforts which he made
to secure the recall of his father, Metellus Numidicus, from
exile.

over the ground I tread? Do I fly with plumage
bestowed by Calais and Zethus—I, whom thou seest
already trampling the snow-clad brow of this ridge?
Art *thou* overcome by the cold, by the Alps? Then
'tis time I sought to compensate thee for the frosts;
I will give thee a summer near the Syrtes."[1] Thus
dost thou brace thy troops with thy words and
cheer them by thine example, ever the first to essay
whatever tasks thou dost order; and the others
willingly obey when the lawgiver makes himself
the servant of his own laws.

And what a staff thou hadst, and what a Master
of the Forces![2] He it was who pushed on the line
of men behind thee—right willing men, 'tis true.
To him, of all men, Sulla might well have given
precedence in fighting, Fabius in talent, Metellus[3]
in filial loyalty, Appius in eloquence, Fulvius[4] in
energy, Camillus in skill. And if it should be asked
how great is the man who wields the Prefect's[5]
office where Gaul extends her wide lands—he is a
man scarce equalled in goodness by him to whom,
with the senate as witness, Trajan entrusted a
drawn sword to be used even against himself.[6]
Under thy judge he who now gives laws to the
Goths—he, our skin-clad foe—doth respect the

---

[4] Q. Fulvius Flaccus (consul in 237, 224, 212, and 209 B.C.),
a great general. Along with Ap. Claudius Pulcher he took
Capua in 212 B.C.

[5] The new Praetorian Prefect of Gaul was Magnus. See n.
on 23. 455.

[6] It is related that Trajan, on handing to a praetorian
prefect the sword which was the badge of his office, said,
"Take this, to be used in my defence if I act well, against me
if I act ill." (Aur. Vict. *Caes.* 13, Cass. Dio LXVIII. 16. 1; cf.
Plin. *Pan.* 67.)

pellitus ravum praeconem suspicit hostis.
quid loquar hic illum qui scrinia sacra gubernat,
qui, cum civilis dispenset partis habenas,   565
sustinet armati curas, interprete sub quo
flectitur ad vestras gens effera condiciones?
quid laudare Petrum parvis, temeraria Clio,
viribus aggrederis? cuius dignatur ab ore
Caesar in orbe loqui, licet et quaestore diserto   570
polleat; attamen hic nuper, placidissime princeps,
obside percepto nostrae de moenibus urbis
visceribus miseris insertum depulit ensem.
et quia lassatis nimium spes unica rebus
venisti, nostris, petimus, succurre ruinis   575
Lugdunumque tuam, dum praeteris, aspice victor:
otia post nimios poscit te fracta labores.
cui pacem das, redde animum: lassata iuvenci
cervix deposito melius post sulcat aratro
telluris glaebam solidae. bove, fruge, colono,   580
civibus exhausta est. stantis fortuna latebat;
dum capitur, vae quanta fuit! post gaudia, princeps,

---

563. suscipit *LCFP.*

---

[1] The reference is obviously to Theodoric II, but it is mere
hyperbole or sanguine prophecy. The Gallic rising had roused
the Visigoths to war, and it was not till the following year,
when Aegidius drove them back from the walls of Arles, that
they submitted and made a treaty with Majorian. *Iudice*
refers to the praetorian prefect, as head of the judicature.
There may have been a truce with Theodoric at the time when
the Panegyric was delivered. It is also possible that there were
some Visigoths in the conquered garrison of Lugdunum. The
variant reading *suscipit* in *v.* 563 might possibly mean " is

V. PANEGYRIC ON MAIORIANUS

hoarse-voiced usher of the court.[1] Why tell here of
him who controls the Sacred Bureau,[2] who, while
he guides the reins of a civil office, supports also the
cares of a man-at-arms; with whom as spokesman a
wild race is won over to your terms?[3] But why,
my rash Muse, dost thou essay with thy puny
strength to praise Petrus? Through his lips Caesar
deigns to speak all over the world, although he hath
also a tower of strength in his eloquent quaestor;[4]
nay, this man lately, O most gracious Emperor, took
hostages and thrust off from the walls of our city
the sword that had been driven into our hapless flesh.
And since thou hast come hither as the only hope
for our exhausted fortunes, we pray and beseech thee,
save our ruins, and, as thou passest on, let thine
eye survey thy Lugdunum in thine hour of victory;
broken, she asks thee for rest after toils too great
to bear. Give fresh heart to her to whom thou
givest peace. When the steer's neck is wearied he
will afterwards furrow the solid clods all the better
if the plough is laid aside for a time. The town is
drained of her oxen, her provender, her farmers,
her citizens. In her days of strength her fortune
was unnoticed, but in the hour of her capture, alas,
how great it was! When joy has come, my

adopting," *i.e.* he is copying the Roman legal procedure in his
own domain; but *suspicit* is almost certainly right.
  [2] As Imperial secretary (*magister epistularum*) Petrus (on
whom see 3. 5 n.) controlled one of the three great bureaux of
the civil service.
  [3] The Burgundians, who had been received into Lugdunum
by the Gallo-Roman insurgents.
  [4] The quaestor was probably Domnulus, who is mentioned
as a poet in 14 § 2; cf. *Epist.* IX. 13. 4, IX. 15. 1 carm. 38.
Epist. IV. 25 is addressed to him. On the *quaestor sacri Palatii*
as mouthpiece of the Emperor see n. on 1. 25.

delectat meminisse mali.   populatibus, igni
etsi concidimus, veniens tamen omnia tecum
restituis: fuimus vestri quia causa triumphi,   585
ipsa ruina placet.   cum victor scandere currum
incipies crinemque sacrum tibi more priorum
nectet muralis, vallaris, civica laurus
et regum aspicient Capitolia fulva catenas,
cum vesties Romam spoliis, cum divite cera   590
pinges Cinyphii captiva mapalia Bocchi,
ipse per obstantes populos raucosque fragores
praecedam et tenui, sicut nunc, carmine dicam
te geminas Alpes, Syrtes te, te mare magnum,
te freta, te Libycas pariter domuisse catervas,   595
ante tamen vicisse mihi.   quod lumina flectis
quodque serenato miseros iam respicis ore,
exsultare libet: memini, cum parcere velles,
hic tibi vultus erat; mitis dat signa venustas.
annue: sic vestris respiret Byrsa tropaeis,   600
sic Parthus certum fugiat Maurusque timore
albus eat; sic Susa tremant positisque pharetris
exarmata tuum circumstent Bactra tribunal.

---

[1] Pictures or models of conquered places were often exhibited
in Roman triumphal processions.   Bocchus is used as a typical
name of a north-African king.

V. PANEGYRIC ON MAIORIANUS

Emperor, 'tis pleasant to remember the evil days. Prostrated though we are by devastation and by fire, thou by thy coming dost restore all things; and since we were the cause of thy triumph, our very fall is pleasing. When thou shalt step into the victor's chariot and after the manner of our forefathers the mural, castrensian and civic crowns shall entwine thy sacred hair, and the golden Capitol shall behold kings in chains; when thou shalt clothe Rome with spoils and shalt depict in costly wax the captured huts of some African Bocchus,[1] then I myself will walk before thee amid the obstructing throngs and the clamour of hoarse shouts, and in my puny strain, as now, I will tell how thou hast subdued two Alpine ranges,[2] the Syrtes, the Great Sea, the narrower waters, and the Libyan hordes; but first I will tell how thou didst conquer for my benefit. I am fain to leap for joy that thou dost turn thine eyes and already regardest the unfortunate with brightened countenance. I remember well, when thou wert minded to be merciful, such was ever thy look; a benign graciousness gives the sign. Grant my prayer: so may Byrsa[3] draw breath again through thy victories; so may the Parthian flee in good earnest and the Moor go his way white with fear; so may Susa tremble and the Bactrians lay aside their quivers and stand disarmed around thy tribunal!

[2] The Alps and the Pyrenees. Majorian was going to proceed to Spain.
[3] 2. 351 n.

VI

PRAEFATIO PANEGYRICI DICTI AVITO AVGVSTO

Pallados armisonae festum dum cantibus ortum
    personat Hismario Thracia vate chelys,
et dum Mopsopium stipantur per Marathonem
    qui steterant fluvii quaeque cucurrit humus,
dulcisonum quatitur fidibus dum pectine murmur,   5
    has perhibent laudes laude probasse deam :
" diva, Gigantei fudit quam tempore belli
    armatus partus vertice dividuo,
quam neque Deliacis peperit Latona sub antris,
    fixura errantem Cyclada pignoribus,   10
nec quae Cadmeis pariens Alciden in oris
    suspendit triplici nocte puerperium,
nec cuius pluvio turris madefacta metallo est,
    cum matrem impleret filius aurigena :
sed te, cum trepidum spectaret Phlegra Tonantem,
    impulit excussam vertice ruptus apex ;   16
cumque deos solae traherent in proelia vires
    confusum valde te sine robur erat :
protulit ut mox te patrius, Sapientia, vertex,
    tum mage vicerunt, te cum habuere dei.   20
te propter cessit, manibus constructa tremendis,
    iam prope per rutilum machina tensa polum.

---

[1] The Ismarian (Thracian) bard is Orpheus.
[2] The meaning of this absurdity will be clear from 2. 70–74 and 23. 185–194.
[3] *i.e.* Attic.
[4] When Leto (Latona), fleeing from the persecution of Hera (Juno), reached the floating island of Delos, it suddenly became stationary. There Artemis (Diana) and Apollo were born.

VI

PREFACE TO THE PANEGYRIC ADDRESSED TO THE EMPEROR AVITUS

While the Thracian lyre in the hands of the Ismarian [1] bard celebrated in ringing song the glorious birth of Pallas with her clashing arms; while rivers that stood and earth that ran [2] were thronging close in Mopsopian [3] Marathon, and the quill twanged out its sweet notes on the strings, the goddess, 'tis said, commended with her praise these praises: "Hail, divine one, whom a birth full-armed sent forth from the opened head at the time of the giant-war, whom Latona bore not in the depths of the Delian cave, fain to fix the wandering Cyclad for her offspring's sake [4]; no, nor she who in bringing forth Alcides in the land of Cadmus delayed her travail for three nights, nor she whose tower was steeped in the rain of metal, when the gold-begotten son began to cumber his mother; but while Phlegra [5] beheld the Thunderer alarmed, the crown of his head burst open and thou wert shot forth from its summit; and as brute force and naught else was impelling the gods to battle, their might without thee had been sorely confounded; but after thy father's head had brought thee forth, O goddess of Wisdom, then the gods, with thee to aid, were victorious as ne'er before. Thanks to thee that great pile gave way which was built by those dread hands and at last well-nigh pierced the

---

[5] The plains of Phlegra were the scene of the battle between gods and giants.

Pindus, Othrys, Pholoe dextris cecidere Gigantum,
    decidit et Rhoeti iam gravis Ossa manu.
sternitur Aegaeon, Briareus, Ephialta Mimasque,   25
    Arctoas sueti lambere calce rotas.
Enceladus patri iacuit fratrique Typhoeus;
    Euboicam hic rupem sustinet, hic Siculam."
Hinc sese ad totam genetricem transtulit Orpheus
    et docuit chordas dicere Calliopam.   30
assurrexerunt Musae sub laude sororis
    et placuit divae carmine plus pietas.
quod si maternas laudes cantasse favori est
    nec valeo priscas aequiperare fides,
publicus hic pater est, vovi cui carmen, Avitus: 35
    materia est maior si mihi Musa minor.

VII

PANEGYRICVS

Phoebe, peragrato tandem visurus in orbe
quem possis perferre parem, da lumina caelo:
sufficit hic terris.   nec se iam signifer astris

VI 30. decuit *MPTF*.

---

[1] The snaky extremities of the giants, ending in mouths
instead of feet, are treated with elaborate absurdity in 9. 76–87.

flaming firmament. Pindus, Othrys, and Pholoe fell
from the grasp of the giants; down at last fell
ponderous Ossa from Rhoetus' hand; Aegeon was
laid low, and Briareus and Ephialtes and Mimas,
who were wont to lick the northern Wain with their
feet.[1] Enceladus fell by thy father's hand, Typhoeus
by thy brother's; and now the one supports an
Euboean[2] mountain, the other a Sicilian."

Then Orpheus changed his theme, making his
mother the whole burden of his song, and teaching
the strings to hymn Calliope. The Muses rose in
homage at this praise of their sister, and the goddess
was gladdened even more by a son's devotion than
by his song. But if it is well pleasing to sing a
mother's praises, and if I lack the power to match
the ancient lyre, yet in Avitus, to whom I have
vowed my song, we have here the *father* of his people,
and though my muse be weaker, my theme is
greater.

VII

PANEGYRIC [3]

O Sun-god, now at last in the circle of thy wander-
ings thou canst see one that thou art able to brook
as thine equal; so give thy rays to heaven, for he
is sufficient to lighten the earth. Nor need the

---

[2] A far-fetched epithet. Typhoeus was buried under the
island of Inarime (Verg. *Aen.* IX. 716, Lucan V. 101), the
modern Ischia, near "Euboean" Cumae (Verg. *Aen.* VI. 2).
According to another version he, like Enceladus, was buried
under Etna.

[3] Jan. 1, A.D. 456. See Introd., p. xxxvii.

THE POEMS OF SIDONIUS

iactet, Marmaricus quem vertice conterit Atlans:
sidera sunt isti.   quae sicut mersa nitescunt,   5
adversis sic Roma micat, cui fixus ab ortu
ordo fuit crevisse malis.   modo principe surgit
consule; nempe, patres, collatos cernere fasces
vos iuvat et sociam sceptris mandasse curulem:
credite, plus dabitis: currus.   iam necte bifrontes, 10
anceps Iane, comas duplicique accingere lauro.
principis anterior, iam consulis iste coruscat
annus, et emerita trabeis diademata crescunt.
incassum iam, Musa, paves quod propulit Auster
vela ratis nostrae; pelago quia currere famae   15
coepimus, en sidus, quod nos per caerula servet.

Forte pater superum prospexit ab aethere terras:
ecce viget quodcumque videt; mundum reparasse
aspexisse fuit; solus fovet omnia nutus.
iamque ut conveniant superi, Tegeaticus ales   20
nunc plantis, nunc fronte volat.   vix contigit arva
et toto descendit avo: mare terra vel aer
indigenas misere deos.   germane Tonantis,

---

7. surgit *M* : surget.   *Vid. Class. Quart. loc. cit. p.* 19.
20. ales *Bitschofsky* : archas.
21–23. *dist. ego ; vid. Class. Quart. ib. ; cf.* 7. 360 *sq.*

---

[1] *Marmaricus* is used by poets for "African"; cf. 11. 103,
23. 56. Marmarica lay between Egypt and the Greater
Syrtes, and was therefore far from the Atlas range. In 5.
337, *Marmarides* is used in its strict sense, and in *v.* 448
below the Marmaricans are distinguished from the Massylians,
another north-African people.
[2] See 5. 63 n.
[3] "double," because it encircles two brows.
[4] For the meaning of *trabea* see n. on XV. 150 sq.
[5] Mercury. *Tegeaticus* means no more than "Arcadian":
see n. on 1. 7. The "feet" and the "brow" allude to the
wings attached to his sandals and to his forehead.   According

118

VII. PANEGYRIC ON AVITUS

Zodiac, that is grazed by the head of Marmaric[1] Atlas, make boast of its constellations; for this man also hath his stars, and as stars sink only to shine forth once more, so doth Rome's light flash forth out of her calamities; since from her very beginning it hath been her fixed destiny to grow greater by misfortunes.[2] Now she begins to rise once more with an emperor for consul. Surely, O Senators, it delights you to see the fasces of two dignities combined and to think that ye have assigned a curule chair to bear the sceptre company! Believe me, ye shall yet give more—a triumphal chariot! Now bind, O two-headed Janus, the locks of thy twin brows, encircling them with a double[3] wreath of laurel. Last year was illustrious as the emperor's, this year is glorious as the consul's; and the diadem that has served us so well is enhanced by the state robes of a magistrate.[4] Now, O Muse, idle is the fear thou dost feel because the breeze hath driven out to sea the sails of my bark; as I have begun to speed over the ocean of fame—behold the star that is to protect me throughout the blue expanse!

It chanced that the father of the gods looked forth from heaven upon the earth. Lo! whatever he beholds is quickened; to view the world is to renew it; his mere nod revives all things. Thereupon, to bid the gods assemble, the winged god of Tegea[5] speeds his flight now with his feet, now with his brow. Scarce has he descended the whole length of his grandfather[6] and touched the fields when sea, earth, and air send their native divinities. First

to another idea the second pair of wings was attached to his hat (*petasus*).

[6] Atlas: cf. Verg. *Aen.* IV. 258. For the fusion of the god with his domain cf. 2. 333 and 426-8, 22. 41-46.

THE POEMS OF SIDONIUS

prime venis, viridi qui Dorida findere curru
suetus in attonita spargis cito terga serenum;   25
umentes Nymphas Phorcus comitatur ibique
glaucus, Glauce, venis, vatum et certissime Proteu,
certus eras. longo veniunt post ordine divi:
pampineus Liber, Mars trux, Tirynthius hirtus,
nuda Venus, fecunda Ceres, pharetrata Diana,   30
Iuno gravis, prudens Pallas, turrita Cybebe,
Saturnus profugus, vaga Cynthia, Phoebus ephebus,
Pan pavidus, Fauni rigidi, Satyri petulantes.
convenere etiam caelum virtute tenentes,
Castor equo, Pollux caestu, Perseius harpe,   35
fulmine Vulcanus, Tiphys rate, gente Quirinus.
quis canat hic aulam caeli, rutilantia cuius
ipsa pavimentum sunt sidera?
                              Iam pater aureo
tranquillus sese solio locat, inde priores
consedere dei (fluviis quoque contigit illo,   40
sed senibus, residere loco, tibi, maxime fluctu
Eridane et flavis in pocula fracte Sygambris,
Rhene tumens, Scythiaeque vagis equitate catervis
Hister et ignotum plus notus, Nile, per ortum):
cum procul erecta caeli de parte trahebat   45

35. Perseius *def. Brakman*: tum Perseus *Mohr*, Danaeius
Wilamowitz.

---

[1] Colour-names in ancient literature are notoriously
vague; a good example of this is found in 10. 5 sq., where
first *viridis* and then *caeruleus* is applied both to Nereus and
to his dress. In 15. 132 the dress of Glaucus is called *viridis*.
The adjective *glaucus*, unlike *caeruleus*, is never applied to
the deep blue of the sky, but there is regularly an element
of blue in its connotation. It is applied to the sea and other
expanses of water, to water-deities, to plants (especially,
like Greek γλαυκός, to the grey-green of the olive), to the

120

comes the Thunderer's own brother, who, accustomed as he is to cleave the sea with his green chariot, now quickly spreads calm over the amazed surface. Phorcus comes with the dripping nymphs, Glaucus too, green as his name[1]; Proteus also, surest of seers, was there in sure presence.[2] After them comes a long array of divine beings; Liber, lord of the vine, fierce Mars, the shaggy hero of Tiryns, naked Venus, fruitful Ceres, Diana with her quiver, staid Juno, wise Pallas, tower-crowned Cybele, Saturn the exile, fair young Phoebus, pavid Pan, the uncouth Fauns, the wanton Satyrs. There also assembled those that inhabit heaven by virtue of their prowess—Castor by the steed, Pollux by the boxing-glove, Perseus by the scimitar, Vulcan by the thunderbolt, Tiphys by the ship, Quirinus by his people. Who could sing here below of heaven's great hall, whose floor the flaming stars themselves compose?

Now the great Father serenely sat him down on his golden throne; then the chiefest gods took their seats (and even to the rivers, such of them as are aged, the right to be seated in that place has been given,—Eridanus, mightiest in his torrent, the swelling Rhine, that the yellow-haired Sygambrian breaks to fill his cups, Danube, crossed on horseback by Scythia's nomad hordes, and Nile, known all the better for his unknown source). Lo! afar, from a lofty tract of sky, came Rome, dragging her slow

human eye (5. 240), and to many other things (including animals). No uniform translation is possible; such words as "blue," "green," "blue-green" (the meaning here), "blue-grey," "grey-green" will serve at various times. A full list of citations is now available in the *Thesaurus Linguae Latinae*.

[2] *i.e.* not in one of his numerous disguises (Semple, p. 88).

pigros Roma gradus, curvato cernua collo
ora ferens; pendent crines de vertice, tecti
pulvere, non galea, clipeusque impingitur aegris
gressibus, et pondus, non terror, fertur in hasta.
utque pii genibus primum est adfusa Tonantis,   50
" testor, sancte parens," inquit, " te numen et illud,
quidquid Roma fui: summo satis obruta fato
invideo abiectis; pondus non sustinet ampli
culminis arta domus nec fulmen vallibus instat.
quid, rogo, bis seno mihi vulture Tuscus haruspex   55
portendit? iaciens primae cur moenia genti
ominibus iam celsa fui, dum collis Etrusci
fundamenta iugis aperis mihi, Romule pauper?
plus gladio secura fui cum turbine iuncto
me Rutulus, Veiens pariterque Auruncus et Ae-
        quus,   60
Hernicus et Volscus premerent. sat magna videbar
et tibi dum rumpit vitiatum femina ferro
corpus et ad castum remeas, pudor erute, vulnus.
iam cum vallatam socio me clausit Etrusco
Tarquinius: pro Muci ignes! pro Coclitis undae!   65
pro dolor! hic quonam est qui sub mea iura redegit
Samnitem, Gurges, Volsci qui terga cecidit,
Marcius, et Senones fundens dictator et exul?
Fabricii vitam vellem, mortes Deciorum,
vel sic vincentem vel sic victos: mea redde   70

---

[1] For similar utterances on the perils of greatness and the
blessed security of a low estate see commentators on Hor. C.
II. 10. 9–12, Vollmer on Stat. Silv. II. 7. 90.

[2] Cf. 357 sq. The twelve vultures which appeared to
Romulus were interpreted as portending a duration of twelve
centuries for Rome. According to the usual dating of the
foundation of the city this period ended in A.D. 447. In the
middle of the fifth century many people recalled the old
augury with superstitious dread. See Gibbon, c. 35, last par.

VII. PANEGYRIC ON AVITUS

VII. PANEGYRIC ON AVITUS

steps along, with neck bent and head bowed; her hair hung limply down, covered not with a helmet but with dust; at each feeble step her shield knocked against her, and in her spear there was no terror, but only heaviness. Flinging herself at the feet of gracious Jove she cried: " O holy Father, I call thee to witness—thee and that divinity of other days, all that I, Rome, have been: wholly overwhelmed by my exalted fortune, I envy the very outcast; a narrow house has not a spacious roof to support, and the lowly vales are not harassed by the lightning.[1] What, pray, did the Tuscan seer foretell for me from the twelve vultures?[2] Why is it that when but beginning to build walls for my infant people I was already raised on high by omens of greatness, when Romulus in his poverty dug foundations for me on the ridge of the Tuscan hill? Through my sword I knew greater safety than now, when in a massed hurricane Rutulian, Veientine, Aequian, Hernican, and Volscian bore down upon me. Mighty enough I seemed even to thee when the woman stabbed with the knife her sullied body, and her ravished honour returned with that chaste wound.[3] Tarquin with his Etruscan ally shut me within my new-built rampart. Alas for the fire that Mucius, the water that Horatius braved! Woe is me! Where is there here a Gurges [4]—the man who brought the Samnite under my sway? Where the Marcius who cut down the flying Volscian, or he who routed the Senones, a dictator and an exile?[5] Would that I had Fabricius as he lived, the Decii as they died, victory such as his or defeat like theirs:

[3] Lucretia.   [4] Q. Fabius Maximus Gurges.
[5] Camillus : cf. 2. 526 sq.

123

principia. heu! quo nunc pompae ditesque triumphi
et pauper consul?   Libycum mea terruit axem
cuspis et infido posui iuga tertia Poeno.
Indorum Ganges, Colchorum Phasis, Araxes
Armeniae, Ger Aethiopum Tanaisque Getarum   75
Thybrinum tremuere meum.   me Teutone iuncto
quondam fracte subis Cimber, gladiisque gravatas
ante manus solas iussi portare catenas.
vae mihi! qualis eram, cum per mea iussa iuberent
Sulla, Asiatogenes, Curius, Paulus, Pompeius   80
Tigrani, Antiocho, Pyrrho, Persae, Mithridati
pacem ac regna, fugam, vectigal, vincla, venenum.
Sauromatem taceo ac Moschum solitosque cruentum
lac potare Getas ac pocula tingere venis
vel, cum diffugiunt, fugiendos tum mage Persas.   85
nec terras dixisse sat est: fulgentibus armis
tot maria intravi duce te longeque remotas
sole sub occiduo gentes.   victricia Caesar
signa Caledonios transvexit ad usque Britannos;
fuderit et quamquam Scotum et cum Saxone Pictum,
hostes quaesivit, quem iam natura vetabat   91
quaerere plus homines.   vidit te frangere Leucas,
trux Auguste, Pharon, dum classicus Actia miles
stagna quatit profugisque bibax Antonius armis
incestam vacuat patrio Ptolomaida regno.   95

80. *fort.* Asiatogenes *Luetjohann* : Asiagenes.
81. Perseo *Luetjohann* : perso (perse *M*) *codd.*
82. ac *add. ego* : *an* et? patria regna *Mohr.*

---

[1] The correspondences are : Sulla, Mithridates, poison (a
flagrant inaccuracy); Asiaticus, Antiochus, tribute; Curius,

give me back my beginnings! Alas! Where now
are those pageants, those triumphs rich of a consul
poor? My spears affrighted Libya's clime, and I
laid the yoke even a third time upon the faithless
Carthaginian. Ganges of the Indian, Phasis of the
Colchian, Araxes of Armenia, Ger of the Ethiopians,
Tanais of the Getae, all trembled before my Tiber.
I bethink me too of the Cimbrian and the leagued
Teuton shattered of old, when I ordered hands till
then loaded with the sword to carry naught but chains.
Alas for what I was when at my bidding Sulla,
Asiaticus, Curius, Paulus, Pompeius demanded of
Tigranes, Antiochus, Pyrrhus, Perseus, and Mithridates peace and realms, banishment, tribute, chains,
and poison![1] I say naught of the Sauromatians or
of the Moschans or of the Getae, whose wont it is
to drink bloody milk and stain their cups with
severed veins; or of the Persians,[2] most to be shunned
when they shun the foe. Nor is it enough to speak
of the land alone, for with thee to guide me I have
entered many a sea and nations far away under the
setting sun. Caesar took his victorious legions over
even to the Caledonian Britons, and although he
routed the Scot, the Pict and the Saxon, he still
looked for foes where nature forbade him to look
any more for men. Leucas saw the fierce Augustus
shatter Egypt, when the warriors of the fleet shook
the waters of Actium and the tippler Antonius by the
rout of his arms ousted the unclean daughter of the
house of Ptolemy from her ancestral kingdom. And

Pyrrhus, flight; Paulus, Perseus, chains; Pompeius,
Tigranes, peace and realms (the latter referring perhaps to
the two provinces of Sophene and Gordyene).
[2] *i.e.* The Parthians.

cumque prius stricto quererer de cardine mundi,
nec limes nunc ipsa mihi.   plus, summe deorum,
sum iusto tibi visa potens quod Parthicus ultro
restituit mea signa Sapor positoque tiara
funera Crassorum flevit dum purgat.   et hinc iam   100
(pro dolor!) excusso populi iure atque senatus
quod timui incurri; sum tota in principe, tota
principis, et fio lacerum de Caesare regnum,
quae quondam regina fui; Capreasque Tiberi
et caligas Gai Claudi censura secuta est   105
et vir morte Nero; tristi Pisone verendum
Galbam sternis, Otho, speculo qui pulcher haberi
dum captas, ego turpis eram; mihi foeda Vitelli
intulit ingluvies ventrem, qui tempore parvo
regnans sero perit; lassam post inclitus armis   110
Vespasianus habet, Titus hinc, post hunc quoque
    frater;
post quem tranquillus vix me mihi reddere Nerva
coepit, adoptivo factus de Caesare maior;
Vlpius inde venit, quo formidata Sygambris
Agrippina fuit, fortis, pius, integer, acer.   115
talem capta precor.   Traianum nescio si quis
aequiperet, ni fors iterum tu, Gallia, mittas

---

¹ *i.e.* "the precincts of my own city are not intact"
(Semple, p. 89).

² Phraates IV : see n. on 2. 457.

³ *i.e.* successive Caesars are reducing Rome's dominion
more and more.

⁴ A reference to the nickname *Caligula* (= little military
boot) given to Gaius in his boyhood by the soldiers, because
he went about the barracks dressed like a soldier. For the
allusions to Claudius and Otho in this passage see nn. on 5.
322 sq.

VII. PANEGYRIC ON AVITUS

I, who complained aforetime that the world's limits
were too narrow, am now not even a boundary to
myself.[1] O chiefest of the gods, I seemed to thee
more powerful than is meet, inasmuch as the Parthian
Sapor[2] freely restored my standards and, laying
aside his royal tiara, wept for the deaths of the
Crassi as he made atonement therefor. And hence
now, woe is me! I have fallen upon the fate I
feared, after wresting their rights from senate and
people; I am merged in the Emperor, wholly the
Emperor's property, and through Caesar I who
was once a queen am becoming a mangled realm.[3]
Tiberius with his Capri and Gaius with his soldier's
boots[4] were followed by Claudius with his censorship and Nero, who in death played the man; Galba,
to whom the stern Piso gave a claim to reverence,
was laid low by Otho, who, while he sought by his
mirror to seem beautiful, made me ugly. Then
Vitellius, with his loathsome gluttony, thrust his
paunch upon me, and though he reigned but a short
time he perished all too late. Thus sore wearied
was I when Vespasian, famed man of war, possessed
me, and after him Titus, after Titus his brother; and
after him the tranquil Nerva scarce began to make me
myself again,—Nerva, who made himself greater by
the Caesar he adopted. Then came Trajan, by whose
doing Agrippina[5] became a terror to the Sygambrians, an emperor gallant, faithful, righteous and
vigorous. In my captivity I pray for such another.
I know not if anyone can match Trajan—unless
perchance Gaul should once more[6] send forth a man

[5] Colonia Agrippina (Cologne).
[6] Trajan was a native of Spain, which was now included in
the " Prefecture of the Gauls."

qui vincat." lacrimae vocem clausere precantis,
et quidquid superest luctus rogat. undique caeli
assurgunt proceres, Mars, Cypris, Romulus et qui 120
auctores tibi, Roma, dei ; iam mitior ipsa
flectitur atque iras veteres Saturnia donat.

Iuppiter ista refert : " Fatum, quo cuncta reguntur
quoque ego, non licuit frangi. sat celsa laborant
semper, et elatas nostro de munere vires 125
invidit Fortuna sibi ; sed concipe magnos,
quamquam fracta, animos. si te Porsenna soluto
plus timuit de ponte fremens, si moenia capta
mox Brenni videre fugam, si denique dirum
Hannibalem iuncto terrae caelique tumultu 130
reppulimus (cum castra tuis iam proxima muris
starent, Collina fulmen pro turre cucurrit,
atque illic iterum timuit natura paventem
post Phlegram pugnare Iovem) : torpentia tolle
lumina, detersam mentem caligo relinquat. 135
te mirum est vinci ; incipies cum vincere, mirum
non erit. utque tibi pateat quo surgere tandem
fessa modo possis, paucis, cognosce, docebo.

" Est mihi, quae Latio se sanguine tollit alumnam,
tellus clara viris, cui non dedit optima quondam 140
rerum opifex natura parem ; fecundus ab urbe

126. fortuna *M* : natura.
128. fremens *M* : tremens.

---

[1] The Roman army was encamped between the Colline and
Esquiline Gates when Hannibal approached Rome (Livy
XXVI. 10. 1); the battlemented Colline Gate is called
Collina turris also by Juvenal (VI. 291) and Claudian (*Gild.*
86). Livy mentions the blinding storms of rain and hail,
which occurred on two consecutive days (*ib.* 11. 2 sq.), but
makes no mention of lightning; Sidonius probably borrowed
this (and not only this) from the grandiose description by
Silius (XII. 605–728; cf. XIII. 15–20). Cf. Juv. VII. 163.
[2] See n. on 6. 15.

who should even surpass him." Tears choked the suppliant's voice, and her grief served for what remained of her petition. On all sides the chiefs of heaven rise in her honour, Mars, Venus, Romulus and the gods that made Rome great; even Saturn's daughter is moved to greater gentleness and forgoes her ancient wrath.

Then answered Jupiter: " Fate, whereby all things—yea, I myself—are governed, might not be violated. Whatever has reached its highest bourne must needs be afflicted, and Fortune hath grudged to aid a power that hath been exalted by *my* bounty. But broken though thou art, be of right good cheer. If Porsenna feared thee more than ever when he raged indignant at the severing of the bridge, if the walls that Brennus captured soon saw his flight, if, last of all, we drove back Hannibal with a wild outburst from earth and sky alike (his camp already stood nigh to thy walls when in front of the Colline tower a thunderbolt rushed down,[1] and Nature feared that there once again, as in Phlegra's [2] combat, Jove was fighting in terror), raise thy drooping eyes, let the dark mist be wiped away and vanish from thy soul. 'Tis a marvel that thou shouldst be conquered, but when thou beginnest to conquer, 'twill be no marvel. And now, that it may be plain to thee how thou mayest rise again, worn out as thou art, hearken and I will declare it in few words.

" I have a land which carries its head high as sprung from Latin blood,[3] a land famed for its men, a land to which Nature, the blessed creator of all things, vouchsafed no peer in days gone by.

---

[3] This claim of the Arverni is mentioned in Lucan I. 427 sq., a passage recalled by Sidonius in *Epist.* VII. 7. 2.

pollet ager, primo qui vix proscissus aratro
semina tarda sitit vel luxuriante iuvenco
arcana exponit piceam pinguedine glaebam.
assurrexit huic, coxit quod torridus Auster,   145
Niliacum Libycumque solum, collataque semper
arida Mygdoniae damnarunt Gargara falces;
Apulus et Calaber cessit.   spes unica rerum,
hanc, Arverne, colens nulli pede cedis in armis,
quosvis vincis equo.   testis mihi Caesaris esto   150
hic nimium Fortuna pavens, cum colle repulsus
Gergoviae castris miles vix restitit ipsis.
hos ego tam fortes volui, sed cedere Avitum
dum tibi, Roma, paro, rutilat cui maxima dudum
stemmata complexum germen, palmata cucurrit   155
per proavos, gentisque suae te teste, Philagri,
patricius resplendet apex.   sed portio quanta est
haec laudum, laudare patres, quos quippe curules
et praefecturas constat debere nepoti?
sint alii per quos se postuma iactet origo,   160
et priscum titulis numeret genus alter: Avite,

---

[1] *Proscindere* is the technical term for the first ploughing.
Here no further ploughing is required, so the oxen have a lazy
time. [This explanation of *luxuriante* is given by Dr. Semple,
p. 91.]

[2] The Patrician Philagrius to whom Avitus was related is
no doubt the man mentioned in *Epist*. II. 3. 1 as a remote
ancestor of our poet's old schoolfellow, Magnus Felix (see n.
on *Carm*. 9. 1).   He cannot be the Philagrius to whom *Epist*.
VII. 14 is addressed, but he may be the one mentioned in *Carm*.
24. 93.   Modern authorities treat the two (or three) men as
one.

[3] *i.e.* their distinctions came to them because it was ordained
that a descendant should be Emperor; it was his destined

VII. PANEGYRIC ON AVITUS

From the city extend rich and fruitful fields; scarce are they cloven with the early ploughing [1] when they thirst for the tardy seeds, and while the ox enjoys luxurious ease they display clods made black by some fatness mysteriously at work. To this soil the tilth of Nile and Libya, baked by the scorching south wind, hath yielded pride of place, and Gargarus, compared with such land, hath always been condemned by Phrygian sickles as withered; the Apulian and the Calabrian have likewise owned defeat. O Arvernian, who dwellest therein, sole hope for the world, thou yieldest to none when thou fightest on foot, and on thy steed thou art a match for any man! Let Fortune, Caesar's attendant goddess, be my witness, who was sore dismayed in this land when his warriors were forced back from Gergovia's hill and scarce halted their flight at their very camp. I ordained that these men should be thus gallant, but all the time I was making ready, O Rome, to present to thee Avitus, whose natal tree, rich in noble branches, hath long shone illustrious, whose forefathers have time after time been adorned with the palm-decked robe, and whose race, as Philagrius bears witness, is irradiated by a Patrician's dignity. [2] But how small a part of his meed of praise is such praise of his forefathers, who manifestly owe their curule rank and prefectures to their descendant! [3] There may be others of whom the later scions of their race will make boast; another may recount the ancient honours of his line; but thou alone, Avitus, dost

greatness that was the real cause of their dignities. Thus it is he who ennobles his ancestors, not his ancestors who ennoble him (*v.* 162).

nobilitas tu solus avos.   libet edere tanti
gesta viri et primam paucis percurrere vitam.

   " Solverat in partum generosa puerpera casti
ventris onus ; manifesta dedi mox signa futuri   165
principis ac totam fausto trepidi patris aulam
implevi augurio.   licet idem grandia nati
culparet fata et pueri iam regna videret,
sed sibi commissum tanto sub pignore cernens
mundi depositum, ne quid tibi, Roma, periret,   170
iuvit fortunam studio.   lactantia primum
membra dedit nivibus, glaciemque inrumpere plantis
iussit et attritas parvum ridere pruinas.
surgentes animi Musis formantur et illo
quo Cicerone tonas ; didicit quoque facta tuorum   175
ante ducum ; didicit pugnas libroque relegit
quae gereret campo.   primus vix coeperat esse
ex infante puer, rabidam cum forte cruentis
rictibus atque escas ieiuna fauce parantem
plus catulis stravit (fuerant nam fragmina prop-
      ter)   180
arrepta de caute lupam, fractusque molari
dissiluit vertex et saxum vulnere sedit.
sic meus Alcides, Nemeae dum saltibus errat,
occurrit monstro vacuus, non robora portans,
non pharetras ; stetit ira fremens atque hoste pro-
      pinquo   185
consuluit solos virtus decepta lacertos.

   "Parva quidem, dicenda tamen : quis promptior isto

167. *sq. dist. ego ; vid. Class. Quart. loc. cit. pp.* 19 *sq.*
185. fremens *Buecheler et Wilamowitz*: tremens *codd.
plerique.*

132

ennoble thy forefathers. Fain am I to relate the deeds of this great man and in few words to run through his earliest years.

" His noble mother had been released from her chaste travail; anon I gave plain tokens of the emperor that was to be, and filled with happy augury the whole palace of the anxious father. He, 'tis true, murmured at his son's high destiny, already seeing his boy a sovereign; nevertheless, discerning in this great pledge the whole world's trust committed to his keeping, he seconded fortune's bounty by his own diligence, lest thou, O Rome, shouldst suffer loss. First he surrendered the suckling's limbs to the snows; he compelled him while a little child to break the ice with his feet and to laugh at the frost as he trod it down. His growing mind was moulded by the Muses and by the Cicero that bestows on thee tones of thunder; he learned also the deeds of thy leaders of former days; he learned of battles and read in the written page what he should perform in the field. Scarce had he changed infancy for boyhood when, seeing a she-wolf ravening with bloody jaws agape as with hungry mouth she sought food, chiefly for her cubs, he snatched a stone (for there were pieces of rock hard by) and laid her low. Shattered by the boulder her head split open, and the stone sank down in the wound. Even so my Hercules, as he roamed the glens of Nemea, faced the monster empty-handed, carrying neither club nor quiver; in raging wrath he took his stand, and with the enemy nigh that brave spirit, taken unawares, looked for aid to naught but his own strong arms.

" Small things, yet worthy to be told are these:—Who was quicker than he to lower to the scent the

tensa catenati summittere colla Molossi
et lustris recubare feras interprete nare
discere non visas et in aere quaerere plantas?   190
iam si forte suem latratibus improbus Vmber
terruit, albentes nigro sub gutture lunas
frangere ludus erat colluctantique lacerto
vasta per adversas venabula cogere praedas.
quam pulchrum, cum forte domum post lustra re-
    vertens   195
horrore splenderet apri virtusque repugnans
proderet invitum per fortia facta pudorem!
sic Pandioniis castae Tritonidos arvis
Hippolytus roseo sudum radiabat ab ore,
sed simul a gemino flagrans cum Cressa furore   200
transiit adfectu matres et fraude novercas.

    "Quid volucrum studium, dat quas natura rapaces
in vulgus prope cognatum?   quis doctior isto
instituit varias per nubila iungere lites?
alite vincit aves, celerique per aethera plausu   205
hoc nulli melius pugnator militat unguis.

    "Nec minus haec inter civilia iura secutus
eligitur primus, iuvenis, solus, mala fractae
alliget ut patriae poscatque informe recidi
vectigal.   procerum tum forte potentior illic,   210
post etiam princeps, Constantius omnia praestat,

---

[1] Hounds.
[2] "Pandionian" means "Attic," from Pandion, king of
Athens, father of Procne and Philomela. "Tritonis" means
Pallas Athena; cf. 15. 179.   [3] Falconry.
[4] Sidonius makes it clear that Constantius was not yet
Emperor. He does not actually say that Constantius was in
Gaul at the time, and some have supposed that the embassy
went to Ravenna, where Constantius was persuaded to use his
influence with Honorius. But the description of Constantius
as *potentior illic* seems to imply that he was commanding in

taut necks of the leashed Molossians,[1] to learn by the
guidance of their nostrils that wild beasts he could not
see were lurking in the den, and to seek for tracks in
the air? Again, if haply the irrepressible Umbrian
hound frightened a boar by his barking, it was sport
to this lad to smash the white crescents under the
monster's black throat and with straining arm to
drive a huge spear through the confronting quarry.
What a beautiful sight when, returning home from
the chase, he would appear all the more resplendent
for the boar's bristling hideousness, and his gallantry
in its own despite baulked his shrinking modesty
by this evidence of brave deeds! Thus in the
Pandionian fields of chaste Tritonis [2] was Hippolytus
wont to diffuse a sunny radiance from his glowing
countenance—though it was then that the Cretan
woman, fired by a double frenzy, overpassed a
mother's love and a stepmother's guile.

"What of his devotion to the birds that nature
creates to prey upon the common throng of creatures
almost their kin? [3] Who more skilfully trains them
to clash in divers contests amid the clouds? With a
bird he vanquishes birds; with a swift whirring
through the upper air the warrior claw fights for
none more gallantly than for him.

"And amid these sports he followed the law none
the less, and, young though he was, he was chosen
first and alone to bind up the wounds of his shattered
homeland and to make claim for the abolishment of
a hideous tax. It chanced that Constantius [4] was
chief lord in those parts—he who anon was emperor;

Gaul. It is indeed quite probable that *patriae* (209) refers to
Auvergne. We learn from Greg. Tur. II. 9 that the "generals
of Honorius" acted with great severity towards the supporters

indole defixus tanta et miratus in annis
parvis grande bonum vel in ore precantis ephebi
verba senis.
        " Ducis hinc pugnas et foedera regum
pandere, Roma, libet. variis incussa procellis   215
bellorum regi Getico tua Gallia pacis
pignora iussa dare est, inter quae nobilis obses
tu, Theodore, venis; quem pro pietate propinqui
expetis in media pelliti principis aula
tutus, Avite, fide. probat hoc iam Theudoris
    altum   220
exemplum officii. res mira et digna relatu,
quod fueris blandus regi placuisse feroci.
hinc te paulatim praelibat sensibus imis
atque nimis vult esse suum; sed spernis amicum
plus quam Romanum gerere. stupet ille repul-
    sam   225
et plus inde places. rigidum sic, Pyrrhe, videbas
Fabricium, ingestas animo cum divite fugit
pauper opes, regem temnens, dum supplice censu
pignus amicitiae vili mendicat ab auro.

224. nimis Mohr: animis.

---

of Jovinus in the land of the Arvernians, but Sidonius can
scarcely be alluding to such an early date (Jovinus fell in
A.D. 413). Constantius was so often and so long in Gaul that
we cannot fix the reference with any certainty. If the *vectigal*
was a tax levied by the government, only the Emperor could
remit it, and we must then suppose that Avitus persuaded
Constantius to use his influence with Honorius to that end.
It may, however, refer to the requisitions for the pay and
provisioning of the army (*annona militaris*).

    [1] The Theodorus here mentioned is not otherwise known.
It is scarcely likely that he is the man mentioned in *Epist.*
III. 10. 1. The Gothic king is Theodoric I (419–451). It is
thought that the hostages referred to here were given to him
on the occasion of his treaty with the Romans which gave him

and he granted all that was asked, marvelling at
such great talent and astonished at such full-grown
virtue in those boyish years, at such elderly speech
on the lips of the suppliant youth.

" And now, O Rome, I would fain relate the battles
wherein he commanded and the compacts he made
with kings. Thy land of Gaul, buffeted by divers
tempests of war, was bidden to give to the Gothic
king sureties of peace, and among them, a noble
hostage, went Theodorus.[1] Avitus, in loving duty
to his kin, sought him out in the midst of the skin-
clad monarch's court, and his loyalty won him safety.
Theodoric soon looked with favour on this sublime
devotion. Marvellous indeed is it and worthy to be
recorded that by thy gentle winsomeness, Avitus,
thou didst find grace with a fierce king. Little by
little he began to know thee in his inmost soul, and
he desired exceedingly to have thee as one of his
own; but thou didst scorn to act the friend rather
than the Roman. The king marvelled at this rebuff,
but esteemed thee all the more for it. Even thus
did Pyrrhus see Fabricius immovable, when that
poor man with rich soul shunned the riches thrust
upon him, despising the king in that he made his
wealth play the suppliant and begged with paltry
gold for a bond of friendship.

sovereignty over Aquitanica Secunda and Novempopulana
(Introd., p. xvii). This is possible if we accept one of the two
dates usually given for that agreement (426 and 430), but
not if, with Stein (p. 482), we place it in 439. The giving
of hostages does not necessarily imply that the Gothic kingdom was now independent; see Stein, *loc. cit.*, n. 3. See also
n. on 495 sqq. Some eminent historians (*e.g.* Mommsen) have
erred seriously through ignorance of the meaning of *expetis*
(*v.* 219). In Sidonius and other late Latin writers this verb
often means " seek out," " visit."

"Aetium interea, Scythico quia saepe duello est   230
edoctus, sequeris; qui, quamquam celsus in armis,
nil sine te gessit, cum plurima tute sine illo.
nam post Iuthungos et Norica bella subacto
victor Vindelico Belgam, Burgundio quem trux
presserat, absolvit iunctus tibi.   vincitur illic   235
cursu Herulus, Chunus iaculis Francusque natatu,
Sauromata clipeo, Salius pede, falce Gelonus,
vulnere vel si quis plangit cui flesse feriri est
ac ferro perarasse genas vultuque minaci
rubra cicatricum vestigia defodisse.   240
" Inlustri iam tum donatur celsus honore.
squameus et rutilis etiamnunc livida cristis

232. tute *L. Mueller* : tu.
238. feriri C^aF : perire.

---

[1] It is important to note that *interea* is often used in poetry
to introduce a new action subsequent to, not contempor-
aneous with, the events just described.   For this use in Virgil
see D. W. Reinmuth in *Amer. Journ. Phil.* LIV. (1933), pp.
323–339, especially 328–330.   " Meanwhile" is often a
misleading translation.

[2] The Huns were for years the mainstay of Aëtius' army,
and "Scythian warfare" in all probability means war waged
by means of Hunnish forces.   It is scarcely likely that the
meaning is "hostilities with the Goths" (n. on 5. 219), which
had apparently gone on with little intermission from about
A.D. 425 to 430, and in which Aëtius had played an important
part.   The details are obscure, though it is certain that
Theodoric made at least one unsuccessful attempt to take
Arles.

[3] The Iuthungi were subdued by Aëtius in A.D. 430; the
contest with the Noricans and the Vindelicians no doubt took
place in the course of the same expedition.   All modern
authorities infer from this passage that Avitus took part in
the campaign against the Iuthungi and their neighbours, but
Sidonius does not say so.

[4] The Burgundians rose in A.D. 435 and were crushed in

VII. PANEGYRIC ON AVITUS

"Anon[1] thou didst follow Aëtius, because he had learnt many a lesson from the Scythian warfare[2]; and he, glorious in arms though he was, did no deed without thee, though thou didst many without him. For when he had finished with the Iuthungi[3] and the war in Noricum, and had subdued the Vindelicians, thereafter in partnership with thee did he deliver the Belgians, whom the fierce Burgundian had harassed.[4] There the Herulian found in thee his match in fleetness, the Hun in javelin-throwing, the Frank in swimming, the Sauromatian in use of shield, the Salian in marching, the Gelonian in wielding the scimitar; and in bearing of wounds thou didst surpass any mourning barbarian[5] to whom wailing means self-wounding and tearing the cheeks with steel and gouging the red traces of scars on his threatening face.

"Even thus early this hero was glorified by bestowal of the title of Illustrious.[6] Wearing his scale-armour, his face still bearing the mark of the

the following year. It is obvious from this passage that Roman forces were used in the campaign; Bury (I. 249) must be wrong in thinking that the Huns were put in independent charge of it.

[5] The construction is *vel* (= *et*) *vulnere* ("in the matter of a wound") *vincitur* ("is surpassed") *si quis* (= *quisquis*) *plangit*.

[6] The *viri inlustres* were the highest class of the senatorial order. As Avitus had not yet held any of the high offices of state which gave a right to the title, it must have been bestowed as an honorary distinction. It is somewhat surprising to find a Gallo–Roman reaching that dignity at such an early stage in his career. It is obvious that in this period he held a high military rank, and the Prefectship which soon followed shows that he was already a marked man. But as the Praetorian Prefect became *inlustris* as a matter of course, one is tempted to suspect that Sidonius has antedated the conferment of the title on Avitus.

THE POEMS OF SIDONIUS

ora gerens vix arma domum sordentia castris
rettulerat : nova bella iterum pugnamque sub ipsis
iam patriae muris periurus commovet hostis.   245
Litorius Scythicos equites tum forte subacto
celsus Aremorico Geticum rapiebat in agmen
per terras, Arverne, tuas ; qui proxima quaeque
discursu, flammis, ferro, feritate, rapinis
delebant, pacis fallentes nomen inane.   250
huius tum famulum quidam truculentior horum,
mox feriende, feris ; ruit ille et tristia fata
commendat domino absenti partemque futuram
vindictae moriens Stygium spe portat ad amnem.
et iam fama viro turres portasque tuenti   255
intuitu pavidae plebis perfert scelus actum.
excutitur, restat, pallet, rubet, alget et ardet,
ac sibimet multas vultum variata per unum
ira facit facies, vel, qui mos saepe dolenti,   259
plus amat extinctum ; tandem prorumpit et arma,
arma fremit, pinguisque etiamnum sanguine fertur
lorica, obtusus per barbara vulnera contus
atque sub assiduis dentatus caedibus ensis.
includit suras ocreis capitique micantem
imponit galeam, fulvus cui crescit in altum   265
conus et iratam iaculatur vertice lucem.
et iam scandit equum vulsisque a cardine portis
emicat ; adsistunt socio Virtusque Dolorque
et Pudor : armatas pilo petit impiger alas

245. periurus *Wilamowitz* : periturus.

---

[1] *Celsus* may mean " made glorious."
[2] For the conquest of the Aremoricans by Litorius and his
subsequent march against the Goths, who were besieging
Narbonne, see Introd., p. xvi. The present passage refers to
a lawless body of Hunnish auxiliaries, no doubt detached from
the main body of Litorius's forces.

burnished helmet, scarce had he brought home his
stained arms from the field when there came fresh
wars and a battle this time under the very walls of
his own city, stirred up by a faithless foe. Litorius,
elated [1] by the conquest of the Aremoricans,[2] was
hurrying his Scythian horsemen against the Gothic
host through the land of the Arvernian, and they
with raid and fire and sword and barbarity and
pillage were destroying all things near them, betraying and making void the name of peace. A servant
of Avitus was wounded by one of these, more savage
than his fellows, soon to be wounded in turn; the
victim fell, and falling commended his woeful fate to
the vengeance of his absent master, and as he died
he carried with him to the Stygian stream a hopeful
foretaste of the revenge that was to come. Now
Rumour brought knowledge of the dastard deed to
our leader as he kept his ward of towers and gates,
regardful of the scared populace. He starts, halts,
grows pale, grows red, grows cold and hot; his
anger in its changing phases takes many forms in
that one countenance, and, as is oft the mourner's
way, he loves the lost one more than ever. At
length he dashes forward, shouting again and again
for his arms, and they bring him his corselet, still
clotted with gore, his lance blunted by wounds dealt
upon the barbarians, and his sword notched by
unceasing slaughter. He cases his legs in greaves
and puts upon his head a gleaming helmet, whereon
a golden crest-base rises aloft, darting an angry
flash from on high. Next he mounts his charger,
and tearing the gates from their hinges rushes
forth; Valour and Grief and Honour range themselves with their ally; eagerly he charges with his

pugnando pugnam quaerens, pavidumque per ag-
    men   270
multorum interitu compensat quod latet unus.
sic Phrygium Emathia victorem cuspide poscens
Aeacides caeso luctum frenavit amico,
per mortes tot, Troia, tuas (nam vilia per se
agmina) contentus ruere strictumque per amplos   275
exserere gladium populos; natat obruta tellus
sanguine, dumque hebetat turba grave caedua telum
absens in cuncto sibi vulnere iam cadit Hector.
proditus ut tandem tanti qui causa tumultus,
inquit Avitus: ' Age, Scythica nutrite sub Arcto,
qui furis et caeso tantum qui fidis inermi,   281
congredere armato. multum tibi praestitit ira
iam mea: concessi pugnam iubeoque resistas;
certantem mactasse iuvat.' sic fatur et aequor
prosilit in medium, nec non ferus advenit hostis. 285
ut primum pectus vel comminus ora tulere,
hic ira tremit, ille metu. iam cetera turba
diversis trepidat votis variosque per ictus
pendet ab eventu. sed postquam prima, secunda
tertiaque acta rota est, venit ecce et celsa cruen-
    tum   290
perforat hasta virum, post et confinia dorsi
cedit transfosso ruptus bis pectore thorax,
et dum per duplicem sanguis singultat hiatum
dividua ancipitem carpserunt vulnera vitam.

       273–5. *dist. ego.*
       274. nam *ego dubitanter*: iam.

---

   [1] *i.e.* fighting his way through the ranks in order to meet
the hiding murderer.
   [2] Achilles after the slaying of Patroclus by Hector.

pike the armed ranks, seeking a fight by fighting,[1] and amid the fear-stricken throng he makes the death of many pay for the absence of the one that lurks concealed. Even so did the scion of Aeacus,[2] ranging with his spear in search of the Phrygian victor, hold back his mourning when his friend was slain, content to rush in a tide of death-dealing among Troy's host (for in themselves he counted those hordes as naught), and to wield the drawn sword through multitudinous throngs; the ground was submerged and swam in blood, and as the falling ranks blunted his heavy weapon he saw already in every wound he dealt the absent Hector fall. When at last he who was the cause of that great havoc stood revealed, then said Avitus: 'Ho! thou fellow reared 'neath the Scythian Bear, who ragest like a madman and hast such boldness from slaying the unarmed, come, meet one who is armed! Already my wrath has allowed thee a great boon; I have granted thee a fight, and I bid thee stand thy ground; I choose to slaughter a resisting foe.' Thus he spake, and bounded forth into the midst of the plain; and the barbarous foe likewise came. When first they approached, breast to breast and face to face, the one shook with anger, the other with fear. Now the general throng stands in sore suspense, with prayers on this side or on that, and as blow follows blow they hang on the issue. But when the first bout, the second, the third have been fought, lo! the upraised spear comes and pierces the man of blood; his breast was transfixed and his corselet twice split, giving way even where it covered the back; and as the blood came throbbing through the two gaps the separate wounds took away the life that each of them might claim.

" Haec post gesta viri (temet, Styx livida, testor)
intemerata mihi praefectus iura regebat ;   296
et caput hoc sibimet solitis defessa ruinis
Gallia suscipiens Getica pallebat ab ira.
nil prece, nil pretio, nil milite fractus agebat
Aetius ; capto terrarum damna patebant   300
Litorio ; in Rhodanum proprios producere fines
Theudoridae fixum, nec erat pugnare necesse,
sed migrare Getis.   rabidam trux asperat iram
victor ; quod sensit Scythicum pro moenibus hostem,
imputat ; et nil est gravius, si forsitan umquam   305
vincere contingat, trepido.   postquam undique nul-
          lum
praesidium ducibusque tuis nil, Roma, relictum est,
foedus, Avite, novas ; saevum tua pagina regem
lecta domat ; iussisse sat est te, quod rogat orbis.
credent hoc umquam gentes populique futuri ?   310
littera Romani cassat quod, barbare, vincis.
iura igitur rexit ; namque hoc quoque par fuit, ut tum
assertor fieret legum qui nunc erit auctor,
ne dandus populis princeps, caput, induperator,
Caesar et Augustus solum fera proelia nosset.   315
    " Iam praefecturae perfunctus culmine tandem
se dederat ruri (numquam tamen otia, numquam
desidia imbellis, studiumque et cura quieto
armorum semper) : subito cum rupta tumultu

---

[1] The prefecture of Avitus began in A.D. 439, the year in
which Litorius was defeated near Toulouse (Introd., pp. xvi f.,
and it seems to have lasted for some years. Litorius, though
finally defeated, inflicted heavy losses on the Goths, and
it was perhaps this fact, as much as the diplomacy of Avitus,
that persuaded the king to come to terms with the
Romans.

VII. PANEGYRIC ON AVITUS

" After these valiant deeds (I call even thee, dark Styx, to witness) he was my prefect,[1] administering the laws without corruption. Gaul when she received him as her head was worn out with the familiar devastation and pale with affright at the Gothic wrath. Aëtius was broken; naught could he do by prayer or bribe or with his soldiers; and when Litorius was captured the destitution of the land stood revealed. Theodoric was resolved to advance his own boundaries to the Rhone, and the Goths needed not to fight, but only to migrate. The fierce victor whetted his raging wrath; he counted it a sin against him that he had known the presence of the Scythian foe [2] before his walls, and naught is more grievous than a frightened man if he ever chance to be victorious. When there was no support anywhere and no resource, O Rome, was left to thy leaders, Avitus renewed the treaty; the reading of his scroll subdued the king; Avitus had but to order that which the world begged for. Will future races and peoples ever believe this?—a Roman's letter annulled a barbarian's conquests. So he administered the laws; for this also was fitting, that at that time he should become the champion of the laws who will now be their maker, lest he who was to be given to the peoples as prince, head, emperor, Caesar, and Augustus should have no knowledge save of savage battles.

" Now he had discharged the prefect's majestic office, and he had devoted himself to country life (though never with him was there idleness or unwarlike sloth, but even in those peaceful days arms were ever his study and his care)—when suddenly the bar-

[2] The Huns under Litorius.

barbaries totas in te transfuderat Arctos,   320
Gallia.   pugnacem Rugum comitante Gelono
Gepida trux sequitur ; Scirum Burgundio cogit ;
Chunus, Bellonotus, Neurus, Bastarna, Toringus,
Bructerus, ulvosa vel quem Nicer alluit unda
prorumpit Francus ; cecidit cito secta bipenni   325
Hercynia in lintres et Rhenum texuit alno ;
et iam terrificis diffuderat Attila turmis
in campos se, Belga, tuos.   vix liquerat Alpes
Aetius, tenue et rarum sine milite ducens
robur in auxiliis, Geticum male credulus agmen   330
incassum propriis praesumens adfore castris.
nuntius at postquam ductorem perculit, Hunos
iam prope contemptum propriis in sedibus hostem
exspectare Getas, versat vagus omnia secum
consilia et mentem curarum fluctibus urget.   335
tandem nutanti sedit sententia celsum
exorare virum, collectisque omnibus una
principibus coram supplex sic talibus infit :
' orbis, Avite, salus, cui non nova gloria nunc est
quod rogat Aetius, voluisti, et non nocet hostis ;   340
vis : prodest.   inclusa tenes tot milia nutu,
et populis Geticis sola est tua gratia limes ;
infensi semper nobis pacem tibi praestant.
victrices, i, prome aquilas ; fac, optime, Chunos,

336. nutanti *M* : cunctanti.

---

[1] The incursion of Attila and his hordes gathered from many
nations, A.D. 451.   The support of the Visigoths was vital to
the Romans.   Avitus certainly made a good ambassador,
but the probability is that Theodoric acted largely from self-
interest, already detecting Attila's intention to push his conquests beyond the Loire.

[2] The Bellonoti (Balloniti, or perhaps Ballonoti, in Val.
Flacc. VI. 161) were a Sarmatian people.   For the other
peoples here mentioned, see Hodgkin II. 106 ff.

barian world, rent by a mighty upheaval, poured the whole north into Gaul.[1] After the warlike Rugian comes the fierce Gepid, with the Gelonian close by; the Burgundian urges on the Scirian; forward rush the Hun, the Bellonotian,[2] the Neurian, the Bastarnian, the Thuringian, the Bructeran, and the Frank, he whose land is washed by the sedgy waters of Nicer.[3] Straightway falls the Hercynian forest, hewn to make boats, and overlays the Rhine with a network of its timber; and now Attila with his fearsome squadrons has spread himself in raids upon the plains of the Belgian. Aëtius had scarce left the Alps, leading a thin, meagre force of auxiliaries without legion-aries, vainly with ill-starred confidence expecting that the Gothic host would join his camp. But tidings came that struck the leader with dismay; in their own land were the Goths awaiting the Huns, a foe they now almost despised. Perplexed, he turned over every plan, and his mind was beset with surging cares. At length in his wavering heart was formed the fixed resolve to make appeal to a man of high estate; and before an assemblage of all the nobles he thus began to plead: ' Avitus, saviour of the world, to whom it is no new glory to be besought by Aëtius, thou didst wish it, and the enemy no longer does harm;[4] thou wishest it, and he does good. All those thousands thou dost keep within bounds by thy nod; thine influence alone is a barrier-wall to the Gothic peoples; ever hostile to us, they grant peace to thee. Go, display the victorious eagles;[5] bring it to pass, O noble hero, that the Huns,

---

[3] The Neckar.

[4] See *vv.* 306-311.

[5] *i.e.* in order that the Gothic soldiers may rally to them.

quorum forte prior fuga nos concusserat olim,   345
bis victos prodesse mihi.'   sic fatur, et ille
pollicitus votum fecit spem.   protinus inde
avolat et famulas in proelia concitat iras.
ibant pellitae post classica Romula turmae,
ad nomen currente Geta ; timet aere vocari   350
dirutus, opprobrium, non damnum barbarus horrens.
hos ad bella trahit iam tum spes orbis Avitus,
vel iam privatus vel adhuc.   sic cinnama busto
collis Erythraei portans Phoebeius ales
concitat omne avium vulgus ; famulantia currunt   355
agmina, et angustus pennas non explicat aer.

   " Iam prope fata tui bis senas vulturis alas
complebant (scis namque tuos, scis, Roma, labores) :
Aetium Placidus mactavit semivir amens ;
vixque tuo imposito capiti diadema, Petroni :   360
ilico barbaries, nec non sibi capta videri
Roma Getis tellusque suo cessura furori ;
raptores ceu forte lupi, quis nare sagaci
monstrat odor pinguem clausis ab ovilibus auram,
irritant acuuntque famem portantque rapinae   365

---

¹ *i.e.* by serving in the Roman ranks : cf. *prodest, v.* 341.
The meaning is that the Huns serving under Litorius had by
their flight before the Goths caused a Roman disaster (A.D.
339) : now a second defeat of the Huns will put them once more
at the service of Rome.

² *Aere dirutus* (Cic. *Verr.* II. 5. 33, etc.) was applied to a
soldier whose pay was stopped as a punishment.

³ A play on the two meanings of *privatus* : Avitus was
n o w *privatus* ("out of office" ; his Prefectship was over)
or s t i l l *privatus* (*i.e.* a subject : he was soon to become
Emperor).   For the latter meaning of *privatus* cf. *v.* 593
below.

⁴ See nn. on 2. 417 and (for *Eryth.*) 2. 447.

⁵ See *v.* 55 n.

⁶ See 5. 305 sqq. n.   Placidus was one of the names of

whose flight aforetime shook us, shall by a second
defeat be made to do me service.'[1] Thus he spake,
and Avitus consenting changed his prayer into hope.
Straightway he flies thence and rouses up the
Gothic fury that was his willing slave. Rushing to
enroll their names, the skin-clad warriors began to
march behind the Roman trumpets; those barbarians
feared the name of ' pay-docked soldiers,'[2] dreading
the disgrace, not the loss. These men Avitus swept
off to war, Avitus even thus early the world's hope,
though now (or still) a plain citizen.[3] Even so the
bird of Phoebus, when bearing the cinnamon to
his pyre on the Erythraean hill,[4] rouses all the
common multitude of birds; the obedient throng
hies to him, and the air is too narrow to give their
wings free play.

" Now destiny was well-nigh bringing to fulfilment the sign of the twelve flying vultures[5] (Thou
knowest, O Rome, thou knowest all thy troubles).
Placidus,[6] the mad eunuch, slaughtered Aëtius.
Scarce was the diadem set on the head of Petronius
when all at once came a barbarian flood, and the
Goths had visions of Rome captured by them and of
the whole earth ready to surrender to their frenzy;
as ravening wolves, whose keen scent has caught a
whiff of fatlings wafted from a fenced sheepcote,
goad and sharpen their hunger, and carry in their

Valentinian III. That feeble emperor is perhaps intentionally
described in terms strictly applicable to the chamberlain
Heraclius, who helped him in the assassination of Aëtius. It
was Petronius Maximus who appointed Avitus to the military
command of Gaul, dignifying that office, apparently for the
first time, with the title *magister peditum equitumque* (or
mag. utriusque militiae; see v. 377 and n. on 5. 553). Another
view is that Avitus was made *mag. mil. praesentalis.*

in vultu speciem, patulo ieiunia rictu
fallentes; iam iamque tener spe frangitur agnus
atque absens avido crepitat iam praeda palato.
quin et Aremoricus piratam Saxona tractus
sperabat, cui pelle salum sulcare Britannum   370
ludus et assuto glaucum mare findere lembo.
Francus Germanum primum Belgamque secundum
sternebat, Rhenumque, ferox Alamanne, bibebas
Romani ripis et utroque superbus in agro
vel civis vel victor eras. sed perdita cernens   375
terrarum spatia princeps iam Maximus, unum
quod fuit in rebus, peditumque equitumque magis-
          trum
te sibi, Avite, legit. collati rumor honoris
invenit agricolam, flexi dum forte ligonis
exercet dentes vel pando pronus aratro   380
vertit inexcoctam per pinguia iugera glaebam.
sic quondam ad patriae res fractas pauper arator,
Cincinnate, venis veterem cum te induit uxor
ante boves trabeam dictatoremque salignae
excepere fores atque ad sua tecta ferentem   385
quod non persevit, turpique e fasce gravata
vile triumphalis portavit purpura semen.
   " Vt primum ingesti pondus suscepit honoris,
legas qui veniam poscant, Alamanne, furori,
Saxonis incursus cessat, Chattumque palustri   390
alligat Albis aqua; vixque hoc ter menstrua totum

---

¹ *i.e.* the inhabitants of Germania Prima (capital Mogunt-
iacum, Mainz) and Belgica Secunda (capital Durocortorum
Remorum, Rheims).

eyes a vision of their spoil, beguiling their famishment with jaws opened wide; every moment their expectant hope sees a young lamb mangled, and the prey beyond their reach is already crunched in their greedy mouths. The Aremorican region too expected the Saxon pirate, who deems it but sport to furrow the British waters with hides, cleaving the blue sea in a stitched boat. The Frank began to lay low the First German and the Second Belgian[1]; the bold Alaman was drinking the Rhine from the Roman bank and proudly lording it on both sides, a citizen[2] or a conqueror. But Maximus, now emperor, seeing such loss of widespread lands, took the sole availing course in such distress and chose for himself Avitus as Master of Horse and Foot. The tidings of the rank bestowed found him farming, plying the bent mattock's tooth or stooping over the curved plough as he turned up the unsunned clods in his fertile acres. Thus aforetime Cincinnatus came, a poor ploughman, to heal his country's broken fortunes, when his wife put the old robe upon him, standing before the oxen, and his doors of willow-wood now opened for a dictator, who bore back to his dwelling what he had not sowed, and thus the triumphal purple, weighted with a mean load, carried common seed.

" No sooner had he taken up the burden of the office thrust upon him than the Alaman sent envoys to crave pardon for their frenzy, the Saxon's raiding abated and the marshy water of Albis confined the Chattian; and scarce had the moon viewed all this

---

[2] *i.e.* an Alamannian tribesman, a member of the Alamannian community on the right bank of the Rhine; on the other bank he is an alien invader. *Civis* does not here mean " Roman citizen."

luna videt, iamque ad populos ac rura feroci
tenta Getae pertendit iter, qua pulsus ab aestu
Oceanus refluum spargit per culta Garunnam;
in flumen currente mari transcendit amarus   395
blanda fluenta latex, fluviique impacta per alveum
salsa peregrinum sibi navigat unda profundum.
hic iam disposito laxantes frena duello
Vesorum proceres raptim suspendit ab ira
rumor, succinctum referens diplomate Avitum   400
iam Geticas intrare domos positaque parumper
mole magisterii legati iura subisse.

" Obstupuere duces pariter Scythicusque senatus
et timuere, suam pacem ne forte negaret.
sic rutilus Phaetonta levem cum carperet axis   405
iam pallente die flagrantique excita mundo
pax elementorum fureret vel sicca propinquus
saeviret per stagna vapor limusque sitiret
pulvereo ponti fundo, tunc unica Phoebi
insuetum clemens exstinxit flamma calorem.   410

" Hic aliquis tum forte Getes, dum falce recocta
ictibus informat saxoque cacuminat ensem,
iam promptus caluisse tubis, iam iamque frequenti
caede sepulturus terram non hoste sepulto,
claruit ut primum nomen venientis Aviti,   415
exclamat: ' periit bellum, date rursus aratra.

400. succinctum *ego*: succincto.

---

[1] Sidonius likes to dwell on the tidal bores of the Garonne:
cf. 22. 18 sq.; *ib.* 105 sqq.; *Epist.* VIII. 12. 5.

[2] *Scyth.*, *i.e.* Gothic (5. 219 n.).

[3] The lightness of Phaethon helped to throw the chariot-
horses into confusion: Ovid, *Met.* II. 161 sq.

VII. PANEGYRIC ON AVITUS

throughout three monthly courses, when he set
himself on the march to the peoples and lands possessed by the bold Goth, where the ocean driven
onwards by the tide spreads the retreating Garonne
over the fields—for as the sea invades the river the
salt water climbs over the sweet flow, and the briny
flood, driven along the river-bed, rides on deeps that
are strange to it.[1] Here the chiefs of the Visigoths
were letting loose the war they had planned, when
suddenly their fury was checked by tidings that
Avitus, armed with an imperial writ, was already
entering the home of the Goths and, having laid
aside for a little the pomp of the Master's office, had
taken upon himself the authority of an ambassador.

"The Scythian[2] leaders and senate alike were
thunderstruck, and feared lest he should deny their
peaceful intent. Even thus, when the flaming
chariot was pulling the light[3] Phaethon this way and
that and the daylight was already dim, when the
harmony of the elements was stirred to fury by a
blazing world, when the hot breath came close and
ranged madly over the drying pools, and the parched
mud thirsted on the dusty bottom of the sea, then
Phoebus' gentle fire alone quenched that unwonted
heat.

"Hereupon, as it chanced, one of the Goths, who
had re-forged his pruning-hook and was shaping a
sword with blows on the anvil and sharpening it
with a stone, a man already prepared to rouse himself to fury at the sound of the trumpet and looking
at any moment with manifold slaughter to bury the
ground under unburied foes, cried out, as soon as the
name of the approaching Avitus was clearly proclaimed: 'War is no more! Give me the plough

153

THE POEMS OF SIDONIUS

otia si replico priscae bene nota quietis,
non semel iste mihi ferrum tulit.   o pudor! o di!
tantum posse fidem! quid foedera lenta minaris,
in damnum mihi fide meum? compendia pacis   420
et praestare iubes nos et debere.   quis umquam
crederet? en Getici reges, parere volentes,
inferius regnasse putant! nec dicere saltim
desidiae obtentu possum te proelia nolle:
pacem fortis amas.   iam partes sternit Avitus;   425
insuper et Geticas praemissus continet iras
Messianus; adhuc mandasti, et ponimus arma.
quid restat quod posse velis? quod non sumus hostes
parva reor; prisco tu si mihi notus in actu es,
auxiliaris ero: vel sic pugnare licebit.'   430
  " Haec secum rigido Vesus dum corde volutat,
ventum in conspectum fuerat.   rex atque magister
propter constiterant; hic vultu erectus, at ille
laetitia erubuit veniamque rubore poposcit.
post hinc germano regis, hinc rege retento   435
Palladiam implicitis manibus subiere Tolosam.
haud secus insertis ad pulvinaria palmis
Romulus et Tatius foedus iecere, parentum
cum ferro et rabidis cognato in Marte maritis
Hersilia inseruit Pallantis colle Sabinas.   440

---

¹ Messianus was one of Avitus's trusted officers, who afterwards went with him to Rome and received the title of patrician. He accompanied his master in his flight and was killed at Placentia, A.D. 456.
² The king is Theodoric II, the brother Friedrich (Fridericus). These two had in A.D. 453 murdered their brother Thorismund, who had succeeded Theodoric I. There is an interesting description of Theodoric II in *Epist* I. 2.
³ *Palladiam.* An epithet already applied by Martial and Ausonius to Toulouse as a home of the liberal arts.

again! If I recall the familiar old days of idle peace, he hath time and again taken the sword from me. O shame! O ye gods above! To think that faithful friendship should have such power! Why dost thou threaten me with tedious treaties, dealing loyally with me to my loss? Thou dost bid us both give to thee and owe to thee the advantages of peace. Who could have believed it? Lo! the Gothic kings are fain to yield obedience, and deem their royal power of less account than that. Nor can I even say that thou dost shun battle to screen a craven spirit; brave art thou, albeit thou lovest peace. Avitus is already ending the strife of parties, and Messianus[1] too, sent on before, is curbing the Gothic wrath. Thou hast as yet but sent thine orders, Avitus, and we are laying down our arms. What further power canst thou desire? I count it a small thing that we are not thine enemies; nay, if I have gained a right knowledge of thee in action aforetime, thine auxiliary will I be; thus at least I shall have leave to fight.'

"While the Visigoth revolved these thoughts in his stern heart they had come into view. The king and the Master took their stand near together, the Master with confident look, while the other blushed with joy and by his blush sued for clemency. Then Avitus kept on one side of him the king,[2] on the other side the king's brother, and with joined hands they entered Tolosa, city of Pallas.[3] Even thus with hand clasped in hand beside the couches of the gods did Romulus and Tatius establish their treaty, when Hersilia on the hill of Pallas thrust the Sabine women between their father's weapons and the husbands who were furiously battling against their kindred.

" Interea incautam furtivis Vandalus armis
te capit, infidoque tibi Burgundio ductu
extorquet trepidas mactandi principis iras.
heu facinus! in bella iterum quartosque labores
perfida Elisseae crudescunt classica Byrsae.   445
nutristis quod, fata, malum? conscenderat arces
Euandri Massyla phalanx montesque Quirini
Marmarici pressere pedes rursusque revexit
quae captiva dedit quondam stipendia Barce.
exsilium patrum, plebis mala, principe caeso   450
captivum imperium ad Geticas rumor tulit aures.
luce nova veterum coetus de more Getarum
contrahitur; stat prisca annis viridisque senectus
consiliis; squalent vestes ac sordida macro
lintea pinguescunt tergo, nec tangere possunt   455
altatae suram pelles, ac poplite nudo
peronem pauper nodus suspendit equinum.

" Postquam in consilium seniorum venit honora
pauperies pacisque simul rex verba poposcit,
dux ait: ' optassem patriïs securus in arvis   460
emeritam, fateor, semper fovisse quietem,
ex quo militiae post munia trina superbum

---

[1] It must not be forgotten that Jupiter is still addressing
Rome.

[2] Accounts of the murder of Petronius Maximus differ a
great deal, and we have no means of knowing what Sidonius
means by *Burgundio*.

[3] 2. 351 n.

[4] Avitus had gone to Toulouse to negotiate on behalf of
Petronius Maximus. These negotiations were apparently
not completed when news of the Emperor's death on May 31
arrived. Theodoric formed the plan of making Avitus Emperor and summoned his council. Avitus is represented as
appearing before the council in ignorance of the scheme on

VII. PANEGYRIC ON AVITUS

" Meanwhile, when thou [1] wert off thy guard, the Vandal with stealthy arms captured thee, and the Burgundian with his traitorous leadership extorted from thee the panic-fury that led to an emperor's slaughter.[2] Alas for the deed! Once more for war and for a fourth season of trouble the faithless war-trumpets of Dido's Byrsa [3] blare forth. O Destiny, what ill hast thou been fostering? A Massylian band had climbed Evander's height, Marmarican feet trampled Quirinus' hills, and Barce carried back the tribute that once she paid in her days of captivity. Rumour brought to Gothic ears the exile of the senate, the ills of the common folk, the Emperor's murder and the captivity of the Empire. At dawn of day a meeting of Gothic elders was assembled in the wonted fashion [4]; there stand they, old in years but hale in counsel; their dress is unkempt, tarnished and greasy are the linen garments on their lean backs; their coats of skin are drawn up high and cannot reach the calf; their knees are bare and their boots of horse-hide are held up by a common knot.

" When this company of elders, venerable for all their poverty, entered the council, and the king called for the proposals of peace, the general said: ' I confess that I would fain have cherished evermore in tranquillity among my paternal acres the rest that my toil has earned, now that after holding three commands [5] I have reached a fourth glory and held the

foot and merely making a strong plea for peace between the two nations.

[5] By *militiae munia* Sidonius certainly means military commands, not posts in the civil service. We learn from *v.* 315 that Avitus had held no civil office before he became *praefectus praetorio*.

praefecturae apicem quarto iam culmine rexi.
sed dum me nostri princeps modo Maximus orbis
ignarum, absentem procerum per mille repulsas   465
ad lituos post iura vocat voluitque sonoris
praeconem mutare tubis, promptissimus istud
arripui officium, vos quo legatus adirem.
foedera prisca precor, quae nunc meus ille teneret,
iussissem si forte, senex cui semper Avitum   470
sectari crevisse fuit.   tractare solebam
res Geticas olim; scis te nescisse frequenter
quae suasi nisi facta.   tamen fortuna priorem
abripuit genium; periit quodcumque merebar
cum genitore tuo.   Narbonem tabe solutum   475
ambierat (tu parvus eras); trepidantia cingens
milia in infames iam iamque coegerat escas;
iam tristis propriae credebat defore praedae,
si clausus fortasse perit, cum nostra probavit
consilia et refugo laxavit moenia bello.   480
teque ipsum (sunt ecce senes) hoc pectore fultum
hae flentem tenuere manus, si forsitan altrix
te mihi, cum nolles, lactandum tolleret.   ecce
advenio et prisci repeto modo pignus amoris.
si tibi nulla fides, nulla est reverentia patris,   485
i durus pacemque nega.'

"Prorumpit ab omni

---

¹ Theodoric I.
² See Introd., p. xvi.   The result of the siege of Narbonne
is described in 23. 59 sqq.   The relief of the town is elsewhere
attributed to Litorius.   We may assume that the arrival of
Litorius (and possibly a severe engagement with his troops)
inclined Theodoric to make a temporary peace, negotiated by
Avitus.   The Goths withdrew, but soon renewed hostilities,
which ended with the bloody battle of Toulouse.   It is most
probable that Avitus joined the army of Litorius on its way
to Narbonne and held a high command in it.

VII. PANEGYRIC ON AVITUS

supreme honour of the Prefecture.   But as Maximus, late sovereign of our western world, after a thousand refusals from our chieftest men, summoned me, all unsuspecting and far away, to serve amid the clarions of war after controlling the laws, and ordained that I should now hear the blaring trumpets instead of the court-usher's voice, then did I right readily embrace the duty, that I might go as ambassador to you.   I crave of you the old treaty, which even now that aged man, my one-time friend,[1] for whom to follow Avitus was always to grow greater, would be maintaining if only I had bidden him.   In former days I was wont to guide the doings of the Goths; thou knowest that my counsel was often acted on before thou wert aware of it.   But fate hath taken away from me my guardian-spirit of former days, and all my services have faded from sight along with thy father.   He had surrounded Narbo,[2] and it was enfeebled with wasting famine (thou wert then a child): hemming in those panic-stricken thousands he had all but driven them to eat of loathsome things, and already he had begun gloomily to think that some of his due spoil would be lost if haply the besieged perished within, when he gave ear to my advice, and withdrawing his arms relieved the walls from war.   And thee thyself (See! there are old men to witness it), these hands of mine have held weeping close to this breast, when perchance thy nurse was taking thee away from me to give thee suck and thou wert loth to go.   Behold! I come and seek now a fresh pledge of our old love.   If thou hast no loyalty, no reverence for thy father, then go thy harsh way and refuse peace.'

" From all the council arose murmurs and shout-

murmur concilio fremitusque, et proelia damnans
seditiosa ciet concordem turba tumultum.
tum rex effatur : ' dudum, dux inclite, culpo
poscere te pacem nostram, cum cogere possis   490
servitium, trahere ac populos in bella sequaces.
ne, quaeso, invidiam patrio mihi nomine inuras :
quid mereor, si nulla iubes ? suadere sub illo
quod poteras, modo velle sat est, solumque moratur,
quod cupias, nescisse Getas.   mihi Romula dudum
per te iura placent, parvumque ediscere iussit   496
ad tua verba pater docili quo prisca Maronis
carmine molliret Scythicos mihi pagina mores ;
iam pacem tum velle doces.   sed percipe quae sit
condicio obsequii : forsan rata pacta probabis.   500
testor, Roma, tuum nobis venerabile nomen
et socium de Marte genus (vel quidquid ab aevo,
nil te mundus habet melius, nil ipsa senatu),
me pacem servare tibi vel velle abolere
quae noster peccavit avus, quem fuscat id unum,   505
quod te, Roma, capit ; sed di si vota secundant,
excidii veteris crimen purgare valebit
ultio praesentis, si tu, dux inclite, solum

---

[1] The following lines refer to the episode described in *vv.*
215–226. That passage seems to imply that the visit to
Theodorus was the first occasion on which Avitus met Theodoric I. The most probable date for the visit is A.D. 430 or a
little later. *Vv.* 233–235 do not necessarily rule out A.D. 430
(see n.). Between that year and 435, when Avitus took part
in the war against the Burgundians, the Goths seem to have
been comparatively quiet, and Avitus may have remained at
the Gothic court for a considerable time, acting as tutor to
the young prince. There is no need to assume any further
sojourn among the Goths, apart from the official missions
described in this poem. As for *vv.* 481–483, they are probably
an empty rhetorical flourish.

ing; the insurgent crowd, condemning war, raised a friendly uproar. Then out spake the king: ' O leader renowned, I have long been blaming thee for begging peace from us when thou hast power to enforce bondage and draw willing peoples to war in thy train. I beseech thee, brand me not with obloquy by bringing up my father's name. What blame can be mine if thou give me no orders? What thou mightest have advised in his day thou needst now but desire; the only hindrance is that the Goths have not learnt what thou wouldst have. [1] Thanks to thee the laws of Rome have long been pleasing to me; when I was a child my father bade me learn lines by heart at thine instruction, that those strains of Virgil's ancient page, taught to thy willing pupil, might soften my Scythian ways; even then thou didst teach me to desire peace. But hear now the terms of my obedience, and perhaps thou wilt be pleased to sanction a compact. I swear, O Rome, by thy name, revered by me, and by our common descent from Mars [2] (for among all things that have been since the beginning of time the world hath naught greater than thee and thou hast naught greater than the senate): I desire to keep the peace with thee and to wipe out the transgressions of my grandsire,[3] whose one blot is that he captured thee; but if the gods bless my prayer, the guilt of that ancient destruction can be atoned for by avenging that of to-day [4]—if only thou, renowned leader,

[2] Jord. *Get.* 5 states that Mars is said to have dwelt for a long time among the Goths. With this tradition he associates Verg. *Aen.* III. 35, where Mars is said to be a tutelary deity of the *Getica arva*.

[3] Alaric, who captured Rome, A.D. 410.

[4] *i.e.* the capture by Geiseric.

Augusti subeas nomen. quid lumina flectis?
invitum plus esse decet. non cogimus istud,   510
sed contestamur: Romae sum te duce amicus,
principe te miles. regnum non praeripis ulli,
nec quisquam Latias Augustus possidet arces;
qua vacat, aula tua est. testor, non sufficit istud,
ne noceam; atque tuo hoc utinam diademate fiat, 515
ut prosim! suadere meum est; nam Gallia si te
compulerit, quae iure potest, tibi pareat orbis,
ne pereat.' dixit pariterque in verba petita
dat sanctam cum fratre fidem. discedis, Avite,
maestus, qui Gallos scires non posse latere   520
quod possint servire Getae te principe. namque
civibus ut patuit trepidis te foedera ferre,
occurrunt alacres ignaroque ante tribunal
sternunt; utque satis sibimet numerosa coisse
nobilitas visa est, quam saxa nivalia Cotti   525
despectant, variis nec non quam partibus ambit
Tyrrheni Rhenique liquor, vel longa Pyrenei
quam iuga ab Hispano seclusam iure cohercent,
aggreditur nimio curarum pondere tristem
gaudens turba virum. procerum tum· maximus
    unus,   530
dignus qui patriae personam sumeret, infit:
' quam nos per varios dudum fortuna labores

521. quod *Mohr* : quid.

VII. PANEGYRIC ON AVITUS

shouldst take upon thee the name of Augustus.
Why dost thou avert thine eyes? Thine unwilling-
ness becomes thee all the more. We do not force
this on thee, but we adjure thee: with thee as
leader I am a friend of Rome, with thee as Emperor
I am her soldier. Thou art not stealing the
sovereignty from any man; no Augustus holds the
Latian hills, a palace without a master is thine. I
protest, it is not enough that I do thee no harm; I
would that thine imperial diadem might bring me
the means to do thee service. My part is but to
urge thee; but if Gaul should compel thee, as she
has the right to do, the world would cherish thy
sway, lest it perish.' He spake, and straightway with
his brother gave his solemn pledge in the form of
words desired. But thou, Avitus, didst depart in
sadness, knowing it could not be hidden from the
Gauls that the Goths could be at their service if
thou wert Emperor. Yea, when it was revealed to
the anxious citizens that thou wert carrying back
with thee a treaty, they eagerly rushed to meet
thee, and without thy knowing it they spread a
tribunal for thee beforehand, and when the crowds
of nobles deemed they were assembled in sufficient
multitude—those on whom the snowy rocks of the
Cottian Alps look down, those around whom in their
sundry regions wind the waters of the Tuscan sea
or the Rhine, and those whom the long ridges of the
Pyrenees shut off from Spanish rule—then did that
throng approach with joy that man oppressed by a
crushing load of care. Thereupon the oldest of all those
lords, one right worthy to be his country's spokesman, thus began: ' Of the cruel fortune that hath
long harassed us with divers hardships under a boy-

principe sub puero laceris terat aspera rebus,
fors longum, dux magne, queri, cum quippe dolentum
maxima pars fueris, patriae dum vulnera lugens   535
sollicitudinibus vehementibus exagitaris.
has nobis inter clades ac funera mundi
mors vixisse fuit.   sed dum per verba parentum
ignavas colimus leges sanctumque putamus
rem veterem per damna sequi, portavimus um-
    bram   540
imperii, generis contenti ferre vetusti
et vitia ac solitam vestiri murice gentem
more magis quam iure pati.   promptissima nuper
fulsit condicio proprias qua Gallia vires
exsereret, trepidam dum Maximus occupat ur-
    bem;   545
orbem sat potuit, si te sibi tota magistro
regna reformasset.   quis nostrum Belgica rura,
litus Aremorici, Geticas quis moverit iras,
non latet: his tantis tibi cessimus, inclite, bellis.
nunc iam summa vocant; dubio sub tempore reg-
    num   550
non regit ignavus.   postponitur ambitus omnis
ultima cum claros quaerunt: post damna Ticini
ac Trebiae trepidans raptim respublica venit
ad Fabium; Cannas celebres Varrone fugato
Scipiadumque etiam turgentem funere Poenum   555
Livius electus fregit.   captivus, ut aiunt,
orbis in urbe iacet; princeps perit, hic caput omne
nunc habet imperium.   petimus, conscende tribunal,

---

546. orbem sat potuit *Leo*: orbem ego sat potui *MC*, orbem
immo potuit *TF*.

[1] Referring to Valentinian III.
[2] This refers to Avitus's organisation of resistance to
Attila; see *vv.* 316–356.

emperor,[1] tearing our prosperity to shreds, it would belike be tedious to make plaint, O mighty leader, since verily thou wert the chiefest figure among the mourners, lamenting ever thy country's wounds and tortured by uncontrollable anxieties. Amid those calamities, that universal destruction, to live was death. But as we, taught by our fathers' words, paid homage to idle laws and deemed it a hallowed duty to cling to the old order even through disasters, we endured that shadow of Empire, content to bear even the vices of an ancient stock and to tolerate, more from custom than by reason of just claim, a house that had been wont to be invested with the purple. Of late a golden opportunity shone forth, whereby Gaul might make her own strength felt, while Maximus was possessing himself of the panic-stricken capital; and she might well have possessed herself of the world if with thee as Master she had restored to herself all her rightful lands. 'Tis no secret who of us it was that stirred up the Belgian land, the Aremorican shore and the Gothic fury.[2] In this dread warfare we yielded pride of place to thee, renowned one. Now the supreme office calls for thee; in time of peril a realm cannot be ruled by a poltroon. All ambitious rivalry gives place when extremity calls for men of renown. After the losses of Ticinum and Trebia the trembling republic came in haste to Fabius. By the election of Livius the disaster of Cannae, famous for Varro's rout, was undone; undone too was the Carthaginian, still exulting over the deaths of the Scipios. The world, they say, lies captive in the captive city; the Emperor has perished, and now the Empire has its head here. Ascend the tribunal, we beseech thee, and raise up

erige collapsos ; non hoc modo tempora poscunt,
ut Romam plus alter amet.   nec forte reare   560
te regno non esse parem : cum Brennica signa
Tarpeium premerent, scis, tum respublica nostra
tota Camillus erat, patriae qui debitus ultor
texit fumantes hostili strage favillas.
non tibi centurias aurum populare paravit,   565
nec modo venales numerosoque asse redemptae
concurrunt ad puncta tribus ; suffragia mundi
nullus emit.   pauper legeris ; quod sufficit unum,
es meritis dives.   patriae cur vota moraris,
quae iubet ut iubeas ? haec est sententia cunctis : 570
si dominus fis, liber ero.'

                        " Fragor atria complet
Vierni, quo forte loco pia turba senatus
detulerat vim, vota, preces.   locus, hora diesque
dicitur imperio felix, ac protinus illic
nobilium excubias gaudens sollertia mandat.   575

   " Tertia lux refugis Hyperiona fuderat astris :
concurrunt proceres ac milite circumfuso
aggere composito statuunt ac torque coronant
castrensi maestum donantque insignia regni ;
nam prius induerat solas de principe curas.   580
haud alio quondam vultu Tirynthius heros

        572. uierni *M*, Ugerni *Sirmond.* : t(h)ierni.
        580. nam *Mohr* : iam.

   [1] Viernum, or Ugernum, modern Beaucaire, near Arles. The
meeting here referred to was a hastily summoned assembly
of Gallic notabilities, not the representative assembly of Gaul
(on which see Introd. p. xii, Bury I. pp. 207 sq.), which met at
Arles.

the fainting; this time of peril asks not that some other should love Rome more. Nor do thou by any chance deem thyself unequal to sovereignty. When Brennus' host beset the Tarpeian rock, then, thou knowest, Camillus was himself the whole of our state, and he, the destined avenger of his country, covered the smoking embers of the city with the slaughtered enemy. No gold scattered among the people hath secured for thee the verdict of the centuries; this time no venal tribes bought with plenteous coin rush to give their votes; the suffrages of the world no one can buy. Though a poor man, thou art being chosen; rich art thou in thy deserts, and that suffices in itself. Why dost thou hinder the desires of thy country, when she orders thee to give orders to her? This is the judgment of all: " if thou becomest the master I shall be free." '

" Then a great clamour filled the hall of Viernum [1] (for it was in this place, as it chanced, that the senate's devoted throng had brought before him the force of its authority, its desires, and its prayers). Place, hour, and day are declared auspicious for the assumption of empire, and straightway those resourceful nobles joyously order a guard to be set there.

" The third day had spread the sun's light over the retreating stars : the lords of the land assemble in haste and with soldiers all around set him on a mound-platform [2]; there they crown their sorrowing chief with a military collar and present him with the outward emblems of sovereignty (hitherto the only attribute of an Emperor he had assumed was his cares). With such a look did the Tirynthian hero

---

[2] The next stage was the proclamation of the Emperor by the soldiers.

pondera suscepit caeli simul atque novercae
cum Libyca se rupe Gigas subduceret et cum
tutior Herculeo sedisset machina dorso.

  "Hunc tibi, Roma, dedi, patulis dum Gallia
      campis   585
intonat Augustum plausu faustumque fragorem
portat in exsanguem Boreas iam fortior Austrum.
hic tibi restituet Libyen per vincula quarta,
et cuius solum amissas post saecula multa
Pannonias revocavit iter, iam credere promptum
     est   590
quid faciat bellis. o quas tibi saepe iugabit
inflictis gentes aquilis, qui maxima regni
omina privatus fugit, cum forte vianti
excuteret praepes plebeium motus amictum!
laetior at tanto modo principe, prisca deorum   595
Roma parens, attolle genas ac turpe veternum
depone: en princeps faciet iuvenescere maior,
quam pueri fecere senem."

                             Finem pater ore
vix dederat: plausere dei fremitusque cucurrit

---

[1] Juno. Her jealous hatred dogged Hercules from his
birth, and was the prime cause of his "labours." It was while
engaged on one of these (the quest of the golden apples)
that he temporarily took the burden of the heavens from the
shoulders of Atlas (the "giant" of this passage).

[2] *i.e.* the Vandals, now pale with fright.

[3] A very mysterious allusion. Avitus was proclaimed
Emperor in July and reached Rome in September, A.D. 455.
There is no reason to believe that he took a long time over his
journey; the statement sometimes made that he left Gaul in
July has neither common sense nor ancient authority to support
it. It is scarcely credible that he turned aside at this time to
make a demonstration against the "barbarians" in Pannonia.
He may have sent a force under one of his generals; it was

of old take upon him the burden alike of the sky and of his stepmother [1] when the giant withdrew himself from the Libyan mount and the firmament had sunk with greater safety upon the back of Hercules.

" This man I have given thee, Rome, while Gaul throughout her wide plains thunders with plaudits for Augustus, and the north, now stronger, carries the auspicious clamour to the pale-cheeked south.[2] He shall restore Libya to thee a fourth time in chains —and when a man has recovered the lost Pannonias after so many generations by a mere march,[3] 'tis easy to feel sure even now of what he can do by waging war. How he shall, time and again, bring nations under thy yoke, dashing his eagles against them!—that man who as a subject shrank from the glorious omens of sovereignty, when it chanced that as he journeyed a startled bird struck from his shoulders the common cloak he wore. But now be of good cheer with such a man for Emperor, O Rome, ancient mother of gods; lift up thine eyes and cast off thine unseemly gloom. Lo! a prince of riper years shall bring back youth to thee, whom child-princes have made old."

The great Father had scarce ended his utterance when the gods clapped their hands and a shout of

quite in order to give the Emperor credit for a military success won under his auspices. If Avitus did not lead the expedition it may have taken place even after his arrival in Rome. It is, however, probable that *iter* means the journey of Avitus from Gaul to Rome, and that in the course of it there came some good news or friendly overtures from Pannonia, which Sidonius attributes to the prestige of the new Emperor and the fear produced by his journey southward. The contrast of *iter* with *bellis* seems to imply that there was no fighting on this occasion.

concilio.   felix tempus nevere sorores   600
imperiis, Auguste, tuis et consulis anno
fulva volubilibus duxerunt saecula pensis.

VIII

AD PRISCVM VALERIANVM VIRVM
PRAEFECTORIVM

Prisce, decus semper nostrum, cui principe Avito
  cognatum sociat purpura celsa genus,
ad tua cum nostrae currant examina nugae,
  dico: " state, vagae; quo properatis? amat.
destrictus semper censor, qui diligit, exstat;   5
  dura fronte legit mollis amicitia.
nil totum prodest adiectum laudibus illud
  Vlpia quod rutilat porticus aere meo
vel quod adhuc populo simul et plaudente senatu
  ad nostrum reboat concava Roma sophos."   10
respondent illae: " properabimus, ibimus, et nos
  non retines: tanto iudice culpa placet.
cognitor hoc nullus melior; bene carmina pensat
  contemptu tardo, iudicio celeri."
et quia non potui temeraria sistere verba,   15
  hoc rogo, ne dubites lecta dicare rogo.

---

[1] Almost the only information which we have about Priscus
Valerianus is derived from this poem and from *Epist.* V. 10.
The superscription of the poem shows that Valerianus had
risen to be Praetorian Prefect of Gaul, but does not, as some
authorities suppose, state that he held that office at the time
when the verses were written.

[2] For the statue of Sidonius in Trajan's Forum see Introd.,
p. xxxvii.

170

applause rang through the council. The fateful
Sisters spun out a happy time for thy rule, Augustus,
and for thy consular year they drew out with their
whirling spindles a golden age.

VIII

TO PRISCUS VALERIANUS, OF PREFECTORIAN RANK [1]

Priscus, my unceasing pride, whose race is by
right of kinship linked with the majestic purple,
now that Avitus is Emperor: as my trifling effusions
are hurrying off to encounter your judgment, I say,
" Halt, flighty creatures! Whither are you hastening?
He loves me, and he who loves ever shows himself an
unsparing judge; gentle friendship reads with harsh
brow. It boots me not that there is added to the tale
of my merits all the glory of my form in bronze [2]
gleaming red in the Ulpian portico and the huzzas
for me that still re-echo from the recesses of Rome's
hills,[3] while senate and people alike sound my
praises." Then they reply: " We *will* hasten, we
will go, and you shall not hold us back. With such
a man to judge us even censure is sweet. There is
no better critic than he; skilfully does he weigh
poems, and though quick of judgment he is slow to
scorn." And so, as I could not keep my reckless
verses from going, hesitate not, when you have read
them, to let the fire prey on them, I pray you.

[3] *Concava Roma* is a bold expression, in which *concava* is
even more difficult to translate than it is in Verg. *Georg.*
IV. 49 (also referring to echoes), *concava pulsu saxa sonant.*
The circle of Rome's hills suggests the idea of a building with
concave walls, from which echoes are flung back.

IX

AD FELICEM

LARGAM SOLLIVS HANC APOLLINARIS
FELICI DOMINO PIOQVE FRATRI
DICIT SIDONIVS SVVS SALVTEM.

Dic, dic quod peto, Magne, dic, amabo,
Felix nomine, mente, honore, forma,   5
natis, coniuge, fratribus, parente,
germanis genitoris atque matris
et summo patruelium Camillo:
quid nugas temerarias amici,
sparsit quas tenerae iocus iuventae,   10
in formam redigi iubes libelli,
ingentem simul et repente fascem
conflari invidiae et perire chartam?
mandatis famulor, sed ante testor,
lector quas patieris hic salebras.   15
Non nos currimus aggerem vetustum
nec quicquam invenies ubi priorum
antiquas terat orbitas Thalia.
non hic antipodas salumque rubrum,
non hic Memnonios canemus Indos   20
Aurorae face civica perustos;
non Artaxata, Susa, Bactra, Carrhas,
non coctam Babylona personabo,

---

¹ Magnus Felix, son of Magnus (23. 455 n.), was a schoolfellow of Sidonius (v. 330, below). He rose to be Praetorian
Prefect of Gaul and Patrician. He lived in Narbonne. *Epist.*
II. 3, III. 4 and 7, IV. 5 and 10 are addressed to him. See
also *Carm.* 24. 91 and, for his connexion with Philagrius, n.
on 7. 156.

² The wife's name was Attica. An extant epigram records
that she built a church.

IX. TO FELIX

IX

TO FELIX

To the Lord Felix,
His Loving Brother,
Sollius Apollinaris Sidonius
Hereby Gives Heartiest Greeting.

Come tell me, tell me what I want to know, tell me, Magnus,[1] please, Magnus Felix, felicitous in your name, in your intellect, in your eminence, your person, your children, wife,[2] brothers,[3] parents, your father's and mother's brothers,[4] and that chiefest of all cousins, Camillus [5]—why do you demand that the thoughtless scribblings of your friend, broadcast in the frolicsome spirit of early youth, should be put into book-form, and thus a great bundle of enmity should suddenly be produced and paper wasted at the same time? I bow to your commands, but first I declare to you what jolts you are going to suffer here as you read.

I am not speeding over the old road; you shall find here no place where my muse treads in the antique ruts of my predecessors. I shall not here sing of Antipodes or Red Sea or Memnon's Indians burnt by Aurora's torch blazing in her homeland. I shall not trumpet forth Artaxata, Susa, Bactra, Carrhae or brick-built Babylon, which opens out

[3] Probus (24. 94 n.) was a brother of Felix. Araneola, for whose marriage Sidonius wrote *Carm.* 14 and 15, may have been a sister. *Fratres* may mean " brother and sister."
[4] One of the brothers of Magnus was the father of Camillus. He was a proconsul before A.D. 461 (*Epist.* I. 11. 10).
[5] Camillus, as we learn from *Epist.* I. 11. 10 sq., held two high offices of state and received the title of *inlustris*.

quae largum fluvio patens alumno
inclusum bibit hinc et inde Tigrim.   25
non hic Assyriis Ninum priorem,
non Medis caput Arbacen profabor,
nec quam divite, cum refugit hostem,
arsit Sardanapallus in favilla.
non Cyrum Astyagis loquar nepotem,   30
nutritum ubere quem ferunt canino,
cuius non valuit rapacitatem
vel Lydi satiare gaza Croesi ;
cuius nec feritas subacta tunc est,
caesis milibus ante cum ducentis   35
in vallis Scythicae coactus artum
orbatae ad Tomyris veniret utrem.

Non hic Cecropios leges triumphos,
vel si quo Marathon rubet duello,
aut, cum milia mille concitaret,   40
inflatum numerositate Xerxen,
atque hunc fluminibus satis profundis
confestim ebibitis adhuc sitisse ;
nec non Thermopylas et Helles undas
spretis obicibus soli salique   45
insanis equitasse cum catervis
admissoque in Athon tumente ponto
iuxta frondiferae cacumen Alpis
scalptas classibus isse per cavernas.

Non prolem Garamantici Tonantis,   50
regnis principibusque principantem,
porrectas Asiae loquar paterno
actum fulmine pervolasse terras

44. Helles *Luc. Mueller* : hel(l)is.

_____

[1] " Tigris " should be " Euphrates."
[2] Cyrus had slain the son of Tomyris, queen of the Massage-

afar to receive the stream that nourishes it and so drinks the Tigris [1] on both banks within the walls. I shall not here proclaim the earlier Ninus of the Assyrians nor Arbaces, head of the Medes, nor the richness of the pyre on which Sardanapallus burned when he sought refuge from the foe. I shall not tell of Astyages' grandson, Cyrus, who they say was suckled at a bitch's breast, a man whose greed not even the treasure of Lydian Croesus could sate, whose fierceness was not subdued even when, having slain two hundred thousand, he was hemmed within a narrow Scythian valley and drew nigh to the bag of the bereaved Tomyris.[2]

You shall not read here of Athenian triumphs or of any war that may have dyed Marathon red, or how Xerxes, stirring up a thousand thousand men, was puffed up by their multitudinousness, or how, when rivers of great depth had been drunk up in a trice, he still thirsted, or the tale of Thermopylae, or how, scorning the barriers of land and sea, he rode with his mad hordes over the waters that Helle named [3] and, letting into Athos waves that rose well-nigh to the summit of that leafy Alp, he passed on shipboard through the deep channel he had cut.

I shall not relate how the offspring of the Garamantian Thunder-god,[4] lording it over lords and kingdoms, was sped on by his father's thunderbolt and swept through Asia's widespread lands; how

tae. Soon afterwards she enticed the Persians into a narrow pass, and slew Cyrus and all his men. She ordered his head to be cut off and thrown into a bag filled with blood, thus reviling his cruelty : " Sate yourself with the blood for which you thirsted insatiably."

[3] The Hellespont.

[4] Alexander the Great : see 2. 121-126.

et primum Darii tumultuantes
praefectos satrapasque perculisse,   55
mox ipsum solio patrum superbum
cognatosque sibi deos crepantem
captis coniuge, liberis, parente
in casus hominis redire iussum ;
qui cum maxima bella concitasset   60
tota et Persidis undique gregatae
uno constituisset arma campo,
hoc solum perhibetur assecutus,
dormire ut melius liberet hosti.
   Non vectos Minyas loquente silva   65
dicam Phasiaco stetisse portu,
forma percita cum ducis Pelasgi
molliret rabidos virago tauros,
nec tum territa, cum suus colonus
post anguis domiti satos molares   70
armatas tremebundus inter herbas
florere in segetem stuperet hostem
et pugnantibus hinc et hinc aristis
supra belliferas madere glaebas
culmosos viridi cruore fratres.   75
   Non hic terrigenam loquar cohortem
admixto mage vividam veneno,
cui praeter speciem modo carentem
angues corporibus voluminosis
alte squamea crura porrigentes   80
in vestigia fauce desinebant.

65. vescos (vescas F) codd.

---

[1] The "plain" is that of Gaugamela, where Alexander
routed Darius and overthrew the Persian Empire (331 B.C.,
the so-called Battle of Arbela). On the day appointed for
the battle Alexander slept until an alarmingly late hour.
When Parmenio with difficulty awoke him and asked how he

he first laid low in confusion the governors and
satraps of Darius and then the king himself, a
monarch that proudly exulted in the throne of his
father and prated of his kin the gods, but now,
with wife, children and mother captured, was forced
to relapse into a mere mortal's lot, and who, 'tis
said, when he had stirred up a mighty war and had
set in one plain the whole armed force of Persia
gathered from every part, won thereby this one
thing only—that his enemy was disposed to sleep the
better for it.[1]

Nor shall I tell how the Minyae were carried over the
sea by the talking timber [2] and halted in the harbour
of the Phasis, what time the man-like maid, smitten
by the beauty of the Grecian leader, soothed the
raging bulls and knew no terror even when he whom
she had made a tiller of the soil had sown the teeth
of the vanquished serpent and stood trembling amid
the armed shoots, aghast to see a foe burst into
crop and the spikes take sides and fight with one
another, while over the war-breeding clods the
stalky brothers dripped with green blood.

I shall not here speak of the earth-born band
made more live by the venom in their veins, who,
besides a form that had outgrown all limits, had
likewise snakes with coiling bodies, extending their
scaly legs on high and ending in mouths that served

could possibly sleep so long on that most important of all
days, Alexander answered, "Don't you think the victory
is as good as won, now that we are freed from the necessity
of roaming far and wide over desolate country in pursuit
of the elusive Darius?" (Plutarch, *Alex.* 32). The "wife,
children and mother" of Darius were captured at the Battle
of Issus (333 B.C.).

[2] One plank of the *Argo* was endowed with speech.

sic formae triplicis procax iuventus
tellurem pede proterens voraci
currebat capitum stupenda gressu
et cum classica numinum sonabant   85
mox contra tonitrus resibilante
audebat superos ciere planta.
nec Phlegrae legis ampliata rura,
missi dum volitant per astra montes
Pindus, Pelion, Ossa, Olympus, Othrys   90
cum silvis, gregibus, feris, pruinis,
saxis, fontibus, oppidis levati
vibrantum spatiosiore dextra.
     Non hic Herculis excolam labores,
cui sus, cerva, leo, Gigas, Amazon,   95
hospes, taurus, Eryx, aves, Lycus, fur,
Nessus, Libs, iuga, poma, virgo, serpens,
Oete, Thraces equi, boves Hiberae,
luctator fluvius, canis triformis
portatusque polus polum dederunt.   100
     Non hic Elida nobilem quadrigis
nec notam nimis amnis ex amore
versu prosequar, ut per ima ponti
Alpheus fluat atque transmarina
in fluctus cadat unda coniugales.   105
     Non hic Tantaleam domum retexam,
qua mixtum Pelopea per parentem est
prolis facta soror novoque monstro
infamem genuit pater nepotem;
nil maestum hic canitur; nec esculentam   110

---

[1] Cf. 6. 26.
[2] The plains are " enlarged " by the removal of the mountains.

as feet.[1] Thus that arrogant young band of triple-formed monsters, trampling the earth with ravenous feet, would run in marvellous wise with stepping heads; and when the war-trumps of the gods sounded they thereupon dared to challenge the denizens of heaven with foot hissing in reply to the thunder's roar. Nor do you read here of Phlegra's plains enlarged [2] when hurtling mountains flew about among the stars, Pindus, Pelion, Ossa, Olympus, Othrys, with their woods, herds, beasts, frosts, rocks, springs, and towns, all uplifted by the hurlers' right hands that were broader than they.

I shall not here embellish the labours of Hercules,[3] to whom boar, deer, lion, giant, Amazon, host, bull, Eryx, birds, Lycus, thief, Nessus, Libyan, hills, apples, maid, serpent, Oeta, Thracian steeds, Spanish cows, wrestling river, tri-formed dog and the carrying of heaven gave heaven as a reward.

I shall not here celebrate in verse Elis renowned for the four-horse chariots nor her who is so famed for a river's love,[4] telling how Alpheus flows through the lowest deeps of the sea and the water on the other side falls into the connubial waves.

I shall not here recall the house of Tantalus, wherein Pelopea by union with a father became the sister of her children and her father by an unheard-of deed of horror begat an infamous grandson. Nothing doleful is here sung; I do not relate the

---

[3] Cf. 15. 141 sqq. Most of the references are obvious. The "giant" is perhaps Typhoeus, the "host" is probably Busiris, the "thief" is Cacus, the "Libyan" is Antaeus, the "hills" are Calpe and Abyla (the "Pillars of Hercules"), the "maid" is Hesione, the "Thracian steeds" are those of Diomede.

[4] Arethusa.

fletus pingimus ad dapem Thyestae,
fratris crimine qui miser voratis
vivum pignoribus fuit sepulcrum,
cum post has epulas repente flexis
Titan curribus occidens ad ortum   115
convivam fugeret, diem fugaret.

    Nec Phryx pastor erit tibi legendus,
decrescens cui Dindymon reciso
fertur vertice texuisse classem,
cum iussu Veneris patrocinantis   120
terras Oebalias et hospitales
raptor depopulatus est Amyclas,
praedam trans pelagus petens sequacem.
sed nec Pergama nec decenne bellum
nec saevas Agamemnonis phalangas   125
nec periuria persequar Sinonis,
arx quo Palladio dicata signo
pellaci reserata proditore
portantem pedites equum recepit.

    Non hic Maeoniae stilo Camenae   130
civis Dulichiique Thessalique
virtutem sapientiamque narro,
quorum hic Peliaco putatur antro
venatu, fidibus, palaestra et herbis
sub Saturnigena sene institutus,   135
dum nunc lustra terens puer ferarum
passim per Pholoen iacet nivosam,
nunc praesepibus accubans amatis
dormit mollius in iuba magistri;
inde Scyriadum datus parenti   140
falsae nomina pertulisse Pyrrhae

    111. pingimus : pangimus *vulgo*, fingimus *Buecheler*.

---

[1] *i.e.* the sun, when in the middle of its course, suddenly
turned back, making the day retreat.

IX. TO FELIX

weeping of Thyestes at the gluttonous feast, who by his brother's crime, unhappy one, was a living tomb for the children he devoured, while the sun, after that horrible banquet, suddenly turning his car, set toward the east, and fleeing from the feaster put the day to flight.[1]

Nor shall you have to read of the Phrygian shepherd[2] for whom, 'tis said, Dindymon[3] grew smaller and with her lopped crest formed a fleet, when by order of Venus his abettor that ravisher despoiled the land of Oebalia and hospitable Amyclae, seeking across the sea a prey that willingly followed him. Nay, I shall not go over the tale of Troy and the ten years' war and the fierce battalions of Agamemnon and the treachery of Sinon whereby the citadel dedicated to the image of Pallas was laid open through the work of a wily betrayer and admitted the horse that carried foot-soldiers.

I do not here relate with the pen of the Maeonian muse the wisdom of the Dulichian and the valour of the Thessalian[4]; of whom the second is deemed to have been trained in a cave of Pelion under an aged son of Saturn[5] in hunting, in the music of the lyre, in wrestling and in the use of simples; and the boy, as he scoured the wild beasts' haunts, would sometimes repose on any part of snowy Pholoe, at other times he would recline in the well-loved stall, sleeping more comfortably on his tutor's mane; then, says the story, he was given to the father of the Scyrian maids, enduring the false name of

[2] Paris.
[3] Sidonius is here imitating Statius *Silv.* I. 1. 10, the only other passage where the nominative form *Dindymon* occurs. *Dindymus* and *Dindyma* (plur.) are the usual forms.
[4] Ulysses and Achilles.   [5] Chiron.

atque inter tetricae choros Minervae
occultos Veneri rotasse thyrsos;
postremo ad Phrygiae sonum rapinae
tractus laudibus Hectoris trahendi.   145
ast illum, cui contigit paternam
quartum post Ithacam redire lustrum,
nec Zmyrnae satis explicat volumen.
nam quis continuare possit illos
quos terra et pelago tulit labores: 150
raptum Palladium, repertum Achillem,
captum praepetibus Dolona plantis
et Rhesi niveas prius quadrigas
Xanthi quam biberent fluenta tractas,
ereptam quoque quam deus patronus,   155
Philocteta, tibi dedit pharetram,
Aiacem Telamonium furentem
quod sese ante rates agente causam
pugnacis tulit eloquens coronam,
vitatum hinc Polyphemon atque Circen   160
et Laestrygonii famem tyranni,
tum pomaria divitis, Calypso et
Sirenas pereuntibus placentes,
vitatas tenebras facemque Naupli
et Scyllae rabidum voracis inguen   165
vel Tauromenitana quos Charybdis
ructato scopulos cavat profundo?
    Non divos specialibus faventes
agris, urbibus insulisque canto,
Saturnum Latio Iovemque Cretae   170
Iunonemque Samo Rhodoque Solem,
Hennae Persephonen, Minervam Hymetto,
Vulcanum Liparae, Papho Dionen,

---

[1] Or perhaps " by the glorious prospect of dragging Hector."

Pyrrha, and amid the band of stern Minerva's votaries he honoured Venus in secret revels: lastly, when the noise of the Phrygian spoiling reached his ears, he was dragged away by the glories of that Hector who would himself one day be dragged.[1] But as for the other hero, whose hap it was to return to Ithaca, the land of his father, after four lustres had passed, even Smyrna's scroll[2] does not unfold the whole tale. Nay, who could relate the whole succession of toils that he endured on land and sea—the seizing of the Palladium, the finding of Achilles, the capture of swift-footed Dolon, and the four snow-white chariot-horses of Rhesus taken away before they could drink of Xanthus' stream; likewise the snatching of the quiver given to Philoctetes by his patron god and the madness of Ajax son of Telamon because when he stood before the ships and pled his cause the man of words won the prize of the man of arms; then the escape from Polyphemus, from Circe, and from the hunger of the Laestrygonian king, and thereafter the rich man's orchard, and Calypso and the Sirens who charmed men to their doom; his escape likewise from the darkness and the torch of Nauplius[3] and the raging groin of ravening Scylla and the rocks that Charybdis of Tauromenium hollows out by the belching of the deep?

I sing not of the divinities that show favour to special lands, cities, and islands; Saturn to Latium, Jove to Crete, Juno to Samos, the Sun-god to Rhodes, Proserpine to Henna, Minerva to Hymettus, Vulcan to Lipara, Dione to Paphos, Perseus to Argos,

[2] Homer.
[3] Nauplius, by showing false lights on the cliffs of Euboea, wrecked the Greek ships on their way back from Troy.

Argis Persea, Lampsaco Priapum,
Thebis Euhion Ilioque Vestam,   175
Thymbrae Delion, Arcadem Lycaeo,
Martem Thracibus ac Scythis Dianam,
quos fecere deos dicata templa,
tus, sal, far, mola vel superfluarum
consecratio caerimoniarum.   180
    Non cum Triptolemo verendam Eleusin,
qui primas populis dedere aristas
pastis Chaonium per ilicetum,
non Apin Mareoticum sonabo
ad Memphitica sistra concitari.   185
non dicam Lacedaemonos iuventam
unctas Tyndaridis dicasse luctas,
doctos quos patriis palen Therapnis
gymnas Bebrycii tremit theatri;
non sortes Lyciasque Caeritumque,   190
responsa aut Themidis priora Delphis,
nec quae fulmine Tuscus expiato
saeptum numina quaerit ad bidental;
nec quos Euganeum bibens Timavum
colle Antenoreo videbat augur   195
divos Thessalicam movere pugnam;
nec quos Amphiaraus et Melampus
              *   *   *
ex ipsis rapuit deos favillis
per templum male fluctuante flamma
gaudens lumine perdito Metellus.   200

---

[1] See 5. 163 n.
[2] A place struck by lightning. Such places were *loca religiosa, i.e.* a taboo was attached to them. The lightning was ceremonially " buried " (*fulmen condere*) and a sheep sacrificed (hence the name, from *bidens*); then the spot was doubly enclosed by a high kerb and an outer wall. At Rome

IX. TO FELIX

Priapus to Lampsacus, Bacchus to Thebes, Vesta
to Ilium, the Delian god to Thymbra, the Arcadian
to Lycaeus, Mars to Thrace, Diana to Scythia, who
have all been made gods by the dedication of temples
to them, by incense, salt, spelt, meal, and the
hallowing of vain rites.

I shall not trumpet forth the worshipful Eleusis
and Triptolemus, givers of the first corn to folks
wont to find their food in the Chaonian oak-forest;
nor Egyptian Apis aroused by the sounds of the
Memphitic sistrum. I shall not tell how Sparta's
young manhood dedicated the oily wrestling-bout
to the sons of Tyndarus, at whose prowess, learned
in their native Therapnae, the athletes of the
Bebrycian [1] arena trembled. Nor shall my theme be
Lycian or Caerite oracles or the earlier responses
of Themis at Delphi or the divinities that the Tuscan,
when he expiates the lightning, seeks at the fenced
bidental,[2] or the gods whom on Antenor's mount the
seer [3] who drank the waters of Euganean Timavus
saw stirring up the Thessalian battle; nor of those
whom Amphiaraus and Melampus . . . (nor of) the
gods that Metellus [4] snatched even from the midst
of the burning, when the flames surged ruinously
through the temple, and he rejoiced in the loss of

the help of Etruscan experts was frequently enlisted on such
occasions. Sidonius is probably thinking of the Puteal Libonis
in the Roman Forum.

[3] Cornelius, a priest, was said to have seen at Patavium
a vision of the battle of Pharsalia. Sidonius is thinking of
Lucan VII. 192 sqq., where the story is related with considerable scepticism. For *Euganeum* see n. on 2. 189.

[4] L. Caecilius Metellus, Pontifex Maximus, rescued the
Palladium when the temple of Vesta caught fire in 241 B.C.
His bravery cost him his eyesight. The generalising plural
dei is often used of an action affecting one deity.

non hic Cinyphius canetur Hammon
mitratum caput elevans harenis,
vix se post hecatombion litatum
suetus promere Syrtium barathro.
non hic Dindyma nec crepante buxo   205
Curetas Berecynthiam sonantes,
non Bacchum trieterica exserentem
describam et tremulas furore festo
ire in Bassaridas vel infulatos
aram ad turicremam rotare mystas.   210
    Non hic Hesiodea pinguis Ascrae
spectes carmina Pindarique chordas;
non hic socciferi iocos Menandri,
non laesi Archilochi feros iambos,
vel plus Stesichori graves Camenas,   215
aut quod composuit puella Lesbis;
non quod Mantua contumax Homero
adiecit Latiaribus loquelis,
aequari sibimet subinde livens
busto Parthenopam Maroniano;   220
non quod post saturas epistularum
sermonumque sales novumque epodon,
libros carminis ac poeticam artem

216. Lesbis *Luetjohann* : lesbi.
221. post *Leo* : per *codd., quod retineri potest si* valuit (*Luetjohann*) *in v. 225 legas.*

---

[1] It is surprising to find (H)ammon wearing a *mitra* on his horned head. Bacchus is so represented in Sen. *Phaedr.* 756, and Sidonius may have had a confused recollection of that passage. By *Syrtes* here Sidonius may mean "the land near the Syrtes"; the Roman poets are always ready to bring any Libyan lands near to those famous gulfs; see 5. 263 sq. and Lucan IV. 673, *confinis Syrtibus Hammon.* He may, however, be alluding to the fact, that the land extending from the Syrtes to the oasis of Ammon had formerly been covered by the sea; see Strabo I. 3. 4.

his sight. Here no Cinyphian Hammon [1] shall be
sung, who raises his snooded head among the desert
sands and even after auspicious sacrifice of a heca-
tomb will scarce show himself from the depths of
the Syrtes; nor shall I picture Dindyma or the Curetes
sounding on murmuring box-pipe the praises of the
Berecynthian Mother; nor Bacchus, as he brings forth
his triennial festival and invades the Bassarids quivering with the frenzy of the feast and whirls his fillet-
crowned votaries beside the incense-burning altar.

Not here shall you behold the Hesiodic strains of
sluggish Ascra or Pindar's lyre; nor the jests of
Menander, wearer of comedy's sock; nor the
savage lampoons of the injured Archilochus; nor
the graver muse of Stesichorus or the song fashioned
by the Lesbian maid; nor that which Mantua,
defying Homer's supremacy, added to Latin utterance—Mantua, soon jealous that Parthenope matched
her by possessing Virgil's tomb; nor the notes that
Horace was fain to sound when he penned the
praises of Phoebus and roaming Diana after the
medleys of the Epistles,[2] the witty sallies of the

[2] Sidonius seems to be playing on the word *satura* by using
it in its old sense of "medley" and applying it to the *Epistles*,
not the *Satires*, of Horace. Horace refers to his *Satires* as
saturae as well as *sermones*. In Suetonius' life of the poet a
phrase from the *Epistles* is said to occur *in saturis*; but this is
probably an inadvertence, though Hendrickson in *Am. Journ.
Phil.* XVIII (1897), pp. 313–324, uses it, along with the present
passage (wrongly punctuated with commas after *saturas* and
sales) and other inconclusive evidence, to prove that the
ancients assigned the *Epistles* as well as the *Satires* to the
literary *genre* called *satura* (or *satira*). Line 224 refers to the
Carmen Saeculare, the first line of which is *Phoebe silvarumque
potens Diana*, but it was not the latest work of Horace, as is
implied if the reading here given is correct.

THE POEMS OF SIDONIUS

Phoebi laudibus et vagae Dianae
conscriptis voluit sonare Flaccus ;   225
non quod Papinius tuus meusque
inter Labdacios sonat furores
aut cum forte pedum minore rhythmo
pingit gemmea prata silvularum.

  Non quod Corduba praepotens alumnis   230
facundum ciet, hic putes legendum,
quorum unus colit hispidum Platona
incassumque suum monet Neronem,
orchestram quatit alter Euripidis,
pictum faecibus Aeschylon secutus   235
aut plaustris solitum sonare Thespin,
qui post pulpita trita sub cothurno
ducebant olidae marem capellae ;
pugnam tertius ille Gallicani
dixit Caesaris, ut gener socerque   240
cognata impulerint in arma Romam,
tantum dans lacrimas suis Philippis,
ut credat Cremerae levem ruinam,
infra et censeat Alliam dolendam
ac Brenni in trutina Iovem redemptum,   245
postponat Trebiam gravesque Cannas,
stragem nec Trasimenicam loquatur,
fratres Scipiadas putet silendos,
quos Tartesiacus retentat orbis,

---

[1] The *Thebais* and *Silvae* of Statius.
[2] Referring to the long hair and beard typical of the philosopher : cf. *Epist.* IV. 11. 1.
[3] Sidonius wrongly regards the philosopher Seneca as distinct from the writer of tragedies.
[4] Cf. Hor. *A.P.* 276 sq.
[5] Hor. *ib.* 220.   [6] Lucan.

188

IX. TO FELIX

Satires, the new-fangled Epodes, the books of Odes
and the Art of Poetry; nor what Papinius, dear to
you and to me, utters amid the frenzy of the house
of Labdacus, or when in shorter-footed measure
he portrays the begemmed meads of his little
" Silvae." [1]

Nor must you expect to read here the eloquence
called forth by Corduba, great in her sons, of whom
one is devoted to the unkempt [2] Plato and vainly
admonishes his pupil Nero, another [3] rouses again
the stage of Euripides and also follows Aeschylus,
who painted his face with wine-lees, and Thespis,
who was wont to give utterance from waggons, [4]
bards who after treading the stage with their buskins
used to lead away the mate of a fetid she-goat: [5]
third of Corduba's sons was he who sang the fight
of Caesar the Gallic conqueror, [6] how a father and his
daughter's husband drove Rome into a war of
kinsfolk; [7] and so bitterly does he weep for his
Philippi [8] that he deems the disaster of Cremera a
trifle, he avers that Allia [9] and the ransom of Jupiter [10]
in the scales of Brennus are less to be lamented,
he holds Trebia [11] and dire Cannae [12] of less moment,
he has naught to say of Trasimene's slaughter, he
thinks those Scipios not worth a word whom the region
of Tartessus holds, he takes no account of the ruinous

[7] *Cognata arma* probably alludes to Lucan's *cognatas
acies*, I. 4.

[8] *Philippi, i.e.* Pharsalia. Poets (Verg. *Georg.* I. 489 sq.)
often place Philippi and Pharsalia in the same region. The
very first line of Lucan places Pharsalia in Macedonia.

[9] Lucan VII. 409.

[10] *Iovem, i.e.* the Capitol, the habitation of Jupiter.

[11] Lucan II. 46.

[12] *ib.* II. 46, VII. 408.

189

Euphraten taceat male appetitum,   250
Crassorum et madidas cruore Carrhas
vel quos, Spartace, consulum solebas
victrici gladios fugare sica,
ipsum nec fleat ille plus duellum,
quod post Cimbrica turbidus tropaea   255
et vinctum Nasamonium Iugurtham,
dum quaerit Mithridaticum triumphum,
Arpinas voluit movere Sullae.
   Non Gaetulicus hic tibi legetur,
non Marsus, Pedo, Silius, Tibullus,   260
non quod Sulpiciae iocus Thaliae
scripsit blandiloquum suo Caleno,
non Persi rigor aut lepos Properti,
sed nec centimeter Terentianus.
non Lucilius hic Lucretiusque est,   265
non Turnus, Memor, Ennius, Catullus,
Stella et Septimius Petroniusque
aut mordax sine fine Martialis,
non qui tempore Caesaris secundi
aeterno incoluit Tomos reatu,   270

---

[1] This and the previous line probably refer to Lucan I.
10 sqq., though the poet does not there say that the disaster
of Carrhae was of little account compared with the Civil
War; he merely says that the Romans would have done
better to avenge Carrhae than to fight among themselves.
In I. 103–108 he makes the disaster of Carrhae and the death
of Crassus responsible for the Civil War.

[2] Cf. Luc. II. 67–133.

[3] In Martial I. *praef.* (which Sidonius probably had in mind)
Gaetulicus, Marsus and Pedo are mentioned as epigrammatists.
Gaetulicus, after a distinguished official career, was put to
death by Caligula, A.D. 39. He is sometimes credited with
a historical work, but it was probably an epic poem. He is
mentioned again by Sidonius in *Epist.* II. 10. 6. Domitius
Marsus, an Augustan poet, wrote, besides epigrams, versified

attempt on the Euphrates and of Carrhae drenched
with the blood of the Crassi,[1] or of the consuls whose
swords Spartacus was wont to rout with victorious
dagger; nay, he does not bewail more bitterly
that war which the man of Arpinum, wild with
arrogance after his Cimbric trophies and the en-
chainment of Nasamonian Jugurtha, and seeking
next a Mithridatic triumph, was fain to stir up against
Sulla.[2]

Here you shall read no Gaetulicus, Marsus, Pedo,[3]
Silius, or Tibullus, nor the winsome words which
Sulpicia's [4] sprightly muse wrote to her Calenus,
nor the sternness of Persius nor the liveliness of
Propertius, nor yet Terentianus of the hundred
metres.[5] Here is no Lucilius, no Lucretius, Turnus,
Memor,[6] Ennius, Catullus, Stella,[7] Septimius,[8] or
Petronius, no Martial with his constant bite, nor
he who in the days of the second Caesar dwelt at
Tomi,[9] a prisoner never absolved; nor he who later

tales and an epic. Albinovanus Pedo was a friend of Ovid.
He wrote an epic called *Theseis* and a poem (of which an interesting fragment is preserved) on the exploits of Germanicus
in the North.

   [4] Sulpicia, a writer of love-poetry in the time of Domitian.
Calenus was her husband. The *satura* which goes under her
name probably belongs to a later age.

   [5] *centimeter* : apparently a popular designation of writers
on metre, perhaps suggested by the work of Servius, *De Centum
Metris*. The reference is to Terentianus Maurus.

   [6] Turnus, a satirist, Memor, a writer of tragedies, in the
age of Domitian.

   [7] L. Arruntius Stella, a native of Padua, often mentioned
by his friends Martial and Statius. He wrote love-elegies
celebrating Violentilla, who became his wife.

   [8] In all probability Septimius Serenus, mentioned in 14
Praef. 3, a poet of the age of Hadrian, who wrote *opuscula* on
rural themes.   [9] Ovid : cf. 23. 158 sqq.

nec qui consimili deinde casu
ad vulgi tenuem strepentis auram
irati fuit histrionis exsul,
non Pelusiaco satus Canopo,
qui ferruginei toros mariti 275
et Musa canit inferos superna,
nec qui iam patribus fuere nostris
primo tempore maximi sodales,
quorum unus Bonifatium secutus
nec non praecipitem Sebastianum 280
natales puer horruit Cadurcos
plus Pandionias amans Athenas;
cuius si varium legas poema,
tunc Phoebum vel Hyantias puellas
potato madidas ab Hippocrene, 285
tunc Amphiona filiumque Maiae,
tunc vatem Rhodopeium sonare
conlato modulamine arbitreris.

Non tu hic nunc legeris tuumque fulmen,
o dignissime Quintianus alter, 290
spernens qui Ligurum solum et penates
mutato lare Gallias amasti,
inter classica, signa, pila, turmas
laudans Aetium vacansque libro,
in castris hederate laureatis. 295
sed nec tertius ille nunc legetur,
Baetin qui patrium semel relinquens

295. hederate laureatis *Chatelain*: (h)edera ter laureatus.

---

[1] On the stories of Juvenal's banishment see Duff's ed.,
pp. x-xiii, Plessis, *La Poésie latine* 633-641 (discussion of
the present passage on p. 635).
[2] Claudian, *De Raptu Proserpinae*.

by a like misfortune, on the stirring of a breath of
vulgar gossip, became the exiled victim of an angry
actor [1]; nor that son of Egyptian Canopus who of
the dusky bridegroom's marriage and of the denizens
of hell doth sing with his heavenly muse; [2] nor those
who even in their earliest days were the greatest
of our fathers' comrades, of whom one,[3] following
Boniface and the headstrong Sebastian, abhorred in
boyhood his native Cadurcans,[4] loving Pandion's
Athens more: were you to read his varied poems,
then would you think that Phoebus was giving
utterance, and the Boeotian maids, their lips all
moist with draughts of Hippocrene, and Amphion
too and the son of Maia and the bard of Rhodope,
all contributing their melody.

Nor does the reader now find thee here, Quintianus,[5]
the second of the three, with thy thunderbolt, who
spurning thy Ligurian soil and home didst change
thine abode and give Gaul thy love, and didst sing the
praises of Aëtius amid trumpet-calls, standards,
spears, and troops, sparing time for the pen as for the
sword, a bard ivy-crowned in a belaurelled camp.
Nor shall the reader here find that other,[6] the third of
the band, who leaving once for all his native Baetis

[3] The name of this poet is unknown. Sebastian succeeded
his father-in-law Boniface as *magister utriusque militiae* in A.D.
432. After an adventurous career he finally betook himself to
Geiseric, who put him to death in A.D. 450 because he would
not abjure the Catholic faith.

[4] In Aquitaine, S.W. of the Arverni.

[5] *Quintianus*, not otherwise known.

[6] Flavius Merobaudes. The inscription attached to his
statue has been found (C. I. L. vi. 1724, Dessau 2950). Its
date is A.D. 435. The *princeps* (*v.* 300) is Valentinian III;
this reference to him is astonishingly kind after 7. 359 and
532 ff. In 23. 214 he is *pius princeps*.

undosae petiit sitim Ravennae,
plosores cui fulgidam Quirites
et carus popularitate princeps   300
Traiano statuam foro locarunt.

Sed ne tu mihi comparare temptes,
quos multo minor ipse plus adoro,
Paulinum Ampeliumque Symmachumque,
Messalam ingenii satis profundi   305
et nulli modo Martium secundum,
dicendi arte nova parem vetustis
Petrum et cum loquitur nimis stupendum,
vel quem municipalibus poetis
praeponit bene vilicum senatus,   310
nostrum aut quos retinet solum disertos,
dulcem Anthedion et mihi magistri
Musas sat venerabiles Hoeni,
acrem Lampridium, catum Leonem
praestantemque tuba Severianum   315

---

[1] This jest about Ravenna is found in Martial III. 56
and 57, and is repeated by Sidonius in *Epist.* I. 8. 2; cf. *ib.*
I. 5. 6.

[2] *Paulinum*, probably not Pontius Paulinus (*Epist.* VIII.
12. 5), son of Pontius Leontius, whose " Castle " is celebrated
in *Carm.* 22. This line seems to refer to (epistolary ?) writers
of the age of Symmachus, and Gallo-Roman writers seem to
be excluded from this part of the paragraph (see *v.* 311).
The reference may possibly be to Paulinus of Nola, who,
though a native of Gaul, came to be closely associated with Italy.

[3] The Ampelius mentioned here is supposed to be P. Ampelius, who held several high offices of state in the fourth
century. He died not later than 397. He was a corre-
spondent of Libanius.

[4] Valerius Messala is highly praised for his eloquence by
Symmachus, who wrote several letters to him. He is probably
the Messala praised by Rutilius Namatianus, 1. 267 sqq.

[5] Probably not Martius Myro (23. 444).

betook himself to that place of thirst, well-watered
Ravenna,[1] and to whom the acclaiming citizens of
Rome and the Emperor so beloved for his gracious-
ness set up a gleaming statue in Trajan's Forum.

And try not, gentle reader, to compare me with
those whom I, vastly their inferior, worship all the
more, Paulinus,[2] Ampelius,[3] and Symmachus, Messala [4] of genius so profound, Martius,[5] second to
none in these times, Petrus,[6] equal of the ancients
in the modern style of eloquence and a marvel to
all when he speaks, or that steward [7] whom the
senate rightly prefers to the poets of the towns:
or those men of gifted utterance whom our soil
possesses, charming Anthedius,[8] my master Hoënius,
whose muse commands my deepest reverence,
spirited Lampridius,[9] shrewd Leo,[10] and Severi-

---

[6] 3. 5 n.

[7] *Vilicum* is not likely to be a proper name. Juvenal (IV. 77)
uses the word of a *praefectus urbi*. The mention of the Senate
in *v.* 310 makes it probable that Sidonius is thinking of that
passage and referring to a contemporary prefect; in his day
the *praef. urbi* was president of the Senate. We do not possess
a complete list of the city prefects for the period in which this
poem must have been written, and there is no evidence that
any of the known prefects was a poet. Sidonius plays on the
ordinary meaning of *vilicus*, "farm-bailiff."

[8] Anthedius, a friend of Sidonius; 22 *epist.* § 2 ; *Epist.* VIII.
11. 2. Hoënius is not otherwise known.

[9] Lampridius taught rhetoric at Bordeaux. For an appreci-
ation of him see *Epist.* VIII. 11. 3 sqq.; on his poetical talent
Epist. IX. 13. 2 carm. 20 sq. and § 4. He gained favour with
Euric, and Sidonius seems in *Epist.* VIII. 9 to angle for his
good offices with that king.

[10] Leo, a native of Narbonne, descended from Fronto (*Epist.*
VIII. 3. 3), lauded as a poet (cf. 23. 450–4, *Epist* IX. 13. 2,
carm. 20; *ib.* IX. 15. 1, carm. 19 sq.) and as a jurist (23. 447).
He became a minister of Euric, and no doubt helped to
procure the release of Sidonius; see Introd., p. xlix.

et sic scribere non minus valentem,
Marcus Quintilianus ut solebat.
  Nos valde sterilis modos Camenae
rarae credimus hos brevique chartae,
quae scombros merito piperque portet.   320
nam quisnam deus hoc dabit reiectae,
ut vel suscipiens bonos odores,
nardum ac pinguia Nicerotianis
quae fragrant alabastra tincta sucis,
Indo cinnamon ex rogo petitum,   325
quo Phoenix iuvenescit occidendo,
costum, malobathrum, rosas, amomum,
myrrham, tus opobalsamumque servet?
quapropter facinus meum tuere
et condiscipuli tibi obsequentis   330
incautum, precor, asseras pudorem.
germanum tamen ante sed memento,
doctrinae columen, Probum advocare,
isti qui valet exarationi
destrictum bonus applicare theta.   335
novi sed bene, non refello culpam,
nec doctis placet impudens poeta;
sed nec turgida contumeliosi
lectoris nimium verebor ora,
si tamquam gravior severiorque   340
nostrae Terpsichores iocum refutans
rugato Cato tertius labello
narem rhinoceroticam minetur.
non te terreat hic nimis peritus;
verum si cupias probare, tanta   345
nullus scit, mihi crede, quanta nescit.

324. flagrant codd.

---

[1] Severianus, poet and rhetorician : see *Epist.* IX. 13. 4;
IX. 15. 1 carm. 37. He may be the Iulius Severianus who is
the reputed compiler of a collection of rhetorical precepts still

anus,[1] who excels in trumpet-tones and is no less apt
in such writing as Marcus Quintilianus used to pen.

As for these measures of my sadly barren muse, I
rarely commit them to a papyrus-sheet, and then
only to a short one,[2] which would rightly be used
for carrying mackerel or pepper—for what god will
ever grant to my scorned sheet even the small boon
of sniffing pleasant scents and being used for wrapping nard and oily alabaster flasks fragrant with
Nicerotian[3] essences, and cinnamon got from the
Indian[4] pyre where the Phoenix renews his youth by
dying, and costum and malobathrum and roses and
amomum and incense and opobalsamum? Therefore defend my audacious deed and vindicate, I pray
you, in its rash escapade the modesty of a schoolfellow who is but obeying your orders. But remember first to call in that pillar of learning, your
brother Probus, who is able, with all his kindness,
to attach a stern obelus to this scribbling. But I
know it well, I am not clearing myself of guilt, and
a shameless poet does not please the well-instructed.
And yet I shall not dread excessively the pompous
mouthing of an abusive reader, should he, with an
air of superior gravity and sternness, like a third
Cato, spurn the jesting of my Terpsichore, purse his
lips and threaten me with the contemptuous nose of a
rhinoceros. Let not this too consummate pundit
frighten you. If you would get at the real truth, believe
me, nobody knows as many things as he doesn't know.

extant (*Rhet. Min.*, Halm, pp. 350–370), but there is nothing
to prove it. *Tuba* probably refers to Epic poetry.

[2] See Introd., p. lv, n. 1.

[3] An epithet borrowed from Martial (VI. 55. 3, X. 38. 8).
Niceros was a famous perfumer in the time of Domitian.

[4] See n. on *Erythras*, 2. 447.

X

PRAEFATIO EPITHALAMII DICTI RVRICIO ET HIBERIAE

Flucticolae cum festa nurus Pagasaea per antra
    rupe sub Emathia Pelion explicuit,
angustabat humum superum satis ampla supellex;
    certabant gazis hinc polus hinc pelagus;
ducebatque choros viridi prope tectus amictu   5
    caeruleae pallae concolor ipse socer;
nympha quoque in thalamos veniens de gurgite nuda
    vestiti coepit membra timere viri.
tum divum quicumque aderat terrore remoto
    quo quis pollebat lusit in officio.   10
Iuppiter emisit tepidum sine pondere fulmen
    et dixit: "melius nunc Cytherea calet."
Pollux tum caestu laudatus, Castor habenis,
    Pallas tum cristis, Delia tum pharetris;
Alcides clava, Mavors tum lusit in hasta,   15
    Arcas tum virga, nebride tum Bromius.
hic et Pipliadas induxerat optimus Orpheus
    chordis, voce, manu, carminibus, calamis.
ambitiosus Hymen totas ibi contulit artes;
    qui non ingenio, fors placuit genio.   20

---

[1] Ruricius (to whom *Epist.* IV. 16, V. 15, VIII. 10 are
addressed) was a member of a noble family connected with the
gens Anicia. Hiberia, whom he married, was the daughter
of Ommatius, an Arvernian of good family who does not seem
to have taken much part in public life. Ruricius afterwards

X. PREFACE TO RURICIUS

X

PREFACE TO THE EPITHALAMIUM OF RURICIUS AND HIBERIA [1]

When Pelion displayed the marriage-feast of the sea-maiden [2] in a Pagasaean cave beneath an Emathian crag, the stately pageantry of the gods taxed the ground to hold it; on this side the sky, on that the sea vied one with the other in their treasures, and the song and dance were led by the bride's father almost hidden in his green robe and himself of the same hue as his sea-coloured mantle. The nymph also, coming naked from the waves to her marriage, was seized with fear of the bridegroom's draped form. Then every god that was present laid aside his dreadfulness and exhibited a playful version of his special power. Jupiter hurled a thunderbolt that had heither heat nor force, and said, " At this time it is more fitting for our lady of Cythera to show warmth." Pollux then won praise with the boxing-glove, Castor with reins, Pallas with her plumed helm, the Delian goddess with her arrows; Hercules frolicked with his club, Mars with his spear, the Arcadian god with his wand, Bromius with the fawn-skin. At this moment the Muses also had been introduced by the incomparable Orpheus with strings, voice, hand, songs, and reeds. Hymen, eager to show off, mustered there all arts, and he who did not give pleasure by his merit gave pleasure belike by

entered the Church, and in A.D. 485 became Bishop of Limoges. We possess two books of his letters, written mostly before his episcopate. Two letters are addressed to Sidonius.

[2] Thetis, daughter of Nereus, bride of Peleus.

199

Fescennina tamen non sunt admissa priusquam
  intonuit solita noster Apollo lyra.

XI

EPITHALAMIVM

[Inter Cyaneas, Ephyraea cacumina, cautes
qua super Idalium levat Orithyion in aethram
exesi sale montis apex, ubi forte vagantem
dum fugit et fixit trepidus Symplegada Tiphys,
atque recurrentem ructatum ad rauca Maleam,]   5
exit in Isthmiacum pelagus claudentibus alis
saxorum de rupe sinus, quo saepe recessu
sic tamquam toto coeat de lumine caeli,
artatur collecta dies tremulasque per undas
insequitur secreta vadi, transmittitur alto   10
perfusus splendore latex, mirumque relatu,
lympha bibit solem tenuique inserta fluento
perforat arenti radio lux sicca liquorem.
  Profecit studio spatium; nam Lemnius illic
ceu templum lusit Veneri fulmenque relinquens   15
hic ferrugineus fumavit saepe Pyragmon.
hic lapis est de quinque locis dans quinque colores
Aethiops, Phrygius, Parius, Poenus, Lacedaemon,

  2. orithion *codd.*
  11. mirumque *Mohr et in adnot. Luetjohann* : miroque.

---

[1] *ingenio . . . genio*, an antithesis found in several other
places, but the meaning of *genius* varies. Here it probably
means " geniality," " mirthfulness." See n. on 2. 191.
  [2] *i.e.* the Apollo of us poets.
  [3] The first five lines of this difficult poem are an unintelligible
jumble, and *v.* 5 cannot even be construed. *Vv.* 3 and 4
may be by Sidonius; if we retain them and omit *vv.* 1 and 2
sinus will be acc. plur. after *claudentibus*, and should probably
be altered to *sinum*. Corinth is prominent in the Argonautic

his spirit.[1] But Fescennine jests were not admitted until our Apollo [2] had made his song ring forth on the familiar lyre.

XI

EPITHALAMIUM [3]

[Between the Dark-blue Rocks, Ephyra's peaks, where the summit of a sea-worn mountain raises Orithyion above Idalium [4] to the sky, in which place, as it chanced, the wandering Symplegades were fixed fast by the trembling Tiphys even as he fled from them, . . .] there emerges into the sea of the Isthmus a bay enclosed by wings of piled rocks jutting from the cliff; in which retreat, just as if the whole radiance of the sky were concentrated there, the daylight is gathered together into a narrow space, and penetrating the quivering waters it searches out the secluded depths, and so the ripples pass on, bathed in deep-shining brightness, and, wondrous to tell, the water drinks in the sun and the light, pushed into the limpid stream, bores unwetted through the wet with arid ray.

This site favoured a labour of love; for there the Lemnian god amused himself by building a mimic temple for Venus, and swarthy Pyragmon, abandoning the thunderbolt, raised his smoke in the place many a time.   Here is stone from five regions, giving forth five hues, Aethiopian, Phrygian, Parian, Punic,

legend, but it is very surprising to find the Symplegades in its neighbourhood.   For the legend of the storm encountered by the Argonauts off Cape Malea (to which *v.* 5 must refer) see Herodotus IV. 179.

[4] Or " raises up Idalian Orithyion "—whatever that may mean.

purpureus, viridis, maculosus, eburnus et albus.
postes chrysolithi fulvus diffulgurat ardor;   20
myrrhina, sardonyches, amethystus Hiberus, iaspis
Indus, Chalcidicus, Scythicus, beryllus, achates
attollunt duplices argenti cardine valvas,
per quas inclusi lucem vomit umbra smaragdi;
limina crassus onyx crustat propterque hyacinthi   25
caerula concordem iaciunt in stagna colorem.
exterior non compta silex, sed prominet alte
asper ab adsiduo lympharum verbere pumex.
interiore loco simulavit Mulciber auro
exstantes late scopulos atque arte magistra   30
ingenti cultu naturae inculta fefellit,
huic operi insistens, quod necdum noverat illa
quae post Lemniacis damnavit furta catenis.
squameus huc Triton duplicis confinia dorsi,
qua coeunt supra sinuamina tortilis alvi,   35
inter aquas calido portavit corde Dionen.
sed premit adiecto radiantis pondere conchae
semiferi Galatea latus, quod pollice fixo
vellit, et occulto spondet conubia tactu;
tum gaudens torquente ioco subridet amator   40
vulnere iamque suam parcenti pistre flagellat.
pone subit turmis flagrantibus agmen Amorum;
hic cohibet delphina rosis, viridique iuvenco
hic vectus spretis pendet per cornua frenis;

26. iaciunt *Luetjohann in adnot.* : faciunt.

---

[1] The descriptions, if placed in the same order as the stones,
would have been " purple (see 5. 34 sqq. n.), spotted, white,
ivory (5. 37 sq. n.), green."

[2] *Chalcidicus* probably refers to *chalcitis*, a copper-coloured
gem (Plin. *N. H.* XXXVII. 191). *Scythicus* refers to the
Scythian emerald, said by Pliny (*N. H.* XXXVII. 65) to be
the finest of all : cf. Martial IV. 28. 4.

XI. EPITHALAMIUM

Spartan—purple, green, mottled, ivory, white.[1] The yellow glow of topaz flashes through the doorpost; porcelain, sardonyx, Caucasian amethyst, Indian jasper, Chalcidian and Scythian stones,[2] beryl and agate, form the double doors that rise upon silver pivots, and through these doors the shadowy recess beyond pours out the sheen of the emeralds that are within. Onyx thickly encrusts the threshold, and hard by the blue colour of amethyst casts upon the lagoon a harmonious hue. Outside is no dressed stone, but towering walls of rock that has been roughened by the constant lashing of the waters. In the inner part Mulciber mimicked in gold the crags that rise up far and wide, and with his skill to guide him counterfeited with mighty art the artless creations of Nature, plying his work diligently—for not yet did he know of that deception which afterwards he punished with his Lemnian chains. Hither scaly Triton with heart aflame bore amid the waters Venus, seated where the boundaries of his double back meet above the windings of his writhing belly.[3] But Galatea has brought up close to him her weighty, glittering shell, and presses his side, which she pinches with inserted thumb, promising by that stealthy touch connubial bliss; whereupon the lover, rejoicing in that torturing jest, smiles at the wound and anon lashes his beloved with a gentle stroke of his fishy tail. Behind them comes a column of Loves in ardent squadrons; one controls a dolphin with reins of roses, another rides on a green sea-calf, despising bridle's aid and clinging to the horns; others are on

---

[3] The nether half of this merman is fishy, the fore part human; the former is in perpetual motion as he propels himself by lashing the water. Venus is seated on his back, just clear of the agitated fishy half.

THE POEMS OF SIDONIUS

hi stantes motu titubant plantaque madenti   45
labuntur firmantque pedum vestigia pennis.
  Illa recurvato demiserat ora lacerto
mollia; marcebant violae graviorque sopore
coeperat attritu florum descendere cervix.
solus de numero fratrum qui pulchrior ille est   50
deerat Amor, dum festa parat celeberrima Gallis,
quae socer Ommatius, magnorum maior avorum
patriciaeque nepos gentis, natae generoque
excolit auspiciis faustis. sed fulsit ut ille
forte dies, matrem celeri petit ipse volatu,   55
cui fax, arcus, gorytus pendebat. at ille
cernuus et laevae pendens in margine palmae
libratos per inane pedes adverberat alis,
oscula sic matris carpens somnoque refusae
semisopora levi scalpebat lumina penna.   60
tum prior his alacer coepit: " nova gaudia porto
felicis praedae, genetrix. calet ille superbus
Ruricius nostris facibus dulcique veneno
tactus votivum suspirat corde dolorem.
esset si praesens aetas, impenderet illi   65
Lemnias imperium, Cressa stamen labyrinthi,
Alceste vitam, Circe herbas, poma Calypso,
Scylla comas, Atalanta pedes, Medea furores,

---

¹ "as . . . wakefulness." L. C. Purser's rendering. The
context seems to show that this is the meaning, although,
curiously enough, *somno refusa* might also mean "sinking back
in sleep": cf. Lucan VIII. 105, *refusa coniugis in gremium.*
² Hypsipyle.
³ The form *Alceste* occurs also in 15. 165. The only other
certain instance is in an inscription (C. I. L. VI. 34964),
where it does not refer to the mythological character.
⁴ Scylla was the daughter of Nisus, king of Megara. He
had one red lock in his hair, and on its preservation depended
his life and fortune. When Minos was besieging Megara,
Scylla, who had fallen in love with him, severed her father's
204

foot, swaying with the motion, slipping on their dripping soles and steadying their steps with their wings.

Venus had let her soft cheek rest upon her bended arm; the violets about her grew languid and her neck had begun to sink, ever heavier with slumber as the flowers pressed against her. Of all the troop of brothers one alone was missing, the Love-god, the fairest of them all; for he was contriving a glorious marriage-feast for the Gauls, a feast that the bride's father Ommatius, scion of a patrician race and the greatest of his great line, was gracing with splendour for his daughter and her bridegroom amid happy auguries. But when in due course the great day dawned, then the god with swift flight sought his mother, with torch, bow, and quiver slung upon him. Stooping down and resting on the edge of his left hand, with his wings he lashed his feet, as they hung poised in the air, and thus he snatched kisses from his mother; and as she floated back into wakefulness [1] he began to graze her half-slumbering eyes with the light touch of a feather. Then before she could speak he briskly addressed her thus: "I bring you a new joy, Mother, the joy of a happy capture. That proud Ruricius is set aflame by our torch; he has caught the sweet poison and heaves sighs of welcome pain. If those olden times were now, the maid of Lemnos [2] would have lavished on him her sovereignty, the Cretan maid the thread for the labyrinth, Alcestis [3] her life, Circe her magic herbs, Calypso her apples, Scylla [4] the fatal hair, Atalanta her swift feet, Medea her mad passions,

red lock. This story is the subject of the *Ciris*, one of the minor works attributed to Virgil.

Hippodame ceras, cygno Iove nata coronam;
huic Dido in ferrum, simul in suspendia Phyllis,   70
Euadne in flammas et Sestias isset in undas."

His haec illa refert: " Gaudemus, nate, rebellem
quod vincis laudasque virum; sed forma puellae est
quam si spectasset quondam Stheneboeius heros,
non pro contemptu domuisset monstra Chimaerae;   75
Thermodontiaca vel qui genetrice superbus
sprevit Gnosiacae temeraria vota novercae,
hac visa occiderat, fateor, sed crimine vero;
et si iudicio forsan mihi quarta fuisset,
me quoque Rhoetea damnasset pastor in Ida;   80
' vincere vel, si optas, istam da, malo, puellam '
dixerat: hanc dederam formam pro munere formae.
tantus honor geniusque genis; collata rubori
pallida blatta latet depressaque lumine vultus
nigrescunt vincto bacarum fulgura collo.   85
te quoque multimodis ambisset, Hiberia, ludis
axe Pelops, cursu Hippomenes luctaque Achelous,
Aeneas bellis spectatus, Gorgone Perseus;
nec minus haec species totiens cui Iuppiter esset

---

81. *dist. ego*: vincere *passivum est.*
89. minus *ego*: minor. *Vid. Class. Quart., loc. cit., p.* 20.

---

[1] Hippodamia: for *ceras* cf. 2. 492.
[2] Helen crowned Menelaus with a garland to signify that
she had chosen him from among her many suitors. Hygin.
Fab. 78.
[3] Phyllis, daughter of a Thracian king, hanged herself
when Demophon, who had promised to return from Athens
and marry her, did not appear on the appointed day.
[4] When her husband Capaneus had been killed in the assault
of the "Seven" upon Thebes, she leaped into the flames of
his pyre.
[5] Hero threw herself into the sea after the death of Leander.
[6] Bellerophon: see 5. 178.

XI. EPITHALAMIUM

Hippodame [1] her wax, Jupiter's swan-daughter her crown [2]; for him Dido would have rushed upon the sword, Phyllis to the halter,[3] Evadne into the flames,[4] the maid of Sestos into the waves." [5]

His mother answered: " I rejoice, my son, that thou dost both vanquish and praise that stubborn resister. But the maid's beauty is such that if the hero whom Sthenoboea loved in bygone days [6] had beheld her he would not have had to overcome the dread Chimaera through slighting her charms; he who, arrogantly proud of his Amazon mother,[7] spurned the reckless prayers of his Cretan stepmother, would, if he had seen the maid, have been doomed indeed, but on a true charge; nay, if she had chanced to contend with me as a fourth competitor in the trial of beauty, then the shepherd on Rhoetean Ida would have given his verdict even against me. ' Lose the contest,' he would have said to me, ' or, if thou choosest (and this I prefer), give the girl to me;' and I should have given him all that beauty in return for the prize of beauty. Such are the charm and comeliness of her cheeks that compared with their radiance the purple pales into nothingness, and the gleam of the pearls that encircle her neck is dimmed to darkness by the light of her countenance. [8] Her also would men have wooed by all manner of exploits, Pelops attesting his prowess by his chariot, Hippomenes [9] by running, Achelous by wrestling, Aeneas by wars, Perseus by the Gorgon. Yea, hers is the beauty for whose sake Jupiter would so oft have

[7] Hippolytus was the son of Theseus and Hippolyte, queen of the Amazons.

[8] The following passage is discussed in *Class. Quart.* XXVIII (1934), p. 20.

[9] See 5. 165–176, 14. 13–15.

Delia, taurus, olor, Satyrus, draco, fulmen et
    aurum. 90
quare age, iungantur; nam census, forma genusque
conveniunt: nil hic dispar tua fixit harundo.
sed quid vota moror?" dixit currumque poposcit,
cui dederant crystalla iugum, quae frigore primo,
orbis adhuc teneri glacies ubi Caucason auget, 95
strinxit Hyperboreis Tanaitica crusta pruinis
naturam sumens gemmae quia perdidit undae.
perforat hunc fulvo formatus temo metallo;
miserat hoc fluvius cuius sub gurgite Nymphae
Mygdonium fovere Midam, qui pauper in auro 100
ditavit versis Pactoli flumina votis.
splendet perspicuo radios rota margine cingens
Marmaricae de fauce ferae, dum belua curvis
dentibus excussis gemit exarmarier ora;
misit et hoc munus tepidas qui nudus Erythras, 105
concolor Aethiopi vel crinem pinguis amomo,
fluxus odoratis vexat venatibus Indus.
illa tamen pasci suetos per Cypron olores
vittata stringit myrto, quis cetera tensis
lactea puniceo sinuantur colla corallo. 110

---

98. hunc (*sc.* currum) *Mohr* : hanc *codd. Fortasse legendum
est* hoc (*sc.* iugum: *cf.* 22. 24) *et in sequenti versu* hunc (*sc.*
temonem), *ut me monuit W. H. Semple.*

---

[1] *i.e.* Diana. Jupiter assumed this form in order to deceive
Cynosura. The victims of the other disguises mentioned
were (in order) Europa, Leda, Antiope, Mnemosyne (Proser-
pina, according to the usual account, but see 15. 175 sq.),
Semele, Danae. See 15. 174–178. According to Ovid,
Met. VI. 113, in the case of Mnemosyne the appearance
assumed was that of a shepherd.

XI. EPITHALAMIUM

become the Delian goddess,[1] a bull, a swan, a satyr, a serpent, thunder or gold. So let them be straightway united, for they are alike in wealth and beauty and lineage; there is naught that is ill-matched in these victims of thy shaft. But why am I thus delaying their marriage?" Thus she spake and called for her chariot. Its yoke was of crystal, which in early winter, when the ice of the young world began to increase the bulk of Caucasus, was compacted of a piece of the Tanais by dint of the northern frosts, assuming the nature of a gem because it lost the nature of water. The car was pierced by a pole of the yellow metal, metal which had been sent by the river beneath whose waters the nymphs fondled Mygdonian Midas, who, poor in the midst of gold, enriched Pactolus' stream when his prayers had been turned against him. Brightly gleamed the wheels, encircling the spokes with translucent rims; they were got from the jaws of the Libyan beast, while the monster bewailed the disarming of his mouth with the tusks wrenched away. This also was a gift, sent by the Indian, a man like the Ethiopian in hue and with the grease of unguent on his hair, who troubles warm Erythrae[2] as he roams about naked in his fragrant hunting.[3] Her swans, wont to feed in Cyprus, Venus held firmly with reins of be-ribboned myrtle; the rest of their bodies was tense and taut, but their milk-white necks were bent by a circlet of red coral.[4]

[2] See 2. 447 n. Here a district rather than a town seems to be indicated.

[3] "Fragrant hunting" refers to the fragrance cast from his perfumed hair as he hunts.

[4] This seems to mean that the reins are attached to a coral necklet, and the neck is bent back when they are pulled.

Ergo iter aggressi : pendens rota sulcat inanem
aera et in liquido non solvitur orbita tractu.
hic triplex uno comitatur Gratia nexu,
hic redolet patulo Fortunae Copia cornu,
hic spargit calathis, sed flores Flora perennes,   115
hic Cererem Siculam Pharius comitatur Osiris,
hic gravidos Pomona sinus pro tempore portat,
hic Pallas madidis venit inter prela trapetis,
hic distincta latus maculosa nebride Thyias
Indica Echionio Bromii rotat orgia thyrso,   120
hic et Sigeis specubus qui Dindyma ludit
iam sectus recalet Corybas ; cui gutture ravo
ignem per bifores regemunt cava buxa cavernas.

Sic ventum ad thalamos : tus, nardum, balsama,
      myrrhae
hic sunt, hic Phoenix busti dat cinnama vivi.   125
proxima quin etiam festorum adflata calore
iam minus alget hiemps, speciemque tenentia vernam
hoc dant vota loco quod non dant tempora mundo.
tum Paphie dextram iuvenis dextramque puellae
complectens paucis cecinit sollemnia dictis,   130
ne facerent vel verba moram : " feliciter aevum
ducite concordes ; sint nati sintque nepotes ;
cernat et in proavo sibimet quod pronepos optet."

XI. EPITHALAMIUM

So they begin their journey: the poised wheel cleaves the empty air, leaving in the clear expanse no rut to be smoothed out. Here the three Graces attend her, linked in a single embrace; here Plenty casts fragrance from Fortune's open horn; here Flora scatters flowers from baskets, flowers ever blooming; here Egyptian Osiris accompanies Sicilian Ceres; here Pomona carries the folds of her robe loaded with the fruits of the season; here Pallas comes with oil-mills that are oozing between the presses; here the Bacchanal, her side mottled with a dappled fawn-skin, plies the whirling Indian revelry of Bromius with the Theban thyrsus; here the Corybant too, who represents the rites of Dindyma in the caves of Sigeum, unmanned though he now is, feels the old glow return, and from that hoarse throat the hollowed box-wood groans out through its double pipe the fire that is within him.

Thus they come to the bridal; incense, nard, balm, and myrrh are here; here Phoenix presents the cinnamon of his living pyre.[1] Nay, even the winter so near at hand has felt the warm breath of the festival and has grown less cold, and the wedding preserves a suggestion of spring and gives to that spot a boon which the seasons do not give to the world. Then the goddess of Paphos, clasping the right hands of man and maid, chanted the hallowed blessing in but few words, unwilling that even words should bring delay: " Pass your lives in happiness and concord; may ye have children and grand-children; and may your great-grandchildren see in their great-grandparents the bliss which they themselves would fain enjoy ! "

[1] See 2. 417 n.

XII

AD V. C. CATVLLINVM

Quid me, etsi valeam, parare carmen
Fescenninicolae iubes Diones
inter crinigeras situm catervas
et Germanica verba sustinentem,
laudantem tetrico subinde vultu   5
quod Burgundio cantat esculentus,
infundens acido comam butyro?
vis dicam tibi, quid poema frangat?
ex hoc barbaricis abacta plectris
spernit senipedem stilum Thalia,   10
ex quo septipedes videt patronos.
felices oculos tuos et aures
felicemque libet vocare nasum,
cui non allia sordidumque cepe
ructant mane novo decem apparatus,   15
quem non ut vetulum patris parentem
nutricisque virum die nec orto
tot tantique petunt simul Gigantes,
quot vix Alcinoi culina ferret.
    Sed iam Musa tacet tenetque habenas   20
paucis hendecasyllabis iocata,
ne quisquam satiram vel hos vocaret.

14. sordidumque cepe *ego*: sordidaeque caepae (sepe *F*)
codd.; *sed desideratur accusativus.*

---

[1] Catullinus, who appears to have asked Sidonius to write
an epithalamium, is mentioned in *Epist.* I. 11. 3 sq., but is
not otherwise known. In that letter, which has reference to
a supposed " satire " of Sidonius, Catullinus plays an amusing
part, and it is fairly obvious that *v.* 22 contains a reference
to the incident, which occurred at Arles in A.D. 461. The

XII

TO CATULLINUS, SENATOR [1]

Why—even supposing I had the skill—do you bid me compose a song dedicated to Venus the lover of Fescennine mirth, placed as I am among long-haired hordes, having to endure German speech, praising oft with wry face the song of the gluttonous Burgundian who spreads rancid butter on his hair? Do you want me to tell you what wrecks all poetry? Driven away by barbarian thrumming the Muse has spurned the six-footed exercise ever since she beheld these patrons seven feet high. I am fain to call your eyes and ears happy, happy too your nose, for you don't have a reek of garlic and foul onions discharged upon you at early morn from ten breakfasts, and you are not invaded even before dawn, like an old grandfather or a foster-father, by a crowd of giants so many and so big that not even the kitchen of Alcinous could support them.

But already my Muse is silent and draws rein after only a few jesting hendecasyllables, lest anyone should call even these lines satire.

poem may have been written at Arles some time after Catullinus had left. The reference to the Burgundians is not quite clear. Sidonius seems to imply that he was responsible for feeding a certain number of them. Were they members of a Burgundian contingent in the forces of Majorian? Hodgkin (II. 362), though adopting the above view of *v.* 21 and the consequent dating of the poem, conjectures that these verses were written at Lyons—presumably because Lyons was in (though not part of) the Burgundian territory; but he does not explain the reference to the Burgundian meals. For an account of various suggested dates and places see Stevens, p. 66, n. 1. For the superscription of this poem see n. on *Epist.* I. 11. 3.

213

XIII

AD IMPERATOREM MAIORIANVM

Amphitryoniaden perhibet veneranda vetustas,
    dum relevat terras, promeruisse polos.
sed licet in nuda torvus confregerit ulna
    ille Cleonaeae guttura rava ferae,
et quamquam ardenti gladio vix straverit hydram, 5
    cum duplices pareret vulnere mors animas,
captivumque ferens silva ex Erymanthide monstrum
    exarmata feri riserit ora suis,
collaque flammigenae disrumpens fumida furis
    tandem directas iusserit ire boves,   10
taurus, cerva, Gigas, hospes, luctator, Amazon,
    Cres, canis, Hesperides sint monimenta viri,
nulla tamen fuso prior est Geryone pugna,
    uni tergeminum cui tulit ille caput.
haec quondam Alcides; at tu Tirynthius alter,   15
    sed princeps, magni maxima cura dei,
quem draco, cervus, aper paribus sensere sagittis,
    cum dens, cum virus, cum fuga nil valuit,
Eurysthea nos esse puta monstrumque tributum;
    hinc capita, ut vivam, tu mihi tolle tria.   20

3. sed *Mohr*: et.
19. Eurysthea *ego*: hystriones (histr.). *Vid. Class. Quart.
loc. cit. p.* 20.
20. hinc *Luetjohann*: hic.

---

[1] Majorian had punished the rebellious Gallo-Romans in
Lyons by levying a heavy tax. The method adopted was
apparently to assess each man on an increased number of
capita (property-units on which taxation was calculated).
The " three heads " in this poem seem to mean that the taxes
were trebled; or they may even have been quadrupled by
the addition of three *capita* to every former one. Sidonius here
pleads for a remission on behalf of himself and (less obviously)
of others. His appeal was probably successful, otherwise he

XIII. TO MAJORIAN

XIII

TO THE EMPEROR MAJORIAN [1]

Hallowed antiquity records that the son of Amphitryon by succouring earth earned heaven as his reward.   But although with grim look he crushed within his bare arms the tawny [2] throat of the monster of Cleonae; although with his fiery sword he just availed to lay the hydra low, as one death ever brought forth two lives from the wound; although he carried the captured monster from the Erymanthian forest, laughing at the wild boar's disarmed mouth; and although, bursting open the smoking neck of the fire-born thief, he compelled the cows at last to go frontwise; although the bull, the deer, the giant, the host, the wrestler, the Amazon, the Cretan beast, the dog, and the Hesperides [3] are memorials of the hero's prowess—yet none of his fights takes rank before the overthrow of Geryon, from whose one body he took three heads.   Thus Alcides of old; but do thou, as a second Hercules, and our sovereign to boot, and our great God's greatest care—thou, whose arrows made snake, stag, and boar alike to feel thy prowess,[4] when tooth, poison, and flight availed them not—deem us to be Eurystheus [5] and the tax to be the monster, and favour me by taking from it three heads, that I may be able to live.

would scarcely have included it in his collected poems.   It was probably written very soon after the Panegyric.

[2] This is probably the meaning of *rava* here.   There is another word *ravus*, meaning "hoarse," "rough-voiced" (= *raucus*): see *Epist.* VIII. 11. 3 carm. 49; *ib.* IX. 2. 2.   The meaning of the word in Horace is disputed; see commentators on *C.* III. 27. 3, *Epod.* XVI. 33, and G. Ramain in *Revue de Philologie* Sér. III. T. IX (1935), pp. 358–360.

[3] Cf. 9. 95–98 n.   [4] For this exploit of Majorian see 5. 153 sq.

[5] The king who ordered the labours of Hercules.

THE POEMS OF SIDONIUS

Has supplex famulus preces dicavit
responsum opperiens pium ac salubre.
ut reddas patriam simulque vitam
Lugdunum exonerans suis ruinis,
hoc te Sidonius tuus precatur: 25
sic te Sidonio recocta fuco
multos purpura vestiat per annos;
sic lustro imperii perennis acto
quinquennalia fascibus dicentur;
sic ripae duplicis tumore fracto   30
detonsus Vachalim bibat Sygamber.
quod si contuleris tuo poetae,
mandem perpetuis legenda fastis
quaecumque egregiis geris triumphis.
nam nunc Musa loquax tacet tributo,   35
quae pro Vergilio Terentioque
sextantes legit unciasque fisci,
Marsyaeque timet manum ac rudentem,
qui Phoebi ex odio vetustiore
nunc suspendia vatibus minatur.   40

XIV

SIDONIVS POLEMIO SVO SALVTEM

1. Dum post profectionem tuam, mi Polemi, frater
amantissime, mecum granditer reputo quatenus in
votis tuis philosophi Fescennina cantarem, obrepsit

---

[1] *mandem*, a good instance of present subjunctive for future
indicative. There are several examples of this in Sidonius.
[2] A reference not only to the well-known legend of Apollo
and Marsyas, but to Marsyas as symbolising the law (from the
statue of Marsyas in the Roman Forum near the law-courts).

216

XIV. SIDONIUS TO POLEMIUS

This petition thy suppliant servant has offered, waiting for a kind and life-giving answer. That thou mayest give him back his native town and his life withal, releasing Lugdunum from its fallen estate— this thy Sidonius craves of thee: so may the purple, redipped in Sidonian dye, clothe thee for many a year; so, when thou hast completed a lustre of thine everlasting reign, may a quinquennial festival be consecrated to thy rule; so may the Sygambrian, when the commotion on both banks has been quelled, drink the waters of Vachalis with head shorn in humiliation. If thou grant this to thy poet, I will commit [1] to history's undying records, to be read of mankind, all the exploits of thy glorious triumphs. For now my talkative muse is silenced by the tax, and culls instead of Virgil's and Terence's lines the pence and halfpence owed to the Exchequer, and fears the hand and rope of Marsyas,[2] who from his old-time hatred of Phoebus now threatens bards with hanging.

XIV

SIDONIUS TO HIS FRIEND POLEMIUS,[3] GREETING

1. My devoted brother Polemius,

After your departure I considered carefully how far I was entitled to sing a Fescennine strain in celebrating the wedding of a philosopher like you.

---

[3] Polemius, a descendant of the historian Tacitus, became Praetorian Prefect of Gaul (perhaps A.D. 471–2, less probably after 475 : see Stevens, p. 197), and held office for two years. See *Epist.* IV. 14, which is addressed to him.

materia, qua decursa facile dinosci valet magis me
doctrinae quam causae tuae habuisse rationem.
omissa itaque epithalamii teneritudine per asper-
rimas philosophiae et salebrosissimas regulas [1] stilum
traxi; quarum talis ordo est ut sine plurimis novis
verbis, quae praefata pace reliquorum eloquentum
specialiter tibi et Complatonicis tuis nota sunt,
nugae ipsae non valuerint expediri. 2. videris,
utrum aures quorundam per imperitiam temere
mentionem centri, proportionis, diastematum, cli-
matum vel myrarum epithalamio conducibilem non
putent. illud certe consulari viro vere Magno,
quaestorio viro Domnulo, spectabili viro Leone
ducibus audacter adfirmo, musicam et astrologiam,
quae sunt infra arithmeticam consequentia membra
philosophiae, nullatenus posse sine hisce nominibus
indicari; quae si quispiam ut Graeca, sicut sunt, et
peregrina verba contempserit, noverit sibi aut
semper [2] huiuscemodi artis mentione supersedendum
aut nihil omnino se aut certe non ad assem Latiari
lingua hinc posse disserere. 3. quod si aliqui [3]
secus atque assero rem se habere censuerint, do
quidem absens obtrectatoribus manus; sed noverint
sententiam meam discrepantia sentientes sine Marco

---

[1] regiunculas *Stangl*, regiones *Buecheler*.
[2] semper *Buecheler* : super.
[3] aliqui . . . censuerint *ego* : aliquis . . . censuerit.

---

[1] Magnus: 23. 455 n. Domnulus: 5. 570 n. Leo:
9. 314 n. The *spectabiles* ranked between the *inlustres* and

XIV. SIDONIUS TO POLEMIUS

The subject of the poem then crept into my mind, and now that it is completed it is easily seen that I have taken more notice of your learning than of the happy occasion. Thus I have abandoned the melting tones of the nuptial song and trailed my pen over the roughest and most stony teachings of philosophy, which are so constituted that even a trifling effort like this could not have been accomplished without a large number of the new words which (with apologies to all other stylists) are known in a special degree to you and your fellow-Platonists. 2. You shall judge whether certain persons' ears, owing to inexperience, imagine too hastily that the mention of " centrum," " proportio," " diastemata," " climata," " myrae," is unsuited to a marriage-poem. This at least I confidently affirm, following the lead of Magnus, a consular and a man as great as his name, Domnulus, of quaestorian rank, and the Eminent Leo,[1] that music and astronomy, the branches of philosophy which come next in importance to arithmetic, cannot in the least be made intelligible without these terms; and if anyone look down on them, as being Greek and foreign expressions (which they are), let him be assured that he must for ever renounce all mention of this sort of science or else that he cannot treat the subject at all, or at least that he cannot treat it completely, in the Latin tongue. 3. Should some people maintain that the facts are not as I declare them to be, I surrender to those cavillers whom I cannot meet face to face; nevertheless, I would have all who differ from me know that my opinion cannot be condemned without condemning Marcus Varro,

the *clarissimi* in the official hierarchy. See Hodgkin I, 603, 620, Bury I. 19.

Varrone, sine Sereno, non Septimio, sed Sammonico,
sine Censorino, qui de die natali volumen illustre
confecit, non posse damnari. 4. lecturus es hic
etiam novum verbum, id est essentiam; sed scias
hoc ipsum dixisse Ciceronem; nam essentiam nec
non et indoloriam nominavit, addens: " licet enim
novis rebus nova nomina imponere "; et recte dixit.
nam sicut ab eo quod est verbi gratia sapere et
intellegere sapientiam et intellegentiam
nominamus, regulariter et ab eo quod est esse
essentiam non tacemus. igitur, quoniam tui
amoris studio inductus homo Gallus scholae
sophisticae intromisi materiam, vel te potissimum
facti mei deprecatorem requiro. illi Venus vel
Amorum commenticia pigmenta tribuantur cui
defuerit sic posse laudari. vale.

PRAEFATIO EPITHALAMII DICTI POLEMIO
ET ARANEOLAE

Prosper conubio dies coruscat,
quem Clotho niveis benigna pensis,

---

[1] See 9. 267. The Serenus Sammonicus here referred to
is the elder of that name, a very learned man, who was put
to death by Caracalla. His son was a poet, and is usually
identified with Quintus (or Quintius? See Vollmer's ed., p. 3)
Serenus, the author of a still extant medical treatise in verse.

[2] Seneca (*Epist.* 58. 6) confirms Sidonius about *essentia*;
but the word is not found in any extant work of Cicero.
According to Quintilian (II. 14. 2, III. 6. 23, VIII. 3. 33)

Serenus (Sammonicus, not Septimius [1]), and Censorinus, the author of a fine book " On the natal Day." 4. Here also you are going to read a novel word, *essentia*; but you must note that Cicero himself has used that word; for he introduced the two terms *essentia* and *indoloria*,[2] adding: " for it is allowable to apply new names to new notions." And he was quite right, for just as we form, for example, the nouns *sapientia* and *intellegentia* from *sapere* and *intellegere*, so quite legitimately we do not refrain from using *essentia* from *esse*. Therefore, since my interest in your love-affair has led me, a man of Gaul, to introduce such matter as belongs to the philosophical lecture-room, I claim you in a special degree as intercessor on my behalf. Let Venus and all the fictitious gallery of love-gods be bestowed on one who cannot be eulogised in the manner of this poem. Farewell.

PREFACE TO THE EPITHALAMIUM ADDRESSED TO POLEMIUS AND ARANEOLA [3]

Auspicious for the marriage gleams the day, a day for a kindly Clotho to distinguish with snow-

---

essentia (a translation of οὐσία, " being ") was first used by a philosopher called Plautus (this seems to be the correct form, but the MSS. vary). Cicero uses *indolentia*, but it is scarcely credible that he ever used *indoloria*. Both these words are renderings of the Greek word ἀναλγησία, " insensibility," literally " freedom from pain." The form *indoloria* is used by Jerome and Augustine.

[3] For Araneola see n. on 9. 6.

albus quem picei lapillus Indi,
quem pacis simul arbor et iuventae
aeternumque virens oliva signet.   5
eia, Calliope, nitente palma
da sacri laticis loquacitatem,
quem fodit pede Pegasus volanti
cognato madidus iubam veneno.
non hic impietas, nec hanc puellam   10
donat mortibus ambitus procorum;
non hic Oenomai cruenta circo
audit pacta Pelops nec insequentem
pallens Hippomenes ad ima metae
tardat Schoenida ter cadente pomo;   15
non hic Herculeas videt palaestras
Aetola Calydon stupens ab arce,
cum cornu fluvii superbientis
Alcides premeret, subinde fessum
undoso refovens ab hoste pectus;   20
sed doctus iuvenis decensque virgo,
ortu culmina Galliae tenentes,
iunguntur: cito, diva, necte chordas
nec, quod detonuit Camena maior,
nostram pauperiem silere cogas.   25
ad taedas Thetidis probante Phoebo
et Chiron cecinit minore plectro,
nec risit pia turba rusticantem,
quamvis saepe senex biformis illic
carmen rumperet hinniente cantu.   30

---

[1] For this proverbial expression (said to be derived from the
Thracian custom of putting a white pebble in an urn to mark
a lucky day) see commentators on Horace, *Odes* I. 36. 10,
Conington on Persius II. 1. In Martial, whom Sidonius here

white thread, a day to be marked by the white stone of the black Indian[1] and by the olive ever fresh and green, tree at once of peace and of youth. Ho, Calliope! With thy radiant hand deliver to me the eloquence of the sacred spring which Pegasus dug out with his flying foot when his mane was wet with his mother's poison. Here there is no unnatural enmity; this girl is not being bestowed through the deaths of rival suitors. Here no Pelops listens to the bloody terms of Oenomaus[2] in the racing-ground; no Hippomenes[3] pale with dread at the lower turning-point of the course retards the maid of Schoenus with thrice-falling apple; not here does Calydon behold in amazement from her Aetolian height the wrestling of Hercules, when he forced down the horn of the arrogant river, refreshing his breast ever and anon from his watery foe.[4] Nay, a learned young scholar and a comely maid, holding by right of birth the most exalted eminence in Gaul, are being united. Quick, goddess, string the lyre, nor compel my poor talent to keep silence because a greater Muse[5] hath sent forth thundering strains. At the marriage of Thetis, with Apollo's approval, even Chiron made music with lesser quill, nor did the kindly company laugh at his rustic style, although oft the aged double-formed creature broke his song with a whinnying note.[6]

imitates, the stones become pearls (*Indicis lapillis* I. 109. 4; cf. X. 38. 5; see also VIII. 45. 2, XI. 36. 1).

[2] See 2. 491 n.

[3] Cf. 2. 494–496, 5. 167–176, 11. 87.

[4] See 2. 497–499 n.

[5] The identity of this " greater Muse " is unknown.

[6] Cf. 1. 19 sq.

XV

EPITHALAMIVM

Forte procellosi remeans ex arce Capherei,
Phoebados Iliacae raptum satis ulta pudorem,
Pallas Erechtheo Xanthum mutabat Hymetto.
aurato micat aere caput, maiusque serenum
de terrore capit; posito nam fulmine necdum   5
Cinyphio Tritone truces hilaraverat artus.
Gorgo tenet pectus medium, factura videnti
et truncata moras; nitet insidiosa superbum
effigies vivitque anima pereunte venustas;
alta cerastarum spiris caput asperat atrum   10
congeries, torquet maculosa volumina mordax
crinis, et irati dant sibila taetra capilli.
squameus ad mediam thorax non pervenit alvum
post chalybem pendente peplo; tegit extima limbi
circite palla pedes, qui cum sub veste moventur,   15
crispato rigidae crepitant in syrmate rugae.
laevam parma tegit Phlegraei plena tumultus:
hic rotat excussum vibrans in sidera Pindum
Enceladus, rabido fit missilis Ossa Typhoeo;
Porphyrion Pangaea rapit, Rhodopenque Damastor
Strymonio cum fonte levat, veniensque superne   21
intorto calidum restinguit flumine fulmen;
hic Pallas Pallanta petit, cui Gorgone visa

19. rabido *Mohr et Luetjohann*: rapido.

---

[1] See 5. 196 n.
[2] Tritonis (palus) was a lake in N. Africa, now impossible to
identify with certainty. It was near the Lesser Syrtes, with
which it seems to have been united by a river, also called
Tritonis. The lake is often associated with Pallas Athena,
who is called Τριτογένεια, Tritonia, and Tritonis (see 7. 198 and
below, *v.* 179). One legend made her a daughter of the lake-
nymph, another said that she was born on the shores of the lake.

XV

EPITHALAMIUM

It chanced that Pallas was returning from the peak of storm-swept Caphereus[1]; she had avenged to the full the ravished honour of Apollo's Trojan votary, and now she was abandoning Xanthus for Athenian Hymettus. Her head sparkles with gilded bronze, and she begins to show a more serene aspect after her frightfulness; for she has laid aside the thunder-bolt, though she has not yet gladdened her fierce limbs with the waters of African Tritonis.[2] The Gorgon covers the middle of her breast, with power still to make the beholder motionless, though the head be severed. Proudly shines that guileful form, and its beauty still lives though life is ebbing. The dark head bristles with a towering swarm of twisting vipers; those fanged tresses tangle their spotted coils, those angry locks utter horrible hisses. The corselet of scale-armour worn by the goddess reaches not to the waist; where the steel ceases her robe hangs down; the end of her cloak covers her feet with its circling hem, and when they move under her raiment there is a rustling of the stiff folds in the crimped trailing mantle. Her left hand is covered by a shield filled with a likeness of the Phlegraean fray. In one part Enceladus brandishes Pindus, torn from its base, and sends it whirling to the stars, while Ossa is the missile of frenzied Typhoeus; Porphyrion snatches up Pangaeus, Damastor lifts up Rhodope along with Strymon's spring, and when the glowing thunderbolt comes down he hurls the river at it and quenches it. In another part Pallas assails Pallas, but he has seen the Gorgon, and her spear is

225

invenit solidum iam lancea tarda cadaver;
hic Lemnon pro fratre Mimas contra aegida
    torquet,   25
impulsumque quatit iaculabilis insula caelum;
plurimus hic Briareus populoso corpore pugnat,
cognatam portans aciem, cui vertice ab uno
cernas ramosis palmas fruticare lacertis.
nec species solas monstris, dedit arte furorem   30
Mulciber atque ipsas timuit quas finxerat iras.
hastam dextra tenet, nuper quam valle Aracynthi
ipsa sibi posita Pallas protraxit oliva.
hoc steterat genio, super ut vestigia divae
labentes teneat Marathonia baca trapetas.   35

    Hic duo templa micant; quorum supereminet unus
ut meritis sic sede locus, qui continet alta
scrutantes ratione viros quid machina caeli,
quid tellus, quid fossa maris, quid turbidus aer,
quid noctis lucisque vices, quid menstrua lunae   40
incrementa parent, totidem cur damna sequantur.

---

[1] Pallas Athena is elsewhere said to have flayed Pallas the
giant. See Apollodorus I. 6. 2 with Sir J. G. Frazer's note
(vol. I. p. 46 n. 1 in this series).

[2] The digression on the shield ends here. Failure to notice
this has led to serious misunderstanding of the next four
lines, although Sidonius has taken pains to make things
clear: *hastam dextra tenet* is contrasted with *laevam parma
tegit* (*v.* 17).

[3] M. Aracynthus was in Aetolia, but Sidonius seems to
follow Virgil in placing it on the borders of Attica and Boeotia:
see Conington (ed. 5) and Page on Virgil, *Ec.* II. 24.

[4] The olive.

[5] The poet imagines a site in or near Athens (the Acropolis?)
where there are two adjoining temples consecrated to Pallas
Athena, goddess of wisdom and of arts and crafts. The first
temple is a home of philosophy, where Polemius learns all
the doctrines of the sages; the second (described in *vv.* 126 sqq.)

226

XV. EPITHALAMIUM

already too late, and encounters a solid corpse.[1]
Elsewhere is seen Mimas flinging Lemnos against
the aegis in a brother's defence, while the island-
missile shakes heaven with its impact. In yet
another part is the multiple Briareus with his much-
peopled body joining in the fray, carrying in his
person a whole host all akin: you could see his hands
on branching arms sprouting from a single source.
To these monsters Vulcan had given by his skill not
only forms but frenzy, so that he trembled at the
very wrath which his art had counterfeited.[2] The
right hand of Pallas held a spear, which she herself
had lately plucked in the vale of Aracynthus[3] from an
olive she had planted   Arrayed in all this glory she
had now alighted, and where the feet of the goddess
rested there arose the Marathonian berry[4] to take
possession of the gliding mills

Here two temples[5] gleam forth, both in the same
region, a region exalted alike in situation and in
achievements, for it contains the men who by thought
profound inquire what the fabric of the sky, the earth,
the sunken sea, the tempestuous air, the alternations
of day and night, and the monthly waxing of the moon
bring to pass, and why the waxing is ever followed by

is devoted to the textile arts, and there Araneola sits, doing
wonderful embroidery. Her subjects are mostly taken from
the love-stories of mythology. The goddess indicates that
she prefers the subjects which are cultivated in the other
temple; whereupon Araneola mischievously begins to depict
a philosopher (Diogenes the Cynic) in a ridiculous situation.
The goddess, unable to restrain a smile, says, " You are not
going to laugh at philosophers any longer; you are going to
marry one." For an ingenious but unconvincing attempt
to identify and locate the two " temples " see A. von Premer-
stein in *Jahresh. d. österr. arch. Inst.* XV (1912), pp. 28-35.
He seriously misunderstands *vv.* 36 f.

ilicet hic summi resident septem sapientes,
innumerabilium primordia philosophorum:
Thales Mileto genitus vadimonia damnat;
Lindie tu Cleobule iubes modus optimus ut sit;   45
tu meditans totum decoras, Periandre, Corinthon;
Atticus inde Solon " ne quid nimis " approbat unum;
Prienaee Bia, plures ais esse malignos;
tu Mytilene satus cognoscere, Pittace, tempus,
noscere sese ipsum, Chilon Spartane, docebas;   50
asserit hic Samius post docta silentia lustri
Pythagoras solidum princeps quod musica mundum
temperet et certis concentum reddat ab astris,
signaque zodiacus quae circulus axe supremo
terna quater retinet proprio non currere motu,   55
aequis inter se spatiis tamen esse locata
fixaque signifero pariter quoque cernua ferri,
praecipuumque etiam septem vaga sidera cantum
hinc dare, perfectus numerus quod uterque habeatur,
hoc numero adfirmans, hoc ordine cuncta rotari: 60
falciferi zonam ire senis per summa polorum,
Martis contiguum medio Iove pergere sidus,
post hos iam quarto se flectere tramite Solem,
sic placidam Paphien servare diastema quintum,
Arcadium sextum, Lunam sic orbe supremo   65

59. utique *P fortasse ex* utrimque *ortum*: *vid. Class. Quart. loc. cit. p.* 21.   61. zonam *Mohr*: c(h)ronon.
65. sextum *ego*: sexto; *vid. Class. Quart. ib.*

the waning. Here, then, are enthroned the Seven Sages, the sources of numberless philosophers.[1] Thales of Miletus condemns the giving of sureties; Cleobulus of Lindus bids moderation be our ideal; Periander glorifies Corinth as he practises everything; then Solon of Athens approves above all the saying, " Nothing to excess "; Bias of Priene says that the evil-hearted are the majority; Pittacus, that son of Mitylene, taught this lesson—to mark the opportune time, and Spartan Chilo to know oneself. Here the Samian Pythagoras declares, after a philosophic silence of five years, that music is the prime regulator of the universe and gives it a harmony from the unvarying movement of the stars, and that the thrice four signs that the Zodiac-belt holds in high heaven run not on with their own separate motion, but are placed at equal intervals one from another and, being fixed in the sign-bearing belt, are borne with it in descending movement; also that the seven wandering stars give forth the finest music because in planets and notes alike a perfect number is present. He says that by this number the universe is whirled round, and in this arrangement: the circle of the old Sickle-bearer [2] traverses the highest regions of the firmament; next, save that Jupiter comes between, the star of Mars wends its way; after these the Sun winds along the fourth path; in like manner the gentle goddess of Paphos [3] retains the fifth zone, the Arcadian [4] the sixth; and the moon in the last circle

[1] Cf. 2. 156 sqq.
[2] Saturn.
[3] Venus.
[4] Mercury : see 1. 7 n.

ter denas tropico prope currere climate myras.
si quos ergo chelys, si quos lyra, tibia si quos
ediderint cum voce modos, exemplar ad istud
ponderibus positis, quantum proportio suadet,
intervalla sequi septeni sideris edit;   70
harmoniam dicens etiam quod quattuor istis
sic sedeant elementa modis ut pondere magnis
sit locus inferior media tellure (quod autem
perfecte medium est, imum patet esse rotundi);
hinc fieri ut terram levior superemicet unda,   75
altior his quoque sit qui purior eminet aer,
omnia concludat caelum levitate suprema,
pendeat et totum simul hoc ab origine centri.
Thales hic etiam numeris perquirit et astris
defectum ut Phoebi nec non Lunaeque laborem   80
nuntiet anterius; sed rebus inutile ponit
principium, dum credit aquis subsistere mundum.
huius discipuli versa est sententia dicens
principiis propriis semper res quasque creari,
singula qui quosdam fontes decernit habere   85
aeternum irriguos ac rerum semine plenos.

---

¹ *Myrae* or *moerae* are segments of the zodiacal circle, which
extends from tropic to tropic. The sun traverses thirty of these
in about a month. Had Sidonius been speaking of the sun there
would have been no difficulty; but he seems to be confusing
these solar degrees with the (approximately) 30 days of the
moon's monthly revolution.
² Anaximander; but Sidonius in this passage gives a rough
summary of doctrines usually associated with Anaxagoras:
the primal chaos contained an infinite number of particles,
or "seeds" of things; these became separated off, like becoming united with like (*e.g.* gold particles with gold particles):
everything in the world consists predominantly of particles of
the same nature as itself (miniatures of itself as it were)—this
is the doctrine of *homoiomereia*, as it was called by Aristotle
and others. The process of change in individual things is

runs on through nearly thirty degrees within the clime of the tropics.[1] Thus all the tones that have been given forth by harp and lyre and flute and voice follow, he declares, the intervals of the seven planets, the pitch of the sounds being assigned after this pattern according to the dictates of proportion. He also calls by the name of harmony the arrangement of the four elements, which are so placed that those of great weight have the lowest place in the earth at the centre (It is clear that in a round shape what is absolutely the middle must be the lowest part); hence it comes about that water, which is lighter, springs up above the land, and higher than both is air, which is purer and thus soars over them, while sky, with its extreme lightness, encloses all these, and at the same time this whole universe takes its poise from the centre. In this temple also Thales inquires by calculations concerning the heavenly bodies how to announce beforehand the eclipse of the sun and the travail of the moon; but he assigns to things a vain first principle, believing that the universe is evolved from water. His pupil[2] takes a contrary view; he says that everything is always created from its own peculiar first-beginnings, and he holds that individual entities have, as it were, springs ever flowing and full of the seeds of things.

always going on : by addition or separation something quite different may be produced, owing to the predominance of another type of particle. This may be the meaning of *vv.* 85 sq.; but the language is vague and might be variously interpreted. The ancients often attribute Anaxagorean doctrines to Anaximander, and it is not easy to draw a rigid line between the tenets of the two philosophers; but Anaxagoras seems really to have been more influenced by Anaximenes than by Anaximander.

hunc etiam sequitur qui gignere cuncta putabat
hunc aerem pariterque deos sic autumat ortos.
quartus Anaxagoras Thaletica dogmata servat,
sed divinum animum sentit, qui fecerit orbem.   90
iunior huic iunctus residet collega, sed idem
materiam cunctis creaturis aera credens
iudicat inde deum, faceret quo cuncta, tulisse.
post hos Arcesilas divina mente paratam
conicit hanc molem, confectam partibus illis   95
quas atomos vocat ipse leves.   Socratica post hunc
secta micat, quae de naturae pondere migrans
ad mores hominum limandos transtulit usum.
hanc sectam perhibent summum excoluisse Platona,
sed triplici formasse modo, dum primus et unus   100
physica vel logico, logicum vel iungit ad ethos.
invenit hic princeps quid prima essentia distet
a summo sextoque bono: cum denique saxa
sint tantum penitusque nihil nisi esse probentur;
proxima succedant, quibus esse et vivere promptum
    est,   105
addere quis possis nil amplius, arbor et herba;
tertia sit pecorum, quorum esse et vivere motu
non caret et sensu; mortales quarta deinde
respiciat factura suos, quibus esse, moveri,
vivere cum sensu datur, et supereminet illud,   110

88. hunc aerem *def. Brakman.*   104. nisi id, esse *Leo.*

---

[1] Anaximenes.
[2] It is difficult to guess why Sidonius thought that Anaxagoras upheld the doctrines of Thales.
[3] This seems to refer to Diogenes of Apollonia, but he certainly did not regard God as a creator essentially distinct
from the air out of which all else is created.
[4] Arcesilas should be Archelaus.
[5] See n. on 2. 173. There is no reason for attributing this
triple division of philosophy to Socrates or Plato.   It may have

He is followed by one [1] who thought that our air produces all things, and who declares that the gods also have a like origin. Fourth in the line is Anaxagoras, who upholds the dogmas of Thales [2] but feels the presence of a divine mind, creator of the world. Next to him sits a younger colleague,[3] but he, believing air to be the substance from which all creatures come, judges that thence God derived the wherewithal to create everything. After them Arcesilas [4] guesses that this great world-mass is produced by a divine mind but is made up of those particles which he himself calls light atoms. After him shines forth the Socratic school, which passed from nature's massive fabric and transferred its practice to enhancing the moral life of mankind. This school they say the peerless Plato adorned, but he moulded it after a triple pattern,[5] being an unmatched pioneer in his joining of physics to logic and logic to ethics. He is the first to discover how great is the distance between the first essence and the sixth and highest good.[6] For stones, he says, do but exist, and are clearly proved to do naught but exist; next come those things which manifestly both exist and live, but to which you could ascribe no further attribute, trees and plants; the third kind of being is found in the beasts, in whom existing and living are accompanied by motion and sensation; next the fourth creation favours his own fellow-mortals, to whom are given the gifts of existence, movement, life, and sensation, whereto is added the crowning gift of discernment

been first formulated by Xenocrates, but was first emphasised by the Stoics. See Reid on Cic. *Ac.* I. 19.

[6] Needless to say, Plato never propounded this doctrine.

quod sapiunt veroque valent discernere falsum;
quinta creaturas superas substantia prodat,
quas quidam dixere deos, quia corpora sumant
contemplanda homini, paulo post ipsa relinquant
inque suam redeant, si qua est tenuissima, formam—
sic fieri ut pateat substantia summa creator,   116
sexta tamen supraque nihil, sed cuncta sub ipso.
hoc in gymnasio Polemi sapientia vitam
excolit adiunctumque suo fovet ipsa Platoni;
obviet et quamquam totis Academia sectis   120
atque neget verum, veris hunc laudibus ornat.
Stoica post istos, sed concordantibus ipsis,
Chrysippus Zenonque docent praecepta tenere.
exclusi prope iam Cynici, sed limine restant;
ast Epicureos eliminat undique Virtus.   125
    At parte ex alia textrino prima Minervae
palla Iovis rutilat, cuius bis coctus aeno
serica Sidonius fucabat stamina murex.
ebria nec solum spirat conchylia sandix;
insertum nam fulgur habet, filoque rigenti   130
ardebat gravidum de fragmine fulminis ostrum.
hic viridis patulo Glaucus pendebat amictu;
undabant hic arte sinus, fictoque tumore
mersabat pandas tempestas texta carinas.
Amphitryoniadi surgebat tertia vestis: 135
parvulus hic gemino cinctus serpente novercae

119. adiunctumque *PF*: adiunctamque. *Vid. Class. Quart.
loc. cit. p.* 21.
132. patulo *ego*: patruo *CP*, glauco patruo *F*, patrio *T*:
proprio *Leo*, prasino *Purgold*.

---

[1] A good example of the weakened force of *tamen*, common
in late Latin. See Schmalz-Hofmann, *Synt.* p. 672, and the
authorities there cited, especially Löfstedt, *Komm.* 27–33.
[2] *i.e.* probably Polemius, possibly Plato.

and power to distinguish false from true; the fifth class reveals the created beings that dwell on high, whom some have called gods, because they assume bodies that man can view but soon abandon them and return to their own form, a form of the most ethereal fineness: thus he says it comes to pass that the highest being is shown to be the creator; he is, then,[1] the sixth, and there is naught above him, but all else is beneath him. In this school Philosophy ennobles the life of Polemius and herself fosters him close to her own son Plato; and although the Academy opposes all sects by denying that truth exists, that sect extols him[2] with praises that are true. After them, but now in harmony one with the other, Chrysippus and Zeno teach adherence to the Stoic doctrines. The Cynics are by this time almost shut out, but they linger on the threshold; as for the Epicureans, Virtue ejects them from every part.

On the other side is Minerva's weaving-hall. Here the robe of Jupiter first shows its ruddy gleam; Sidonian purple twice boiled in the cauldron coloured the silken threads, and the deep-dyed red showed not only the sheen of purple, for the gleam of lightning was intermingled, and a blaze came from the stiff threads where the purple was weighted with a broken levin-shaft.[3] Here also hung a likeness of green Glaucus in a spreading mantle; here art had fashioned his billowing robe, and an inwoven storm with mimic swelling was submerging curved ships. The third garment that rose before the eyes was dedicated to Amphitryon's son. Here the infant, encircled by the two serpents sent by his stepdame,[4]

---

[3] *i.e.* a representation of lightning wrought in gold thread.
[4] See 7. 582 n.

inscius arridet monstris ludumque putando
insidias, dum nescit, amat vultuque dolentis
exstingui deflet quos ipse interficit angues.
praeterea sparsis sunt haec subiecta figuris :   140
sus, leo, cerva, Gigans, taurus, iuga, Cerberus, hydra,
hospes, Nessus, Eryx, volucres, Thrax, Cacus, Amazon,
Cres, fluvius, Libs, poma, Lycus, virgo, polus, Oete.
hoc opus, et si quid superest quod numina vestit,
virgineae posuere manus.   sed in agmine toto   145
inter Cecropias Ephyreiadasque puellas
Araneola micat ; proprias conferre laborat
ipsa Minerva manus, calathisque evicta recedens
cum tenet haec telas vult haec plus tela tenere.
hic igitur proavi trabeas imitata rigentes   150
palmatam parat ipsa patri, qua consul et idem
Agricolam contingat avum doceatque nepotes
non abavi solum sed avi quoque iungere fasces.
texuerat tamen et chlamydes, quibus ille magister
per Tartesiacas conspectus splenduit urbes   155
et quibus ingestae sub tempore praefecturae
conspicuus sanctas reddit se praesule leges.
attamen in trabea segmento luserat alto

---

144. numina *Wilamowitz* : nomina.

---

[1] Cf. 9. 95-98.

[2] The meaning of *trabea* in later Imperial writers is a vexed
question, but these words strongly confirm the view that it
was strictly a synonym of *tunica palmata* (see 2. 6 n.) : cf.
Auson. 322. 92, *ut trabeam pictamque togam, mea praemia,
consul induerer.*   The word is also used in a less precise way
to denote the consular vestments in general.   In 7. 384 it is
still more loosely used of the dictator's garb (which was,
it is true, the same as the consul's ; but in republican times
the consul wore the *toga praetexta*, as did all other curule
magistrates, and had no distinctive *tunica*).   In 23. 174
the plural is used for " robes of state."

smiles in all innocence upon the monsters and, taking the guileful menace as a game, loves them in his ignorance, and with a countenance of grief bewails the dying of the snakes he himself slays. Moreover, there are added in scattered figures these likenesses—the boar, the lion, the deer, the giant, the bull, the yoke, Cerberus, the hydra, the host, Nessus, Eryx, the birds, the Thracian, Cacus, the Amazon, the Cretan beast, the river, the Libyan, the apples, the Lycian, the maid, the sky, and Oeta.[1] This work and all other vestures fit for gods have been set up in that place by maidens' hands. But amid the whole multitude, among all the damsels of Athens and of Corinth, Araneola shines out. Minerva herself strives to match her own hands with hers, but retires beaten from the work-baskets, and when Araneola holds the web she herself prefers to hold weapons. So here this maid copies the stiff-broidered consular vestment of her great-grandfather, making with her own hands a palm-decked robe [2] for her father, wherewith he, a consul likewise, shall match his grandfather Agricola [3] and teach his grand-children to link up in their chain of consulships their grandsire as well as their grandsire's grandsire. She had also woven the mantles in which he as Master shone before all eyes in the cities of Spain and in which conspicuous, when the prefecture was thrust upon him, he dispensed the hallowed laws from the president's seat. But on a high strip of broidery upon the consular robe she had playfully fashioned

[3] Agricola was Praetorian Prefect of Gaul twice (his second term of office was in A.D. 418) and consul in 421. He may have been an ancestor, possibly even the father, of the Emperor Avitus, who had a son named Agricola. See also n. on 23. 455.

quod priscis inlustre toris.   Ithacesia primum
fabula Dulichiique lares formantur et ipsam   160
Penelopam tardas texit distexere telas.
Taenaron hic frustra bis rapta coniuge pulsat
Thrax fidibus, legem postquam temeravit Averni,
et prodesse putans iterum non respicit umbram.
hic vovet Alceste praelato coniuge vitam   165
rumpere, quam cernas Parcarum vellere in ipso
nondum pernetam fato restante salute.
hic nox natarum Danai lucebat in auro,
quinquaginta enses genitor quibus impius aptat
et dat concordem discordia iussa furorem;   170
solus Hypermestrae servatus munere Lynceus
effugit; aspicias illam sibi parva paventem
et pro dimisso tantum pallere marito.
iamque Iovem in formas mutat quibus ille tenere
Mnemosynam, Europam, Semelen, Ledam, Cyno-
        suram   175
serpens, bos, fulmen, cygnus, Dictynna solebat.
iamque opus in turrem Danaae pluviamque metalli
ibat et hic alio stillabat Iuppiter auro,
cum virgo aspiciens vidit Tritonida verso
lumine doctisonas spectare libentius artes;   180
commutat commota manus ac pollice docto
pingere philosophi victricem Laida coepit,
quae Cynici per menta feri rugosaque colla

167. salute *Buecheler*: salutem *codd.* praestante salutem
vulgo, fortasse recte.
182. Laida: livida *codd.*

---

[1] Orpheus.
[2] See ll. 89 sq. n.
[3] *i.e.* the gold threads of the embroidery.
[4] See note on *v.* 6, above.

all the famous tales of old-time marriages. First
the story of Ithaca and the Dulichian home were
figured, and she wove in Penelope herself unweaving
the slow-growing web. There also is the Thracian,[1]
whose wife has twice been snatched from him;
vainly he beats upon the portal of Taenarus with the
throbs of his lyre, after breaking the ordinance of
Avernus, and he looks not back a second time upon
the shade, deeming that this is in his favour.
Then there is Alcestis, who puts her husband before
herself and vows to cut short her life, which you
could see there in the very wool of the Fateful
Sisters, not yet spun to the end, for by her destiny
life still remains to her. There also shines forth in
gold the night of the Danaids; their impious father
girds upon them fifty swords, and the discord forced
upon them stirs a concordant frenzy. Lynceus
alone escapes, saved by the grace of Hypermestra;
you could see her there, fearing little for herself
and pale only with anxiety for the husband she has
suffered to depart. The broiderer likewise changes
Jove into the shapes in which he was wont to embrace
Mnemosyne, Europa, Semele, Leda, Cynosura,
becoming serpent, bull, lightning, swan, and Dictynna.[2] Then the work passed into Danae's tower
and the rain of metal; and here Jupiter was dripping
with another kind of gold [3] when the maid, looking
at Tritonis,[4] saw that the eyes of the goddess were
averted and that she was gazing with more pleasure
at the arts that give forth learned utterance. Then
the maiden's hand was moved to motive new, and
with cunning thumb she began to portray Lais,
the philosopher's vanquisher, who all over the chin
and wrinkled neck of the boorish Cynic severed

rupit odoratam redolenti forcipe barbam.
subrisit Pallas castoque haec addidit ore: 185
" non nostra ulterius ridebis dogmata, virgo
philosopho nuptura meo; mage flammea sumens
hoc mater sine texat opus. consurge, sophorum
egregium Polemi decus, ac nunc Stoica tandem
pone supercilia et Cynicos imitatus amantes   190
incipies iterum parvum mihi ferre Platona."
haerentem tali compellat voce magister:
" perge libens, neu tu damnes fortasse iugari,
quod noster iubet ille senex qui non piger hausit
numina contemplans Anyto pallente venenum." 195
   Dixerat; ille simul surgit vultuque modesto
tetrica nodosae commendat pallia clavae.
amborum tum diva comas viridantis olivae
pace ligat, nectit dextras ac foedera mandat,
Nymphidius quae cernat avus. probat Atropos omen
fulvaque concordes iunxerunt fila sorores.   201

XVI

EVCHARISTON AD FAVSTVM EPISCOPVM

Phoebum et ter ternas decima cum Pallade Musas
Orpheaque et laticem simulatum fontis equini

190. cygnos *Wilamowitz.*
195. contemplans *Wilamowitz*: condempnans, condemp-
nens, contempnens *codd.*

---

[1] The Cynics' neglect of personal comfort gained them a
bad reputation. This Cynic's beard is not over-clean; the
dainty Lais, on the other hand, perfumes even her scissors.
Possibly, however, *odoratam* means " perfumed."
[2] " The Master " seems to be Plato.
[3] The *pallium* and the *clava* (a thick staff) mark the philosopher: cf. *Epist.* IV. 11. 1, IX. 9. 14.
[4] It is uncertain whether he was the bride's or the bridegroom's grandfather. He may be the Nymphidius to whom
Epist. V. 2 is addressed.

the odorous beard with fragrant scissors.[1] Pallas
smiled, and opened her virgin lips to add these
words: "No more shall you laugh at our dogmas—
you maid that are bride-to-be of my philosopher;
rather now put on the bridal veil and let a matron
do this piece of broidery. Rise, Polemius, bright
jewel among our sages; now at last put away the
Stoic frown, and imitating the Cynic lovers you shall
begin to bring me a second little Plato." As he
hesitated, the Master [2] addressed him thus: "Proceed with willing heart, and do not haply condemn
marriage, which the old teacher enjoins who promptly
drained the poison with his eyes fixed on the gods,
while Anytus' cheek grew pale."

When these words are spoken he arises and with
modest mien commends the austere cloak to the
keeping of the knotted cudgel.[3] Then the goddess
binds the hair of each with green olive, the emblem of
peace, joins their hands, and ordains the contract
which the grandfather Nymphidius [4] is to ratify.
Atropos approves the omen and the sister Fates
with one accord unite the golden life-threads of the
two.

XVI

THANKSGIVING TO BISHOP FAUSTUS [5]

Thrust far from thee, O lyre of mine, Phoebus
and the nine Muses together with Pallas as tenth,
Orpheus and the fabled water of the horse's spring,

[5] Faustus was a native of Britain (*Epist.* IX. 9. 6). He
entered the monastery of Lérins (104 n.) at an early age,
becoming its abbot in A.D. 433 in succession to Maximus

Ogygiamque chelyn, quae saxa sequacia flectens
cantibus auritos erexit carmine muros,
sperne, fidis; magis ille veni nunc spiritus, oro,   5
pontificem dicture tuum, qui pectora priscae
intrasti Mariae, rapiens cum tympana siccus
Israel appensi per concava gurgitis iret
aggeribus vallatus aquae mediasque per undas
pulverulenta tuum clamaret turba triumphum; 10
quique manum Iudith ferientem colla Olophernis
iuvisti, exciso iacuit cum gutture truncus
et fragilis valido latuit bene sexus in ictu;
expresso vel qui complens de vellere pelvem
inficiensque dehinc non tacto vellere terram 15
firmasti Gedeona, tubis inserte canoris
spiritus, et solo venit victoria cantu;
quique etiam adsumptum pecorosi de grege Iesse
adflasti regem, plaustro cum foederis arcam
imponens hostis nullo moderante bubulco 20
proderet obscaenum turgenti podice morbum;
quique trium quondam puerorum in fauce sonasti,
quos in Chaldaei positos fornace tyranni

14. pelvem *Luetjohann*: pellem.

(*v.* 112). He was consecrated Bishop of Riez (Reii) probably
about A.D. 460 and became a leading ecclesiastical figure.
His opposition to the Arian creed caused his banishment after
Euric had extended his territory in 476 or 477 and gained
control of Riez. He was later allowed to return. His writings
include two books *De Gratia*, two *De Spiritu Sancto*, and some
letters. Some works have been falsely attributed to him.
After his death his writings were condemned as heretical.

and the Theban lute that with its music moved the
stones to follow it and raised by its strains the eagerly
listening walls.   Rather do thou come, O great Spirit,
I pray, to speak of thy pontiff—thou who didst enter
into the heart of Miriam [1] in olden times, when Israel
seizing their timbrels marched dry-shod through
the trough of the suspended sea, walled in by ram-
parts of water, and thy people, dust-covered as they
passed through the midst of the waves, acclaimed thy
triumph:

1   Who didst aid the hand of Judith as it smote
the neck of Holophernes, when the trunk was laid
prostrate with the throat cut through and the strong
blow gloriously disguised the weak sex [2]:

4   Who, filling the basin from the wrung fleece and
then bedewing the earth without touching the
fleece, didst hearten Gideon [3]; thou Spirit that wert
infused into the sounding trumpets, so that victory
came from their blast alone [4]:

8   Who didst also inspire the king that was called
from amid the sheep of Jesse,[5] the possessor of rich
flocks, when the enemy set the Ark of the Covenant
on a wain with no drover to guide it and betrayed
the loathsome disease by the swelling of the secret
parts [6]:

2   Who didst once sound in the mouths of the three
youths who when put in the Chaldean tyrant's

---

[1] Miriam, *Exod.* 15. 20; crossing of the Red Sea, c. 14.
[2] *Judith* 13. 8–10.   [3] *Judges* 6. 36–40.
[4] *Judges* 7. 19 sqq.   [5] 1 *Sam.* 16. 11–13; 18. 2.
[6] Ark and emerods, 1 *Sam.* cc. 5 and 6. But this story
has nothing to do with King David; Sidonius has confused
the story of the Philistines and the ark with that of 2 *Sam.*
6. 2 sqq.

roscida combusto madefecit flamma camino;
quique volubilibus spatiantem tractibus alvi　25
complesti Ionam, resonant dum viscera monstri
introrsum psallente cibo vel pondera ventris
ieiuni plenique tamen vate intemerato
ructat cruda fames, quem singultantibus extis
esuriens vomuit suspenso belua morsu;　30
quique duplex quondam venisti in pectus Helisei,
Thesbiten cum forte senem iam flammeus axis
tolleret et scissam linquens pro munere pellem
hispidus ardentes auriga intraret habenas;
quique etiam Heliam terris missure secundum　35
Zachariae iusti linguam placate ligasti,
dum faceret serum rugosa puerpera patrem,
edita significans iusso reticere propheta,
gratia cum fulsit, nosset se ut lex tacituram;
quique etiam nascens ex virgine semine nullo,　40
ante ullum tempus deus atque in tempore Christus,
ad corpus quantum spectat, tu te ipse creasti;
qui visum caecis, gressum quoque reddere claudis,
auditum surdis, mutis laxare loquelam

33. pallam *cod. Helmstad.*

---

[1] *Daniel* 3. 13 sqq.; the " dew-like flame " *ib.* 50 (Vulgate):
*et [Angelus Domini] fecit medium fornacis quasi ventum
roris flantem, et non tetigit eos omnino ignis neque contristavit,
nec quidquam molestiae intulit.* This occurs in a passage
of 67 verses (numbered 24–90) which does not appear in the
Hebrew text, but which is found in Theodotion's version
(from which the Vulgate took it) and in the Septuagint :
it doubtless occurred also in all the old Latin versions. Curiously enough, as Professor A. Souter informs me, no Latin
Father quotes the above verse. Even Jerome in his commentary on *Daniel* fails to do so, though he makes some comments
on the interpolated passage after pointing out that it does not
occur in the Hebrew.

furnace were but wetted with a dew-like flame when the oven itself was consumed[1]:

Who didst fill Jonah,[2] as he traversed the rolling tracts of the whale's belly, while the inward parts of the monster resounded with the psalms sung by the swallowed food, and a hunger that was clogged within belched forth the load of a full but fasting stomach without hurting the prophet, whom the beast, ravenous yet holding off his bite, disgorged from his retching entrails:

Who aforetime didst pass in a double portion into the breast of Elisha, when the time came for the fiery chariot to bear aloft the Tishbite in his old age, and the rough-clad charioteer, leaving as a gift his torn coat of skin, entered the flaming car[3]:

Who also, when minded to send to earth the second Elias,[4] didst in thy mercy bind the tongue of righteous Zacharias,[5] till such time as a mother in wrinkled eld should make him a father in his old age; and who in bidding the prophet to be silent about thy message didst give token that with the dawn of Grace the Law must know that silence was coming upon it:

Who also, born of a pure virgin, before all time God and in time Christ, didst create thyself, as touching the body; who wert wont to give to the blind sight, to the lame the power to walk, to the deaf hearing, and to loosen the tongue of the

---

[2] *Jonah*, c. 2.

[3] 2 (4) *Kings* 2. 9 sqq. Sidonius is again confused: Elisha rent his own clothes and "took up the mantle of Elijah that fell from him."

[4] *Malachi* 4. 5, *Matth.* 11. 14, 17. 12, *Mark* 9. 13 (12 Vulg.), *Luke* 1. 17.

[5] *Luke* 1. 5 sqq.

suetus ad hoc etiam venisti, ut mortua membra   45
lecto, sandapila, tumulo consurgere possint;
quique etiam poenas suscepta in carne tulisti,
sustentans alapas, ludibria, verbera, vepres,
sortem, vincla, crucem, clavos, fel, missile, acetum,
postremo mortem, sed surrecturus, adisti,   50
eripiens quidquid veteris migraverat hostis
in ius per nostrum facinus, cum femina prima
praeceptum solvens culpa nos perpete vinxit;
(qui cum te interitu petiit nec repperit in te
quod posset proprium convincere, perdidit omne   55
quod lapsu dedit Eva suo; chirographon illum,
quo pervasus homo est, haec compensatio rupit.
expers peccati pro peccatoribus amplum
fis pretium veteremque novus vice faenoris Adam,
dum moreris, de morte rapis. sic mortua mors est,
sic sese insidiis quas fecerat ipsa fefellit;   61
nam dum indiscrete petit insontemque reosque,
egit ut absolvi possent et crimine nexi);

---

[1] *Coloss.* 2. 14. The Greek is ἐξαλείψας τὸ καθ’ ἡμῶν χειρόγραφον τοῖς δόγμασιν and the Latin (Vulgate) is *delens quod adversus nos erat chirographum decreti.* These very difficult words have been much discussed both by the ancient Fathers and by modern theologians. Sidonius was no theologian, but there is perhaps something to be said for his interpretation: man had by his fall been, as it were, compelled to sign a bond whereby he was made over to the devil in default of paying a seemingly impossible ransom; Christ has made himself the ransom.

[2] *Pervasus* is very difficult. In legal Latin and in many late authors *pervadere, pervasio,* and *pervasor* are used with reference to an act of wanton appropriation. The act may be a flagrant theft (property stolen from a church is called *pervasa* in Paulin. Petricord. *Vit. Mart.* VI. 247) or the unlawful occupation of a dwelling. In the latter meaning we find *pervadere* and *pervasor* used metaphorically by Christian

mute, and didst come that dead bodies might be
able to rise from bed, bier, and tomb; who didst
in thine adopted flesh suffer torments, enduring
buffets, scoffs, stripes, thorns, casting of lots, chains,
the cross, the nails, the gall, the spear, the vinegar,
and finally didst meet death, though only to rise
again, delivering whatsoever had passed into the
dominion of the old Enemy through our trans-
gression, when the first woman broke the com-
mandment and so fettered us with abiding guilt
(But the Enemy, when he sought thy destruction
nor found in thee aught that he could prove to
be his own, lost all that Eve gave him by her fall;
and this recompense of thine dissolved the bond [1] by
which man became a robber's possession.[2] Free from
sin thou didst become an ample ransom for sinners,
and thou, the new Adam, didst by dying pay the
price and snatch the old Adam from death. Thus
Death is dead, caught in the very trap himself had
made; for attacking without distinction innocent
and guilty, he brought it to pass that even those
enslaved by sin received the power to be absolved):

writers with reference to demoniac possession. In this sense
the devil is called *pervasor* by Paulinus, *op. cit.* VI. 44; the
same metaphor (probably suggested by *Matth.* 12. 29, *Luke* 11.
24) is developed more fully by Sedulius in relating the story
of the boy possessed by an unclean spirit (*Matth.* 17. 14–18,
Mark 9. 17–27, *Luke* 9. 38–42, A.V. numbering): Christ
compels the spirit *pervasa migrare domo* (*Pasch. Carm.* III.
309; so in the prose version, *Pasch. Op.* III. 25, *pervasae
domus habitaculo migraturus*). Sidonius may have had this
image in his mind: in virtue of the "bond" the Evil One
has seized possession of man and made of him a dwelling-
place. On the other hand the meaning of *pervasus* here may
be simply "seized," "snatched away," "stolen." The
translation given attempts to cover both meanings.

quique etiam iustos ad tempus surgere tecum
iussisti cineres, cum tectis tempore longo   65
inrupit festina salus infusaque raptim
excussit tumulis solidatas vita favillas:
da Faustum laudare tuum, da solvere grates,
quas et post debere iuvat. te, magne sacerdos,
barbitus hic noster plectro licet impare cantat.   70

   Haec igitur prima est vel causa vel actio laudum,
quod mihi germani, dum lubrica volvitur aetas,
servatus tecum domini per dona probatur
nec fama titubante pudor; te respicit istud
quantumcumque bonum; merces debebitur illi,   75
ille tibi. sit laus, si labi noluit, eius;
nam quod nec potuit, totum ad te iure redundat.
praeterea quod me pridem Reios veniente,
cum Procyon fureret, cum solis torridus ignis
flexilibus rimis sitientes scriberet agros,   80
hospite te nostros excepit protinus aestus
pax, domus, umbra, latex, benedictio, mensa, cubile.
omnibus attamen his sat praestat quod voluisti
ut sanctae matris sanctum quoque limen adirem.
derigui, fateor, mihi conscius atque repente   85
tinxit adorantem pavido reverentia vultum;
nec secus intremui quam si me forte Rebeccae
Israel aut Samuel crinitus duceret Annae.

78. venientem codd.
85. derigui Luetjohann : dirigui.

---

¹ Matth. 27. 52 sq.
² We do not know the name of any brother of Sidonius.
³ i.e. although a reward in heaven will be his due, you will
have made him what he is.
⁴ The mother is probably (as Krusch conjectured) Mother
Church, not the mother of Faustus, and s. m. limen is the
threshold of the cathedral church.

XVI. TO BISHOP FAUSTUS

4   Who didst likewise bid the ashes of the just
to rise with thee at the appointed time,[1] when
salvation of a sudden burst upon them who had
long been covered up, and a flood of life poured
into them and swept their re-knit ashes from the
tomb—

8   Do thou grant that I may praise thy servant Faustus,
that I may pay my debt of gratitude, which even
after this payment I am glad to owe. Thee, great
priest, this lyre of mine doth hymn, albeit with a
quill unequal to the task.

The first cause and burden of my praises is that
when my brother [2] was at an age that is prone to slip
his virtue was preserved with thy help through the
grace of our Lord, and stands approved—yea,
and with no wavering in his good report. This
blessing in all its immensity is to be ascribed to thee;
the reward will be due to him, but he will be due
to thee.[3] If he has of his own free will refused to
stumble, let the praise be his; but that he could not
have stumbled even if he would redounds by right
entirely to thy credit. I praise thee too because
when I came aforetime to Reii, while Procyon was
raging and the sun's parching fire was marking the
thirsty fields with winding cracks, thy hospitality
straightway greeted my hot discomfort with peace,
home, shade, water, benediction, bed, and board.
But a far greater boon than all these was that thou
wert willing for me to approach also the hallowed
threshold of the hallowed mother.[4] I stood stock-
still, I confess, as I felt my unworthiness, and all at
once fearful awe coloured my face as it thrilled with
adoration; yea, I trembled as if Israel were bringing
me to Rebecca or long-haired Samuel to Hannah.

249

THE POEMS OF SIDONIUS

quapropter te vel votis sine fine colentes
adfectum magnum per carmina parva fatemur.   90
  Seu te flammatae Syrtes et inhospita tesqua
seu caeno viridante palus seu nigra recessu
incultum mage saxa tenent, ubi sole remoto
concava longaevas adservant antra tenebras;
seu te praeruptis porrecta in rupibus Alpis   95
succinctos gelido libantem caespite somnos,
anachoreta, tremit (quae quamquam frigora portet,
conceptum Christi numquam domat illa calorem),
qua nunc Helias, nunc te iubet ire Iohannes,
nunc duo Macarii, nunc et Paphnutius heros,   100
nunc Or, nunc Ammon, nunc Sarmata, nunc Hilarion,
nunc vocat in tunica nudus te Antonius illa
quam fecit palmae foliis manus alma magistri;
seu te Lirinus priscum complexa parentem est,
qua tu iam fractus pro magna saepe quiete   105
discipulis servire venis vixque otia somni,
vix coctos capture cibos abstemius aevum
ducis et insertis pinguis ieiunia psalmis,
fratribus insinuans quantos illa insula plana

108. pingis *CTF* : pinguas *Caduceus, fortasse recte.*

---

[1] Probably the prophet Elijah and John the Baptist, though
there were Egyptian anchorites who bore these names.
The Macarii, Hilarion, and Antonius are mentioned in *Epist.*
VII. 9. 9. *Sarmata* is unknown; it may be either the man's
name or a description of him, "the Sarmatian." For the
others see *Dict. Chr. Biog.* and Dom E. C. Butler in *C. M. H.*,
I. 521 sqq. The "master" of St. Anthony was Paulus
(Thebaeus).

[2] Lirinus (*Lerina* in Pliny), modern St.-Honorat, one of the
Lérins-group of islands opposite Antibes.

[3] *Montes* is used by ecclesiastical writers to denote bishops
and priests. There is here, of course, a frigid contrast between
montes and *plana insula.* Caprasius was associated with
Honoratus in the foundation of the monastery. *Lupus =* St.

Wherefore I honour thee without ceasing even in my prayers, and now I acknowledge in paltry verse my great affection.

Whether thou dost tarry roughly garbed in a cheerless wilderness by the sun-fired Syrtes or choosest rather a marsh full of green slime or the dark recesses of rocks where deep sunless caves maintain an age-long gloom; or whether the Alps, stretching afar with their long line of precipitous crags, tremble before thee, great anchorite, as thou snatchest brief slumber on the chill ground (and with all their cold they never overcome the warm glow that Christ hath set in thy heart); for this is the way that thou art urged to go, now by Elias, now by John,[1] now by the two Macarii, now by the great Paphnutius, now by Or, now by Ammon, now by Sarmata, now by Hilarion; and another time the call comes from Antonius, clad only in that tunic which the kindly hand of his master made of palm-leaves:

4 Or whether Lirinus[2] hath welcomed thee, its erstwhile father, whither thou, instead of resting long when thy strength is exhausted, dost often come to serve thy disciples, and thou wilt scarce repose thyself in sleep or take cooked food, but livest a life of self-denial and makest thy fasts rich with intervals of psalmody, meanwhile instilling lessons into the brethren, telling how many great eminences[3]

Lupus of Troyes. Honoratus became Bp. of Arles, and Maximus (see *Epist.* VIII. 14. 2) succeeded him at Lérins and subsequently became Bp. of Riez; in each of these offices his successor was Faustus. St. Eucherius was a monk at Lérins and afterwards Bp. of Lyons. His theological writings were potent for many centuries. Hilarius was a monk of Lérins, who followed Honoratus to Arles but subsequently returned to his old monastery. He afterwards became Bp. of Arles.

miserit in caelum montes, quae sancta Caprasi 110
vita senis iuvenisque Lupi, quae gratia patrem
mansit Honoratum, fuerit quis Maximus ille,
urbem tu cuius monachosque antistes et abbas
bis successor agis, celebrans quoque laudibus illis
Eucherii venientis iter, redeuntis Hilari; 115
seu te commissus populus tenet et minor audet
te medio tumidos maiorum temnere mores;
seu tu sollicitus curas qua languidus esca
quave peregrinus vivat, quid pascat et illum,
lubrica crura cui tenuat sub compede carcer; 120
seu mage funeribus mentem distractus humandis,
livida defuncti si pauperis ossa virescant,
infastiditum fers ipse ad busta cadaver;
seu te conspicuis gradibus venerabilis arae
contionaturum plebs sedula circumsistit, 125
expositae legis bibat auribus ut medicinam:
quidquid agis, quocumque loci es, semper mihi
    Faustus,
semper Honoratus, semper quoque Maximus esto.

XVII

AD V. C. OMMATIVM

Quattuor ante dies quam lux Sextilis adusti
  prima spiciferum proferat orbe caput

113. monachosque *Sirmondus* : monachusque.

---

[1] The preacher is seated, as was usual; the congregation
stands, as was the common, but not universal, custom at
this time. Augustine (*De Catechizandis Rudibus*, c. 13,
a very interesting chapter) expresses approval of the practice
adopted in some "transmarine" (*i.e.* Italian) churches,
where seats were provided for all. He would have them provided everywhere, at least for the infirm and the physically tired.

that flat island hath sent soaring to the skies, of
what kind was the holy life of old Caprasius and young
Lupus, what favour was destined for Honoratus their
founder, and who was that Maximus over whose city
and monks thou, twice his successor, wert set as
bishop and abbot; and thou dost also acclaim in
these praises the coming of Eucherius and the
return of Hilarius:

6   Or whether the people committed to thy charge
now have thee among them, and the lesser folk,
with thee in their midst, dare to despise the proud
ways of the great; or whether thou dost anxiously
take heed what food the sick or the stranger has
and how even he is fed whose legs the prison wastes
until they slide loosely beneath the fetters; or
whether the burial of the dead has all thy thoughts,
and loathing not the body of one of the poor although
a green hue be spreading over the livid remains,
thou with thine own hands dost bear it to the tomb;
or whether thou art about to preach from the conspicuous steps of the holy altar, and the eager crowd
take their stand around thee[1] that their ears may
drink in the healing medicine of the Law's exposition
—whatever thou doest, wherever thou art, I wish
thee for evermore the blessings of thy three names,
Fortunate, Honoured, Greatest.

XVII

TO OMMATIUS, SENATOR[2]

Four days before the first dawn of August raises
above the earth its corn-wreathed head there will

[2] For Ommatius see 11. 52 n.

natalis nostris decimus sextusque coletur,
  adventu felix qui petit esse tuo.
non tibi gemmatis ponentur prandia mensis,　　5
  Assyrius murex nec tibi sigma dabit;
nec per multiplices abaco splendente cavernas
  argenti nigri pondera defodiam;
nec scyphus hic dabitur rutilo cui forte metallo
  crustatum stringat tortilis ansa latus.　　10
fercula sunt nobis mediocria, non ita facta
  mensurae ut grandis suppleat ars pretium.
non panes Libyca solitos flavescere Syrte
  accipiet Galli rustica mensa tui.
vina mihi non sunt Gazetica, Chia, Falerna　　15
  quaeque Sarepteno palmite missa bibas.
pocula non hic sunt inlustria nomine pagi
  quem posuit nostris ipse triumvir agris.
tu tamen ut venias petimus; dabit omnia Christus,
  hic mihi qui patriam fecit amore tuo.　　20

16. Sarepteno *T, quod Graecae formae respondet*: Seraptano
C F, Saraptano *cett. Hic aut* Sarepteno *aut* Sarapteno
legendum censeo (de forma Σάραπτα *vide Pauly-Wissowa s.v.*
Sarepta). *Latina forma* Sareptensis *apud Hieronymum invenitur.*
18. quem *ego*: quod. *Vide Class. Quart., loc. cit.*

---

[1] It should have been unnecessary to point out that *nostris*
is not *nostrorum*; but everyone since Mommsen's day has
inferred from this line that two of Sidonius's children were
twins! *Nostris* is Dative of the Agent.
[2] Sidonius speaks as a Lyonese to an Arvernian. "Celtic
Gaul" and Aquitaine, which included Auvergne, were made
separate provinces by Augustus and remained so.

be celebrated by my family a sixteenth birthday,[1] which craves to be made lucky by your coming. You shall not have a meal set for you on jewelled tables, nor shall Assyrian purple provide your dining-couch. I shall not bury in the manifold recesses of a glittering side-board masses of dark old silver-plate; nor shall there be offered here a cup whose twisted handles clasp sides overlaid with ruddy gold. Our salvers are of moderate size, and not so made that their artistry atones for their lack of bulk. The rustic table of your Gallic[2] friend will not receive loaves that were wont to make the fields yellow by the Libyan Syrtes. As for wines, I have none of Gaza, no Chian or Falernian, none sent by the vines of Sarepta[3] for you to drink. There are here no cups distinguished by the name of that canton which the triumvir himself established in our land.[4] Nevertheless, we beg you to come; Christ will provide all things, by whose grace this has been made a real homeland[5] for me through your love.

[3] The Zarephath of 1 *Kings* 17. 9 f. (Sarepta in *Luke* 4. 26), between Tyre and Sidon. There is an interesting reminiscence of this passage in Corippus, *In Laudem Iustini* III. 87 f. : *dulcia Bacchi munera quae Sarepta* (note the quantity) *ferax, quae Gaza crearat.*

[4] Cass. Dio, XLVI. 50, states that Lug(u)dunum was founded in 43 B.C. by Munatius Plancus and M. Aemilius Lepidus (who was about to become a triumvir), and that the first inhabitants were refugees from Vienna (mod. Vienne). As the district round Vienne was famous for its wine, I believe that Sidonius means "cups of the wine of Vienne." The Viennenses are rather loosely described as a *pagus*, but that is no serious objection. "Our (or possibly "my") land" refers to the territory of Lyons. See *Class. Quart. loc. cit.*, p. 21.

[5] This refers to the poet's new home in Auvergne.

THE POEMS OF SIDONIUS

XVIII

DE BALNEIS VILLAE SVAE

Si quis Avitacum dignaris visere nostram,
  non tibi displiceat: sic quod habes placeat.
aemula Baiano tolluntur culmina cono
  parque cothurnato vertice fulget apex.
garrula Gauranis plus murmurat unda fluentis   5
  contigui collis lapsa supercilio.
Lucrinum stagnum dives Campania nollet,
  aequora si nostri cerneret illa lacus.
illud puniceis ornatur litus echinis:
  piscibus in nostris, hospes, utrumque vides.   10
si libet et placido partiris gaudia corde,
  quisquis ades, Baias tu facis hic animo.

XIX

DE PISCINA SVA

Intrate algentes post balnea torrida fluctus
  ut solidet calidam frigore lympha cutem;
et licet hoc solo mergatis membra liquore,
  per stagnum nostrum lumina vestra natant.

---

[1] See introductory note to *Epist*. II. 2. With *nostram*
understand *villam*.

[2] For the conical roof cf. *Epist*. II. 2. 5. Apparently a
prominent bathing-establishment at Baiae had a roof of that
kind.

[3] *Cothurnato* gives the idea of dignity, possibly also of
height, as in Pliny, *Epist*. IX. 7. 2, of which this is probably
a rather loose reminiscence. There Pliny tells us of two villas
which he possessed on the shores of Lake Como. One was on
a height, with a view of the lake, the other was down on the
lake-side. The former he called Tragedy because it seemed to be
supported on buskins (*cothurni*), the latter he named Comedy
because it seemed to rest on humble " socks " (*socculi*).

XIX. ON HIS SWIMMING-BATH

XVIII
ON THE BATHS OF HIS COUNTRY HOUSE

Whoe'er you be, if you deign to visit our Avitacum,[1]
let it not dissatisfy you: so may what *you* possess
satisfy *you*. Here a roof[2] rises that rivals the cone
of Baiae, and no whit inferior shines the peaked top
with its proud crest.[3] There the chattering water
that falls from the brow of the neighbouring hill
babbles more busily than the streams that flow from
Gaurus. Rich Campania would be ill-pleased with
the Lucrine mere if she beheld the waters of our lake.
That other shore is adorned by red sea-urchins, but
in our fish, O stranger, you see both characters.[4]
If you are willing, and if you share our joys with
contented heart, gentle visitor, whoever you be,
you can create a Baiae here in your fancy.

XIX
ON HIS SWIMMING-BATH

Enter ye the chill waves after the steaming baths,
that the water by its coldness may brace your heated
skin; and though you plunge your limbs in this
liquid alone,[5] our pond makes your eyes swim.

---

[4] The meaning seems to be " You can see in our fish both
characteristics of the *echini* of Baiae," *i.e.* both " fishiness "
and redness (cf. *Epist.* II. 2. 17), or possibly redness and prickli-
ness. But the text may be corrupt. It is just possible that
utrumque vides is a corruption of *acumen idem*, "there is the
same sharpness," the fish having a sharp flavour (cf. Plin. *N. H.*
XIV. 124, *saporis quaedam acumina*) and the *echini* sharp
prickles.

[5] Perhaps the point is " Although it is only water, with no
stronger liquor in it." For another explanation see Semple,
op. cit., p. 113.

XX

AD ECDICIVM SORORIVM SVVM

Natalis noster Nonas instare Novembres
  admonet: occurras non rogo, sed iubeo.
sit tecum coniunx, duo nunc properate; sed illud
  post annum optamus tertius ut venias.

XXI

DE PISCIBVS NOCTE CAPTIS

Quattuor haec primum pisces nox insuit hamis;
  inde duos tenui, tu quoque sume duos.
quos misi, sunt maiores; rectissimus ordo est;
  namque animae nostrae portio maior eras.

XXII

SIDONIVS PONTIO LEONTIO SVO SALVTEM

1. Dum apud Narbonem quondam Martium dictum
sed nuper factum moras necto, subiit animum quos-

---

[1] Ecdicius was the son of the Emperor Avitus, and therefore
the brother of Sidonius' wife, Papianilla. He was the hero of
the last resistance of Auvergne to the Goths (see Introd.,
p. xlvi). *Epist.* II. 1 and III. 3 are addressed to him. This
poem shows that the birthday of Sidonius was the 5th of
November. Klotz (Pauly-Wissowa, *R.-E.* s.v. *Sidonius*) thinks
the word *instare* may mean that the birthday was the day
before the Nones (*i.e.* the 4th). Obviously he misunderstood
natalis, although the meaning found here occurs even in Ovid
and Tibullus. The meaning " birthday " does not fit the
rest of the sentence.

[2] The owner of " Burgus " was Pontius Leontius of Bordeaux, " easily the first of the Aquitanians " (*Epist.* VIII. 12.5).
The poem is very obscure in places, and gives no adequate idea
of the arrangement of the buildings. The name of this

XXII. SIDONIUS TO LEONTIUS

XX

TO HIS BROTHER-IN-LAW ECDICIUS [1]

The genius of my birth reminds me that the Nones of November are at hand. I do not invite you, I order you to come to me. Bring your wife with you; hasten—a couple this time, but next year I hope there will be three of you.

XXI

FISH CAUGHT AT NIGHT

This night for the first time fixed four fishes on my hooks. Of these I have kept two; do you also take two. Those I am sending are the largest; the arrangement is perfectly just, for you are the larger portion of my heart.

XXII

SIDONIUS TO HIS FRIEND PONTIUS LEONTIUS, GREETING [2]

1. As I was trying to spin out the days at Narbo [3] —which was named of old and has in recent times become in reality the town of Mars—it occurred to

Burgus is believed to survive in the modern Bourg-sur-Gironde. Stevens, p. 65 n. 1, refers to Naufroy, *Histoire de Bourg-sur-Gironde* (1898), p. 9, which I have not been able to consult.

[3] Narbo Martius was the full name of the town, but the origin of *Martius* is uncertain. In A.D. 462, the town was occupied by Theodoric II. For its struggles with Theodoric I see 7. 475 sqq. See also n. on 23. 59–87.

piam secundum amorem tuum hexametros concinnare
[vel condere], quibus lectis oppido scires, etsi utrique
nostrum disparatis aequo plusculum locis lar familiaris
incolitur, non idcirco tam nobis animum dissidere
quam patriam. 2. habes igitur hic Dionysum inter
triumphi Indici oblectamenta marcentem; habes et
Phoebum, quem tibi iure poetico inquilinum factum
constat ex numine, illum scilicet Phoebum Anthedii
mei perfamiliarem, cuius collegio vir praefectus non
modo musicos quosque verum etiam geometras,
arithmeticos et astrologos disserendi arte supervenit;
siquidem nullum hoc exactius compertum habere
censuerim quid sidera zodiaci obliqua, quid plane-
tarum vaga, quid exotici sparsa praevaleant. 3. nam
ita his, ut sic dixerim, membris philosophiae claret
ut videatur mihi Iulium Firmicum,[1] Iulianum Ver-
tacum, Fullonium Saturninum, in libris matheseos
peritissimos conditores, absque interprete ingenio
tantum suffragante didicisse. nos vestigia doctrinae
ipsius adorantes coram canoro cygno ravum anserem
profitemur. quid te amplius moror ? Burgum tuam,
quo iure amicum decuit, meam feci, probe sciens vel
materiam tibi esse placituram, etiamsi ex solido
poema displiceat.

---

[1] Iulium Firmicum *solus exhibet Vatican. 3421.*

[1] The two mentions of Phoebus are not very clear. The
first seems to allude to the fact that Paulinus, son of Pontius,
is a poet (n. on 9. 304), the second to some poetical society
or institute of which Anthedius was president. On Anthedius
see 9. 312 n.

XXII. SIDONIUS TO LEONTIUS

me to put together some hexameters after your own heart. I hoped that when you read them you might feel well assured that, although our respective household gods are set in places a bit farther from one another than they ought to be, it does not follow that our souls are as far apart as our homes. 2. Here, then, you can find Dionysus bemused amid the delights of his Indian triumph, and Phoebus [1] also, who, as is well known, is for you a god no longer but rather, through a poet's privilege, an inmate of your house—that same Phoebus who is a great crony of my friend Anthedius, head of the Apolline college, a man who surpasses in the art of lecturing not only all musicians but all geometers, arithmeticians, and astrologers; for I should think no one knows more perfectly the special influences of the various heavenly bodies—the slanting signs of the zodiac, the roaming planets, or the scattered stars of the extra-zodiacal region. 3. He is indeed so eminent in these members (if I may so term them) of philosophy that he seems to me to have mastered without an interpreter, solely by dint of his own genius, the greatest savants among writers on astrology, Iulius Firmicus, Iulianus Vertacus, and Fullonius Saturninus. Following reverently the footsteps of such [2] learning, I pretend to no higher title than a hoarse gander in the presence of a tuneful swan. But why delay you further? I have made your home, " The Castle," my own, using a friend's proper privilege, knowing full well that my subject-matter will please you even though the poem should be entirely displeasing.

[2] *Ipsius* is here a mere demonstrative. See critical note on *Epist.* I. 9. 7.

THE POEMS OF SIDONIUS

BVRGVS PONTII LEONTII

Bistonii stabulum regis, Busiridis aras,
Antiphatae mensas et Taurica regna Thoantis
atque Ithaci ingenio fraudatum luce Cyclopa
portantem frontis campo per concava montis
par prope transfossi tenebrosum luminis antrum,　5
hospes, adi, si quis Burgum taciturus adisti.
et licet in carmen non passim laxet habenas
Phoebus et hic totis non pandat carbasa fandi,
quisque tamen tantos non laudans ore penates
inspicis, inspiceris : resonat sine voce voluntas ;　10
nam tua te tacitum livere silentia clamant.

Ergo age, Pierias, Erato, mihi percute chordas ;
responsent Satyri, digitumque pedemque moventes
ludant, et tremulo non rumpant cantica saltu.
quidquid forte Dryas vel quidquid Hamadryas
　　umquam　　　　　　　　　　　　　　　　15
conexis sibimet festum plausere Napaeis,
dependant modo, Burge, tibi, vel Naidas istic,
Nereidum chorus alme, doce, cum forte Garunna
huc redeunte venis pontumque in flumine sulcas.
pande igitur causas, Erato, laribusque sit ede　20
quis genius ; tantum non est sine praesule culmen.

8. totus *TF*.

262

XXII. CASTLE OF PONTIUS LEONTIUS

THE CASTLE OF PONTIUS LEONTIUS

Stranger, whoever you may be, that have visited the Castle and yet are fain to keep silence about it, may you visit the stalls of the Bistonian king,[1] the altars of Busiris,[2] the table of Antiphates,[3] the Tauric realm of Thoas,[4] and the Cyclops who was robbed of his sight by the cunning of the man of Ithaca and bears on the wide expanse of his forehead, as he ranges through his mountain-cave, a gloomy cavern well-nigh as vast, the socket of his pierced eye: and although Phoebus suffers not all and sundry to give free rein to song and does not here spread out fully the sails of eloquence for every man, yet whoever you are who, with no praise on your lips, view that splendid home, you are thereby put on view yourself; your inclination loudly heralds itself though without voice, for your silence proclaims you dumb with jealousy.

Come then, Erato, strike the Pierian strings for me. Let the Satyrs accompany the strain, playing their part with movement of finger and of foot, but not interrupting the melody with jerky leaps. All the festive dances that Dryads or Hamadryads hand in hand with the nymphs of the glen have ever danced may they now bestow on thee alone, great Castle! Kindly choir of Nereids, teach the Naiads there at the season when the Garonne flows back thither and ye come, cleaving the sea in the midst of the river.[5] Reveal then, O Erato, the origin of the house, and declare what protecting spirit watches that home; for so great an edifice cannot lack a divine guardian.

[5] See 7. 393 n. and *vv.* 105–113 below.

THE POEMS OF SIDONIUS

Forte sagittiferas Euan populatus Erythras
vite capistratas cogebat ad esseda tigres,
intrabat duplicem qua temo racemifer arcum.
marcidus ipse sedet curru; madet ardua cervix   25
sudati de rore meri, caput aurea rumpunt
cornua et indigenam iaculantur fulminis ignem
(sumpserat hoc nascens primum, cum transiit olim
in patrium de matre femur); fert tempus utrumque
veris opes rutilosque ligat vindemia flores;   30
cantharus et thyrsus dextra laevaque feruntur,
nec tegit exertos, sed tangit palla lacertos;
dulce natant oculi, quos si fors vertat in hostem,
attonitos, solum dum cernit, inebriat Indos.
tum salebris saliens quotiens se concutit axis,   35
passim deciduo perfunditur orbita musto.
Bassaridas, Satyros, Panas Faunosque docebat
ludere Silenus iam numine plenus alumno,
sed comptus tamen ille caput; nam vertice nudo
amissos sertis studet excusare capillos.   40
    Corniger inde novi fit Ganges pompa triumphi;
cernuus inpexam faciem stetit ore madenti et
arentes vitreis adiuvit fletibus undas;
coniectas in vincla manus post terga revinxit
pampinus; hic sensim captivo umore refusus   45
sponte refrondescit per bracchia roscida palmes.

---

¹ *Eryth.* : n. on 2. 447.
² Both the Latin and the translation are rather strained.
One is tempted to suspect that a line has dropped out of the
text. The "double arch" can scarcely be anything but the
double yoke, illustrations of which may be seen in the ordinary
dictionaries of antiquities. The pole was passed through the
connecting-piece between the two yokes. Those editors who
punctuate so as to connect *v.* 24 with *v.* 25 make *duplicem
arcum* unintelligible.

It chanced that Bacchus, having laid waste Erythrae,[1] the famed haunt of bowmen, was subjecting vine-bridled tigers to his chariot where a pole that bore clustering grapes entered the double arch.[2] In the car sat the god himself, all languorous; his proud neck sweated with exuded wine; from his head sprang golden horns, which hurled forth his native levin-fire (this he had first received at his birth long before, when he passed from his mother into his father's thigh). Both his temples were covered with the bounties of springtime, and the vintage crop fastened the red flowers in their place; his right hand carried a goblet and his left a thyrsus, and his arms were bare, the cloak just touching without hiding them. There was charm in his swimming eyes, and if he chanced to turn them upon the enemy he dazed those Indians by his mere look and made them drunken. Whenever the wheel jolted, forced upward by rough places, the track was soaked all over with a falling shower of new wine. Bassarids, Satyrs, Pans and Fauns were being taught to frolic by Silenus; he was now filled with the divinity that he had reared, but his head was in orderly array; for on his bare pate he took pains to palliate the loss of hair with a garland.

The next show in this new triumph is horned Ganges. With hanging head he has taken his place; his face is unkempt and his cheeks bedewed, and with his glassy tears he has helped to replenish his parched stream. His hands have been cast into chains, and a vine-branch has fastened them behind his back; and gradually the water thus held prisoner has caused fresh growth, and of its own accord the vine-shoot sends forth new leafage all over those dewy arms.

Nec non et rapti coniunx ibi vincta mariti
it croceas demissa genas vetitaque recondi
lampade cum Solis radiis Aurora rubebat.

Adfuit hic etiam post perdita cinnama Phoenix, 50
formidans mortem sibi non superesse secundam.
succedit captiva cohors, quae fercula gazis
fert onerata suis ; ebur hic hebenusque vel aurum
et niveae piceo raptae de pectore bacae
gestantur ; quicumque nihil sustentat, odoros   55
mittitur in nexus ; videas hic ipsa placere
supplicia et virides violis halare catenas.

Vltima nigrantes incedunt praeda elephanti ;
informis cui forma gregi : riget hispida dorso
vix ferrum passura cutis ; quippe improba cratem 60
nativam nec tela forant, contracta vicissim
tensaque terga feris crepitant usuque cavendi
pellunt excussis impactum missile rugis.

Iamque iter ad Thebas per magnum victor agebat
aera et ad summas erexerat orgia nubes,   65
cum videt Aonia venientem Delion arce.
grypas et ipse tenet : vultus his laurea curvos
fronde lupata ligant ; hederis quoque circumplexis
pendula lora virent ; sensim fera subvolat ales
aerias terraeque vias, ne forte citato   70
alarum strepitu lignosas frangat habenas.
aeternum nitet ipse genas ; crevere corymbis

55. odoros *edit. Baret* : odoris.

[1] The " stolen husband " is probably Tithonus, though he
is not the only beautiful youth that Aurora carried off.
Commentators wrongly take the husband to be Ganges.
[2] 2. 417 n.
[3] Apollo. The " Aonian height " is Mt. Helicon, sacred
to Apollo and the Muses. In *v.* 96 below *Aonios colles* means
" Boeotian hills." Boeotia (especially Thebes and Orchomenos)
was famous for its worship of Dionysus.

There also walks in chains the wife of a stolen husband,[1] Aurora. Her saffron-hued countenance is downcast, but her lamp may not be hidden, and she is flushed with the glow of the sun's rays.

Here also appears the Phoenix,[2] who has lost his cinnamon and fears that after this no second death can be his. Then comes a company of prisoners bearing trays laden with their treasures; here are carried ivory and ebony and gold and snow-white gems snatched from pitch-black bosoms. Whoever does not support a load is consigned to fragrant bonds, and it is plain that their very punishment is pleasing, for the verdant chains breathe forth the odour of violets.

Last of the spoil, the dusky elephants advance, a troop of unshapely shape. On their backs is a skin rough and stiff, that will scarce let steel pass through it; for even ruthless javelins fail to pierce that natural barrier, and the hide crackles as it stretches and contracts in turn and with practised defence repels the smiting missile by shaking out its wrinkles.

Now the conqueror was speeding his way to Thebes through the vast air and had taken up his revelling rout to the clouds, when he saw the god of Delos[3] approaching from the Aonian height. This god likewise wields the rein, but his steeds are gryphons; curbs of leafy laurel bind their hooked beaks; the hanging reins are green with ivy intertwined. Slowly and steadily do those winged beasts fly along their paths in air and over land, lest haply by a violent flapping of their wings they break the woody reins. The countenance of the god shines with an eternal radiance; clusters of ivy-berries stand out upon his

tempora et auratum verrit coma concolor axem ;
laeva parte tenet vasta dulcedine raucam
caelato Pythone lyram, pars dextra sagittas   75
continet atque alio resonantes murmure nervos.
ibant Pipliades pariter mediumque noveno
circumsistentes umbrabant syrmate currum.
pendet per teretes tripodas Epidaurius anguis
diffusus sanctum per colla salubria virus.   80
hic et crinisatas iungebat Pegasus alas,
portans doctiloquo facundum crure Crotonem.

Vt sese iunxere chori, consurgit uterque
fratris in amplexus, sed paulo segnior Euan,
dum pudet instabiles, si surgat, prodere plantas.   85
tum Phoebus "quo pergis ? " ait, "num forte nocentes,
Bacche, petis Thebas ? te cretus Echione nempe
abnegat esse deum.   linque his, rogo, moenia, linque,
et mecum mage flecte rotas.   despexit Agaue
te colere et nosmet Niobe ; riget inde superba,   90
vulnera tot patiens quot spectat vulnera ventris,
optantemque mori gravius clementia fixit ;
parcere saepe malum est sensumque inferre dolori.
ipsa autem nato occiso Pentheia mater
amplius ut furiat numquid non sana futura est ?   95
ergone Aonios colles habitare valemus,

82. Crotonem *Wilamowitz* : Creontem.
90. superba *Luetjohann* : superbum.

---

[1] *i.e.* different from that of the lyre-strings.
[2] Croton (Crotos, Crotus) was a son of Pan and Eupheme,
nurse of the muses.   He became the constellation Sagittarius.
Crure alludes to metre ; *pede* would have been clearer.
[3] Pentheus.
[4] The mother of Pentheus.   She had cast a slight on the
parentage of Bacchus, who exacted vengeance by driving her
and her sisters into a frenzy, in which they slew Pentheus.
[5] *i.e.* just as Niobe's preservation was a cruel mercy,

brow and his gilded car is swept by tresses of like hue.
On his left he holds a sonorous lyre of ineffable sweet-
ness, with Python graven upon it; on his right
are arrows and strings that echo with a different
twang.[1] With him advance the Muses, all gathered
around him and casting on the midst of his chariot
the shadow of their ninefold robes. The serpent
of Epidaurus hangs loosely coiled about the shapely
tripod, with a hallowed essence diffused throughout his
health-giving neck. Joined to them also is Pegasus
with his hairy wings, carrying on his back Croton,[2]
whose skilled foot brings forth eloquent utterance.

When the two bands came together each god arose
to give a brotherly embrace, but Bacchus a little more
slowly than the other, for he was shy of betraying
his unsteady feet by rising. Then Phoebus said,
"Whither away? Can it be, Bacchus, that thou
art seeking guilty Thebes? True, Echion's descendant [3] denies thy godhead: nevertheless, leave
the city to them, I pray thee; yea, do so, and rather
make thy wheels go my way. Agaue [4] scorned
thy worship and Niobe mine; hence was Niobe
turned to stone in her pride, herself suffering a
wound for every wound that she saw her offspring
suffer; and as she longed for death my mercy gave
her that rigid form, a boon worse than death; 'tis
oft an ill service to spare and to inflict on pain longer
suffering. So shall not even Pentheus' mother,
having slain her son, regain her senses only to
become more frenzied still? [5] Nay, can we dwell
on the Aonian heights [6] when in time to come an

so the restoration of Agaue's sanity will result in a madness
more terrible than before, because it will enable her to realise
what she has done. *Numquid non* is often used in Late Latin
for *nonne*.   [6] See n. on *v.* 66.

cum patris extincti thalamis potietur adulter,
frater natorum, coniunx genetricis habendus,
vitricus ipse suus? cordi est si iungere gressum,
dicam qua pariter sedem tellure locemus.   100
  " Est locus, irrigua qua rupe, Garunna, rotate,
et tu qui simili festinus in aequora lapsu
exis curvata, Durani muscose, saburra,
iam pigrescentes sensim confunditis amnes.
currit in adversum hic pontus multoque recursu   105
flumina quas volvunt et spernit et expetit undas.
at cum summotus lunaribus incrementis
ipse Garunna suos in dorsa recolligit aestus,
praecipiti fluctu raptim redit atque videtur
in fontem iam non refluus sed defluus ire.   110
tum recipit laticem quamvis minor ille minorem
stagnanti de fratre suum, turgescit et ipse
Oceano propriasque facit sibi litora ripas.
hos inter fluvios, uni mage proximus undae, est
aethera mons rumpens alta spectabilis arce,   115
plus celsos habiturus eros vernamque senatum.
quem generis princeps Paulinus Pontius olim,
cum Latius patriae dominabitur, ambiet altis
moenibus, et celsae transmittent aera turres;
quarum culminibus sedeant commune micantes   120
pompa vel auxilium; non illos machina muros,
non aries, non alta strues vel proximus agger,
non quae stridentes torquet catapulta molares,

111. minorem *Luetjohann* : minore.
114. uni : Durani *Wilamowitz*.

---

[1] Oedipus.   [2] The Dordogne.
[3] *i.e.* by the spring tides.

adulterer[1] shall possess himself of his murdered father's bride, to be reckoned brother of his sons, husband of his mother, and stepfather to himself? If thou art fain to go with me, I will tell thee in what land we should make our joint habitation.

" There is a place where two rivers, the Garunna, sped whirling down from a dripping mountain-crag, and the mossy Duranius,[2] which rushes with like swoop to the plain and at last flows out from a bend in its sandy channel, gradually commingle their slowing streams. Here the sea rushes up against the current and with constant coming and going repels or courts the waters that the rivers roll down. But when the Garunna, repulsed by the waxing of the moon,[3] once more gathers its own tidal flood upon its back, then it returns, speeding in headlong billows, and now seems to flow, not backwards, but downwards to its source. Then even the Duranius, though as the lesser it receives from its flooding brother but a lesser share of the water, is likewise swollen by the ocean, and its banks become sea-shores. Between these rivers, but nearer to one than to the other, there is a mountain piercing the sky, conspicuous in its towering height but destined to have owners still more elevated and to be the birthplace of senators. Some day, when his land shall be under Latin sway, Paulinus Pontius, the founder of the family, shall surround that hill with walls, and the towers shall soar beyond earth's atmosphere; thus on their summits shall rest, shining with a common radiance, the two lights of Stateliness and Succour. Those walls no engine, no battering-ram, no high-piled structure or near-built mound, no catapult hurling the hissing stones,

271

sed nec testudo nec vinea nec rota currens
iam positis scalis umquam quassare valebunt.   125
cernere iam videor quae sint tibi, Burge, futura
(diceris sic); namque domus de flumine surgunt
splendentesque sedent per propugnacula thermae.
hic cum vexatur piceis aquilonibus aestus,
scrupeus asprata latrare crepidine pumex   130
incipit; at fractis saliens e cautibus altum
excutitur torrens ipsisque aspergine tectis
impluit ac tollit nautas et saepe iocoso
ludit naufragio; nam tempestate peracta
destituit refluens missas in balnea classes.   135
ipsa autem quantis, quibus aut sunt fulta columnis!
cedat puniceo pretiosus livor in antro
Synnados, et Nomadum qui portat eburnea saxa
collis et herbosis quae vernant marmora venis;
candentem iam nolo Paron, iam nolo Caryston;   140
vilior est rubro quae pendet purpura saxo.

    " Et ne posteritas dubitet quis conditor extet,
fixus in introitu lapis est; hic nomina signat
auctorum; sed propter aqua, et vestigia pressa
quae rapit et fuso detergit gurgite caenum.   145

---

[1] This has wrongly been taken as a reference to nautical
sports such as are described in *Epist.* II. 2. 19; but Sidonius
merely says that there is a gap between rocks through which
water flows from the river into the baths, which are built on
the bank. When a storm arises boats are sometimes driven
through this inlet right into the baths, where they are apt to
have ridiculous experiences.

[2] For these marbles see 5. 34–39 nn.

[3] The next eight lines are desperately obscure. Sidonius is
writing to one who knew the house, and he is more intent on
ingenious conceits than on intelligibility. *Paries* (146) is
possibly the front wall of the house, on the inner side of which
is the atrium. The decorative slabs (*vv.* 146 f.) are on the
inside of the wall. *Vv.* 150–155 describe the atrium, which

no tortoise-roof, no mantlet, no wheel rushing onwards
with ladders already in position shall ever have power
to shake. Methinks I see the future that is in
store for thee, O Castle (for so thou shalt be called).
The house rises from the river's brim and gleaming
baths are set within the circuit of the battlements:
here when the surging waters are troubled by the
murky north-wind, the eaten, jagged rock sends
forth a roar from the scarred bank; then from a
cleft in the crags a torrent leaps forth and is shot
aloft, showering spray on to the very roofs; it lifts up
men in boats and often mocks them with a sportive
shipwreck; for when the storm is over the flood
retreats and strands whole fleets that have been
forced up into the baths.[1] But the columns that
support the baths, of what manner and size are they?
Before them must bow the costly dark hue in the
purple quarry of Synnada and the Numidian hill
that bears stones like ivory and the marble that
burgeons with grass-like veins; henceforth I spurn
gleaming Paros and Carystos; poorer now seems
the purple suspended in the blushing rock.[2]

"Lest posterity should be uncertain whom the
building boasts as its stablisher, a stone is set in
the ground at the entrance with the names of the
founders clearly graven upon it; and there is water
near at hand which clears away all footprints and
wipes off all mud with its flooding stream. [3] The

is crescent-shaped (*lunata atria*, 157). With much diffidence
I have made two alterations in the text. The meaning may
be that a *porticus duplex*, i.e. a double row of pillars, runs
straight through from the entrance, thus dividing the floor
into "two floor-spaces." At the far end the two rows bend
round in opposite directions, following the rounded wall until
they come near to the *paries* from which they started. Then

273

sectilibus paries tabulis crustatus ad aurea
tecta venit, fulvo nimis abscondenda metallo;
nam locuples fortuna domus non passa latere
divitias prodit, cum sic sua culmina celat.
haec post assurgit duplicemque supervenit aream 150
porticus ipsa duplex, duplici non cognita plaustro;
quam rursum molli subductam vertice curvae
obversis paulum respectant cornibus alae.
ipsa diem natum cernit sinuamine dextro,
fronte videns medium, laevo visura cadentem. 155
non perdit quicquam trino de cardine caeli
et totum solem lunata per atria servat.
sacra tridentiferi Iovis hic armenta profundo
Pharnacis immergit genitor; percussa securi
corpora cornipedum certasque rubescere plagas 160
sanguineo de rore putes; stat vulneris horror
verus, et occisis vivit pictura quadrigis.
Ponticus hinc rector numerosis Cyzicon armis
claudit; at hinc sociis consul Lucullus opem fert,
compulsusque famis discrimina summa subire 165
invidet obsesso miles Mithridaticus hosti.
enatat hic pelagus Romani militis ardor
et chartam madido transportat corpore siccam.

150. aream *ego* : aedem.
152. quam rursum *ego* : quarum unam.

---

each row turns inward for a short distance (*obversis* =
" turning athwart " or " turning so as to face one another "),
and thus " looks back upon " the " double colonnade." The
winding pillars on each side form the *alae*. Sidonius
welcomed the word because it made a ludicrous combination
with *cornibus* (" wings " and " horns "). *Duplici . . . plaustro*
means " not exposed to the north."

house-wall is faced with slabs of cut marble up to the gilded ceiling, which is right fitly concealed by the yellow metal, for the rich prosperity of the house, brooking no secrecy, reveals its wealth when thus it hides its roof. Behind this part there soars, passing high above a double floor, a colonnade likewise double, unknown to the double Wain. This again diverges gently backward, and finally these curving wings turn their horns inward for a little way, and so look back upon it. Its right bend sees the dawn, its front the noonday light, its left the fading day. It loses none of these three quarters of the heavens, but preserves the whole of the sun in the crescent hall. There can be seen the father of Pharnaces plunging into the deep the horses sacrificed to the trident-bearing Jove[1]; you would think the bodies of the steeds had in very truth been smitten by the axe and that real gashes were reddening with spurts of blood; each ghastly wound seems true, and that slain team makes the picture live. Next is seen on one side the ruler of Pontus beleaguering Cyzicus with multitudinous host; but on the other side Lucullus brings aid, and the warriors of Mithridates, forced to undergo the direst straits of hunger, envy their besieged foe. Here a bold Roman soldier is swimming to land, carrying across the water a scroll all dry despite his dripping body.[2]

---

[1] Appian, *Bell. Mith.* c. 70, says that Mithridates, before proceeding against Cotta in 74 B.C., sacrificed a chariot team of four horses by flinging them into the sea, but he does not say that the horses were first slaughtered. The " trident-bearing Jove " is Neptune.

[2] For this story see Flor. I. 40 (III. 5) 16.

THE POEMS OF SIDONIUS

" Desuper in longum porrectis horrea tectis
crescunt atque amplis angustant fructibus aedes. 170
huc veniet calidis quantum metit Africa terris,
quantum vel Calaber, quantum colit Apulus acer,
quanta Leontino turgescit messis acervo,
quantum Mygdonio committunt Gargara sulco,
quantum, quae tacitis Cererem venerata choreis, 175
Attica Triptolemo civi condebat Eleusin,
cum populis hominum glandem linquentibus olim
fulva fruge data iam saecula fulva perirent.
porticus ad gelidos patet hinc aestiva triones;
hinc calor innocuus thermis hiemalibus exit 180
atque locum in tempus mollit; quippe illa rigori
pars est apta magis; nam quod fugit ora Leonis,
inde Lycaoniae rabiem male sustinet Vrsae.
arcis at in thermas longe venit altior amnis
et cadit in montem patulisque canalibus actus 185
circumfert clausum cava per divortia flumen.
occiduum ad solem post horrea surgit opaca
quae dominis hiberna domus : strepit hic bona flamma
appositas depasta trabes ; sinuata camino
ardentis perit unda globi fractoque flagello 190
spargit lentatum per culmina tota vaporem.
continuata dehinc videas quae conditor ausus
aemula Palladiis textrina educere templis.
hac celsi quondam coniunx reverenda Leonti,

181. in *add. Mohr.*

---

[1] The sun is (or rather was) in Leo in July.
[2] " Falls into (not down or from) the mountain " : a
characteristically feeble paradox. The meaning is that
trenches are dug in the mountain-side to form conduits, and
the water falls into them.

276

" Higher up the granaries multiply with their long stretch of buildings and with produce within so abundant that even their vast space is cramped. Hither shall come as great a harvest as is reaped in Africa's warm fields or cultivated by the Calabrian or the brisk Apulian, as rich a crop as swells for the stacks of Leontini, or as Gargarus commits to its Lydian furrow, or as Attic Eleusis, that worshipped Ceres with mystic dances, used to garner for her citizen Triptolemus, when long ago the tribes of mankind renounced the acorn and the golden age was perishing now that the golden grain was given. Then there is a summer portico exposed on one side to the chill north: at the other end a harmless warmth comes out from the winter baths and tempers the air of the place when the season requires; so this end is best suited to the cold weather; for the part that fights shy of the Lion's mouth [1] is thereby unfitted to endure the rage of Lycaon's Bear. Into the warm baths of the mansion comes a stream from far above, which falls into the mountain,[2] being forced through open channels till at last it circulates its waters under cover through divergent tunnels. Behind the shaded granaries there rises toward the west a structure that is the winter home of the master and mistress; here a goodly fire crackles, which devours the great logs that are piled near at hand; the glowing cloud that comes forth in billows curls upward from the stove, then fades away, and with its blast now broken it spreads a mitigated heat all over the roof. Joined to the room may be seen the weaving-chambers, which the founder dared to build in a style that vied with the temples of Pallas. Some day it shall be blazoned

qua non ulla magis nurus umquam Pontia gaudet 195
inlustris pro sorte viri, celebrabitur aede
vel Syrias vacuasse colus vel serica fila
per cannas torsisse leves vel stamine fulvo
praegnantis fusi mollitum nesse metallum.
parietibus posthinc rutilat quae machina iunctis 200
fert recutitorum primordia Iudaeorum.
perpetuum pictura micat; nec tempore longo
depretiata suas turpant pigmenta figuras.

"Flecteris ad laevam: te porticus accipit ampla
directis curvata viis, ubi margine summo 205
pendet et artatis stat saxea silva columnis.
alta volubilibus patet hic cenatio valvis;
fusilis euripus propter; cadit unda superne
ante fores pendente lacu, venamque secuti
undosa inveniunt nantes cenacula pisces. 210
comminus erigitur vel prima vel extima turris;
mos erit hic dominis hibernum sigma locare.
huius conspicuo residens in culmine saepe
dilectum nostris Musis simul atque capellis
aspiciam montem; lauri spatiabor in istis 215
frondibus, hic trepidam credam mihi credere
        Daphnen.
iam si forte gradus geminam convertis ad Arcton
ut venias in templa dei qui maximus ille est,

---

[1] The distaff is called "Syrian" because the lady is working
with wool already dyed in Syrian purple.

[2] Perhaps rather "on the extreme edge is perched" (cf.
collis margine, 24. 66). The "forest of columns" was perhaps
built on an overhanging ledge at one end of the hill.

[3] Sidonius plays on the literal meaning of *cenaculum*,
"dining-room," and the derived meaning, "upper chamber."

278

forth by fame that in this sanctuary the worshipful
lady of the great Leontius, than whom no other wife
of the Pontian house ever rejoiced more in her
husband's illustrious rank, stripped the Syrian [1]
distaff and twisted the silken strands along the
light reeds and spun the pliant metal, making the
spindle swell with thread of gold. Next to this,
with wall abutting, there stands a resplendent
structure, which shows depicted the beginnings of
the circumcised Jews. The brightness of the
picture is everlasting: time brings no degeneration
in the colours to mar the painted forms.

" You turn left, and a spacious colonnade receives
you, its shape curved but its passages straight.
To the extreme edge clings [2] a crowded forest of close-
set columns. Here is built a lofty dining-room
with folding-doors. A conduit of cast metal is
near; there is a suspended tank in front of the
door: into it the water falls from above, and
fishes, advancing with the flow, find the end of their
swimming in an upper room—but a watery one.[3]
Close at hand rises the first, or, if it please you better,
the last of the towers. There the masters of the
house will be wont to set their dining-couch in
winter. Often-times on its far-seen roof will I sit
and view that mountain beloved by my Muses and
by the goats; I will walk amid those laurel boughs,
and there I shall believe that the timorous Daphne
believes in me. Then if you chance to turn your
steps towards the two Bears to reach the temple of
that God who is greatest of all, you find the wine-

The tank is a *cenaculum* in the latter sense, but fishes generally find the end of their career in a *cenaculum* of the other
sort.

deliciis redolent iunctis apotheca penusque;
hic multus tu, frater, eris.   220
                          " Iam divide sedem,
cessurus mihi fonte meo, quem monte fluentem
umbrat multicavus spatioso circite fornix.
non eget hic cultu, dedit huic natura decorem.
nil fictum placuisse placet, non pompa per artem
ulla, resultanti non comet malleus ictu   225
saxa, nec exesum supplebunt marmora tofum.
hic fons Castaliae nobis vice sufficit undae.
cetera dives habe; colles tua iura tremiscant;
captivos hic solve tuos, et per iuga Burgi
laeta relaxatae fiant vineta catenae."   230
   Confirmat vocem iamiam prope sobrius istam
Silenus, pariterque chori cecinere faventes:
" Nysa, vale Bromio, Phoebo, Parnase bivertex.
non istum Naxus, non istum Cirrha requirat,
sed mage perpetuo Burgus placitura petatur."   235

   5. Ecce, quotiens tibi libuerit pateris capacioribus
hilarare convivium, misi quod inter scyphos et
amystidas tuas legas. subveneris verecundiae meae,
si in sobrias aures ista non venerint; nec iniuria hoc
ac secus atque aequum est flagito, quandoquidem
Baccho meo iudicium decemvirale passuro tem-
pestivius quam convenit tribunal erigitur. 6. si

---

   [1] As *Bacchus* is used in poetry for " wine," there is a
double meaning here.
   [2] *i.e.* Delphi.

store and the larder fragrant with mingled delights. This place will see much of you, my brother.[1]

" Now agree upon a division of haunts: you shall leave to me my spring, which flows from the mountain, shadowed by an arched covering of ample circuit, much pitted. This needs no embellishment, for Nature has given it beauty. It seems good to me that there no counterfeiting should seem good; no artificial splendour there; no hammer with reechoing blow shall dress those stones, no marble workmanship take the place of the weather-worn tuff. That spring contents me instead of Castalia's fountain. All else you may have to enrich you: the hills may tremble before your power; here set your captives free, and may their loosened bonds become joyous vineyards all over the Castle's hilly slopes! "

Silenus, now all but sober, confirmed this utterance, and the bands of revellers likewise sang their approval: " Nysa, Bromius bids thee farewell; twin-crested Parnassus, Phoebus bids farewell to thee. Let Naxus no longer seek the one or Cirrha [2] the other, but rather let the Castle be our goal, to give delight for evermore."

5. See, I have sent you something to read amid your bumpers and wassailings whenever you choose to cheer the feast with extra-large cups. You will save my blushes if these lines do not find their way to sober ears. This is not an unlawful or an inequitable demand on my part, since the treatment I deprecate amounts to setting up a premature tribunal for my Bacchus, where he would be subjected to a judgment of decemviral severity. 6. Again, should

quis autem carmen prolixius eatenus duxerit esse
culpandum, quod epigrammatis excesserit paucitatem,
istum liquido patet neque balneas Etrusci neque
Herculem Surrentinum neque comas Flavii Earini
neque Tibur Vopisci neque omnino quicquam de
Papinii nostri silvulis lectitasse; quas omnes de-
scriptiones vir ille praeiudicatissimus non distichorum
aut tetrastichorum stringit angustiis, sed potius, ut
lyricus Flaccus in artis poeticae volumine praecipit,
multis isdemque purpureis locorum communium
pannis semel inchoatas materias decenter extendit.
haec me ad defensionis exemplum posuisse sufficiat,
ne haec ipsa longitudinis deprecatio longa videatur.
vale.

XXIII

AD CONSENTIVM

Cum iam pro meritis tuis pararem,
Consenti, columen decusque morum,
vestrae laudibus hospitalitatis
cantum impendere pauperis cicutae,
ultro in carmina tu tubam recludens   5
converso ordine versibus citasti
suetum ludere sic magis sodalem.
paret Musa tibi, sed impudentem

---

[1] These poems are numbered respectively I. 5, III. 1, III.
4, and I. 3 in the *Silvae* of Statius.

[2] Hor. *A. P.* 15, *purpureus, late qui splendeat, unus et
alter adsuitur pannus.*

282

anyone consider that such a lengthy poem deserves
censure for going beyond the brevity of an epigram,
it is perfectly clear that he has not been in the
habit of reading the " Baths of Etruscus " or the
" Hercules of Surrentum " or the " Locks of Flavius
Earinus " or the " Tiburtine Home of Vopiscus," [1]
or indeed anything from the little " Silvae " of our
Statius; for that man of most assured reputation
does not cramp any of these descriptions within
the narrow limits of two-lined or four-lined poems,
but rather does what the lyric poet Horace enjoins
in the " Art of Poetry ": once he has introduced
his subject, he appropriately enlarges it by the repeated use of stock " purple patches." [2] Let this
suffice as a specimen of my self-defence, lest this
justification of length should itself seem too long.
Farewell.

XXIII

TO CONSENTIUS

Consentius,[3] pillar and ornament of manners, I
was already preparing to devote the strains of
my poor reed to the praises of your hospitality,
as you well deserve, when you forestalled me and,
reversing the order of things, brought out your
trumpet and in verses challenged your old crony,
who is more used to that kind of pastime, to produce
a poem.   Well, the Muse answers your call, but she

---

[3] Consentius of Narbonne, to whom *Epist.* VIII. 4 is addressed, is mentioned as a poet in *Epist.* IX. 15. 1, carm.
22 sqq. The present poem cannot have been written before
A.D. 462, when Theodoric II occupied Narbonne (*vv.* 69–73), or
after 466, when he was murdered. See Introd., p. lvii.

multo cautius hinc stilum movebit;
nam cum carmina postules diserte,   10
suades scribere, sed facis tacere.
nuper quadrupedante cum citato
ires Phocida Sestiasque Baias,
inlustres titulisque proeliisque
urbes per duo consulum tropaea,   15
(nam Martem tulit ista Iulianum
et Bruto duce nauticum furorem,
ast haec Teutonicas cruenta pugnas,
erectum et Marium cadente Cimbro),
misisti mihi multiplex poema,   20
doctum, nobile, forte, delicatum.
ibant hexametri superbientes
et vestigia iuncta, sed minora,
per quinos elegi pedes ferebant;
misisti et, triplicis metrum trochaei   25
spondeo comitante dactyloque,
dulces hendecasyllabos, tuumque
blando faenore Sollium ligasti.
usuram petimurque reddimusque;
nam quod carmine pro tuo rependo,   30
hoc centesima laudium tuarum est.
    Quid primum venerer colamque pro te?
ni fallor, patriam patremque iuxta;
qui quamquam sibi vindicare summum
possit iure locum, tamen necesse est   35
illam vincere quae parit parentes.
salve, Narbo potens salubritate,
urbe et rure simul bonus videri,

will move her shameless pen much more cautiously on this account; for in making such an eloquent demand for a song you urge one to write but constrain one to be silent. Lately, when on galloping steed you were travelling to Phocis [1] and the Sestian Baiae, cities conspicuous in the records of the great and famed for battles through the trophies won by two consuls (for the first of these towns bore the brunt of Caesar's armed might and the frenzy of a navy under Brutus' [2] command, the other, bathed in blood, endured the Teuton fray, with Marius proudly standing as the Cimbrian fell), you sent me a manifold poem, skilful, striking, powerful, exquisite. Hexameters marched in their pride, and elegiacs advanced beside them, but with lesser steps that covered but five feet. You sent also graceful hendecasyllables, where spondee and dactyl accompany three trochees, and you have put your Sollius in a charming debt. Now I am asked for interest, and pay it; what I am now disbursing in consideration of your poem is one per cent. of the praises due to you.

To what must I first pay reverence and worship on account of you? To your fatherland, methinks, and after that to your father. He might indeed justly claim the first place for himself, but the parent of parents must needs have precedence. Hail, Narbo, surpassing in thy healthiness, gladdening the eye with thy town and thy countryside alike, with thy

---

[1] *Phocida = Massiliam* (Marseilles), a colony of Phocaea. This confusion of Phocis and Phocaea is probably borrowed from Lucan (III. 340, V. 53), though it occurs elsewhere. The "Sestian Baiae" is Aquae Sextiae (Aix) founded by C. Sextius Calvinus in 122 B.C., and renowned for its warm springs.

[2] *i.e.* Decimus Brutus.

muris, civibus, ambitu, tabernis,
portis, porticibus, foro, theatro,   40
delubris, capitoliis, monetis,
thermis, arcubus, horreis, macellis,
pratis, fontibus, insulis, salinis,
stagnis, flumine, merce, ponte, ponto;
unus qui venerere iure divos   45
Lenaeum, Cererem, Palem, Minervam
spicis, palmite, pascuis, trapetis.
solis fise viris nec expetito
naturae auxilio procul relictis
promens montibus altius cacumen,   50
non te fossa patens nec hispidarum
obiectu sudium coronat agger;
non tu marmora bratteam vitrumque,
non testudinis Indicae nitorem,
non si quas eboris trabes refractis   55
rostris Marmarici dedere barri
figis moenibus aureasque portas
exornas asaroticis lapillis;
sed per semirutas superbus arces,
ostendens veteris decus duelli,   60
quassatos geris ictibus molares,
laudandis pretiosior ruinis.
sint urbes aliae situ minaces,
quas vires humiles per alta condunt,
et per praecipites locata cristas   65
numquam moenia caesa glorientur:
tu pulsate places fidemque fortem
oppugnatio passa publicavit.
      Hinc te Martius ille rector atque
magno patre prior, decus Getarum,   70
Romanae columen salusque gentis,
Theudoricus amat sibique fidum
286

walls, citizens, circuit, shops, gates, porticoes, forum, theatre, shrines, capitol, mint, baths, arches, granaries, markets, meadows, fountains, islands, salt-mines, ponds, river, merchandise, bridge and brine; thou who hast the best title of all to worship as thy gods Bacchus, Ceres, Pales and Minerva in virtue of thy corn, thy vines, thy pastures, and thine olive-mills! Thou hast put thy trust in thy men alone, and seeking no aid from Nature thou dost soar to heights that leave mountains far behind. No gaping fosse, no mound with its barrier of bristling stakes surrounds thee; no marble workmanship, no gilding or glass, no shining Indian tortoiseshell, no bars of ivory broken off from the mouths of Marmaric elephants dost thou fix upon thy walls; thou adornest no golden gates with mosaic; but proud among thy half-demolished strongholds thou dost display thy glory won in the old war, and though thy great stones have been battered down thou art prized more highly for those glorious ruins.[1] Let other cities menace by their sites—cities built on high by lowly powers; let walls set on precipitous ridges boast that they have never been felled; as for thee, shattered as thou art thou dost win favour; the widespread fame of that assault hath made thy staunch loyalty renowned.

Hence that martial ruler, the superior even of his great sire, glorious ornament of the Goths, pillar and saviour of the Roman race, Theodoric, loves thee, and

---

[1] For the attack on Narbo by Theodoric I see n. on 7. 475. It is not certain that Theodoric II met with resistance when he occupied the town in A.D. 462. Sidonius seems here to attribute all the damage to "the old war." In *Carm.* 22 *epist.* 1 he seems to imply recent fighting, but the reference may be merely to warlike preparations.

adversos probat ante per tumultus.
sed non hinc videare forte turpis,
quod te machina crebra perforavit;   75
namque in corpore fortium virorum
laus est amplior amplior cicatrix.
in castris Marathoniis merentem
vulnus non habuisse grande probrum est;
inter Publicolas manu feroces   80
trunco Mucius eminet lacerto;
vallum Caesaris opprimente Magno
inter tot facies ab hoste tutas
luscus Scaeva fuit magis decorus.
laus est ardua dura sustinere;   85
ignavis, timidis et improbatis
multum fingitur otiosa virtus.

  Quid quod Caesaribus ferax creandis,
felix prole virum, simul dedisti
natos cum genitore principantes?   90
nam quis Persidis expeditionem
aut victricia castra praeteribit
Cari principis et perambulatum
Romanis legionibus Niphaten,
tum cum fulmine captus imperator   95
vitam fulminibus parem peregit?

  His tu civibus, urbe, rure pollens
Consenti mihi gignis alme patrem,

---

¹ After the fighting at Dyrrhachium it was found that the
shield of Caesar's centurion, Scaeva, was pierced in 120
places (Caes. *B.C.* III. 53. 4). Lucan devotes a long passage
(VI. 140–262) to his extraordinary feats.

from thy fierce resistance of yore he gains assurance
of thy present loyalty. And thou canst not be considered unsightly because many an engine of war
hath pierced thee, for on the body of the brave the
greater the scar, the greater the honour. In the
campaign of Marathon it was a sore disgrace for a
soldier to have had no wound. Amid the Publicolae
with their bold hands Mucius with his maimed arm
shone conspicuous. When Magnus was over-
whelming Caesar's rampart, then amid a multitude
of faces unharmed by the enemy Scaeva [1] with one
eye lost was comelier than all. Hard to win is the
glory of enduring adversity; it is the indolent, the
coward and the dastard that are wont to feign prowess
without toil.

Nor is this all. Fruitful mother of Caesars and
blest in an offspring of heroes, thou didst give us at
one time father and sons [2] holding imperial sway
together. Who shall leave unmentioned the campaign against Persia or the victorious warfare of
Carus our prince and the marching of Roman legions
over Niphates at that time when the Emperor was
overwhelmed by lightning and a life that was itself
like lightning met its end?

Strong in such citizens and in thy city and thy
countryside, thou didst graciously bless me by
bringing to life the father of Consentius, a man in

[2] Referring to the Emperor Carus (A.D. 282–283) and his
sons Carinus and Numerianus, who were associated with him
as Caesars and succeeded him as joint rulers (283–4). Carus
seems to have been born not at Narbo (Narbonne) but at
Narbona, or rather Narona, in Illyria. The cause of his death
on his Persian expedition may have been assassination, not
lightning.

illum cui nitidi sales rigorque
Romanus fuit Attico in lepore.   100
hunc Miletius et Thales stupere
auditum potuit simulque Lindi est
notus qui Cleobulus inter arces,
et tu qui, Periandre, de Corintho es,
et tu quem dederat, Bias, Priene,   105
et tu, Pittace, Lesbius sophistes,
et tu qui tetricis potens Athenis
vincis Socraticas, Solon, palaestras,
et tu, Tyndareis satus Therapnis,
Chilon, legifero prior Lycurgo.   110
non hic, si voluit vacante cura
quis sit sideribus notare cursus,
diversas Arato vias cucurrit;
non hunc, cum geometricas ad artes
mentem composuit, sequi valebat   115
Euclides spatium sciens Olympi;
non hunc, si voluit rotare rhythmos,
quicquam proposito virum morari
Chrysippus potuisset ex acervo.
hic cum Amphioniae studebat arti   120
plectro, pollice, voce tibiaque,
Thrax vates, deus Arcas atque Phoebus
omni carmine post erant et ipsas
Musas non ita musicas putares.
hic si syrmate cultus et cothurno   125
intrasset semel Atticum theatrum,
cessissent Sophocles et Euripides;

---

¹ The meaning is that Chrysippus, who solved, or rather
dismissed, the problem of the Sorites by arbitrarily choosing
a stopping-place, could not have interrupted periods which
were so skilfully constructed and rounded off that no break

XXIII. TO CONSENTIUS

whom sparkling wit and Roman sternness were
set amid Attic elegance. Hearing him Milesian
Thales might well have been amazed, and Cleobulus
too, renowned among the eminences of Lindus, and
Periander of Corinth, and Bias, whom Priene gave
to the world, and Pittacus, the Lesbian master of
wisdom, and Solon, who ruled grave Athens and
surpassed the school of Socrates, and Chilon, scion of
Tyndarean Therapnae, a man to be esteemed before
Lycurgus the law-giver. This sage of ours, when in
times of leisure he chose to mark the courses of the
stars, did not stray from the paths that Aratus trod.
When he set his mind on the lore of geometry,
Euclid, who knew the measure of the heavens, could
not have followed him. When he chose to build
rhythmical periods, Chrysippus could not have
treated them like the Sorites and hindered him
from completing each scheme.[1] When he devoted
himself to the art of Amphion with quill, thumb,
voice and flute, the Thracian bard, the Arcadian god
and Phoebus lagged behind him in every kind of
song, and the very Muses might be deemed less
musical. If clad in long cloak and buskin he had
once entered the Athenian theatre, Sophocles and
Euripides would have given way before him; if

could be made in the middle of them. The word *acervus*
(corresponding to Greek σωρός, from which comes σωρείτης) is
used also by Cicero, *Ac.* II. 49, and Horace, *Epist.* II. 1.
47, in connexion with the fallacy of the Sorites; see Reid
and Wilkins respectively on the passages just cited. The
Sorites took various forms; the simplest form is represented by the question "How many grains make a heap?
Does one?" The answerer would then be led on to add one,
then another one, and so on, and the process would end in
his discomfiture.

aut si pulpita personare socco
comoedus voluisset, huic levato
palmam tu digito dares, Menander.   130
hic cum senipedem stilum polibat
Zmyrnaeae vice doctus officinae
aut cum se historiae dabat severae,
primos vix poterant locos tueri
torrens Herodotus, tonans Homerus.   135
non isto potior fuisset, olim
qui Pandioniam movebat arte
orator caveam tumultuosus,
seu luscum raperetur in Philippum,
causam seu Ctesiphontis actitaret,   140
vir semper popularitate crescens
et iuste residens in arce fandi,
qui fabro genitore procreatus
oris maluit expolire limam.
quid vos eloquii canam Latini,   145
Arpinas, Patavine, Mantuane,
et te, comica qui doces, Terenti,
et te, tempore qui satus severo
Graios, Plaute, sales lepore transis,
et te multimoda satis verendum   150
scriptorum numerositate, Varro,
et te, qui brevitate, Crispe, polles,
et qui pro ingenio fluente nulli,
Corneli Tacite, es tacendus ori,
et te Massiliensium per hortos   155
sacri stipitis, Arbiter, colonum

---

132. vice *C*, incude *F*, cute *ceteri.*   *Vid. Class. Quart., loc. cit. pp.* 21 *sq.*
135. terrens *codd.*

---

[1] Cf. 2. 185; 9. 148.

again he had chosen to write comedies and make the stage resound with the sock, Menander would have lifted an appealing finger and yielded him the palm. When he skilfully embellished the six-footed style after the manner of Smyrna's school,[1] or when he devoted himself to austere history, Homer with his thunder and Herodotus with his rushing flow were scarcely able to keep the first place. Not above him would that stormy orator have been ranked who in olden times was wont to sway the theatre in Pandion's town by his art, whether he launched himself against the one-eyed Philip or pled insistently the cause of Ctesiphon,—a man ever advancing in favour and justly placed on the topmost pinnacle of oratory, a smith's son who preferred to sharpen his tongue to a fine edge.[2] Why should I sing of the masters of Latin utterance,[3] the man of Arpinum, the man of Padua, the bard of Mantua, Terence, producer of comedies, Plautus, who though born in a serious age surpasses by his brightness the wit of the Greeks; Varro, too, right worshipful for the many-sided multitudinousness of his books, Crispus, master of brevity, Cornelius Tacitus, whom by reason of his fertile genius no tongue must tacitly ignore, Arbiter,[4] whose *Gardens of Massilia* make him the peer of the

[2] 2. 187 sq. n.

[3] With this descriptive catalogue of Latin writers cf. 2. 182–192.

[4] Referring to Petronius Arbiter. The extant remains of his *Satyricon* do not enable us to explain *hortos Massil.*, though there is evidence that Massilia was mentioned in that work. The hero, Encolpius, is dogged by the wrath of Priapus, who was worshipped especially at Lampsacus, on the Hellespont (cf. 9. 174). The "sacred tree-stock" refers to the rude wooden images of Priapus. For a fuller discussion see *Class. Quart., loc. cit.* p. 22.

Hellespontiaco parem Priapi,
et te carmina per libidinosa
notum, Naso tener, Tomosque missum,
quondam Caesareae nimis puellae   160
ficto nomine subditum Corinnae?
quid celsos Senecas loquar vel illum
quem dat Bilbilis alta Martialem,
terrarum indigenas Hibericarum?
quid quos duplicibus iugata taedis   165
Argentaria Polla dat poetas?
quid multos varii stili retexam?
arguti, teneri, graves, dicaces,
si Consentius adfuit, latebant.

    Huic summi ingenii viro simulque   170
summae nobilitatis atque formae
iuncta est femina quae domum ad mariti
prisci insignia transferens Iovini
implevit trabeis larem sophistae.
sic intra proprios tibi penates,   175
Consenti, patriae decus superbum,
fastis vivit avus paterque libris.

    Haec per stemmata te satis potentem,
morum culmine sed potentiorem,
non possim merita sonare laude,   180
nec si me Odrysio canens in antro,
qua late trepidantibus fluentis
cautes per Ciconum resultat Hebrus,
princeps instituisset ille vatum,
cum dulces animata saxa chordae   185

    157. Priapi *ego* : Priapo.   *Vid. Class. Quart., loc. cit. p.* 22.
166. pallidat *codd.*

---

    [1] There is no ground for this identification of Ovid's Corinna
with Julia, daughter of Augustus, or for the suggestion that
his relations with Julia were the cause of his banishment.

dweller of the Hellespont as worshipper of the sacred tree-stock, Priapus; and languishing Ovid, famed for his lascivious poems and banished to Tomi, too much erstwhile the slave of Caesar's daughter, whom he called by the feigned name of Corinna?[1] Why cite the great Senecas, or Martial, given to the world by lofty Bilbilis—all natives of Spanish lands? Why speak of the poets whom Argentaria Polla, twice yoked in wedlock, presents to us?[2] Why rehearse the names of many masters of divers styles? Tuneful, melting, grave or witty, if Consentius appeared they shrank into obscurity.

To this man supreme alike in genius, nobility, and comeliness, was linked a lady who brought to her husband's home the trappings of honour worn by Jovinus of old and filled the dwelling of a scholar with robes of state.[3] Thus within your walls, Consentius, proud glory of your country, your grandfather still lives on by the lustre of his dignities and your father by his books.

[4] Mighty as you are through this lineage, and yet mightier by your lofty character, I could not sound your praises worthily even if the great father of bards, singing in Odrysian cave where Hebrus with his bustling waters re-echoes among the rocks of the Ciconians, had taught me, while the sweet strings by the power of their music drew the animated stones

---

[2] Lucan and presumably Statius; but the idea that Lucan's widow married Statius has no foundation.

[3] The elder Consentius had married a daughter of the usurper Jovinus (411–413).

[4] With the passage which follows compare 2. 69–74. This is the seventh mention of Orpheus in these poems, and there are nearly as many in the *Epistles*.

ferrent per Rhodopen trahente cantu
et versa vice fontibus ligatis
terras currere cogerent anhelas,
nec non Hismara solibus paterent
aurita chelyn expetente silva   190
et nulli resolubiles calori
curvata ruerent nives ab Ossa,
stantem aut Strymona Bistones viderent,
cum carmen rapidus latex sitiret;
nec si Peliaco datus bimembri   195
ad Centaurica plectra constitissem,
hinnitum duplicis timens magistri;
nec si me docuisset ille fari,
iussus pascere qui gregem est clientis
Amphrysi ad fluvium deus bubulcus,   200
quod ferrugineos Cyclopas arcu
stravit sub Liparensibus caminis
vibrans plus grave fulmen in sagitta.
   Iam primo tenero calentem ab ortu
excepere sinu novem sorores,   205
et te de genetrice vagientem
tinxerunt vitrei vado Hippocrenes:
tunc, hac mersus aqua, loquacis undae
pro fluctu mage litteras bibisti.
hinc tu iam puer aptior magistro   210
quidquid rhetoricae institutionis,
quidquid grammaticalis aut palaestrae est,
sicut iam tener hauseras, vorasti.
et iam te aula tulit piusque princeps
inter conspicuous statim locavit,   215
consistoria quos habent, tribunos;

207. texerunt *codd.*; vitrei *CPF*: vitreae *T*; *cf.* 9. 285.
210. hinc *Luetjohann*: tunc.

296

adown the slopes of Rhodope and, reversing the order of things, bound rivers fast and forced the land to rush panting along, and Mount Ismarus was laid bare to the sun, as the trees, all ears, hied them towards the lyre, and the snows that no heat could melt fell headlong down from bowing Ossa, and the Bistones saw Strymon standing still, its rushing waters athirst for song; nay, not if I had been given in charge to the twy-formed denizen of Pelion [1] and had taken my place by the Centaur's lyre, dreading the neigh of my double-bodied teacher; nor if I had been taught to give utterance by him who was commanded to feed the flock of his servant by the river Amphrysus,[2] a god turned herdsman because with his bow he laid prostrate the grimy Cyclopes down among the furnaces of Lipara, launching in his arrow a bolt more crushing than theirs.

The moment that your warm infant form saw the light, the nine Sisters welcomed you to their arms, and they took you, a wailing babe, from your mother and dipped you in the crystal pool of Hippocrene. At that moment, when they steeped you in the fount, it was no mere flow of prattling water that you drank, but rather the lore of letters. Hence when you had grown to boyhood and were more fitted for a teacher's care [3] you devoured all the course of rhetoric and of the grammarian's school even as you imbibed it in infancy. Next the Court claimed you and the good Emperor straightway set you among the honourable tribunes of his Consistory [4]; and the

[1] Chiron.   [2] Apollo.

[3] Or perhaps " more capable than your teacher " (so the *Thes. Ling. Lat.*).

[4] He was *tribunus et notarius* under Valentinian III. On this office see *C. M. H.*, I. 38.

iamque et purpureus in arce regni
praeesse officiis tuis solebat,
mores nobilitate quod merebant:
tantum culminis et decus stupendum   220
scripti annalibus indicant honores.
hinc tu militiam secutus amplam,
castrensem licet ampliare censum
per suffragia iusta debuisses,
sollemnis tamen abstinens lucelli   225
fama plus locuples domum redisti
solum quod dederas tuum putando.
tum si forte fuit quod imperator
Eoas soceri venire in aures
fido interprete vellet et perito,   230
te commercia duplicis loquelae
doctum solvere protinus legebat.
o, sodes, quotiens tibi loquenti
Byzantina sophos dedere regna,
et te seu Latialiter sonantem   235
tamquam Romulea satum Subura,
seu linguae Argolicae rotunditate
undantem Marathone ceu creatum
plaudentes stupuere Bosphorani,
mirati minus Atticos alumnos!   240
hinc si foedera solverentur orbis,
pacem te medio darent feroces
Chunus, Sauromates, Getes, Gelonus;
tu Tuncrum et Vachalim, Visurgin, Albin,
Francorum et penitissimas paludes   245
intrares venerantibus Sygambris
solis moribus inter arma tutus,

---

[1] Theodosius II, whose daughter Eudoxia was married
to Valentinian III.
[2] Stein (I. 547, n. 2) remarks that the choice of so young
an official for this important duty indicates that a good

wearer of the purple himself in the citadel of the
Empire was wont to preside over your boards—an
honour which your noble virtue well deserved. This
great eminence and wondrous glory stands recorded
in the yearly roll of public dignities. Thereupon
you undertook a duty of wide power, and although you
might well have enlarged your service-pay by the
lawful bestowal of your good offices, you held aloof
from that common pursuit of paltry gain, and you
returned home made richer in reputation by deeming
as yours only what you had given away. At that
time if there chanced to be aught that the Emperor
wished to be brought to the ears of the Empress's
father in the East [1] through an interpreter both
honest and skilled, he would straightway choose you
as one well-instructed to hold intercourse in the two
tongues.[2] O how often—let me say it—how often
did the Byzantine realm give you a " bravo ! " as you
spoke ! How often did the dwellers by the
Bosphorus applaud and marvel at you, both when
you uttered the Latin speech like one born in the
Roman Subura and when you poured forth the
finished elegance of the Greek tongue like a son of
Marathon, so that they admired the natives of
Athens less ! Thus if the world's treaties had been
dissolved, your mediation would have made fierce
peoples, the Hun, the Sarmatian, the Goth, the
Gelonian, offer peace ; safe in the midst of arms through
your sheer goodness you would have penetrated even
to the Tungrian and the Vachalis, the Visurgis, the
Albis, and the remotest fens of the Franks, and the
Sygambrians would have done you reverence ; the

knowledge of Greek was now rare among the governing class
in the western Empire. This is probably true, though we
read of some other cases where duties of very high responsibility were entrusted to one of the *tribuni et notarii*.

tu Maeotida Caspiasque portas,
tu fluxis equitata Bactra Parthis
constans intrepidusque sic adires   250
ut fastu posito tumentis aulae
qui supra satrapas sedet tyrannus
ructans semideum propinquitates
lunatam tibi flecteret tiaram.
tu si publica fata non vetarent   255
ut Byrsam peteres vel Africanae
telluris Tanaiticum rebellem,
confestim posito furore Martis
post piratica damna destinaret
plenas mercibus institor carinas,   260
et per te bene pace restituta
non ultra mihi bella navigarent.
    Iam si seria forte terminantem
te spectacula ceperant theatri,
pallebat chorus omnis histrionum   265
tamquam si Arcitenens novemque Musae
propter pulpita iudices sederent.
coram te Caramallus aut Phabaton
clausis faucibus et loquente gestu
nutu, crure, genu, manu, rotatu   270
toto in schemate vel semel latebit,
sive Aeetias et suus Iason
inducuntur ibi ferusque Phasis,
qui iactos super arva Colcha dentes
expavit, fruticante cum duello   275
spicis spicula mixta fluctuarent;
sive prandia quis refert Thyestae
seu vestros, Philomela torva, planctus,
discerptum aut puerum cibumque factum
iamiam coniugis innocentioris;   280

256. ut : et C.

Maeotid mere and the Caspian gates and Bactra,
where the roving Parthians ride, you would have
approached so resolute and fearless that the tyrant
who sits enthroned above his satraps mouthing boasts
of his kinship with demigods would have laid aside
the arrogance of his pompous court and bowed his
crescent [1] tiara before you. Had the fortunes of
Rome allowed you to seek Byrsa and the rebel from
the Tanais [2] in Afric's land, the frenzy of war would
straightway have been laid aside, and the trader,
after all his losses at the hands of pirates, would
have begun to dispatch ships laden with merchandise;
and thus, peace being firmly restored through you,
I should no longer have been troubled with wars
afloat on the seas.

And when you chanced to put aside serious
concerns and were attracted by the shows of the
theatre, the whole company of actors would grow
pale, as if the god of the bow and the nine Muses
were sitting as judges beside the stage. [3] In your
presence a Caramallus or a Phabaton, with his closed
lips and his action that speaks through nod, leg, knee,
hand, and spin, will for once be unnoticed all through
his piece, whether the daughter of Aeëtes and her
Jason are being shown, with the barbarous Phasis, that
was affrighted at the teeth thrown upon the Colchian
field, when a martial host sprouted up amid a surging
mass of corn-spikes and spear-heads commingled:
or whether the feast of Thyestes is represented or the
lamentations of the wild-eyed Philomela or the dis-
membered boy given as food to the husband who
thus at the last became the more innocent of the two:

---

[1] Cf. 2. 51 n.   [2] Geiseric.
[3] The following passage refers to performances of *pantomimi*.

seu raptus Tyrios Iovemque taurum
spreto fulmine fronte plus timendum;
seu turris Danaae refertur illic,
cum multum pluvio rigata censu est,
dans plus aurea furta quam metalla;   285
seu Ledam quis agit Phrygemque ephebum
aptans ad cyathos facit Tonanti
suco nectaris esse dulciorem;
seu Martem simulat modo in catenas
missum Lemniacas, modo aut repulso   290
formam imponit apri caputque saetis
et tergum asperat hispidisque malis
leve incurvat ebur, vel ille fingit
hirtam dorsa feram repanda tela
attritu adsiduo cacuminantem;   295
seu Perseia virgo vindicata
illic luditur harpe coniugali,
seu quod carminis atque fabularum
clausa ad Pergama dat bilustre bellum.
quid dicam citharistrias, choraulas,   300
mimos, schoenobatas, gelasianos
cannas, plectra, iocos, palen, rudentem
coram te trepidanter explicare?
nam circensibus ipse quanta ludis
victor gesseris intonante Roma   305
laetam par fuit exarare Musam.

　　Ianus forte suas bifrons Kalendas
anni tempora circinante Phoebo
sumendas referebat ad curules.
mos est Caesaris hic, die bis uno   310
(privatos vocitant) parare ludos.

---

¹ According to one version of the legend Mars in his jealousy
changed himself into a wild boar and slew Adonis.

or whether it is the Tyrian ravishment and Jove turned bull, with his chief menace in his brow, for he has flung the thunderbolt aside: or whether the scene is the tower of Danae, when it was drenched with a shower of riches and conferred secret joys more golden than the metal: or whether one plays Leda, or by setting the Phrygian youth to serve the wine-cups makes him sweeter to Jove than the nectar-juice: or whether one counterfeits Mars put in Lemnian chains or again invests him, a lover rejected, with a wild boar's [1] form, roughening his head and back with bristles, curving the smooth ivory upward from his shaggy jaws, and the hairy-backed monster is shown sharpening his up-bent weapons by diligent rubbing: or whether Perseus' maid rescued by her lover's falchion is represented, or such song and story as the ten years' war at beleaguered Pergamum affords. Why should I tell how the harpists, flute-players, mimes, rope-walkers and clowns quail as they display before you their reeds, quills, jests, bouts, and ropes? Nay, it was rather the duty of my Muse to record with joy your own great exploits when you were conqueror at the circensian games amid the thunderous plaudits of Rome.[2]

Phoebus was beginning a new yearly circle, and two-faced Janus was bringing back his Calends, the day when the new magistrates take their seats. It is Caesar's custom to provide games (called "private")

[2] "Rome" must not be taken literally: these games were held at Ravenna, where Valentinian III resided. The description which follows, though by no means without originality, is considerably influenced by Statius, *Theb.* VI. 389 sqq., which describes the chariot-race held at Nemea by the seven chieftains on their way to Thebes.

tunc coetus iuvenum, sed aulicorum,
Elei simulacra torva campi
exercet spatiantibus quadrigis.
et iam te urna petit cietque raucae   315
acclamatio sibilans coronae;
tum qua est ianua consulumque sedes,
ambit quam paries utrimque senis
cryptis carceribusque fornicatus,
uno e quattuor axe sorte lecto   320
curvas ingrederis premens habenas.
id collega tuus simulque vobis
pars adversa facit; micant colores,
albus vel venetus, virens rubensque,
vestra insignia. continent ministri   325
ora et lora manus iubasque tortas
cogunt flexilibus latere nodis
hortanturque obiter iuvantque blandis
ultro plausibus et voluptuosum
dictant quadrupedantibus furorem.   330
illi ad claustra fremunt repagulisque
incumbunt simul ac per obseratas
transfumant tabulas et ante cursum
campus flatibus occupatur absens.
impellunt, trepidant, trahunt, repugnant,   335
ardescunt, saliunt, timent, timentur,
nec gressum cohibent, sed inquieto
duratum pede stipitem flagellant.
tandem murmure bucinae strepentis

---

320. sorte *ego* : forte.   321. fremens *codd.*

[1] *i.e.* of the Olympic games.
[2] *urna.* The lot assigned to each competitor a particular
carcer, and hence, on this and similar occasions, a particular
chariot, as the chariots and teams were supplied by the
Emperor, and were already in their respective *carceres* (*v.* 331).

twice in that one day. Then a company of young
men, all of the Court, goes through a grim mimicry
of the field of Elis[1] with four-horse chariots racing
over the course. Now the urn[2] demanded you and
the whistling cheers of the hoarse onlookers summoned you. Thereupon, in the part where the door
is and the seat of the consuls, round which there
runs a wall with six vaulted chambers on each side,
wherein are the starting-pens, you chose one of the
four chariots by lot and mounted it, laying a tight
grip on the hanging reins. Your partner[3] did the
same, so did the opposing side. Brightly gleam the
colours, white and blue, green and red, your several
badges. Servants' hands hold mouth and reins and
with knotted cords force the twisted manes to hide
themselves, and all the while they incite the steeds,
eagerly cheering them with encouraging pats and instilling a rapturous frenzy. There behind the barriers
chafe those beasts, pressing against the fastenings,
while a vapoury blast comes forth between the wooden
bars and even before the race the field they have
not yet entered is filled with their panting breath.
They push, they bustle, they drag, they struggle,
they rage, they jump, they fear and are feared;
never are their feet still, but restlessly they lash the
hardened timber. At last the herald with loud blare

---

[3] Cf. 362. The four competitors were paired off, and each
competitor endeavoured to bring victory to his side by fair
means or by means which in modern times would be considered
foul. The "colleague" of Consentius apparently tries to force
the pace and fluster his opponents in order to leave a clear
field for his partner, who conserves the energies of his team
until the time comes to make a spurt for victory. In the last
lap one of the opposing side tries to help his partner by an
egregious foul, with disastrous results.

suspensas tubicen vocans quadrigas   340
effundit celeres in arva currus.
non sic fulminis impetus trisulci,
non pulsa Scythico sagitta nervo,
non sulcus rapide cadentis astri,
non fundis Balearibus rotata   345
umquam sic liquidos poli meatus
rupit plumbea glandium procella.
cedit terra rotis et orbitarum
moto pulvere sordidatur aer;
instant verberibus simul regentes,   350
iamque et pectora prona de covinno
extensi rapiuntur et iugales
trans armos feriunt vacante tergo,
nec cernas cito, cernuos magistros
temones mage sufferant an axes.   355
iam vos ex oculis velut volantes
consumpto spatio patentiore
campus clauserat artus arte factus,
per quem longam, humilem duplamque muro
euripus sibi machinam tetendit.   360
ut meta ulterior remisit omnes,
fit collega tuus prior duobus,
qui te transierant; ita ipse quartus
gyri condicione tum fuisti.
curae est id mediis, ut ille primus,   365

---

[1] It was usual to start the race from a white line made on
the course itself; but on this occasion the start is made from
the *carceres*. This seems to have been the older method.

[2] *Euripus* is applied to a canal or large tank. In some
circuses the long central barrier (*spina*) was filled with water.
In earlier times *euripus* was applied to the moat which Julius
Caesar built round the interior of the Circus Maximus to
protect the spectators when wild beasts were exhibited. This
was filled up by Nero.

of trumpet calls forth the impatient teams and launches the fleet chariots into the field.[1] The swoop of forked lightning, the arrow sped by Scythian string, the trail of the swiftly-falling star, the leaden hurricane of bullets whirled from Balearic slings has never so rapidly split the airy paths of the sky. The ground gives way under the wheels and the air is smirched with the dust that rises in their track. The drivers, while they wield the reins, ply the lash; now they stretch forward over the chariots with stooping breasts, and so they sweep along, striking the horses' withers and leaving their backs untouched. With charioteers so prone it would puzzle you to pronounce whether they were more supported by the pole or by the wheels. Now as if flying out of sight on wings, you had traversed the more open part, and you were hemmed in by the space that is cramped by craft, amid which the central barrier has extended its long low double-walled structure.[2] When the farther turning-post freed you all from restraint once more, your partner went ahead of the two others, who had passed you; so then, according to the law of the circling course, you had to take the fourth track.[3] The drivers in the middle were intent

---

[3] The races were run counter-clockwise; thus the competitors had the spectators on their right and the *spina* on their left. The coveted position was the inside one, *i.e.* the one nearest to the *spina*, which gave the shortest course. On this occasion Consentius' partner has the inside position and Consentius the next. The two opponents get so far ahead of Consentius that they are entitled to move inward in front of him, and he has to change over to the outside position (363 sq.). Having gained this advantage, the two opponents hope that the horses of Consentius' partner will swerve outward far enough to allow one of his enemies to dash in and

pressus dexteriore concitatu
partem si patefecerit sinistram
totas ad podium ferens habenas,
curru praetereatur intus acto.
tu conamine duplicatus ipso   370
stringis quadriiugos et arte summa
in gyrum bene septimum reservas;
instabant alii manu atque voce,
passim et deciduis in arva guttis
rectorum alipedumque sudor ibat.   375
raucus corda ferit fragor faventum
atque ipsis pariter viris equisque
fit cursu calor et timore frigus.
itur sic semel, itur et secundo,
est sic tertius atque quartus orbis;   380
quinto circite non valens sequentum
pondus ferre prior retorquet axem,
quod velocibus imperans quadrigis
exhaustos sibi senserat iugales;
iam sexto reditu perexplicato   385
iamque et praemia flagitante vulgo
pars contraria nil timens tuam vim
securas prior orbitas terebat,
tensis cum subito simul lupatis,
tensis pectoribus, pede ante fixo,   390
quantum auriga suos solebat ille
raptans Oenomaum tremente Pisa,
tantum tu rapidos teris iugales.
hic compendia flexuosa metae

389. simul *ego* : sinum. *Vid. Class. Quart., loc. cit. pp. 22 sq.*

seize the inside position (365–369). In the fifth lap Consentius'
partner has to withdraw; thus the opponents secure the two
inner tracks. Consentius, acting on the traditional principle

that if haply the first man, embarrassed by a dash of
his steeds too much to the right, should leave a space
open on the left by heading for the surrounding seats,
he should be passed by a chariot driven in on the near
side.   As for you, bending double with the very force
of the effort you keep a tight rein on your team and
with consummate skill wisely reserve them for the
seventh lap.   The others are busy with hand and
voice, and everywhere the sweat of drivers and flying
steeds falls in drops on to the field.   The hoarse roar
from applauding partisans stirs the heart, and the
contestants, both horses and men, are warmed by
the race and chilled by fear.   Thus they go once
round, then a second time; thus goes the third lap,
thus the fourth; but in the fifth turn the foremost
man, unable to bear the pressure of his pursuers,
swerved his car aside, for he had found, as he gave
command to his fleet team, that their strength was
exhausted.   Now the return half of the sixth course
was completed and the crowd was already clamouring
for the award of the prizes; your adversaries, with
no fear of any effort from you, were scouring the
track in front with never a care, when suddenly you
tautened the curbs all together, tautened your chest,
planted your feet firmly in front, and chafed the
mouths of your swift steeds as fiercely as was the
wont of that famed charioteer of old when he swept
Oenomaus [1] along with him and all Pisa trembled.
Hereupon one of the others, clinging to the shortest

that all's fair in the circus, rushes up as close as possible to
the inside car as it passes the turning-post, and succeeds in
exciting the horses, so that they plunge wildly and take a
crooked course.   Consentius watches his opportunity, gains
the inside position, and dashes ahead (394–399).

[1] Cf. 2. 490 sqq.

unus dum premit, incitatus a te   395
elatas semel impetu quadrigas
iuncto non valuit plicare gyro;
quem tu, quod sine lege praeteriret,
transisti remanens, ab arte restans.
alter dum popularitate gaudet,   400
dexter sub cuneis nimis cucurrit.
hunc, dum obliquat iter diuque lentus
sero cornipedes citat flagello,
tortum tramite transis ipse recto.
hic te incautius assecutus hostis   405
sperans anticipasse iam priorem
transversum venit impudens in axem;
incurvantur equi, proterva crurum
intrat turba rotas quaterque terni
artantur radii, repleta donec   410
intervalla crepent volubilisque
frangat margo pedes; ibi ipse quintus
curru praecipitatus obruente
montem multiplici facit ruina,
turpans prociduam cruore frontem.   415
miscet cuncta fragor resuscitatus,
quantum non cyparissifer Lycaeus,
quantum non nemorosa tollit Ossa
crebras inrequieta per procellas,
quantum nec reboant volutae ab Austro   420
Doris Trinacris aut voraginoso

---

¹ *i.e.* the first-mentioned of the two opponents of Consentius,
the one whom Consentius had first passed.

² This man's attention had been distracted (*vv.* 400–404)
and, seeing Consentius pass him on the inside, he assumed
that his own partner, who had occupied that position a moment
before, had gone ahead. He then attempted to simplify
that partner's path to victory by fouling Consentius' wheel

route round the turning-post, was hustled by you, and his team, carried away beyond control by their onward rush, could no more be wheeled round in a harmonious course. As you saw him pass before you in disorder, you got ahead of him by remaining where you were, cunningly reining up. The other adversary, exulting in the public plaudits, ran too far to the right, close to the spectators; then as he turned aslant and all too late after long indifference urged his horses with the whip, you sped straight past your swerving rival. Then the enemy in reckless haste overtook you and, fondly thinking that the first man [1] had already gone ahead, shamelessly made for your wheel with a sidelong dash.[2] His horses were brought down, a multitude of intruding legs entered the wheels, and the twelve spokes were crowded, until a crackle came from those crammed spaces and the revolving rim shattered the entangled feet; then he, a fifth [3] victim, flung from his chariot, which fell upon him, caused a mountain of manifold havoc, and blood disfigured his prostrate brow. Thereupon arose a riot of renewed shouting such as neither Lycaeus with its cypresses ever raises, nor the forests of Ossa, troubled though they be by many a hurricane; such echoing roar as not even the Sicilian sea, rolled onward in billows by the south wind, gives forth, nor Propontis, whose wild deeps

---

Venit (407) does not mean "dashed against"; Consentius' car could not have won after such an impact. How the blow was eluded and how the horses were brought down we are not told explicitly; indeed the end of the description is so vague that I long understood it to mean that one of the men inadvertently fouled his partner's car; but several things seem to rule out this interpretation.

[3] "a fifth," the other four being the horses.

THE POEMS OF SIDONIUS

quae vallat sale Bosphorum Propontis.
hic mox praecipit aequus imperator
palmis serica, torquibus coronas
coniungi et meritum remunerari,   425
victis ire iubens satis pudendis
villis versicoloribus tapetas.

   Iam vero iuvenalibus peractis
quem te praebueris sequente in aevo,
intra aulam soceri mei expetitus   430
curam cum moderatus es Palati,
chartis posterioribus loquemur,
si plus temporibus vacat futuris;
nunc quam diximus hospitalitatem
paucis personet obsequens Thalia.   435

   O dulcis domus, o pii penates,
quos (res difficilis sibique discors)
libertas simul excolit pudorque!
o convivia, fabulae, libelli,
risus, serietas, dicacitates,   440
occursus, comitatus unus idem,
seu delubra dei colenda nobis
tecta inlustria seu videnda Livi,   445
sive ad pontificem gradus ferendi,   443
sive ad culmina Martii Myronis,
sive ad doctiloqui Leonis aedes   446
(quo bis sex tabulas docente iuris
ultro Claudius Appius lateret
claro obscurior in decemviratu;
at si dicat epos metrumque rhythmis   450

445. transposuit Luetjohann.

---

[1] Note the plurals; the two members of the winning
pair receive the same prizes. One of them had not finished
the course, but he had done his best for his side. Thus
unselfish " team-work " was encouraged.

312

are a rampart to the Bosphorus. Next the just
emperor ordered silken ribands to be added to the
victors' palms and crowns to the necklets of gold,[1]
and true merit to have its reward; while to the
vanquished in their sore disgrace he bade rugs of
many-coloured hair to be awarded.

As for your conduct in after-time, when the days
of youth were over, when you were welcomed to the
Court of my wife's father and were charged with the
oversight of the Palace [2]—of this I will tell in a later
writing if the future allows me more free time; but
now let my obedient Muse proclaim in a few ringing
words the hospitality of which I have made mention.

O charming home, O holy hearth, graced by that
double glory, so hard to win, so hard to make one—
free speech and modesty! O feasts and talks and
books, laughter, seriousness, and witty saws, happy
meetings, and fellowship ever the same, whether
God's temple was to be reverently honoured by us
or the glorious house of Livius [3] was to be visited
or our way led to the Bishop [4] or to the towering
house of Martius Myro or to the house of the eloquent
Leo! [5] (If Leo had been expounding the Twelve
Tables of the Law, Appius Claudius would have lain
low of his own accord, and in that decemvirate so
illustrious he would have been a meaner figure;
if, again, Leo should sound an epic strain, guiding

---

[2] The *cura palatii* entailed the oversight of the palaces and
other royal buildings. The holder of this office in the western
Empire received the rank of *spectabilis*. In the eastern
Empire the *cura palatii* was a very exalted office.

[3] A poet of Narbonne.

[4] Probably Hermes, who succeeded Rusticus in A.D. 462.

[5] See 9. 314 n. Martius Myro is not otherwise known:
see n. on 9. 306.

flectat commaticis tonante plectro,
mordacem faciat silere Flaccum,
quamvis post satiras lyramque tendat
ille ad Pindaricum volare cygnum);
seu nos, Magne, tuus favor tenebat,   455
multis praedite dotibus virorum,
forma, nobilitate, mente, censu
(cuius si varios eam per actus,
centum et ferrea lasset ora laude,
constans, ingeniosus efficaxque,   460
prudens arbiter, optimus propinquus,
nil fraudans genii sibi vel ulli
personas, loca, tempus intuendo);
seu nos atria vestra continebant,
Marcelline meus, perite legum   465
(qui, verax nimis et nimis severus,
asper crederis esse nescienti;
at si te bene quispiam probavit,
noscit quod velit ipse iudicare;
nam numquam metuis loqui quod aequum est,   470
si te Sulla premat ferusque Carbo,
si tristes Marii trucesque Cinnae,
et si forte tuum caput latusque
circumstent gladii triumvirales);
seu nos Limpidii lares habebant,   475
civis magnifici virique summi,
fraternam bene regulam sequentis;
seu nos eximii simul tenebat
nectens officiositas Marini,

469. quid PT.

---

[1] "Pindaric swan"; Hor. *C.* IV. 2. 25: the "Odes"
(*lyram*) are those of the first three books.

the metre in brief measured clauses to the thundering
note of the lyre, he would force the carping Flaccus
to silence, even though that bard after his Satires
and his Odes should strive to soar to the heights of
the Pindaric swan.[1])   It was the same when we were
entertained by the kindliness of Magnus,[2] one who is
endowed with many a manly grace, with comeliness,
birth, intellect, and wealth; truly, were I to go
through the list of his diverse achievements, he would
wear out a hundred tongues, even tongues of iron,
with the telling of his praise—that man so staunch,
so talented, so efficient, wise mediator, best of kinsmen, stinting neither himself nor others of enjoyment, regardful as he ever is of persons, places and
seasons.   It was the same when we found ourselves
in the hall of my own Marcellinus,[3] learned in the
law, who being immeasurably truthful and strict is
deemed harsh by the ignorant; but if anyone has
proved him well, then he knows that our friend's
judgment is what he would like his own to be;
for Marcellinus is never afraid to utter what is right—
nor would he be were Sulla or savage Carbo or gloomy
Marii or ferocious Cinnas threatening him, or if the
swords of the triumvirs flashed about his head and
side.   It was the same when the home of Limpidius [4]
welcomed us; a splendid patriot he and a great man,
who follows well his brother's pattern; or it might
be that the excellent Marinus [4] with his engaging

[2] Magnus of Narbonne, an eminent Gallo-Roman noble,
praefectus praetorio Galliarum 458–9, consul 460; father of
Magnus Felix (9. 1 n.); identified by Sundwall with the
grandson of Agricola and father of Araneola (15. 151 sqq.).
See 5. 558; 14, § 2; 24. 90; *Epist.* I. 11. 10.

[3] Mentioned in *Epist.* II. 13. 1.

[4] Limpidius and Marinus are not otherwise known.

cuius sedulitas sodalitasque   480
aeterna mihi laude sunt colendae;
seu quoscumque alios videre fratres
cordi utrique fuit, quibus vacasse
laudandam reor occupationem;
horum nomina cum referre versu   485
adfectus cupiat, metrum recusat.

Hinc nos ad propriam domum vocabas,
cum mane exierat novum et calescens
horam sol dabat alteram secundam.
hic promens teretes pilas trochosque,   490
hic talos crepitantibus fritillis
nos ad verbera iactuum struentes,
tamquam Naupliades, repertor artis,
gaudebas hilarem ciere rixam.
hinc ad balnea, non Neroniana   495
nec quae Agrippa dedit vel ille cuius
bustum Dalmaticae vident Salonae,
ad thermas tamen ire sed libebat
privato bene praebitas pudori.
post quas nos tua pocula et tuarum   500
Musarum medius torus tenebat,
quales nec statuas imaginesque
aere aut marmoribus coloribusque
Mentor, Praxiteles, Scopas dederunt,
quantas nec Polycletus ipse finxit   505
nec fit Phidiaco figura caelo.

Sed iam te veniam loquacitati
quingenti hendecasyllabi precantur.
tantum, etsi placeat, poema longum est.
iamiam sufficit, ipse et impediris   510

492. iactuum *ego*: tractuum. *Vid. Class. Quart., loc. cit.*
p. 23.

courtesy was likewise entertaining us, a man whose
attentiveness and sociableness have earned my
everlasting praise. It was just the same if we both
took a fancy to visit any other of the brethren, to
spare time for whom I deem a glorious occupation;
but though my affection would fain record their
names in verse, metre forbids.

Afterwards you would bid us to your own home,
when the early morning had passed and the sun with
its gathering warmth was bringing the second hour
to second [1] our wishes. Then you would bring out
the shapely balls and hoops or the dice which with
rattling box marshal us for the hurtling throw, and
like Nauplius' son,[2] inventor of the art, you would
exult in the raising of a merry quarrel. Hence to
the baths; they were not those of Nero or those
given by Agrippa or by him whose tomb Dalmatian
Salonae views,[3] but we were pleased to go to baths
fittingly provided for privacy and modesty. After
the bath your cups and a couch in the midst of your
Muses would claim us: no statues or likenesses to
compare with these were ever fashioned in bronze or
marble or colours by Mentor, Praxiteles, or Scopas:
Polycletus himself did not mould any so great, nor
did Phidias with his chisel.

But now five hundred hendecasyllables crave your
pardon for their wordiness. A poem of this size,
even if it should please, is too long. Now at last
I've had enough of it; and you yourself are finding

---

[1] *alteram secundam*: for the pun cf. 2. 1. Others would
translate " the fourth hour."

[2] Palamedes, the reputed inventor of dice.

[3] Diocletian.

multum in carmine perlegens amicum,
dormitantibus otiosiorem.

XXIV

PROPEMPTICON AD LIBELLVM

  Egressus foribus meis, libelle,
hanc servare viam, precor, memento,
quae nostros bene ducit ad sodales,
quorum nomina sedulus notavi;
antiquus tibi nec teratur agger,   5
cuius per spatium satis vetustis
nomen Caesareum viret columnis;
sed sensim gradere: et moras habendo
adfectum celerem moves amicis.
  Ac primum Domiti larem severi   10
intrabis trepidantibus Camenis:
tam censorius haud fuit vel ille
quem risisse semel ferunt in aevo;
sed gaudere potes rigore docto:
hic si te probat, omnibus placebis.   15
hinc te suscipiet benigna Brivas,
sancti quae fovet ossa Iuliani,
quae dum mortua mortuis putantur,
vivens e tumulo micat potestas.
hinc iam dexteriora carpis arva   20
emensusque iugum die sub uno

---

[1] Milestones.   The book is to avoid the high-road.
[2] A *grammaticus*, to whom *Epist.* II. 2 is addressed.

it an encumbrance to read through such a long bit of your friend in verse, a friend who is more of an idler than a man in a doze.

XXIV

L'ENVOI

When you pass out by my door, little book, pray remember to keep this route; it leads conveniently to some comrades of mine whose names I have carefully put down. Do not tread the old road, through whose whole length the name of Caesar shows bright on very old pillars; [1] go by easy stages: by such slow progress you can call forth prompt affection from our friends.

First of all you shall enter the home of the strict Domitius,[2] where our Muse will be very nervous; for even the man who, they say, laughed only once in his life [3] was not as critical as he. Yet you may take pleasure in his sage severity, for if he approve of you, you will satisfy everybody. Next you shall be taken in hand by kindly Brivas,[4] which cherishes the bones of the holy Julian; those bones are deemed dead by the dead, but a living power flashes forth from that tomb. From here you wind through fields more to the right, and having traversed a hill-ridge on the same day, on the morrow you behold

[3] Marcus Crassus, grandfather of the triumvir. The allegation was first made by Lucilius (1299 sq. Marx).

[4] Brioude (Haute-Loire). St. Julian suffered martyrdom in A.D. 304. The Emperor Avitus was buried in the church at Brioude. "The dead" means those who are "dead in their sins" (Coloss. 2. 13; Ephes. 2. 1).

flavum crastinus aspicis Triobrem;
tum terram Gabalum satis nivosam
et, quantum indigenae volunt putari,
sublimem in puteo videbis urbem.   25
hinc te temporis ad mei Laconas
Iustinum rapies suumque fratrem,
quorum notus amor per orbis ora
calcat Pirithoumque Theseumque
et fidum rabidi sodalem Orestae.   30
horum cum fueris sinu receptus,
ibis Trevidon et calumniosis
vicinum nimis, heu, iugum Rutenis.
hic docti invenies patrem Tonanti,
rectorem columenque Galliarum,   35
prisci Ferreolum parem Syagri,
coniunx Papianilla quem pudico
curas participans iuvat labore,
qualis nec Tanaquil fuit nec illa
quam tu, Tricipitine, procreasti,   40

---

¹ Triober, or Triobris, mod. Truyère, tributary of the Oltis
(Lot), which is a tributary of the Garonne. The Gabales
(or Gabali; also Gabalitani, *Epist.* V. 13. 2, VII. 6. 7) were an
Aquitanian people on the border of Narbonese Gaul, occupying
the N.W. slopes of the Cevennes.

² Such local tales of wonderful things to be seen in water
are common enough. An unfounded view, perhaps suggested
by Savaron's note, that *puteus* here means " hill " (Fr. *puy*,
which, however, comes from *podium*), has found general
acceptance. S. Reinach, *Rev. Arch.* Sér. V. I. 3 (1916),
suggests *orbem* for *urbem* and boldly takes *sublimem orbem*
to mean the moon, which is proverbially invisible in French
wells.

³ *i.e.* the Castor and Pollux of his day.

⁴ *Epist.* V. 21 is written to Iustinus and his brother Sacerdos.

⁵ Conjectured without very much reason to be mod. Tréves
(Dép. Gard).

the yellow Triober.[1] Next you shall see the land of
the Gabales, where the snow lies deep, and, according to what the natives would have us believe, you
will view a towering city in a well.[2] Next you shall
hasten to those two Spartans of my time,[3] Iustinus
and his brother,[4] whose love is the theme of every
tongue in the world, thrusting into nothingness
Pirithous and Theseus and the faithful comrade of
mad Orestes. After they have received you with
open arms you shall go to Trevidos [5] and to the hill
which is, alas! only too near to those slanderers,
the Ruteni.[6] Here you will find the father of the
learned Tonantius,[7] the governor and pillar of the
Gallic lands, Ferreolus, peer of old Syagrius,[8] to
whom Papianilla gives all the help a good wife can,
sharing his cares—a woman surpassing Tanaquil and
the daughter of Tricipitinus [9] and that votary of

[6] Their town (orig. Segodunum) is the modern Rodez on the
upper course of the Aveyron, tributary of the Garonne. The
name survives also in the district-name Le Rouerge.

[7] To the young Tonantius *Epist.* IX. 13 is addressed.
His father, Tonantius Ferreolus, was related through his wife
Papianilla (*v.* 37) to Sidonius, whose wife had the same name.
He was a very eminent man of distinguished ancestry (*Epist.*
VII. 12. 1 sqq.); Praetorian Prefect of Gaul 451, when he
helped to secure Gothic support against Attila (*Epist.* VII.
12. 3); a little later his diplomacy saved Arles from Thorismund (*ib.*). In A.D. 469 he was sent to Rome with Thaumastus
and Petronius to prosecute Arvandus (*Epist.* I. 7. 4). He
became a Patrician (the date is uncertain). Besides his estate
at Trevidos he had one called Prusianum near Nîmes (*Epist.*
II. 9. 7).

[8] Afranius Syagrius of Lyons, maternal grandfather of
Tonantius Ferreolus. To him Symmachus wrote a number of
letters and Ausonius dedicated a book of poems. He was
consul in A.D. 381 (less probably 382). See *Epist.* I. 7. 4,
V. 17. 4.

[9] Lucretia, daughter of Sp. Lucretius Tricipitinus.

qualis nec Phrygiae dicata Vestae
quae contra satis Albulam tumentem
duxit virgineo ratem capillo.
hinc te Laesora, Caucason Scytharum
vincens, aspiciet citusque Tarnis,   45
limosum et solido sapore pressum
piscem perspicua gerens in unda.
hic Zeti et Calais tibi adde pennas
nimbosumque iugum fugax caveto;
namque est assiduae ferax procellae;   50
sed quamvis rapido ferare cursu,
lassum te Vorocingus obtinebit.
nostrum hic invenies Apollinarem,
seu contra rabidi Leonis aestus
vestit frigore marmorum penates,   55
sive hortis spatiatur in repostis,
quales mellifera virent in Hybla,
quales Corycium senem beantes
fuscabat picei latex Galaesi;
sive inter violas, thymum, ligustrum,   60
serpyllum, casiam, crocum atque caltam,
narcissos hyacinthinosque flores
spernit quam pretii petitor ampli
glaebam turifer advehit Sabaeus;
seu ficto potius specu quiescit   65
collis margine, qua nemus reflexum
nativam dare porticum laborans
non lucum arboribus facit, sed antrum.

52. vorocingus *C*, voracingus *PT*, veracingus *F*.

---

[1] Claudia, the Vestal, drew along the Tiber the boat containing the image of Magna Mater from Pessinus. The idea that she dragged it by her hair is probably taken from Claudian, *Carm. Min.* XXX. (XXIX.) 18.

XXIV. L'ENVOI

Phrygian Vesta [1] who against the fiercely swelling waters of Tiber dragged the ship by her virtuous hair. Next Laesora,[2] which overtops the Scythian Caucasus, shall behold you; so shall the rapid Tarnis,[3] which carries in its translucent waters a fish that haunts the mud, loaded with solid savouriness. Here put on the wings of Zetus and Calais and take flight from that cloudy mountain-ridge, for it is rife with constant gales. But however speedily you are rushing along, Vorocingus [4] shall harbour your wearied frame. Here you will find my dear Apollinaris. He may be clothing his home in a cold wrapping of marble against the heat of the raging Lion; or he may be walking in his secluded gardens, which are like those that bloom on honey-bearing Hybla or those others, the joy of the old man of Corycus, which the waters of black Galaesus darkened; [5] or there among his violets, thyme, privet, serpyllum, casia, saffron, marigolds, narcissus, and blooms of hyacinth he may be rejecting the earthy lump that the Sabaean carrier of frankincense brings from afar, seeking a great price; or he may have chosen to rest in his mimic grotto on the edge of the hill, where the trees take a backward sweep, striving to make a natural portico, and thereby create not a

[2] A mountain, modern Lozère.

[3] Modern Tarn.

[4] Vorocingus, the estate of Apollinaris, was near the Prusianum of Tonantius Ferreolus (v. 34 n.): see *Epist.* II. 9. 1 and 7. The view that this Apollinaris is identical with the one mentioned in the n. on v. 85 (see Stevens, pp. 195 f.) raises grave difficulties.

[5] An allusion to Virgil's charming description of the garden cultivated near Tarentum by a humble Corycian, *Georg.* IV. 125 sqq. *V.* 59 is a paraphrase of Virgil, v. 126; *Corycium senem* is taken from the same sentence (v. 127).

quis pomaria prisca regis Indi
hic nunc comparet aureasque vites   70
electro viridante pampinatas,
cum Porus posuit crepante gaza
fulvo ex palmite vineam metalli
gemmarum fluitantibus racemis?
   Hinc tu Cottion ibis atque Avito   75
nostro dicis " ave," dehinc " valeto."
debes obsequium viro perenne;
nam, dent hinc veniam mei propinqui,
non nobis prior est parens amico.
hinc te iam Fidulus, decus bonorum   80
et nec Tetradio latens secundus
morum dotibus aut tenore recti,
sancta suscipit hospitalitate.
exin tende gradum Tribusque Villis
Thaumastum expete, quemlibet duorum :   85
quorum iunior est mihi sodalis
et collega simul graduque frater;
quod si fors senior tibi invenitur,
hunc pronus prope patruum saluta.
hinc ad consulis ampla tecta Magni   90

81. latens *ego* : satis.   *Vid. Class. Quart., loc. cit. p.* 23.

---

[1] There are many ancient and mediæval references to
" golden vines " and similar extravagances of the East. These
became a favourite ingredient of the " Alexander-romance."
For an interesting description of such wonders in the palace of
King Porus see *Epist. Alexandri ad Aristotelem,* edited, with
Iulius Valerius, by B. Kuebler, p. 193; Pfister's *Kleine Texte
zum Alexanderroman,* p. 22. For the " golden vine " at Jeru-
salem see Josephus *B. Iud.* V. 5. 4, Tac. *Hist.* V. 5 *ad fin.,*
Flor. I. 40 (III. 5) 30. The earliest mention of such a thing
seems to be in Herodotus VII. 27.
  [2] Cottion cannot be identified.
  [3] A kinsman of Sidonius; *Epist.* III. 1 is addressed to him.

grove but rather a cavern. In that place who would now bring into comparison the ancient orchards of the Indian king and the golden vines [1] with their tendrils of verdant electrum in the days when Porus made a metal vineyard with treasure rustling on the yellow branches and clusters of gems swaying about?

Thence you shall go to Cottion [2] and say to my Avitus [3] "Good-day" and then "Good-bye." To that man you owe eternal duty, for (may my near and dear ones forgive me for this!) I put not even a parent before a friend. Next Fidulus, [4] glory of all good men and no humble second even to Tetradius [5] in gifts of character or in steadfast rectitude, shall receive you with pious hospitality. Thence wend your way and at Three Manors [6] visit Thaumastus— either of the two Wonders: [7] the younger is my bosom-friend and also my colleague and in standing my brother; but if you chance to find the elder, bow low and salute him as almost my uncle. Hence pass on to the spacious abode of the consul Magnus [8]

[4] Not otherwise known.

[5] A lawyer, to whom *Epist.* III. 10 is written. There is a play on the words *Tetradius* (which suggests "four") and *secundus*.

[6] Not otherwise known.

[7] This seems to refer to Thaumastus and his younger brother Apollinaris; Sidonius is punning on the word *Thaumastus*, which means "wonderful." Thaum. is mentioned in *Epist.* I. 7. 4, V. 6. 1, and *Epist.* V. 7 is addressed to him. Apollinaris is mentioned in *Epist.* V. 6. 1; *Epist.* IV. 6, V. 3 and 6 are written to him. These brothers were kinsmen (probably cousins) of Sidonius. Simplicius seems to have been another brother; *Epist.* IV. 4 and 12 are addressed to him and Apollinaris; cf. VII. 4. 4. In V. 6. 1 Sidonius writes of Thaumastus in terms which remind one of the present passage.

[8] See 23. 455 n.

Felicemque tuum veni, libelle;
et te bybliotheca qua paterna est,
qualis nec tetrici fuit Philagri,
admitti faciet Probus probatum;
hic saepe Eulaliae meae legeris,   95
cuius Cecropiae pares Minervae
mores et rigidi senes et ipse
quondam purpureus socer timebant.
    Sed iam sufficit: ecce linque portum;
ne te pondere plus premam saburrae,   100
his in versibus ancoram levato.

92. qua *Luetjohann* : quae *codd.*

XXIV. L'ENVOI

and to your friend Felix,[1] O book of mine, and where their father's library stands, a library such as not even the austere Philagrius[2] had, Probus,[3] having given you approbation, will cause you to be admitted. Here you will often be read by my kinswoman Eulalia,[4] of whose character, worthy of Athenian Minerva, strict greybeards and even her husband's father[5] in the days when he wore the purple used to stand in awe.

But enough! Away with you, put out from the harbour, and, lest I weight you further with a load of sandy ballast, up with the anchor even while these verses sound!

[1] See 9. 1 n.
[2] See n. on 7. 156.
[3] See 9. 6 and 333; *Epist.* IV. 1 is written to him.
[4] Wife of Probus and cousin of Sidonius.
[5] Magnus. The " purple " is that of the consulship.

LETTERS OF GAIUS SOLLIUS APOLLINARIS SIDONIUS

GAI SOLLII APOLLINARIS SIDONII EPISTVLARVM

LIBER PRIMVS

I

SIDONIVS CONSTANTIO SVO SALVTEM

1. Diu praecipis, domine maior, summa suadendi auctoritate, sicuti es in his quae deliberabuntur consiliosissimus, ut, si quae mihi[1] litterae paulo politiores varia occasione fluxerint, prout eas causa persona tempus elicuit, omnes retractatis exemplaribus enucleatisque uno volumine includam, Quinti Symmachi rotunditatem, Gai Plinii disciplinam maturitatemque vestigiis praesumptuosis insecu-

---

[1] mihi *add. R.*

---

* This letter was written about A.D. 469. Constantius of Lyons was a priest much admired by Sidonius for his character (see esp. III. 2) and for his literary ability (see II. 10. 3). He seems to be the Constantius who wrote a life of Remigius of Auxerre, but the extant life of Remigius attributed to him (*A. SS.* Iul, VII., 200–220) is probably by a later writer.

[1] The respectful address *domine maior* seems to occur only in Sidonius (cf. I. 11. 17, II. 3. 1, III. 6. 3, IV. 3. 1, IV. 17. 1, VIII. 4. 1). M. B. O'Brien (*Titles of address in Christian Latin epistolography*, Washington, D.C., 1930) wrongly attributes the use also to Claudianus Mamertus,

LETTERS OF GAIUS SOLLIUS APOLLINARIS SIDONIUS

BOOK I

I

SIDONIUS TO HIS FRIEND CONSTANTIUS, GREETING *

1. My honoured Lord,[1] you have this long while been pressing me (and you have every claim on my attention, for you are a most competent adviser on the matters about to be discussed) to collect all the letters making any little claim to taste that have flowed from my pen on different occasions as this or that affair, person, or situation called them forth, and to revise and correct the originals and combine all in a single book.[2] In so doing, I should be following, though with presumptuous steps, the path traced by Quintus Symmachus with his rounded style and by Gaius Plinius with his highly-developed

misled by the fact that Sidonius *Epist.* IV. 3 is reproduced in editions of Claudianus, to whom the letter was addressed. The use of comparative adjectives (especially *maior, prior, senior*) in titles is derived from the use of the comparative for the superlative, which arose early in colloquial Latin and ultimately became fairly common in the literature. For the use of *dominus* as an honorary title in letters see the article in *Thesaurus linguae Latinae*, especially 1925 f., 1929. 30–1930. 66; also O'Brien, *op. cit.*, p. 83.

[2] For the meaning of *volumen* here see Introd., p. lxi, n. 1.

turus. 2. nam de Marco Tullio silere melius puto,
quem in stilo epistulari nec[1] Iulius Titianus sub
nominibus inlustrium feminarum digna similitudine
expressit; propter quod illum ceteri quique Fron-
tonianorum utpote consectaneum aemulati, cur
veternosum dicendi genus imitaretur, oratorum
simiam nuncupaverunt. quibus omnibus ego immane dictu est quantum semper iudicio meo cesserim
quantumque servandam singulis pronuntiaverim
temporum suorum meritorumque praerogativam.
3. sed scilicet tibi parui tuaeque examinationi has
non recensendas (hoc enim parum est) sed defae-
candas, ut aiunt, limandasque commisi, sciens te
inmodicum esse fautorem non studiorum modo
verum etiam studiosorum. quam ob rem nos nunc
perquam haesitabundos in hoc deinceps famae
pelagus impellis. 4. porro autem super huiusmodi
opusculo tutius conticueramus, contenti versuum
felicius quam peritius editorum opinione, de qua
mihi iam pridem in portu iudicii publici post livi-
dorum latratuum Scyllas enavigatas sufficientis
gloriae ancora sedet. sed si et hisce deliramentis

---

[1] silere . . . nec. *Sic Wilamowitz*; me *pro* melius *et
ordinem turbatum exhibent codd.*

---

[1] There were two writers of this name, father and son.
The reference here is evidently to the elder, who seems to
have fully earned and often received the nickname "ape";
see *Vit. Maximin.* 27. 5 : *dictus est simia temporis sui, quod
cuncta esset imitatus.*

[2] *Aemulari* often means " be jealous of," sometimes, as
here, " be hostile to " or " disparage ": Fronto's disciples

artistry. 2. Marcus Tullius, indeed, I think I had better not mention, for even Julius Titianus [1] in his fictitious letters of famous women failed to produce a satisfactory copy of that writer's epistolary style, and for his pains was called " ape of the orators " by all the other disciples of Fronto, who were, as might be expected, spiteful toward this member of their own school for copying an outworn mode of writing.[2] Now in the first place I have always, in my own judgment, fallen terribly short of all the authors I have named; and secondly, I have always strenuously proclaimed that we must uphold the well-earned right of each of them to the foremost place in his own age. 3. But you see I have obeyed your command, and now submit to your scrutiny these epistles of mine, not merely for revision (which would not suffice) but also for purging, as the saying is, and polishing; for I know you are an enthusiastic friend not only to literary pursuits but to men of letters as well; and that is why, whilst I shiver on the brink, you are launching me upon this new sea of ambition. 4. It would have been safer, though, for me never to have said a word about a petty work of this sort, and to have been content with the reputation I won by my published verses, which have obtained a success out of proportion to their skill; thus I have sailed past Scyllas with their envious barkings, I have reached the harbour of public approval, and I have long been safely anchored to a sufficiency of fame. However, if Jealousy refrains

would have run down a man who aped Cicero's style, but they would scarcely have been jealous of him. *Oratorum* (if the reading is correct) probably means " Cicero and all his tribe."

genuinum molarem invidia non fixerit, actutum tibi
a nobis volumina numerosiora percopiosis scatur-
ientia sermocinationibus multiplicabuntur. vale.

II

SIDONIVS AGRICOLAE SVO SALVTEM

1. Saepenumero postulavisti ut, quia Theudorici
regis Gothorum commendat populis fama civilitatem,
litteris tibi formae suae quantitas, vitae qualitas
significaretur. pareo libens, in quantum epistularis
pagina sinit, laudans in te tam delicatae sollicitudinis
ingenuitatem. igitur vir est et illis dignus agnosci
qui eum minus familiariter intuentur: ita personam
suam deus arbiter et ratio naturae consummatae
felicitatis dote sociata cumulaverunt; mores autem
huiuscemodi, ut laudibus eorum nihil ne regni
quidem defrudet invidia. 2. si forma quaeratur:
corpore exacto, longissimis brevior, procerior emi-
nentiorque mediocribus. capitis apex rotundus, in
quo paululum a planitie frontis in verticem caesaries
refuga crispatur. cervix non sedet enervis sed stat
nervis.[1] geminos orbes hispidus superciliorum

---

[1] enervis sed stat add. ego; codd. varie turbati.

---

* It is generally agreed that this Agricola was a son of the
Emperor Avitus (and therefore a brother-in-law of Sidonius).
See II. 12. 1 sq. He rose to high office, perhaps to the
Praetorian Prefecture of the Gauls. Eventually he entered
the priesthood. We cannot with certainty date this letter
early in the reign of Theodoric, as many do. The last sentence
of § 9 seems to imply that Sidonius was at the Gothic court
when he wrote it; in that case it would have been quite

from fastening a jaw-tooth on these new absurdities as well, there will straightway pour in upon you roll after roll gushing with exuberant garrulity.   Farewell.

II

SIDONIUS TO HIS DEAR AGRICOLA, GREETING *

1. Seeing that report commends to the world the graciousness of Theodoric,[1] King of the Goths, you have often asked me to describe to you in writing the dimensions of his person and the character of his life. I am delighted to do so, subject to the limits of a letter, and I appreciate the honest spirit which prompts so nice a curiosity. Well, he is a man who deserves to be studied even by those who are not in close relations with him. In his build the will of God and Nature's plan have joined together to endow him with a supreme perfection; and his character is such that even the jealousy which hedges a sovereign has no power to rob it of its glories. 2. Take first his appearance. His figure is well-proportioned, he is shorter than the very tall, taller and more commanding than the average man. The top of his head is round, and on it his curled hair retreats gently from his even forehead. His neck is not squat and sinewless but erect and sinewy. Each eye is encircled by a shaggy arch of

natural for Agricola to ask him for a description of Theodoric and his ways. Even though Agricola, as the son of Avitus, must have heard a good deal about the Gothic king, he would be interested in reading an up-to-date record of Sidonius's impressions.

[1] Theodoric II. (reigned A.D. 453–466).

coronat arcus; si vero cilia flectantur, ad malas
medias palpebrarum margo prope pervenit. aurium
legulae, sicut mos gentis est, crinium superiacentium
flagellis operiuntur. nasus venustissime incurvus.
labra subtilia nec dilatatis oris angulis ampliata. pilis
infra narium antra fruticantibus cotidiana succisio.
barba concavis hirta temporibus, quam in subdita
vultus parte surgentem stirpitus tonsor assiduus
genis ut adhuc vesticipibus evellit. 3. menti, gut-
turis, colli, non obesi sed suculenti, lactea cutis, quae
propius inspecta iuvenali rubore suffunditur; namque
hunc illi crebro colorem non ira sed verecundia facit.
teretes umeri, validi lacerti, dura bracchia, patulae
manus, recedente alvo pectus excedens.[1] aream
dorsi humilior inter excrementa costarum spina
discriminat. tuberosum est utrumque musculis
prominentibus latus. in succinctis regnat vigor
ilibus. corneum femur, internodia poplitum bene
mascula, maximus in minime rugosis genibus honor;
crura suris fulta turgentibus et, qui magna sustentat
membra, pes modicus. 4. si actionem diurnam,
quae est forinsecus exposita, perquiras: antelucanos
sacerdotum suorum coetus minimo comitatu expetit,
grandi sedulitate veneratur; quamquam, si sermo

<hr>

[1] excedens *Luetjohann* : accedens.

<hr>

[1] *i.e.* he does not let his moustache grow.

brow; when his eyelids droop, the extremities of
the lashes reach almost half-way down the cheeks.
The tips of his ears, according to national fashion,
are hidden by wisps of hair that are trained over
them. His nose is most gracefully curved; his lips
are delicately moulded and are not enlarged by any
extension of the corners of the mouth. Every day
there is a clipping of the bristles that sprout beneath
the nostril-cavities.[1] The hair on his face grows
heavily in the hollows of the temples, but as it
springs up upon the lowest part of the face the
barber constantly roots it out from the cheeks,
keeping them as though they were still in the
earliest stage of manly growth. 3. His chin, throat
and neck suggest not fat but fullness; the skin is
milk-white, but if closely looked at it takes on a
youthful blush, for this tint is frequently produced
in his case by modesty, not by ill-temper. His
shoulders are well-shaped, his upper arms sturdy,
his forearms hard, his hands broad. The chest is
prominent, the stomach recedes; the surface of his
back is divided by a spine that lies low between
the bulging ribs; his sides swell with protuberant
muscles. Strength reigns in his well-girt loins.
His thigh is hard as horn; the upper legs from joint
to joint are full of manly vigour; his knees are
completely free from wrinkles and full of grace; the
legs have the support of sturdy calves, but the feet
which bear the weight of such mighty limbs are of
no great size. 4. And now you may want to know
all about his everyday life, which is open to the
public gaze. Before dawn he goes with a very small
retinue to the service conducted by the priests of
his faith, and he worships with great earnestness,

secretus, possis animo advertere quod servet istam
pro consuetudine potius quam pro ratione reverentiam. reliquum mane regni administrandi cura
sibi deputat. circumsistit sellam comes armiger;
pellitorum turba satellitum ne absit, admittitur, ne
obstrepat, eliminatur, sicque pro foribus immurmurat
exclusa velis, inclusa cancellis. inter haec intro-
missis gentium legationibus audit plurima, pauca
respondet; si quid tractabitur, differt; si quid
expedietur, accelerat. hora est secunda: surgit e
solio aut thesauris inspiciendis vacaturus aut stabulis.
5. si venatione nuntiata procedit, arcum lateri
innectere citra gravitatem regiam iudicat; quem
tamen, si comminus avem feramque aut venanti aut
vianti fors obtulerit, manui post tergum reflexae
puer inserit nervo lorove fluitantibus; quem sicut
puerile computat gestare thecatum, ita muliebre
accipere iam tensum. igitur acceptum modo sinuatis [1] e regione capitibus intendit, modo ad talum
pendulum nodi parte conversa languentem chordae
laqueum vagantis digito superlabente prosequitur;
et mox spicula capit implet expellit; quidve cupias
percuti prior admonet ut eligas [2]; eligis quid feriat:

[1] sinuatis *FR*: insinuatis.
[2] ut eligas *add. ego.*

---

[1] Or possibly "if one talks to him in private."
[2] One end of the string is permanently knotted to one
"horn" of the bow, the other end has a loop, which can be
easily slipped on to the other horn. Theodoric raises one foot,
keeping the heel on the ground, and rests the strung end of the
bow on that foot, while the other end rests against his body
or is firmly held in one hand. He then stoops, bending the bow
at the same time. Taking hold of the string at the end where
it is tied to the bow, he runs his fingers along it, thus

though (between ourselves [1]) one can see that this devotion is a matter of routine rather than of conviction. The administrative duties of his sovereignty claim the rest of the morning. Nobles in armour have places near his throne; a crowd of guards in their dress of skins is allowed in so as to be at hand, but excluded from the presence so as not to disturb; and so they keep up a hum of conversation by the door, outside the curtains but within the barriers. Meanwhile deputations from various peoples are introduced, and he listens to a great deal of talk, but replies shortly, postponing business which he intends to consider, speeding that which is to be promptly settled. The second hour comes: he rises from his throne, to pass an interval in inspecting his treasures or his stables. 5. When a hunt has been proclaimed and he sallies forth, he considers it beneath his royal dignity to have his bow slung at his side; but if in the chase or on the road chance presents bird or beast within his range, he puts his hand behind his back, and an attendant places the bow in it, with the string or thong hanging loose; for he thinks it childish to carry the bow in a case, and womanish to take it over ready strung. When he takes it he either holds it straight in front of him and bends the two ends and so strings it, or he rests upon his raised foot the end which has the knot, and runs his finger along the loose string until he comes to the dangling loop; [2] then he takes up the arrows, sets them in place, and lets them fly. Or he may urge you first to choose what quarry you wish to be struck down: you choose what he is to

straightening it out, until they reach the loop, which he duly attaches.

quod elegeris ferit; et, si ab alterutro errandum est,
rarius fallitur figentis ictus quam destinantis obtutus.
6. si in convivium venitur, quod quidem diebus
profestis simile privato est, non ibi impolitam con-
geriem liventis argenti mensis cedentibus suspiriosus
minister imponit; maximum tunc pondus in verbis
est, quippe cum illic aut nulla narrentur aut seria.
toreumatum peripetasmatumque modo conchyliata
profertur supellex, modo byssina. cibi arte, non
pretio placent, fercula nitore, non pondere. scypho-
rum paterarumque raras oblationes facilius est ut
accuset sitis quam recuset ebrietas. quid multis?
videas ibi elegantiam Graecam abundantiam Galli-
canam celeritatem Italam, publicam pompam priva-
tam diligentiam regiam disciplinam. de luxu autem
illo sabbatario narrationi meae supersedendum est,
qui nec latentes potest latere personas. 7. ad
coepta redeatur. dapibus expleto somnus meridia-
nus saepe nullus, semper exiguus. quibus horis viro

---

[1] *Toreuma* should mean a piece of ornamental metal-work,
e.g. a chased vase or cup; but Sirmond is undoubtedly right
in thinking that Sidonius connected the word with *torus*,
as did Prudentius (*Psychom.* 370) and Salvian (*Ad Eccl.* IV.
33). For other examples in Sidonius see II. 13. 6, IX. 13. 5
v. 14. Sirmond takes it to mean the coverings of the couch,
but this does not suit the epithet *sericatum*, "covered with
silk," in Bk. II., and the expression *rutilum toreuma bysso* in
Bk. IX., *loc. cit.*, does not favour, though it does not absolutely
exclude, such an interpretation. All difficulty disappears if we
suppose that the word was regarded as an ornate substitute for
torus, "couch," or, more strictly, the mattress of the couch,
over which a covering (*peristroma*) was placed. *Peripetasma*
is applied to a spreading drapery, whether a hanging or a
covering. Here the reference is probably to the *peristromata*,
which often hung down far over the side of the couch, and

strike, and he strikes what you have chosen. Should a mistake be made by either, it is more often the eyesight of the selector than the aim of the bowman that is at fault. 6. When one joins him at dinner (which on all but festival days is just like that of a private household), there is no unpolished conglomeration of discoloured old silver set by panting attendants on sagging tables; the weightiest thing on these occasions is the conversation, for there are either no stories or only serious ones. The couches, with their spreading draperies, show an array sometimes of scarlet cloth, sometimes of fine linen.[1] The viands attract by their skilful cookery, not by their costliness, the platters by their brightness, not by their weight. Replenishment of the goblets or wine-bowls comes at such long intervals that there is more reason for the thirsty to complain than for the intoxicated to refrain. To sum up: you can find there Greek elegance, Gallic plenty, Italian briskness; the dignity of state, the attentiveness of a private home, the ordered discipline of royalty. But as to the luxury of the days of festival I had better hold my tongue, for even persons of no note cannot fail to note it. 7. To resume the story: after satisfying his appetite he never takes more than a short midday sleep, and often goes without it. In the hours when the gaming-board [2]

---

[1] *toreumatum peripetasmatumque* may be regarded as a hendiadys.

[2] *Tabula* may here be used for *tabula lusoria* or as the name of a particular board-game, on which see R. G. Austin in *Greece and Rome* IV. (1935), pp. 77–79. In any case the game described in this passage is one of those in which both dice and pieces were used, as in the various forms of backgammon.

tabula cordi, tesseras colligit rapide, inspicit sollicite,
volvit argute, mittit instanter, ioculanter compellat,
patienter exspectat. in bonis iactibus tacet, in
malis ridet, in neutris irascitur, in utrisque philo-
sophatur. secundas fastidit vel timere vel facere,
quarum opportunitates spernit oblatas, transit
oppositas. sine motu evaditur, sine colludio evadit.
putes illum et in calculis arma tractare: sola est
illi cura vincendi. 8. cum ludendum est, regiam
sequestrat tantisper severitatem, hortatur ad ludum
libertatem communionemque. dicam quod sentio:
timet timeri. denique oblectatur commotione
superati et tum demum credit sibi non cessisse
collegam, cum fidem fecerit victoriae suae bilis
aliena. quodque mirere, saepe illa laetitia minimis
occasionibus veniens ingentium negotiorum merita
fortunat. tunc petitionibus diu ante per patro-
ciniorum naufragia iactatis absolutionis subitae
portus aperitur; tunc etiam ego aliquid obsecra-
turus feliciter vincor, quando mihi ad hoc tabula
perit, ut causa salvetur. 9. circa nonam recrudescit
molis illa regnandi. redeunt pulsantes, redeunt

---

¹ We do not know enough about the game to understand this.
Secundae (sc. *tesserae*?) is obviously a technical term. Probably at certain junctures the player was allowed the option
of a second throw. The translation given of *oppositas* accords
with Dr. Semple's view.

² *Tabula* may here be the name of the game, but more
probably it is a collective term for a player's pieces, as

attracts him he is quick to pick up the dice; he examines them anxiously, spins them with finesse, throws them eagerly; he addresses them jestingly and calmly awaits the result. If the throw is lucky, he says nothing; if unlucky, he smiles; in neither case does he lose his temper, in either case he is a real philosopher. As for a second throw, he is too proud either to fear it or to make it; when a chance of one is presented he disdains it, when it is used against him he ignores it.[1] He sees his opponent's piece escape without stirring, and gets his own free without being played up to. You would actually think he was handling weapons when he handles the pieces on the board; his sole thought is of victory. 8. When it is the time for play he throws off for a while the stern mood of royalty and encourages fun and freedom and good-fellowship. My own opinion is that he dreads being feared. Further, he is delighted at seeing his defeated rival disgruntled, and it is only his opponent's ill-temper which really satisfies him that the game has not been given him. Now comes something to surprise you; the exultation which comes upon him on these trivial occasions often speeds the claims of important transactions. At such times the haven of a prompt decision is thrown open to petitions which have for a long time previously been in distress through the foundering of their advocates. I myself at such times, if I have a favour to ask, find it fortunate to be beaten by him, for I lose my pieces[2] to win my cause. 9. About the ninth hour the burden of royal business is taken up afresh. Back come the im-

perire was a technical term in such games for " to be taken."

summoventes; ubique litigiosus fremit ambitus,
qui tractus in vesperam cena regia interpellante
rarescit et per aulicos deinceps pro patronorum
varietate dispergitur, usque ad tempus concubiae
noctis excubaturus. sane intromittuntur, quamquam raro, inter cenandum mimici sales, ita ut
nullus conviva mordacis linguae felle feriatur; sic
tamen quod illic nec organa hydraulica sonant nec
sub phonasco vocalium concentus meditatum acroama
simul intonat; nullus ibi lyristes choraules meso-
chorus tympanistria psaltria canit, rege solum illis
fidibus delenito, quibus non minus mulcet virtus
animum quam cantus auditum.   10. cum surrexerit,
inchoat nocturnas aulica gaza custodias; armati
regiae domus aditibus assistunt, quibus horae primi
soporis vigilabuntur. sed iam quid meas istud ad
partes, qui tibi indicanda non multa de regno sed
pauca de rege promisi? simul et stilo finem fieri
decet, quia et tu cognoscere viri non amplius quam
studia personamque voluisti et ego non historiam
sed epistulam efficere curavi.   vale.

portunate petitioners, back come the marshals to
drive them off; everywhere the rivalry of the disputants makes an uproar. This continues till evening; then the royal supper interrupts and the
bustle fades away, distributing itself among the
various courtiers whose patronage this or that party
enjoys; and thus they keep watch till the night-
watches. It is true that occasionally (not often) the
banter of low comedians is admitted during supper,
though they are not allowed to assail any guest with
the gall of a biting tongue. In any case no hydraulic
organs are heard there, nor does any concert-party
under its trainer boom forth a set performance in
chorus; there is no music of lyrist, flautist or dance-
conductor, tambourine-girl or female citharist; for the
king finds a charm only in the string music which com-
forts the soul with virtue just as much as it soothes
the ear with melody. 10. When he rises from the
table, the night-watch is first posted at the royal
treasury and armed sentries are set at the entrances
to the palace, who will keep guard through the
hours of the first sleep.

But I have already exceeded my part, for I
promised to tell you a little about the king, not a
long story about his rule; it is also fitting that my
pen should come to a stop because you desired to
hear only of the tastes and personality of the great
man and because I took it upon myself to write a
letter, not a history. Farewell.

III

SIDONIVS PHILOMATHIO SVO
SALVTEM

1. I nunc et legibus me ambitus interrogatum senatu move, cur adipiscendae dignitati hereditariae curis pervigilibus incumbam; cui pater socer avus proavus praefecturis urbanis praetorianisque, magisteriis Palatinis militaribusque micuerunt. 2. et ecce Gaudentius meus, hactenus tantum tribunicius, oscitantem nostrorum civium desidiam vicariano apice transcendit. mussitat quidem iuvenum nostrorum calcata generositas, sed qui transiit derogantes in hoc solum movetur, ut gaudeat. igitur venerantur hucusque contemptum ac subitae stupentes dona

---

* Philomathius is mentioned in V. 17. 7. It is unfortunately impossible to date this letter, as we do not know when Gaudentius held the vicariate referred to.

[1] There is no other evidence that the great-grandfather of Sidonius held any such public office, or that any of the kinsmen referred to ever held the Prefecture of the City; Sidonius himself held it in A.D. 468. *Magisterium* was the office of a *magister*, and *mag. mil.* obviously refers to the *magisterium militum* held by Avitus (Introd., p. xx, *Carm.* 7. 377 sq., n. on 359 sqq.), but *Palatinis magisteriis* is puzzling. We do not read elsewhere that any relation of Sidonius was ever *magister officiorum* or one of the *magistri scriniorum* (on these offices see Bury, I. p. 29). It is just possible, though scarcely likely, that Sidonius's father held one of these posts after being *tribunus et notarius*, under Honorius, or, if he became chief (*primicerius*) of the *tribuni et notarii*, he may have received the honorary title of *magister officiorum* on his retirement from office, as seems sometimes to have happened. Or did the mysterious great-grandfather hold one of those offices? On the whole, it seems probable that when Sidonius says

III

SIDONIUS TO HIS FRIEND PHILOMATHIUS, GREETING *

1. Go to now—indict me by the Electoral Corruption Acts and propose my dismissal from the Senate for striving with unsleeping labours to win a *hereditary* position, seeing that my father, my father-in-law, my grandfather and my great-grandfather won the distinctions of praetorian and city prefectures and Masterships at court and in the army.[1] 2. And lo! my friend Gaudentius, till now only of tribunician rank, has overclimbed the yawning idleness of our countrymen by winning the dignity of a vicarius.[2] Of course our young lordlings are muttering about "trampling on good birth," but when a man has risen over the heads of backbiters the only effect on him is a feeling of elation. So they worship a man whom till yesterday they belittled, and, full of wonderment at the

---

[1] "Palatine and military Masterships" he is speaking loosely and grandiloquently of a Mastership of soldiers and the "Palatine" post of *tribunus et notarius*. The name "Palatine" was applied to offices connected with the great departments of the Imperial civil service which had their headquarters at Rome under the immediate control of the Emperor.

[2] He had been *tribunus et notarius* (on this office see Bury I. 23, C.M.H. I. 38), and was now *Vicarius Septem Provinciarum per Gallias*. The provinces in each praetorian prefecture were grouped so as to form a number of dioceses (*dioeceses*), each of which was administered by a *vicarius*. The *Septem Provinciae* were Viennensis, Narbonensis I and II, Novem Populi (Novempopulana), Aquitanica I and II, Alpes Maritimae; but the *Vicarius Septem Provinciarum* seems at this time to have exercised supervision over all the Gallic provinces.

fortunae quem consessu despiciebant, sede suspiciunt. ille obiter stertentum oblatratorum aures rauci voce praeconis everberat, qui in eum licet stimulis inimicalibus excitentur, scamnis tamen amicalibus deputabuntur. 3. unde te etiam par fuerit privilegio consiliorum praefecturae, in quae participanda deposceris, antiquati honoris perniciter sarcire dispendium, ne, si extra praerogativam consiliarii in concilium veneris, solas vicariorum vices egisse videare. vale.

IV

SIDONIVS GAVDENTIO SVO SALVTEM

1. Macte esto, vir amplissime, fascibus partis dote meritorum; quorum ut titulis apicibusque potiare non maternos reditus, non avitas largitiones, non uxorias gemmas, non paternas pecunias numeravisti, quia tibi e contrario apud principis domum inspecta sinceritas, spectata sedulitas, admissa sodalitas laudi fuere. o terque quaterque beatum te, de cuius

---

[1] He had apparently been assessor to the Vicarius.
[2] The counsellors (*consiliarii*), or assessors (*adsessores*), of the Praetorian Prefect had a position of great dignity. At the end of their year of office they received many privileges, and ranked with the Vicarii.

gifts of an unexpected fortune, they look up to him in the judgment-seat, though they used to look down on him when he was seated by their side. Meanwhile the lucky man makes the husky usher's yells beat upon the ears of those stertorous snarlers; but although they are goaded by feelings of enmity towards him they will be given places on the benches reserved for his friends. 3. So it will be the proper course for you also to repair promptly the loss of your expired office [1] by accepting the earnest invitation addressed to you to occupy the favoured position of Counsellor to the Prefect; [2] for if you come to the Council [3] without the special standing of a counsellor you will be looked upon only as one who has acted as deputy vicarius. Farewell.

IV

SIDONIUS TO HIS FRIEND GAUDENTIUS, GREETING

1. Congratulations, my noble friend, on the office you have won through the dower of your deserts. To win its titles and glories you have not expended a mother's rent-roll, a grandfather's bounty, a wife's jewels or a father's capital; but on the contrary you have won distinction in an emperor's household by well-tested honesty, well-attested assiduity and an approved claim to intimacy. "O three and four times happy thou" [4] by whose elevation joy is brought to your friends, punishment to your detractors and dis-

---

[3] The *Concilium Septem Provinciarum* (Introd., p. xii).

[4] Virg. *Aen.* I. 94.

culmine datur amicis laetitia, lividis poena, posteris
gloria, tum praeterea vegetis et alacribus exemplum,
desidibus et pigris incitamentum; et tamen, si qui
sunt qui te quocumque animo deinceps aemula-
buntur, sibi forsitan, si te consequantur, debeant,
tibi debebunt procul dubio quod sequuntur.
2. spectare mihi videor bonorum pace praefata illam
in invidis ignaviam superbientem et illud militandi
inertibus familiare fastidium, cum a desperatione
crescendi inter bibendum philosophantes ferias
inhonoratorum laudant, vitio desidiae, non studio
perfectionis . . .

* * *

3. . . . appetitus, ne adhuc pueris usui foret,
maiorum iudicio reiciebatur; sic adulescentum
declamatiunculas pannis textilibus comparantes intel-
legebant eloquia iuvenum laboriosius brevia produci
quam porrecta succidi. sed hinc quia istaec satis,
quod subest, quaeso reminiscaris velle me tibi studii
huiusce vicissitudinem reponderare, modo me actionibus iustis deus annuens et sospitem praestet et
reducem. vale.

---

[1] The end of this letter and the beginning of another (of
which § 3 is the conclusion) have apparently been lost.

tinction to your posterity; an example, moreover, to
the energetic and zealous and a spur to the idle and
lazy. And certainly if others in their turn, no
matter in what spirit, become your rivals, such
people, though they may claim credit to themselves
if they catch up with you, will certainly owe it to
you that they follow in your path. 2. I picture
myself looking on (I say this with all respect to the
better sort) at the combination of arrogance and
indolence among your ill-wishers, and at that disdain of public service which is characteristic of the
slothful, when, hopeless themselves of rising in the
world, they play the philosopher over their wine
and praise the leisured lives of those who hold no
office,—not from any eagerness for perfection but
simply through vicious indolence.[1]

* * *

3. Indeed the judgment of our ancestors condemned
the straining after . . . lest it should be taken
advantage of by mere boys. They compared the
short rhetorical exercises of striplings with pieces of
cloth, meaning that it is harder to lengthen the
compositions of young students if too short than to
cut them down if too long. But I have said enough
on this matter: now as to what lies at the bottom
of my remarks—please remember that I am most
anxious to repay this zeal of yours by giving like for
like, provided only that God, who rewards righteous
efforts, keeps me safe and brings me home.
Farewell.

V

SIDONIVS HERONIO [1] SVO SALVTEM

1. Litteras tuas Romae positus accepi, quibus an secundum commune consilium sese peregrinationis meae coepta promoveant, sollicitus inquiris, viam etiam qualem qualiterque confecerim, quos aut fluvios viderim poetarum carminibus inlustres aut urbes moenium situ inclitas aut montes numinum opinione vulgatos aut campos proeliorum replicatione monstrabiles, quia voluptuosum censeas quae lectione compereris eorum qui inspexerint fideliore didicisse memoratu. quocirca gaudeo te quid agam cupere cognoscere; namque huiuscemodi studium de adfectu interiore proficiscitur. ilicet, etsi secus quaepiam, sub ope tamen dei ordiar a secundis, quibus primordiis maiores nostri etiam sinisteritatum suarum relationes evolvere auspicabantur. 2. egresso mihi Rhodanusiae nostrae moenibus publicus cursus usui fuit utpote sacris apicibus accito, et quidem per domicilia sodalium propinquorumque; ubi sane vianti moram non veredorum paucitas sed amicorum multitudo faciebat, quae mihi arto implicita complexu itum reditumque felicem certantibus votis

[1] herenio *LNT*.

---

* On the occasion of this letter and of No. 9 below see Introd., p. xl. Nothing is known of Heronius beyond what may be gathered from these two letters.

[1] On the meaning of *ilicet* see n. on *Carm.* 2. 332.

[2] Lugdunum (Lyons), situated at the confluence of the Rhodanus (Rhone) and the Arar (Saône).

V

SIDONIUS TO HIS FRIEND HERONIUS, GREETING *

1. I received your letter after I had settled down at Rome. I see that you inquire anxiously whether the objects of my journey are prospering according to our common plan. You ask also what the route was like and in what manner I travelled over it, what rivers I viewed made famous by the songs of poets, what cities renowned for their situation, what mountains celebrated as the reputed haunts of deities, what fields claiming the interest of the sight-seer by reason of their memories of battles; for having learnt of these things in books you think it would be a pleasure (so you tell me) to have a more faithful account from those who have seen them with their own eyes. I am delighted therefore that you long to learn how I fare, for interest of this kind proceeds from heartfelt affection. Well,[1] though some things went wrong, I will begin by God's help with my good news; for our ancestors too made it a rule to begin with such, as forming an auspicious start even for a narrative of their misfortunes. 2. When I passed the gates of our native Rhodanusia [2] I found the state-post at my disposal as one summoned by an imperial letter, and, moreover, the homes of intimate friends and relations lined the route; delays on my journey were due not to scarcity of post-horses but to multiplicity of friends, who clasped me to their hearts and vied with one another in their prayers on my behalf for a prosperous journey and

353

conprecabatur. sic Alpium iugis appropinquatum; quarum mihi citus et facilis ascensus et inter utrimque terrentis latera praerupti cavatis in callem nivibus itinera mollita. 3. fluviorum quoque, si qui non navigabiles, vada commoda, vel certe pervii pontes, quos antiquitas a fundamentis ad usque aggerem calcabili silice crustatum crypticis arcubus fornicavit. Ticini cursoriam (sic navigio nomen) escendi, qua in Eridanum brevi delatus cantatas saepe comissaliter nobis Phaethontiadas et commenticias arborei metalli lacrimas risi. 4. ulvosum Lambrum caerulum Adduam, velocem Athesim pigrum Mincium, qui Ligusticis Euganeisque montibus oriebantur, paulum per ostia adversa subvectus in suis etiam gurgitibus inspexi; quorum ripae torique passim quernis acernisque nemoribus vestiebantur. hic avium resonans dulce concentus, quibus nunc in concavis harundinibus, nunc quoque in iuncis pungentibus, nunc et in scirpis enodibus nidorum struis imposita nutabat; quae cuncta virgulta tumultuatim super amnicos margines soli bibuli suco fota fruticaverant. 5. atque obiter Cremonam praevectus adveni, cuius est olim Tityro Mantuano largum suspirata proximitas. Brixillum dein oppidum, dum succedenti

---

[1] Pavia.

[2] *Cursoria* (sc. *navis*), so called from being employed on the Imperial postal service (*cursus publicus*).

[3] The Po. On its banks, according to the legend, the sisters of Phaethon were turned into poplars and their tears into amber.

[4] The modern names of these rivers are Lambro, Adda, Adige, Mincio.

[5] Virg. *Ec.* IX. 28, *Mantua vae miserae nimium vicina Cremonae.* The words are uttered by Moeris, not Tityrus, but Tityrus to Sidonius generally means the Virgil of the *Eclogues*: cf. *Carm.* 4. 1.

homecoming. In this way I drew near to the heights of the Alps. I found the ascent quick and easy; between walls of terrifying precipice on either side, travelling had been simplified by cutting a pathway through the snow. 3. As to the rivers, I found that such of them as were not navigable had convenient fords or at any rate bridges fit for traffic: these our forefathers have constructed on a series of vaulted arches reaching from the foundations up to the roadway with its cobbled surface. At Ticinum [1] I went on board a packet-boat [2] (so they call the vessel) and travelled quickly down-stream to the Eridanus, [3] where I had my laugh over Phaethon's sisters, of whom we have often sung amidst our revels, and over those mythical tears of arboreal ore. 4. I passed the sedgy Lambrus, the blue Addua, the swift Athesis, and the sluggish Mincius, [4] rivers which have their sources in the mountains of Liguria and the Euganeans. In each case I cruised a little way up-stream from the point of confluence so as to view each actually in the midst of its own waters. Their banks and knolls were everywhere clad with groves of oak and maple. A concert of birds filled the air with sweet sounds; their nest-structures quivered, balanced sometimes on hollow reeds, sometimes on prickly rushes, sometimes too on smooth bulrushes: for all this undergrowth, nourished on the moisture of the spongy soil, had sprouted confusedly along the river banks. 5. Proceeding on my way I came to Cremona, whose nearness caused Mantua's Tityrus to sigh profoundly in days of old. [5] Next we entered the town of Brixillum [6] only to quit it, just allowing time

---

[6] Brescello, on the right bank of the Po.

Aemiliano nautae decedit Venetus remex, tantum
ut exiremus intravimus, Ravennam paulo post cursu
dexteriore subeuntes; quo loci veterem civitatem
novumque portum media via Caesaris ambigas utrum
conectat an separet. insuper oppidum duplex pars
interluit Padi, [certa]¹ pars alluit; qui ab alveo
principali molium publicarum discerptus obiectu et
per easdem derivatis tramitibus exhaustus sic
dividua fluenta partitur ut praebeant moenibus
circumfusa praesidium, infusa commercium. 6. hic
cum peropportuna cuncta mercatui, tum praecipue
quod esui competeret, deferebatur; nisi quod, cum
sese hinc salsum portis pelagus impingeret, hinc
cloacali pulte fossarum discursu lintrium ventilata
ipse lentati languidus lapsus umoris nauticis cuspidi-
bus foraminato fundi glutino sordidaretur, in medio
undarum sitiebamus, quia nusquam vel aquae-
ductuum liquor integer vel cisterna defaecabilis
vel fons inriguus vel puteus inlimis. 7. unde pro-
gressis ad Rubiconem ventum, qui originem nomini
de glarearum colore puniceo mutuabatur quique olim
Gallis cisalpinis Italisque veteribus terminus erat,
cum populis utrisque Hadriatici maris oppida divisui
fuere. hinc Ariminum Fanumque perveni, illud

---

¹ certa *seclusi*; *ex gloss.* cetera *corruptela orta videtur.*

---

¹ The harbour constructed by Augustus as a naval station
was connected with the old town, which was three miles
distant, by a causeway, here called " Caesar's road." A large
suburb which grew up between the old town and the harbour-
town (Portus Classis, or simply Classis) was called Caesarea.

² Great confusion has been imported into this sentence
through taking *insuper* as a preposition. The " double
town " is the old town, which is divided into two by the
branch of the Po which runs through it.

for our oarsmen, who were Veneti, to give up their
places to boatmen of Aemilia, and a little later we
reached Ravenna, on a course bearing to the right.
Here Caesar's road [1] runs between the old town and
the new harbour; one could scarcely say whether
it joins or parts them. Moreover, one branch of
the Padus flows through this double town, another
flows by it; [2] for the river is diverted from its main
bed by the intervention of the city embankments,
along whose course are various branch channels
which draw off more and more of the stream. The
effect of this division is that the waters which encircle
the walls provide protection, while those which flow
into the town bring commerce. 6. The whole situation is most favourable to trade, and in particular
we saw large food-supplies coming in. But there
was one drawback: on one side the briny sea-water
rushed up to the gates, and elsewhere the sewer-
like filth of the channels was churned up by the
boat-traffic, and the bargemen's poles, boring into
the glue at the bottom, helped to befoul the current,
slow and sluggish at the best: the result was that
we went thirsty though surrounded by water, [3] finding
nowhere pure water from aqueducts, nowhere a filth-
proof reservoir, nowhere a bubbling spring or mud-
free well. 7. Leaving this place we travelled to the
Rubicon; the name is derived from the red tint
of its gravel. This used to be the dividing line
between Cisalpine Gaul and the old Italy, the
towns on the Adriatic coast being divided between
the two peoples. From this point I came on to
Ariminum and Fanum, the former place celebrated

[3] For this aspersion cf. I. 8. 2, and see note on *Carm.* 9.
298.

Iuliana rebellione memorabile, hoc Hasdrubaliano
funere infectum: siquidem illic Metaurus, cuius ita
in longum felicitas uno die parta porrigitur, ac si
etiam nunc Dalmatico salo cadavera sanguinulenta
decoloratis gurgitibus inferret. 8. hinc cetera
Flaminiae oppida statim ut ingrediebar egressus
laevo Picentes, dextro Vmbros latere transmisi;
ubi mihi seu Calaber Atabulus seu pestilens regio
Tuscorum spiritu aeris venenatis flatibus inebriato
et modo calores alternante, modo frigora vaporatum
corpus infecit. interea febris sitisque penitissimum
cordis medullarumque secretum depopulabantur;
quarum aviditati non solum amoena fontium aut
abstrusa puteorum, quamquam haec quoque, sed
tota illa vel vicina vel obvia fluenta, id est vitrea
Velini gelida Clitumni, Anienis caerula Naris sulpurea,
pura Fabaris turbida Tiberis, metu tamen desiderium
fallente, pollicebamur. 9. inter haec patuit et
Roma conspectui; cuius mihi non solum formas
verum etiam naumachias videbar epotaturus. ubi
priusquam vel pomoeria contingerem, triumphalibus
apostolorum liminibus adfusus omnem protinus

---

[1] After crossing the Rubicon, Caesar promptly occupied
Ariminum (Rimini). Fanum Fortunae (Fano) was an
Umbrian coast-town, near the mouth of the Metaurus (Me-
tauro). The exact site of Hasdrubal's defeat is unknown,
but it was probably not many miles from the mouth of the
river.

[2] A hot dry wind; see commentators on Horace, *Sat.* I.
5. 78.

[3] A lake in the Sabine country, near the Nar (Nera), now
called Piè di Lugo or Lago delle Marmore. Virgil mentions
the *fontes Velini* (*Aen.* VII. 517).

[4] This name is borrowed from Virgil (*Aen.* VII. 715).
Servius says it is the same as the Farfarus (modern Farfa),
a Sabine stream which flows into the Tiber.

through the insurrection of Julius, the latter dyed
with Hasdrubal's life-blood;[1] for here is the
Metaurus, the glory of which river was won in
a single day but has endured through the ages,
as though even now it swept bloody corpses
down its empurpled waters into Dalmatia's seas.
8. As for the other towns on the Flaminian road, I
just entered and then left them, passing on with
Picenum on my left and Umbria on my right; but
there either the wind Atabulus[2] from Calabria or the
malarial district of Etruria intoxicated my lungs
with poisonous blasts of air that brought on sweats
and chills alternately, and infected my whole body
with its atmosphere. Meanwhile fever and thirst
made havoc of the innermost recesses of my heart and
marrow; to their greedy claims I kept promising not
only the deliciousness of springs and the deep-hidden
waters of wells (though I reckoned on these also),
but all the streams that lay on my route or near it,
those of Velinus[3] glassy, of Clitumnus cool, of the
Anio blue, of Nar smacking of sulphur, of the Fabaris[4]
clear, of the Tiber muddy; but caution ever balked my
longing. 9. Amid this distress Rome burst upon
my sight. I thought I could drink dry not only its
aqueducts but the ponds used in its mock sea-fights.
But before allowing myself to set foot even on
the outer boundary of the city I sank on my
knees at the triumphal thresholds of the Apostles,[5]

[5] The churches of St. Peter and St. Paul. St. Peter's,
founded by Constantine and consecrated in A.D. 326, was still
outside the city precincts. The basilica of St. Paul (S. Paolo
fuori le Mura) was founded in A.D. 386. *Triumphalibus* was
perhaps suggested by Porta Triumphalis, the gateway by which
a general's triumphal procession entered Rome.

sensi membris male fortibus explosum esse langu-
orem; post quae caelestis experimenta patrocinii
conducti devorsorii parte susceptus atque etiam
nunc istaec inter iacendum scriptitans quieti pauxillulum operam impendo. 10. neque adhuc principis
aulicorumque tumultuosis foribus obversor. inter-
veni etenim nuptiis patricii Ricimeris, cui filia
perennis Augusti in spem publicae securitatis copu-
labatur. igitur nunc in ista non modo personarum
sed etiam ordinum partiumque laetitia Transalpino
tuo latere conducibilius visum, quippe cum hoc ipso
tempore, quo haec mihi exarabantur, vix per omnia
theatra macella, praetoria fora, templa gymnasia
Thalassio Fescenninus explicaretur, atque etiam
nunc e contrario studia sileant negotia quiescant
iudicia conticescant, differantur legationes vacet
ambitus et inter scurrilitates histrionicas totus
actionum seriarum status peregrinetur. 11. iam
quidem virgo tradita est, iam coronam sponsus, iam
palmatam consularis, iam cycladem pronuba, iam
togam [senator] [1] honoratus, iam paenulam deponit
inglorius, et nondum tamen cuncta thalamorum
pompa defremuit, quia necdum ad mariti domum
nova nupta migravit. qua festivitate decursa cetera
tibi laborum meorum molimina reserabuntur, si

---

[1] senator *seclusit Luetjohann.*

---

[1] See *Carm.* 2. 484 n.
[2] *Thalassio* (or *Talassio*) was properly the cry with which
the bride was greeted by her attendants on entering her new
home, but it became a general expression of good wishes to
the happy couple. Its origin is uncertain. Livy gives a
quaint story to account for it (I. 9. 11 sq.).

and straightway I felt that all the sickness had
been driven from my enfeebled limbs; after which
proof of heavenly protection I found quarters in
a hired lodging, and even now I pen these words
at intervals in my repose, for I am making rest
my business for a little while. 10. Up till now
I have not presented myself at the bustling doors
of the Emperor and his courtiers, for I arrived
here at the moment of the marriage of Ricimer the
patrician, whose union with the daughter of the
immortal Augustus is a hopeful guarantee of the
safety of the state.[1] So for the present, amid
this general rejoicing not merely of individuals
but of classes and parties, the best course for
your friend from over the Alps seemed to be to
lie low, for at the very moment that I am writing
this the shouts of " Thalassio "[2] according to Fescennine custom have hardly ceased to echo in every
theatre, market-place, camp, law-court, church and
playground; on the other hand, the schools[3] are still
silent, business is hushed, lawsuits are stilled, dele-
gations from the provinces are adjourned, place-
seeking takes a holiday, and while buffoons are
making their merry jests all serious business seems
to be away on its travels. 11. And now the bride
has been given away, the bridegroom has put off
his garland, the consular his embroidered robe, the
brideswoman her gay mantle, the man of rank his
toga, and the undistinguished citizen his cloak;
nevertheless, the full pomp of the bridal ceremony
has not yet subsided, for the bride has not yet passed
to her husband's home. When all this gaiety has
run its course I will disclose to you the other struggles

[3] Or possibly "factions," "political antagonisms."

tamen vel consummata sollemnitas aliquando ter-
minaverit istam totius civitatis occupatissimam
vacationem. vale.

VI

SIDONIVS EVTROPIO SVO
SALVTEM

1. Olim quidem scribere tibi concupiscebam, sed
nunc vel maxime impellor, id est cum mihi ducens in
urbem Christo propitiante via carpitur. scribendi
causa vel sola vel maxima, quo te scilicet a profundo
domesticae quietis extractum ad capessenda militiae
Palatinae munia vocem. . . . 2. his additur quod
munere dei tibi congruit aevi corporis animi vigor
integer; dein quod equis, armis, veste sumptu
famulicio instructus solum, nisi fallimur, incipere
formidas et, cum sis alacer domi, in aggredienda pere-
grinatione trepidum te iners desperatio facit; si
tamen senatorii seminis homo, qui cotidie trabeatis
proavorum imaginibus ingeritur, iuste dicere potest
semet peregrinatum, si semel et in iuventa viderit
domicilium legum, gymnasium litterarum, curiam
dignitatum, verticem mundi, patriam libertatis, in

---

* This letter is usually assigned to A.D. 455, when Sidonius
was on his way to Rome in the train of Avitus, but it may
have been written four or five years later, as Sidonius was
again in Rome in the year 459 or (more probably) 460; see
I. 11. 3 n. It seems to have had an immediate effect;
see III. 6. There is no need to assume that either Eutropius or
Sidonius held a public appointment under Avitus; their " old
partnership in the civil service," referred to in III. 6. 1, may
well have been in the reign of Majorian. Eutropius rose to
be Praetorian Prefect of Gaul under Anthemius.

[1] i.e. from Gaul to Rome.

of my toilsome adventure, at least if sooner or later
the completion of the celebration shall end this most
busy holiday of a whole city.   Farewell.

VI

SIDONIUS TO HIS FRIEND EUTROPIUS, GREETING *

1. I have long been wanting to write to you, but
now I am especially drawn to do so at the moment
when by the grace of Christ's atonement I am
treading the path which leads to the City.   My one
reason—at any rate my chief one—is to draw you
out from the depths of your domestic calm and
to invite you to take up the duties of the Palatine
imperial service. . . . 2. Besides all this, you are
by the favour of heaven in the prime of life, and
possess strength of body and mind to correspond; then
you are well furnished with horses, armour, raiment,
money and servants, and (unless I am wrong) you
only dread beginning, and though you have an
energetic spirit at home, an unenterprising nervous-
ness makes you alarmed about attempting foreign
travel [1]—if indeed a man of senatorial descent, who
every day rubs shoulders with the figures of his
ancestors arrayed in robes of state,[2] can fairly say
that he has travelled to foreign parts, when once he
has seen—and seen with the eyes of youth—the
home of laws, the training-school of letters, the
assembly-hall of high dignitaries, the head of the
universe, the mother-city of liberty, the   one

---

[2] Sabinus, consul in A.D. 316, was an ancestor of Eutropius:
see III. 6. 3, and, for the meaning of *trabea*, n. on *Carm.* XV.
150.

qua unica totius orbis civitate soli barbari et servi
peregrinantur. 3. et nunc, pro pudor, si relinquare
inter busequas rusticanos subulcosque ronchantes!
quippe si et campum stiva tremente proscindas aut
prati floreas opes panda curvus falce populeris aut
vineam palmite gravem cernuus rastris fossor in-
vertas, tunc tibi est summa votorum beatitudo.
quin potius expergiscere et ad maiora se pingui
otio marcidus et enervis animus attollat. non
minus est tuorum natalium viro personam suam excolere quam villam. 4. ad extremum, quod tu tibi
iuventutis exercitium appellas, hoc est otium
veteranorum, in quorum manibus effetis enses
robiginosi sero ligone mutantur. esto, multiplicatis
tibi spumabunt musta vinetis, innumeros quoque
cumulos frugibus rupta congestis horrea dabunt,
densum pecus gravidis uberibus in mulctram per
antra olida caularum pinguis tibi pastor includet:
quo spectat tam faeculento patrimonium promovisse
compendio et non solum inter ista sed, quod est
turpius, propter ista latuisse? non nequiter te
concilii tempore post sedentes censentesque iuvenes
inglorium rusticum, senem stantem latitabundum
pauperis honorati sententia premat, cum eos quos

---

[1] *i.e.* all who are not slaves or "barbarians" are citizens
of Rome, so when in Rome they cannot be foreigners.

community in the whole world in which only slaves
and barbarians are foreigners.[1] 3. And now, for
shame if you are to be left behind amongst bumpkin
cowmen and snorting swineherds ! If you can hold
a shaky plough-handle and cut up the field, or if,
stooping over the curved sickle, you can prune the
flowery wealth of the meadow, or if as a down-bent
delver you can turn up with your hoe the vineyard
laden with heavy growth, that, forsooth, is the
supreme happiness to which you aspire! Nay,
rouse yourself, and let your spirit, which is faint
and nerveless through obese idleness, rise to greater
things. A man of your birth must needs cultivate
his reputation just as diligently as his farm. 4. To
conclude, what you are pleased to call the drill of
youth is properly the repose of veterans, in whose
toil-worn hands rusted swords are exchanged for
the mattock of old age. Granted that your vats
will foam with the produce of your extended vineyards, that your barns will show corn heaped in
countless piles until they burst, that your well-fed
shepherd will drive a crowded flock with full udders
to the milking-pail through the odorous entrances
of your sheep-folds : but of what use is it to have
increased your inheritance by so dirty an economy
and at the same time to have remained in obscurity
not only *amid* such surroundings, but (what is more
shameful) *for the sake of them?* Would it not be a
wicked thing if on the day of assembly you in your
old age were to stand behind your juniors while
they are seated and taking part in the debate,—you
an inglorious rustic shrinking from sight and bowing
before the authoritative pronouncement of some
poor man come to high place, having realised with

esset indignum si vestigia nostra sequerentur videris
dolens antecessisse? 5. sed quid plura? si pateris
hortantem, conatuum tuorum socius adiutor, praevius
particeps ero. sin autem inlecebrosis deliciarum
cassibus involutus mavis, ut aiunt, Epicuri dogmatibus
copulari, qui iactura virtutis admissa summum
bonum sola corporis voluptate determinat, testor
ecce maiores, testor posteros nostros huic me noxae
non esse confinem. vale.

VII

SIDONIVS VINCENTIO SVO
SALVTEM

1. Angit me casus Arvandi nec dissimulo quin
angat. namque hic quoque cumulus accedit laudibus imperatoris, quod amari palam licet et capite
damnatos. amicus homini fui supra quam morum
eius facilitas varietasque patiebantur. testatur hoc
propter ipsum nuper mihi invidia conflata, cuius me
paulo incautiorem flamma detorruit. 2. sed quod
in amicitia steti, mihi debui. porro autem in natura
ille non habuit diligentiam perseverandi: libere
queror, non insultatorie, quia fidelium consilia
despiciens fortunae ludibrium per omnia fuit.

---

* Nothing is known of this Vincentius.
[1] See Introd., p. xli.

remorse that men, in whose case it would have been a scandal if they had even followed in our steps, have passed you in the race? 5. Well, what need to say more? If you submit to these exhortations I am ready to be your comrade and helper, the guide and the partner of your efforts. If, however, you let yourself be entangled in the tempting snares of luxury and prefer (as people say) to be tied up with the dogmas of Epicurus, who makes jettison of virtue and defines the supreme good in terms of bodily pleasure alone, then here and now I call our ancestors and our posterity to witness that I have nothing to do with such wickedness. Farewell.

VII

SIDONIUS TO HIS FRIEND VINCENTIUS, GREETING *

1. I am distressed by the fall of Arvandus [1] and do not conceal my distress; for it is the crowning glory of our Emperor that affection may be openly shown even for men condemned to death. I have shown myself this man's friend even more than his easy-going and unstable character justified, as is proved by the disfavour which has lately flared up against me on his account; for I have been rather too heedless and have scorched myself in its flame. 2. But such steadfastness in friendship was a duty which I owed to myself. On the other hand, he never had in his disposition any firmness of principle; and I complain of him frankly (but not spitefully) for scorning the advice of his loyal friends and so becoming the sport of fortune all through.

denique non eum aliquando cecidisse sed tam diu
stetisse plus miror. o quotiens saepe ipse se adversa
perpessum gloriabatur, cum tamen nos ab adfectu
profundiore ruituram eius quandoque temeritatem
miseraremur, definientes non esse felicem qui hoc
frequenter potius esse quam semper iudicaretur!
3. sed damnationis[1] suae ordinem exposcis. salva
fidei reverentia, quae amico debetur etiam adflicto,
rem breviter exponam. praefecturam primam gu-
bernavit cum magna popularitate consequentemque
cum maxima populatione. pariter onere depressus
aeris alieni metu creditorum successuros sibi opti-
mates aemulabatur. omnium colloquia ridere, consilia mirari, officia contemnere, pati de occurrentum
raritate suspicionem, de adsiduitate fastidium, donec,
odii publici mole vallatus et prius cinctus custodia
quam potestate discinctus, captus destinatusque
pervenit Romam, ilico tumens, quod prospero cursu
procellosum Tusciae litus enavigasset, tamquam sibi
bene conscio ipsa quodammodo elementa famu-
larentur. 4. in Capitolio custodiebatur ab hospite
Flavio Asello, comite sacrarum largitionum, qui
adhuc in eo semifumantem praefecturae nuper
extortae dignitatem venerabatur. interea legati
provinciae Galliae, Tonantius Ferreolus praefectorius,
Afranii Syagrii consulis e filia nepos, Thaumastus

---

[1] dampnationis *T* : gubernationis.

---

[1] Minister of Finance. See Bury I. 51.
[2] n. on *Carm.* 24. 34.
[3] n. on *Carm.* 24. 36.

In brief, I am not so much surprised that he has fallen at last as that he has held his own so long. How often he used to boast of himself as one who had often endured ill fortune, whilst we from a deeper feeling for him lamented that his recklessness must some day end in disaster, holding that a man is not fortunate if he is judged to be so only frequently, not always! 3. You ask me to tell the story of his condemnation. I will give you the facts shortly whilst paying all respect to the loyalty which is due even to a fallen friend. He conducted his first term as prefect with great approbation, his second with the greatest depredation. Moreover, he was oppressed by the burden of debt and, dreading his creditors, felt jealous of those nobles who were likely successors to him. He mocked every one of them when they conversed with him, professed astonishment at their suggestions, and ignored their services; if only few sought to accost him he nursed suspicion, if many, contempt; till in the end he was encircled by a wall of general antipathy, and was burdened by guards before he was disburdened of his office. He was arrested and brought in bonds to Rome, priding himself then and there on having sailed safely past the stormy coast of Tuscany, as though the elements were in some way submissive to him, recognising the clearness of his conscience. 4. He was kept under guard on the Capitol by his friend Flavius Asellus, Count of the Sacred Largesses,[1] who respected the lingering aroma of the prefectorian dignity which had just been wrested from him. Meanwhile the deputies of the province of Gaul, Tonantius Ferreolus,[2] of prefectorian rank, grandson of the Consul Afranius Syagrius[3] through

369

quoque et Petronius, maxima rerum verborumque
scientia praediti et inter principalia patriae nostrae
decora ponendi, praevium Arvandum publico nomine
accusaturi cum gestis decretalibus insequuntur.
5. qui inter cetera quae sibi provinciales agenda
mandaverant interceptas litteras deferebant, quas
Arvandi scriba correptus dominum dictasse profite-
batur. haec ad regem Gothorum charta videbatur
emitti, pacem cum Graeco imperatore dissuadens,
Britannos supra Ligerim sitos impugnari oportere
demonstrans, cum Burgundionibus iure gentium
Gallias dividi debere confirmans, et in hunc ferme
modum plurima insana, quae iram regi feroci, placido
verecundiam inferrent. hanc epistulam laesae maiestatis crimine ardere iurisconsulti interpretabantur.
6. me et Auxanium, praestantissimum virum,
tractatus iste non latuit, qui Arvandi amicitias
quoquo genere incursas inter ipsius adversa vitare
perfidum barbarum ignavum computabamus. de-
ferimus igitur nil tale metuenti totam per⟨niciter [1]⟩
machinam, quam summo artificio acres et flammei
viri occulere in tempus iudicii meditabantur, scilicet

---

[1] perniciter machinam *Luetjohann vix probabiliter* : per(i)-
machiam *codd. fere omnes.*

---

[1] n. on *Carm.* 24. 85.
[2] An eminent lawyer, *vir inlustris*. It was at his instance
that Sidonius added Bk. VIII. to his collection of letters.
[3] Anthemius.
[4] *i.e.* the Bretons of Aremorica : see Introd., p. xii, n. 1.
Euric soon acted in accordance with this advice of Arvandus
(*ib.*, p. xxviii).
[5] *i.e.* make him ashamed of his inactivity, shame him out of
his peacefulness.

his daughter, and Thaumastus [1] and Petronius,[2] men possessed of ripe experience and consummate oratorical skill and entitled to rank amongst the chief glories of our native land, followed in his wake, carrying the official resolutions, having been appointed to accuse him on behalf of the province. 5. Amongst other pleas which the provincials had instructed them to urge, they were bringing against him an intercepted letter which Arvandus's secretary (who had been arrested) admitted to have been written at his master's dictation. It appeared to be a message addressed to the king of the Goths, dissuading him from peace with the " Greek Emperor," [3] insisting that the Britanni settled to the north of the Liger [4] should be attacked, and declaring that the Gallic provinces ought according to the law of nations to be divided up with the Burgundians, and a great deal more mad stuff in the same vein, fitted to rouse a warlike king to fury and a peaceful one to shame.[5] The opinion of the lawyers was that this letter was red-hot treason. 6. These proceedings did not escape my excellent friend Auxanius [6] and myself, and we thought it would be disloyal, inhuman and cowardly to disown our friendly relations with Arvandus in his time of danger, no matter how we had been drawn into them. So we promptly reported to the unfortunate man, who had no fear of anything of the sort, the whole machination, which his eager and fiery enemies were most cunningly planning to keep secret till the day of the trial; for they knew,

---

[6] This Auxanius afterwards adopted the monastic life, if, as is probable, he is the Auxanius mentioned in VII. 17. 4. His father had been Praetorian Prefect of Gaul (§ 7 below).

ut adversarium incautum et consiliis sodalium repudiatis soli sibi temere fidentem professione responsi praecipitis involverent. dicimus ergo quid nobis, quid amicis secretioribus tutum putaretur; suademus nil quasi leve fatendum, si quid ab inimicis etiam pro levissimo flagitaretur: ipsam illam dissimulationem tribulosissimam fore, quo facilius exitiosam suscitarent illi persuasionem securitatis.[1] 7. quibus agnitis proripit sese atque in convicia subita prorumpens: " abite degeneres," inquit, " et praefectoriis patribus indigni, cum hac superforanea trepidatione; mihi, quia nihil intellegitis, hanc negotii partem sinite curandam; satis Arvando conscientia sua sufficit; vix illud dignabor admittere, ut advocati mihi in actionibus repetundarum patrocinentur." discedimus tristes et non magis iniuria quam maerore confusi; quis enim medicorum iure moveatur quotiens desperatum furor arripiat? 8. inter haec reus noster aream Capitolinam percurrere albatus; modo subdolis salutationibus pasci, modo crepantes adulationum bullas ut recognoscens libenter audire, modo serica et gemmas et pretiosa quaeque trapezitarum involucra rimari et quasi mercaturus inspicere prensare, depretiari [2] devolvere,

[1] exit. s. i. p. s. *ego desperanter; codices varie et graviter corrupti sunt.*

[2] depretiari *deponens* ἄπ. λεγ. : *fortasse* depretiare *scribendum; cf.* II. 10. 6, *Carm.* 22. 203.

[1] A broad esplanade on the top of the Capitoline Hill. About half-way along it was the historic temple of Jupiter, now a sad ruin owing to the recent Vandal depredations (A.D. 455).

of course, that their opponent was incautious, that he had rejected the advice of his friends and was rashly trusting in his own powers, and so they hoped to entangle him in an avowal through some hasty reply. We told him, therefore, what we and his less open friends thought to be the safe course: we suggested to him that he should make no admission on the assumption that it was a trivial matter, even if his opponents in pressing him for it implied that it was the most trivial matter in the world: we warned him that that very pretence was going to be the most serious danger to him, its aim being to produce more easily in him a fatal sense of security. 7. When he realised our drift he started forward and in a moment burst into violent taunts: " Off with you, degenerate cravens," he said, " unworthy of your prefect-fathers—off with you and your uncalled-for panic! Let me look after this side of the business, since you have no comprehension of it; for Arvandus his consciousness of innocence is enough; only with difficulty shall I bring myself even to allow advocates to defend me on the charge of extortion." We went away disheartened and upset, by grief more than by resentment; for what physician would have a right to become excited when a patient beyond hope of recovery is seized by a fit of madness? 8. Meanwhile our accused friend briskly parades the Capitoline Terrace[1] in festal dress; now he gloats over various knavish salutations given him, now he listens with pleasure to the bursting bubbles of flattery, seeming to recognise them as his due; again, he pries into silk wares, jewels and all the costly cases of the goldsmiths, and (as if he meant to make a purchase) scans them closely, snatches them

et inter agendum multum de legibus, de temporibus, de senatu, de principe queri, quod se non prius quam discuterent ulciscerentur. 9. pauci medii dies, et in tractatorio frequens senatus (sic post comperi; nam inter ista discesseram). procedit noster ad curiam paulo ante detonsus pumicatusque, cum accusatores semipullati atque concreti nuntios a decemviris opperirentur et ab industria squalidi praeripuissent reo debitam miserationem sub invidia sordidatorum. citati intromittuntur: partes, ut moris est, e regione consistunt. offertur praefectoriis ante propositionis exordium ius sedendi: Arvandus iam tunc infelici impudentia concito gradu mediis prope iudicum sinibus ingeritur; Ferreolus circumsistentibus latera collegis verecunde ac leviter in imo subselliorum capite consedit, ita ut non minus legatum se quam senatorem reminisceretur, plus ob hoc postea laudatus honoratusque. 10. dum haec, et qui procerum defuerant adfuerunt: consurgunt partes legatique proponunt. epistula post provinciale mandatum, cuius supra mentio facta, profertur; atque, cum sensim recitaretur, Arvandus necdum interrogatus se dictasse proclamat. re-

---

¹ Criminal charges against senators were at this time regularly judged by five senators chosen by lot, sitting under the presidency of the Prefect of the City. This limitation of number was apparently not enforced in cases of high treason.

up, disparages them and flings them back, and
in the midst of this business makes frequent
criticisms of the laws, the times, the Senate, and the
Emperor for not vindicating him before investigating
his case. 9. A few days elapsed, and then a full
senate met in the Council Chamber (so I learned
afterwards, for I had left Rome in the interval).
Our man makes his way to the Senate-house, having
shortly before been shaved and rubbed down, while
his accusers, in half-mourning and unkempt, await
a summons from the ten judges,¹ having by their
intentional squalor robbed the accused of his due
sympathy, availing themselves of the indignation
which the sight of men in the garb of sorrow
arouses. They are summoned and admitted; the
two sides take their positions as usual, one opposite
the other. Those of prefectorian rank are offered,
before the indictment is begun, the privilege of being
seated. Arvandus, even thus early, with unhappy
self-assertion makes a rush and seizes a place almost
in the laps of his judges; on the other hand, Ferreolus
takes his seat modestly and quietly at the lowest end
of the benches with his colleagues standing on
either side, thus showing that he remembered that
he was a delegate as well as a senator; for which
action he was afterwards all the more complimented
and honoured. 10. Meanwhile those of the magnates
who had not attended at the beginning arrived; the
opponents rose in their places and the delegates set
out their case. After the commission from the
province the letter which we have mentioned above
was produced. It was being slowly read when
Arvandus, without waiting to be questioned, cried
out that he had dictated it. The delegates replied

spondere legati, quamquam valde nequiter, constaret
quod ipse dictasset. at ubi se furens ille quantumque
caderet ignarus bis terque repetita confessione
transfodit, acclamatur ab accusatoribus, conclamatur
a iudicibus reum laesae maiestatis confitentem teneri.
ad hoc et milibus formularum iuris id sancientum
iugulabatur. 11. tum demum laboriosus tarda
paenitudine loquacitatis impalluisse perhibetur, sero
cognoscens posse reum maiestatis pronuntiari etiam
eum qui non adfectasset habitum purpuratorum.
confestim privilegiis geminae praefecturae, quam per
quinquennium repetitis fascibus rexerat, exaugura-
tus et, plebeiae familiae non ut additus sed ut red-
ditus, publico carceri adiudicatus est. illud sane
aerumnosissimum, sicuti narravere qui viderant,
quod, quia se sub atratis accusatoribus exornatum
ille politumque iudicibus intulerat, paulo post, cum
duceretur addictus, miser nec miserabilis erat. quis
enim super statu eius nimis inflecteretur, quem
videret accuratum delibutumque lautumiis aut

---

[1] Arvandus, with his wide legal experience, cannot have
been as ignorant as Sidonius supposes. The reason of his
astounding confidence may have been that Ricimer had
secretly supported his treasonable designs and Arvandus
counted on his potent help. See Stevens, pp. 106 ff. (though
he, like Hodgkin, II. 464, inadvertently takes *adfect. hab.
purp.* to mean " had assumed the purple ").

[2] It was common, perhaps usual, for a person condemned
on his own confession to be committed to prison while awaiting
sentence. Sidonius seems to imply that if Arvandus had not
been a parvenu he would have been put under a milder form
of custody, being committed to the charge of one or two
persons pledged to produce him at the right time.

(very mischievously, indeed) that it should be taken
as an agreed point that he had dictated it. But
when the madman, not realising his blunder, re
peated his avowal two or three times and so dealt
himself his death-blow, the accusers raised a shout
in which the judges joined, declaring that the
accused was guilty of high treason on his own confession. Besides this, thousands of legal precedents
sanctioning the extreme penalty were aimed at his
throat. 11. Then, and not till then, it is reported,
did he show distress. His face grew pale as he
tardily regretted his talkativeness, realising all too
late that a man could be declared guilty of high
treason even although he had not aspired to the
purple.[1] He was instantly deprived by solemn
procedure of the privileges appertaining to the
double prefectship, which he had held by reappoint-
ment for five years, and he was consigned to the
state prison as one not degraded but rather restored
to a plebeian family.[2] The bitterest affliction of all
(as those who watched the scene have related) was
that, because he had marched into the presence of
his judges elegantly dressed and groomed whilst his
accusers were in dark clothing, the pitiable plight in
which he appeared only a little later evoked no pity,
as he was dragged off to prison after his commitment.
For who would distress himself greatly about the
position of one whom he saw being carried off to
the quarries or the convict-prison[3] punctiliously

---

[3] *Ergastula* were slave-prisons, where slaves chosen for hard,
rough labour (often as a punishment) were quartered, being
chained at night and sometimes even working in chains.
Under the Empire there were public *ergastula*, to which convicts as well as slaves were sent.

ergastulo inferri? 12. sed et iudicio vix per hebdo-
madam duplicem comperendinato capite multatus in
insulam coniectus est serpentis Epidauri, ubi usque
ad inimicorum dolorem devenustatus et a rebus
humanis veluti vomitu fortunae nauseantis exsputus
nunc ex vetere senatus consulto Tiberiano triginta
dierum vitam post sententiam trahit, uncum et
Gemonias et laqueum per horas turbulenti carnificis
horrescens. 13. nos quidem, prout valemus, absentes
praesentesque vota facimus, preces supplicationes-
que geminamus, ut suspenso ictu iam iamque
mucronis exserti pietas Augusta seminecem quamquam publicatis bonis vel exsilio muneretur. illo
tamen, seu exspectat extrema quaeque seu sustinet,
infelicius nihil est, si post tot notas inustas contume-
liasque aliquid nunc amplius quam vivere timet.
vale.

---

[1] *Sed et* is not very clear. The meaning seems to be:
"but he was actually (*et*) sentenced to *death* (not merely to
the quarries or the convict-prison)."

[2] The Insula Tiberina, on which stood a temple of Aesculapius.

[3] Under Tiberius the period was ten days. A law of
Theodosius, which allowed a reprieve of thirty days in the case
of an Imperial sentence, presumably caused a similar extension
in the case of the senatorial courts.

dressed and perfumed? 12. But he, indeed,[1] after an adjournment of the sentence for a bare fortnight, was sentenced to death and flung into prison in the island of the Serpent of Epidaurus,[2] where he has been stripped of his elegance to a point at which even his opponents are distressed; and having been spewed out of society as though fortune threw him up in a fit of sickness, he is now dragging out the period of thirty days after his sentence as fixed by an ancient *senatus consultum* of the Emperor Tiberius,[3] living in hourly terror of the hook, the Stairs,[4] and the noose of a savage[5] executioner. 13. As for us, whether at Rome or away from it, we offer vows and reiterate prayers and supplications to the extent of our powers, entreating that the Imperial generosity may, even at the cost of the confiscation of his property or exile, show favour to this half-dead man by holding back the stroke of the sword which threatens every moment to be loosed upon him. But as for him, whether he is now waiting for the worst or already enduring it, he is certainly the most hapless of beings if with the brand of all those ignominies and humiliations upon him there is anything he now dreads more than life. Farewell.

[4] The *Scalae Gemoniae* were on the Capitoline slope, near the old prison, but their exact position is uncertain. To these stairs the executioner dragged by a hook the bodies of criminals, which were exposed there for some days and then dragged to the Tiber.

[5] Sidonius uses *turbulentus* in the sense of *truculentus*.

VIII

SIDONIVS CANDIDIANO SVO
SALVTEM

1. Morari me Romae congratularis; id tamen
quasi facete et fatigationum salibus admixtis: ais
enim gaudere te quod aliquando necessarius tuus
videam solem, quem utique perraro bibitor Araricus
inspexerim. nebulas enim mihi meorum Lugdu-
nensium exprobras et diem quereris nobis matutina
caligine obstructum vix meridiano fervore reserari.
2. et tu istaec mihi Caesenatis furni potius quam
oppidi verna deblateras? de cuius natalis tibi soli
vel iucunditate vel commodo quid etiam ipse sentires,
dum migras iudicavisti;[1] ita tamen quod te Ravennae
felicius exsulantem auribus Padano culice perfossis
municipalium ranarum loquax turba circumsilit.
in qua palude indesinenter rerum omnium lege
perversa muri cadunt aquae stant, turres fluunt
naves sedent, aegri deambulant medici iacent,
algent balnea domicilia conflagrant, sitiunt vivi
natant sepulti, vigilant fures dormiunt potestates,

---

[1] indicasti *F*.

* Candidianus is not mentioned elsewhere.
[1] Modern Cesena, on the Via Aemilia, about 20 miles N.W.
of Ariminum.

VIII

SIDONIUS TO HIS FRIEND CANDIDIANUS, GREETING *

1. You congratulate me on being still in Rome, but you do so in a witty sort of way and with a spice of banter, for you say you are delighted that I, a friend of yours, have at last got a view of the sun, which, as one who drank of the Arar, I have seen (you say) at all events very seldom. You bring up against me the fogs of my countrymen of Lugdunum and complain that with us the daylight is shut out by morning mist and scarcely revealed later by midday heat. 2. And do you talk this balderdash to me, you a native of Caesena,[1] which is an oven rather than a town? You have shown your own opinion of the attractiveness and amenities of that natal soil of yours by quitting it, though in your happier existence as an exile at Ravenna your ears are pierced by the mosquitoes of the Padus, and a chattering company of your fellow-burghers the frogs[2] keeps jumping about on every side of you. In that marshland the laws of nature are continually turned upside down; the walls fall and the waters stand, towers float and ships are grounded, the sick promenade and the physicians lie abed, the baths freeze and the houses burn, the living go thirsty and the buried swim, thieves keep vigil and authorities sleep, clerics prac-

---

[2] The frogs of Ravenna are mentioned by Martial, III. 93. 8. For a few of the features about to be mentioned cf. I. 5. 6. It is impossible to see the point of all the remarks in this section; no doubt they are much exaggerated.

faenerantur clerici Syri psallunt, negotiatores militant milites [1] negotiantur, student pilae senes aleae
iuvenes, armis eunuchi litteris foederati. 3. tu vide
qualis sit civitas ubi tibi lar familiaris incolitur, quae
facilius territorium potuit habere quam terram.
quocirca memento innoxiis Transalpinis esse par-
cendum, quibus caeli sui dote contentis non grandis
gloria datur si deteriorum collatione clarescant.
vale.

IX

SIDONIVS HERONIO [2] SVO
SALVTEM

1. Post nuptias patricii Ricimeris, id est post
imperii utriusque opes eventilatas, tandem reditum

[1] monachi *LNTV*.
[2] herenio *LNTR*.

---

[1] Canon law strictly forbade the clergy to practise usury.

[2] Syrians took a prominent part in trading and in financial
operations all over the Empire. It may be that at this time,
at least in Gaul, the word *Syrus* was used in the special sense
of " banker " or " money-lender " : see Friedlaender, *Sitten-
geschichte*,[10] I. 378, who compares the mediaeval use of " Lom-
bard." With reference to the present passage Hodgkin (I.
861, n. 1) ingeniously suggests that there may be an allusion
to a tradition that " all the bishops of Ravenna for the first
four centuries were of Syrian extraction." This seems very
doubtful.

[3] In the later Empire the trading classes were excluded by
law from the army and from the civil service, and, on the other

tise usury[1] and Syrians[2] sing psalms, business men go soldiering and soldiers do business,[3] the old go in for ball-playing and the young for dicing, the eunuchs for arms and the federates[4] for culture. 3. I bid you look at the nature of the city where you have established your hearth and home, a city which found it easier to secure territory than to secure *terra firma*. So mind that you spare the harmless dwellers beyond the Alps, for they are quite content with the climate with which they have been endowed, and it is no great glory for them if they should shine by comparison with those that are worse. Farewell.

IX

SIDONIUS TO HIS FRIEND HERONIUS, GREETING *

1. Since the wedding of the patrician Ricimer, that is to say after the wealth of two empires has been

hand, soldiers might not go into trade—though some laxity seems to have been allowed in their case. The juxtaposition of *milites* seems to show that *militare* is here used of service in the army, not, as was usual in this period, of a post in the civil service. For *milites* some MSS. read *monachi* ("monks"), which deprives the sentence of all point. Probably *milites* was accidentally omitted in the archetype because of its similarity to *militant* (this is a common form of scribal error); then someone, noticing that a noun was wanted, stupidly inserted *monachi* (perhaps suggested by *clerici* in the preceding sentence).

[4] For the meaning of *foederati* see Introd., p. x, n. 2. The reference here is presumably to the federate troops of the garrison.

* A continuation of the account begun in No. 5. The date of the letter is A.D. 468.

est in publicam serietatem, quae rebus actitandis ianuam campumque patefecit. interea nos Pauli praefectorii tam doctrina quam sanctitate venerandis laribus excepti comiter blandae hospitalitatis officiis excolebamur. porro non isto quisquam viro est in omni artium genere praestantior. deus bone, quae ille propositionibus aenigmata, sententiis schemata, versibus commata, digitis mechanemata facit! illud tamen in eodem studiorum omnium culmen antevenit, quod habet huic eminenti scientiae conscientiam superiorem. igitur per hunc primum, si quis quoquo modo in aulam gratiae aditus, exploro; cum hoc confero, quinam potissimum procerum spebus valeret nostris opitulari. 2. nec sane multa cunctatio, quia pauci de quorum eligendo patrocinio dubitaretur. erant quidem in senatu plerique opibus culti genere sublimes, aetate graves consilio utiles, dignitate elati dignatione communes, sed servata pace reliquorum duo fastigatissimi consulares, Gennadius Avienus et Caecina Basilius, prae ceteris conspiciebantur. hi in amplissimo ordine seposita praerogativa partis armatae facile post purpuratum principem principes erant. sed inter hos quoque

---

[1] Gennadius Avienus belonged to the family of the Corvini (§ 4). He was consul in A.D. 450. In 452 he accompanied Pope Leo I. and Trygetius as ambassador to Attila.

[2] Flavius Caecina Decius Maximus Basilius was Praetorian Prefect of Italy under Majorian (A.D. 458) and again under Severus (463–5); he was consul in A.D. 463.

[3] This refers not only to the personal predominance of Ricimer but to the marked tendency under his régime to exalt the military class (*i.e.* the holders, or former holders, of one of the high military offices) over the class of civil functionaries; for example, an ex-consul who belonged to the military class took precedence over other ex-consuls in the senatorial order. See Stein, p. 563.

scattered to the winds, there has been a reversion to
seriousness in public affairs, and this has opened a door
and a field for the transaction of business. Meanwhile I had been welcomed in the home of Paulus,
a man of prefectorian rank,—a home venerable for
its learning as well as for its virtuousness, where I
was receiving the kindly attentions of a genial
hospitality. Besides, there is not a man anywhere
more excellent than he in every department of
culture. Kind heaven! With what ingenious subtle-
ties he sets forth his theme! What apt figures adorn
his thoughts, what nicely-measured phrases divide
his verses, what works of art he creates with his
fingers! And better still is the coping-stone of all his
studies, namely, that he has a conscience which surpasses his brilliant erudition. And so he was the first
friend through whom I sought to ascertain whether
there was any possible way of approach to gain the
favour of the court; with him I debated the question
who in particular amongst the influential people
would be able to aid my expectations. 2. There
was really little hesitation about this, for there
were very few whose claims as possible protectors
were worth weighing. Certainly there were many in
the Senate who were blessed with wealth and exalted
in lineage, reverend in years and helpful in counsel,
elevated by their dignity and yet accessible through
their condescension; but (with all due respect to the
rest) two consulars of the highest distinction, Gennadius Avienus[1] and Caecina Basilius,[2] were conspicuous above their fellows. In the most elevated rank,
if we leave out of account the privileged military class,[3]
they stood easily next to the Emperor in the purple.
But when we compare the two men we find even in

quamquam stupendi tamen varii mores et genii
potius quam ingenii similitudo.[1] fabor namque super
his aliqua succinctius. 3. Avienus ad consulatum
felicitate, Basilius virtute pervenerat. itaque dignitatum in Avieno iucunda velocitas, in Basilio sera
numerositas praedicabatur. utrumque quidem, si
fors laribus egrediebantur, artabat clientum praevia
pedisequa circumfusa populositas; sed longe in
paribus dispares sodalium spes et spiritus erant.
Avienus, si quid poterat, in filiis generis fratribus
provehendis moliebatur; cumque semper domesticis
candidatis distringeretur, erga expediendas forinsecus ambientum necessitates minus valenter efficax
erat. 4. et in hoc Corvinorum familiae Deciana
praeferebatur, quod qualia impetrabat cinctus
Avienus suis, talia conferebat Basilius discinctus
alienis. Avieni animus totis et cito, sed infructuosius,
Basilii paucis et sero, sed commodius aperiebatur.
neuter aditu difficili, neuter sumptuoso; sed si
utrumque coluisses, facilius ab Avieno familiari-
tatem, facilius a Basilio beneficium consequebare.
5. quibus diu utrimque libratis id tractatus mutuus
temperavit, ut reservata senioris consularis
reverentia, in domum cuius nec nimis raro venti-[2]

---

[1] *genii . . . ingenii.* See nn. on *Carm.* 2. 191 and 10. 20.
[2] Notes 1 and 2 on p. 384 will make this reference clear.

their case that their characters, though both extraordinary, are nevertheless different, and there is more
likeness in their dignity than in their disposition.[1]   I
will make some brief remarks about them.   3. Avienus
had reached the consulship by good fortune, Basilius by
his personal merit; so in the case of Avienus people
commonly remarked upon the happy rapidity of his
dignities and in the case of Basilius upon their tardy
multiplicity.   When either of them happened to go
out of doors, he was encircled by a swarming mass of
clients who preceded him, followed him, or walked at
his side; but though so far there was likeness, the
ambitions and tone of the two companies were very
unlike.   Avienus, so far as his influence extended,
exerted himself in promoting his sons, sons-in-law,
and cousins; and as he was always busy with
candidates from his own family, he was less
helpful in meeting the wants of place-seekers
outside his circle.   4. A further reason which made
the Decian clan preferable to that of the Corvini [2] was that such favours as Avienus when in
office obtained for his relatives Basilius even
when out of office bestowed on outsiders.   Avienus
revealed his mind to all, speedily but rather un-
profitably; Basilius did so to few and tardily, but
more beneficially.   It was not difficult or expensive
to get access to either of them; but if you sought
the company of both you were more likely to get
good-fellowship from Avienus and good deeds from
Basilius.   5. When we had carefully weighed the
considerations in favour of each, the discussion
between us arrived at this compromise, that while
still paying due respect to the elder consular, at
whose house I was indeed a fairly frequent visitor,

tabamus, Basilianis potius frequentatoribus appli-
caremur. ilicet, dum per hunc amplissimum virum
aliquid de legationis Arvernae petitionibus elabora-
mus, ecce et Kalendae Ianuariae, quae Augusti
consulis mox futuri repetendum fastis nomen
opperiebantur. 6. tunc patronus: "heia," inquit,
" Solli meus, quamquam suscepti officii onere pres-
saris, exseras volo in obsequium novi consulis
veterem Musam votivum quippiam vel tumultuariis
fidibus carminantem. praebebo admittendo aditum
recitaturoque solacium recitantique suffragium. si
quid experto credis, multa tibi seria hoc ludo pro-
movebuntur." parui ego praeceptis, favorem ille
non subtraxit iniunctis et impositae devotionis
adstipulator invictus egit cum consule meo, ut me
praefectum faceret senatui suo. 7. sed tu, ni fallor,
epistulae perosus prolixitatem voluptuosius nunc
opusculi ipsius relegendis versibus inmorabere. scio,
atque ob hoc carmen ipsum loquax in consequentibus
charta deportat, quae pro me interim, dum venio,
diebus tibi pauculis sermocinetur. cui si examinis
tui quoque puncta tribuantur, aeque gratum mihi

---

[1] These words show that Sidonius was not the only
delegate, though he must have been the leader of the
mission. Letter V. makes it clear that he had not travelled
along with his colleagues.

[2] *i.e.* as Praefectus Vrbi.

[3] The Panegyric on Anthemius, *Carmen* II.

I should attach myself more particularly to the train of Basilius. Well, while by the aid of this most distinguished man I was devising some move in the matter of the petitions of the Arvernian deputa- tion,[1] lo and behold! the Kalends of January also loomed before us, the day on which the second appearance of Augustus on the list of chief magis- trates was due, for our Emperor was about to become consul. 6. Then my patron said, "Come on, my dear Sollius, though you are sorely busied with the burden of the commission you have undertaken, I wish that you would, in humble duty to the new consul, draw out your old Muse from her retirement, and get her to chant some expression of good wishes, even if she has to strike up a hastily-improvised strain. I will give you the entry by passing you in, I will give you assistance when you are called on to read and support as you go on. Believe me as a man of experience, many serious concerns of yours will be greatly advanced by this sportive performance." I complied with his instructions, and he did not withdraw his support from the work he had charged me with; he gave his personal and irresistible backing to the tribute imposed upon me, and pressed the consul whose praises I had sung to appoint me as president of his Senate.[2] 7. However, unless I am mistaken, you are bored with the length of my letter, and will find it more pleasurable at this point to pass your time in reading the verses of the actual composition.[3] I understand, and accordingly this garrulous sheet carries you the poem itself added at the tail-end, to hold conversation with you on my behalf for a few days, until I arrive. And if it should get good marks from your examination also,

ac si me in comitio vel inter rostra contionante ad
sophos meum non modo lati clavi sed tribulium
quoque fragor concitaretur. sane moneo praeque de-
nuntio quisquilias ipsas[1] Clius tuae hexametris minime
exaeques. merito enim conlata vestris mea carmina
non heroicorum phaleris sed epitaphistarum neniis
comparabuntur. 8. attamen gaude quod hic ipse
panegyricus etsi non iudicium certe eventum boni
operis accepit. quapropter, si tamen tetrica sunt
amoenanda iocularibus, volo paginam glorioso, id est
quasi Thrasoniano fine concludere Plautini Pyrgo-
polinicis imitator. igitur cum ad praefecturam
sub ope Christi stili occasione pervenerim, iuberis
scilicet[2] pro potestate cincti undique omnium
laudum convasatis acclamationibus ad astra portare,
si placeo, eloquentiam, si displiceo, felicitatem.
videre mihi videor ut rideas, quia perspicis nostram
cum milite comico ferocisse iactantiam. vale.

[1] istas *Luetjohann frustra* ; *vid. Mohrii praef. p. xiv.*
[2] iuberis scilicet *ego* : iubeas ilicet *NCT* : iubeo te scilicet
Mohr.

that will be as acceptable to me as if I were holding forth in the Comitium or on the public platform and the clamour not only of the grandees but also of the humble citizens were breaking out in a "Bravo!" for me. I do indeed warn you and give you clear notice that you are on no account to compare this rubbish of mine with the hexameters of your epic Muse; for my strains, if compared with yours, will justly seem to resemble the dirges of tombstone-poets rather than the splendour of heroic bards. 8. Still, I want you to rejoice that this same panegyric, if it has not won critical approval, has at any rate had the practical success of a fine composition. Therefore, if serious subjects really ought to be brightened by jesting, I should like to finish off this column with an ending in a boastful tone, a Thraso-like ending,[1] in fact, and to become an imitator of the Pyrgopolinices of Plautus. So since I have, with Christ's help, been promoted to the Prefectship by the timely use of my pen, you must know that you are commanded by ministerial authority to heap together all the plaudits of all the praises in the world, and to exalt to the skies my eloquence if you are pleased with my work, my good fortune if you are dissatisfied with it. I can imagine myself seeing how you laugh on realising that my arrogance has gone wild in company with the soldier of the comedy. Farewell.

---

[1] Thraso and Pyrgopolinices are two boastful soldiers of Latin comedy, the former in the *Eunuchus* of Terence, the latter in the *Miles Gloriosus* of Plautus.

THE LETTERS OF SIDONIUS

X

SIDONIVS CAMPANIANO SVO
SALVTEM

1. Accepi per praefectum annonae litteras tuas,
quibus eum tibi sodalem veterem mihi insinuas
iudici novo. gratias ago magnas illi, maximas tibi,
quod statuistis de amicitia mea vel praesumere tuta
vel inlaesa credere. ego vero notitiam viri familiari-
tatemque non solum volens sed et avidus amplector,
quippe qui noverim nostram quoque gratiam hoc
obsequio meo fore copulatiorem. 2. sed et tu
vigilantiae suae me, id est famae meae statum
causamque commenda. vereor autem ne famem
populi Romani theatralis caveae fragor insonet et
infortunio meo publica deputetur esuries. sane
hunc ipsum e vestigio ad portum mittere paro, quia
comperi naves quinque Brundisio profectas cum
speciebus tritici ac mellis ostia Tiberina tetigisse;
quarum onera exspectationi plebis, si quid strenue
gerit, raptim faciet offerri, commendaturus se mihi,
me populo, utrumque tibi. vale.

---

* Nothing further is known of Campanianus. The date of
the letter is A.D. 468.
1 The Praefectus Annonae worked under the Prefect of the
City, who was ultimately responsible for the food-supply of
Rome.
2 Probably in a double sense. Sidonius in his new office of

392

X

SIDONIUS TO HIS FRIEND CAMPANIANUS, GREETING *

1. I have received your letter by the Prefect of the Food-Supply ; [1] in it you commend him as an old comrade of yours to me as a new judge.[2] I thank him heartily and you most heartily that you have both decided either to count on my friendship's being safe or at least to believe that nothing has yet impaired it. For my part I accept the acquaintance and intimacy of your excellent friend not only with readiness but with enthusiasm, for I feel sure that our own mutual liking will become closer through this compliance on my part. 2. However, I should wish you also to recommend to his vigilance my own self, that is to say, the upholding and defence of my reputation. For I am afraid that the uproar of the theatre-benches may sound the cry of " starvation in Rome," and that the general famine may be put down to my luckless management. In fact I am proposing to send this very man down to the harbour without a moment's delay, for I have been informed that five ships hailing from Brundisium have reached the mouth of the Tiber with food-stuffs in the shape of wheat and honey ; and if he is at all business-like he will see that their cargoes are promptly placed at the service of the expectant population. By so doing he will commend himself to me, me to the people, and both of us to yourself. Farewell.

Prefect of the City is a " new judge " ; he is also invited to be a fresh judge of the character of the *praefectus annonae*.

XI

SIDONIVS MONTIO SVO SALVTEM

1. Petis tibi, vir disertissime, Sequanos tuos
expetituro satiram nescio quam, si sit a nobis perscripta, transmitti. quod quidem te postulasse
demiror; non enim sanctum est ut de moribus
amici cito perperam sentias. huic eram themati
scilicet incubaturus id iam agens otii idque habens
aevi, quod iuvenem militantemque dictasse prae-
sumptiosum fuisset, publicasse autem periculosum?
cui namque grammaticum vel salutanti Calaber ille
non dixit:

"si mala condiderit in quem quis carmina, ius est
    iudiciumque"?

2. sed ne quid ultra tu de sodali simile credas, quid
fuerit illud quod me sinistrae rumor ac fumus opinio-
nis adflavit longius paulo sed ab origine exponam.

---

* Montius is not otherwise known. The incident here
related is referred to in *Carm.* 12. 22; see note on that poem.
The beginning of the letter seems to show that it was written
very soon after the occurrence, the date of which is A.D. 461.
[1] The point of *perscripta* will be made clear in § 8.
[2] This sentence raises problems even when correctly
construed, but it has been grossly abused through inattention
to the Latin; for example, one of the ablest of recent writers
on Sidonius infers from it that Sidonius still held a government
appointment ("was still *militans*") when he wrote the letter.
Sidonius, who was little, if at all, over thirty at the time, playfully speaks as if his days of youth and official life were far
behind him. He had recently retired from a government
post in Rome (see § 3, *recenti commilitio*, and note on the
passage) and had gone back to Auvergne (§ 4). Now he
assumes the pose of a retired old fogey and talks airily of the

XI

SIDONIUS TO HIS FRIEND MONTIUS, GREETING *

1. You ask me, my most eloquent friend, now that you mean to visit your countrymen the Sequani, to send you some satire or other, if I have finished it.[1] Now I am much surprised that you have made such a request; for it is not decent of you so quickly to believe the worst of a friend's character. So you supposed, did you, that I was likely, after reaching such an age and retiring from active life, to spend pains upon a literary effort which in my young days, when I was in the government service, it would have been audacious for me to have composed and dangerous for me to have published?[2] Who that has even a nodding acquaintance with the schoolmaster has not been told by the poet of Calabria:

" If ribald verse besmirch an honest name,
    The law shall see the offender put to shame "?[3]

2. However, to prevent you from entertaining such notions in future about your comrade, I will risk being rather long and tell from the beginning the whole story of the suspicion that was thrown on me by the chatter and smoke of malicious gossip. Under the

days when he was a young man in the civil service. Even if we take this to refer to some post under Avitus, about five years before the incident related in this letter, it is a jesting absurdity; but it may well refer to the *recens commilitium* of § 3. Thus the present passage throws no real light on the official career of Sidonius.

[3] Horace, *Sat.* II. 1. 82 sq.

temporibus Augusti Maioriani venit in medium
charta comitatum, sed carens indice, versuum plena
satiricorum mordacium, sane qui satis invectivaliter
abusi nominum nuditate carpebant plurimum vitia,
plus homines. inter haec fremere Arelatenses, quo
loci res agebatur, et quaerere quem poetarum publici
furoris merito pondus urgeret, his maxime auctoribus
quos notis certis auctor incertus exacerbaverat.
3. accidit casu ut Catullinus inlustris tunc ab Arvernis
illo veniret, cum semper mihi tum praecipue commilitio recenti familiaris; saepe enim cives magis
amicos peregrinatio facit. igitur insidias nescienti
tam Paeonius quam Bigerrus has tetenderunt, ut
plurimis coram tamquam ab incauto sciscitarentur,
hoc novum carmen an recognosceret. et ille: " si
dixeritis." cumque frusta diversa quasi per iocum
effunderent, solvitur Catullinus in risum intempesti-
voque suffragio clamare coepit dignum poema quod
perennandum apicibus auratis iuste tabula rostralis

---

government of the Emperor Majorian there came into circulation in the court a sheet with no label attached, full of satirical and biting lines, actually making the most savage use of undisguised names, and attacking vices a great deal but men still more. At this the people of Arelate, which was the scene of the incident, began to rage and to cast about among our poets in order to discover which of them deserved to bear the brunt of the general indignation. The chief instigators of this inquiry were the infuriated victims whose identity this mysterious poet had revealed by indications that were no mystery. 3. It so happened that the Illustrious Catullinus [1] arrived at that time from Auvergne. He had always been my friend, and at that moment was particularly intimate with me, as we had recently been partners in the public service; [2] for a sojourn abroad [3] often makes fellow-citizens better friends. Well, Paeonius and Bigerrus [4] together laid a trap for my unsuspecting friend. Designedly taking him off his guard, they asked him before a number of witnesses whether he recognised this new poem. " If you would be good enough to recite it," said he. They proceeded to spout sundry fragments as if it were all a jest; Catullinus burst into laughter, and with unseasonable approbation cried out that the poem deserved by right to be immortalised by being inscribed on a plate in letters of gold, to be set up on the Rostra or

years or more, to the time of Avitus. The whole wording of the sentence is patently against this.

[3] For *peregrinari* used of an inhabitant of Gaul who goes to Rome compare I. 6. 2.

[4] All that is known of Paeonius is contained in this letter; Bigerrus is otherwise unknown.

acciperet aut etiam Capitolina. 4. Paeonius exarsit,
cui satiricus ille morsum dentis igniti avidius impres-
serat, atque ad adstantes circulatores: " iniuriae
communis," inquit, " iam reum inveni. videtis ut
Catullinus deperit risu: apparet ei nota memorari.
nam quae causa festinam compulit praecipitare
sententiam, nisi quod iam tenet totum, qui de parte
sic iudicat? atqui¹ Sidonius nunc in Arverno est;
unde colligitur auctore illo, isto auditore rem textam."
itur in furias inque convicia absentis nescientis
innocentisque; conscientiae, fidei, quaestioni nil
reservatur. sic levis turbae facilitatem qua voluit
et traxit² persona popularis. 5. erat enim ipse
Paeonius populi totus, qui tribuniciis flatibus crebro
seditionum pelagus impelleret. ceterum si re-
quisisses: "qui genus, unde domo?", non eminentius
quam municipaliter natus quemque inter initia
cognosci claritas vitrici magis quam patris fecerit,
identidem tamen per fas nefasque crescere adfectans
pecuniaeque per avaritiam parcus, per ambitum
prodigus. namque ut familiae superiori per filiam
saltim quamquam honestissimam iungeretur, contra
rigorem civici moris splendidam, ut ferunt, dotem
Chremes noster Pamphilo suo dixerat. 6. cumque

¹ atqui *Mohr*: itaque.
² et traxit *L*: contraxit. *Fortasse* attraxit (*Luetjohann*).

¹ This may be (as has been suggested) a reference to the
fact that some of Nero's verses were inscribed in gold letters
and dedicated to Capitoline Jove (Suet. *Ner.* 10); but among
the Romans the idea is older than the age of Nero (see Tac.
Ann. III. 57 and 59, passages unknown to the *Thesaurus*,
s.v. *aureus*), and we are told that the Greeks set up three of
Chilon's wise sayings in letters of gold at Delphi (Plin. *N.H.*
VII. 119). ² Verg. *Aen.* VIII. 114.
³ Pamphilus married the daughter of Chremes. The dowry
was 10 talents (Terence, *Andria*, 950 sq.).

even on the Capitol.[1] 4. Paeonius flared up (the satirist had quite savagely assailed him with the bite of his burning tooth) and said to the loungers who were standing by, " I have now found out the culprit in this attack on us all. You see how Catullinus is dying with laughter; obviously our tale is no news to him. What has made him blurt out such a hasty opinion? Surely a man who pronounces thus on a part of the work already knows the whole of it. Now Sidonius is at present in Auvergne; so we can infer that the thing was concocted with Sidonius as author and this gentleman as audience." They all began to rage and rail against me, absent as I was and unwitting and innocent; no room was left for fair dealing, honesty, or investigation. So Paeonius, who was a power with the populace, led the compliant crowd by the nose. 5. For this Paeonius was a demagogue all over, the sort of man who was always stirring up a sea of riots by his blasts of tribunician violence. But if the question had been asked, " Who is he by birth and whence does he come? " [2]—his parentage had no standing beyond what a provincial town can give, and in the beginning of his career he was better known by the eminence of his stepfather than by that of his father; but he made repeated efforts to rise by fair means or foul, and while his avarice made him stingy his ambition made him a wastrel. Desiring, even if other means should fail, to gain a connexion with a family of higher rank through his daughter (certainly a quite unexceptionable lady), our Chremes, they say, abandoned the hardness characteristic of his native place and promised his Pamphilus a splendid dowry.[3] 6. Later, when the

399

THE LETTERS OF SIDONIUS

de capessendo diademate coniuratio Marcelliniana [1]
coqueretur, nobilium iuventuti signiferum sese in
factione praebuerat, homo adhuc novus in senectute,
donec aliquando propter experimenta felicis audaciae
natalium eius obscuritati dedit hiantis interregni
rima fulgorem. nam vacante aula turbataque
republica solus inventus est, qui ad Gallias adminis-
trandas fascibus prius quam codicillis ausus accingi
mensibus multis tribunal inlustrium potestatum
spectabilis praefectus escenderet, anno peracto
militiae extremae terminum circa vix honoratus,
numerariorum more seu potius advocatorum,
quorum cum finiuntur actiones, tunc incipiunt
dignitates. 7. igitur iste sic praefectorius, sic senator, cuius moribus quod praeconia competentia
non ex asse persolvo, generi sui moribus debeo,
multorum plus quam bonorum odia commovit adhuc
ignoranti mihi, adhuc amico, tamquam saeculo meo
canere solus versu valerem. venio Arelatem, nil
adhuc (unde enim?) suspicans, quamquam putarer

---

[1] Marcelliniana *vel* Marcellini *requiri admonet Mommsen,
recte, ut videtur, nisi* Marcellina *scribas* : marcell(i)ana *codd.*

---

[1] In spite of the confusion in the MSS., it seems reasonable
to believe that the name here connected with the conspiracy
is that of Marcellinus; see Introd., p. xxiii. Sidonius seems to
imply that Marcellinus was a party to the plot; if this is so,
he must have speedily withdrawn without committing himself
deeply. We know that he soon became an active supporter
of Majorian. The "interregnum" occurred between the
death of Avitus and the accession of Majorian. It was an
interregnum in a double sense, as there was no western
Emperor and no Praetorian Prefect of Gaul.

[2] Praetorian Prefects received the rank of *inlustris* as a
matter of course (n. on *Carm.* 7. 241), but Paeonius remained
a *spectabilis* until his appointment was regularised. The
spectabiles ranked below the *inlustres* and above the *clarissimi.*
See Bury I. 19 sqq., Hodgkin I. 603, 620. Since the *vicarii*
ranked as *spectabiles*, it is tempting to conjecture that

conspiracy of Marcellinus [1] to assume the diadem
was being hatched, he presented himself to the
young nobles as their ringleader, still a " new man "
in his old age; till in the end, thanks to some strokes
of lucky audacity on his part, the chink of a gaping
interregnum let in a ray of glory upon the obscurity
of his birth. For the throne being vacant and the
administration in a turmoil, he alone of all men was
found bold enough to assume the government of
Gaul by taking up the fasces before receiving his
patent of office, and to mount for several months
the tribunal of "illustrious" dignitaries as an
"eminent" prefect,[2] so that he had barely gained
his high dignity by the end of the year, toward
the very close of his term of service, like the
official cashiers, or rather the advocates, who
receive their promotion just at the time when their
activities are coming to an end.[3] 7. Well then, this
man, thus risen to prefectorian and senatorial rank (and
if I do not give a full advertisement of his character
it is owing to my respect for the character of his
son-in-law), stirred up ill-feeling against me amongst
the many rather than amongst the good, while I
was still ignorant of his doings, still his friend—as
if I were the only man in my generation who could
write poetry! I came to Arelate, still suspecting
nothing (why should I?), although my enemies did
not expect me to appear; and on the following

Paeonius held the vicariate at the time when he took over
the prefecture. If so, he may have acted partly at least from
patriotic motives; as there was no one to carry on the
Prefect's duties, the Vicar might feel bound to step in.
[3] The *numerarii* (cashiers in the office of the Praetorian
Prefect) might expect to receive the rank of *tribunus*; the
advocates attached to the Prefect's court might become Counts
of the Consistory.

ab inimicis non adfuturus, ac principe post diem viso
in forum ex more descendo. quod ubi visum est,
ilico expavit, ut ait ille, nil fortiter ausa seditio.[1]
alii tamen mihi plus quam deceret ad genua provolvi;
alii, ne salutarent, fugere post statuas, occuli post
columnas; alii tristes vultuosique iunctis mihi
lateribus incedere. 8. hic ego quid sibi haec vellet
in illis superbiae nimiae, nimiae in istis humilitatis
forma mirari, nec ultro tamen causas interrogare,
cum subornatus unus e turba factiosorum dat sese
mihi consalutandum. tum procedente sermone:
" cernis hos? " inquit. et ego: " video," inquam,
" gestusque eorum miror equidem nec admiror."
ad haec noster interpres: " ut satirographum te,"
inquit. " aut exsecrantur aut reformidant." " unde?
cur? quando? " respondi; " quis crimen agnovit?
quis detulit? quis probavit? " moxque subridens:
" perge," inquam, " amice, nisi molestum est, et
tumescentes nomine meo consulere dignare, utrum-
nam ille delator aut index, qui satiram me scripsisse
confinxit, et perscripsisse confinxerit; unde forte sit
tutius, si retractabunt, ut superbire desistant."
9. quod ubi nuntius rettulit, protinus cuncti non

---

[1] Lucan V. 322 sq.

402

day, having visited the Emperor, I walked down in the usual way to the Forum. This was observed, and thereupon panic filled what the poet calls

"The rout that dare not strike a manful blow." [1]

Some indeed threw themselves at my feet with indecent servility; others, to avoid greeting me, ran behind statues and concealed themselves behind columns; others with downcast expression and long faces joined themselves on and walked at my side. 8. At this point I began to wonder what such a show of extravagant haughtiness in one party and extravagant abjectness in another could possibly mean, but I did not go out of my way to inquire into the reasons, until one of the aggressive rabble, who had been put up to the job, presented himself to me so as to make me greet him. Then as we went on talking he asked, "Do you see these gentlemen?" "I do," said I, "and I find their behaviour more puzzling than pleasing." "They look on you as a satirist," said my instructor, "and curse or dread you accordingly." "How so? Why? When?" I replied; "Who discovered the wrongdoing? Who has informed against me? Who has proved the charge?" Then with a smile I added, "Go on, my friend, if you don't mind, and be good enough to inquire as from me of those who are making all this stir whether the informer or spy who invented the story that I had composed a satire also invented the addition that I have finished writing it. So if these people will think over it they will perhaps find it safer to give up their insolent conduct." 9. When the messenger brought back this answer, the whole company, not in a quiet way or one

modeste neque singuli sed propere et catervatim
oscula ac dexteras mihi dederunt. solus Curio
meus, in transfugarum perfidiam invectus, cum
advesperasceret, per cathedrarios servos vispilloni-
bus taetriores domum raptus ac reportatus est.
10. postridie iussit Augustus ut epulo suo circensibus
ludis interessemus. primus iacebat cornu sinistro
consul ordinarius Severinus, vir inter ingentes
principum motus atque inaequalem reipublicae
statum gratiae semper aequalis; iuxta eum Magnus,
olim ex praefecto, nuper ex consule, par honoribus
persona geminatis, recumbente post se Camillo,
filio fratris, qui duabus dignitatibus et ipse decursis
pariter ornaverat proconsulatum patris, patrui
consulatum; Paeonius hinc propter atque hinc
Athenius, homo litium temporumque varietatibus
exercitatus. hunc sequebatur Gratianensis, omni
ab infamia vir sequestrandus, qui Severinum sicut
honore postibat, ita favore praecesserat. ultimus

---

[1] Paeonius is so called as an agitator of the rabble. Cf.
Lucan I. 268–271, IV. 799–801.

[2] One end of the dinner-table was left free for the con-
venience of the service; it is from this end that the "right"
and "left" sides of the couch are reckoned. The usual form
of dining-couch at this time was semicircular (*sigma* or
stibadium), being made to fit the round tables which had long
been fashionable. The "horns" are the two ends of the
couch. In the present case the guests are arranged in a way
which seems to have been usual at the time. On the right
extremity (or "horn") reclines Majorian, the host. Opposite
him, on the left horn, is the guest of honour (the consul). The
other guests are arranged round the couch in strict order of
precedence, beginning with Magnus, next to the consul, and
ending with Sidonius, who is next to Majorian. At the
beginning of the conversation the Emperor was apparently
expected to address the chief guest first and then say a word
to each of the others in order of precedence.

by one, but in a crowd and in a rush, offered me
their lips and their hands. Only my good Curio[1]
upbraided violently the disloyalty of the deserters,
but as evening was coming on he was caught up
by his sedan-bearers, who were more repulsive than
undertakers' men, and so he was carried off to his
house. 10. The next day Augustus invited me to
take part in his banquet on the occasion of the
sports of the circus. The first place on the left horn
of the couch[2] was occupied by Severinus,[3] consul
of the year, a man who through all the great struggles
between the mighty and through all the unstable
fortunes through which the state had passed had
always kept a steady position of influence. At his
side was Magnus,[4] who had formerly had the standing of an ex-prefect and had lately gained that
of an ex-consul,[5] a personality equal to the double
distinction conferred upon him. After him was
placed Camillus,[6] his brother's son, who, having
himself also passed through two high offices, had
added fresh lustre alike to his father's proconsulship
and to his uncle's consulship. Then next to him
came Paeonius, and then Athenius,[7] a man who had
played a busy part in the vicissitudes of litigation
and revolution. After him came Gratianensis,[7] a
man whom no ill-report ought to touch, inferior
to Severinus in rank but having the advantage
of him in favour. Last came I, placed where

---

[3] Nothing further is known of Severinus.

[4] Magnus : n. on *Carm.* 23. 455.

[5] As already mentioned, Magnus had been consul in the
previous year (460).

[6] Camillus : *Carm.* 9. 8.

[7] Not otherwise known.

ego iacebam, qua purpurati latus laevum margine in
dextro porrigebatur.¹ 11. edulium multa parte finita
Caesaris ad consulem sermo dirigitur, isque succinc-
tus; inde devolvitur ad consularem; cum quo
saepe repetitus, quia de litteris factus, ad virum
inlustrem Camillum ex occasione transfertur, in
tantum ut diceret princeps: " vere habes patruum,
frater Camille, propter quem me familiae tuae
consulatum unum gratuler contulisse." tunc ille,
qui simile aliquid optaret, tempore invento: " non
unum," inquit, " domine Auguste, sed primum."
summo fragore, ut nec Augusti reverentia obsisteret,
excepta sententia est. 12. inde nescio quid
Athenium interrogans superiectum Paeonium com-
pellatio Augusta praeteriit, casu an industria ignoro.
quod cum turpiter Paeonius aegre tulisset, quod
fuit turpius, compellato tacente respondit. subrisit
Augustus, ut erat auctoritate servata, cum se com-
munioni dedisset, ioci plenus, per quem cachinnum
non minus obtigit Athenio vindictae, quam conti-
gisset iniuriae. colligit itaque sese trebacissimus
senex et, ut semper intrinsecus aestu pudoris exco-
quebatur, cur sibi Paeonius anteferretur: " non
miror," inquit, " Auguste, si mihi standi locum

---

¹ This is Sidonius's way of saying that he was close to the
emperor, who occupied the right " horn." The mention of
the " left side " of the emperor has no significance, as every
diner reclined on his left side (or elbow); it is due merely to
the author's itch for antithesis; as " right " occurs in the
sentence he cannot refrain from contrasting it with " left,"
just as he can scarcely ever mention " new " without contrasting it with " old," and *vice versa*.

the left side of the wearer of the purple reposed on the right extremity of the couch.[1] 11. When we had got a good way through the courses, Caesar's conversation was directed to the consul, and was only short; then it passed to the consular, and with him it was frequently resumed, being on literary subjects; it was then shifted, when an occasion offered, to the Illustrious Camillus, to the extent that the Emperor remarked, "Truly, my dear Camillus, with such an uncle as you have I am delighted to have bestowed one consulship on your family." Then Camillus, who had similar ambitions for himself, found his opportunity, and said, "Not *one* consulship, my lord Augustus, but *the first*." This reply was received with a roar of applause, not hindered even by respect for Augustus. 12. Then Augustus in his round of remarks, by putting to Athenius some trifling question (whether deliberately or by accident I know not), passed over Paeonius, who was placed above him. Paeonius, with very bad taste, showed annoyance at this, and, what was worse, before the person addressed found words to reply, answered for him. Augustus gave a gentle laugh, being a man who, while keeping his dignity, was full of merriment when he had given himself over to good-fellowship; and by that chuckle Athenius won a revenge quite as great as the injury which he would otherwise have suffered. So this old gentleman, who was a decidedly artful person, pulled himself together, and found a vent for the blaze of shame which constantly burned within him as he thought how Paeonius was favoured above him. " I am not at all surprised, Augustus," said he, " that this fellow should attempt to rob me of my right to

praeripere conetur, qui tibi invadere non erubescit loquendi." 13. et vir inlustris Gratianensis : " multus," inquit, " hoc iurgio satiricis campus aperitur." hic imperator ad me cervice conversa : " audio," ait, " comes Sidoni, quod satiram scribas." " et ego," inquam, " hoc audio, domine princeps." tunc ille, sed ridens : " parce vel nobis." " at ego," inquam, " quod ab inlicitis tempero, mihi parco." post quae ille : " et quid faciemus his," inquit, " qui te lacessunt ? " et ego : " quisquis est iste, domine imperator, publice accuset : si redarguimur, debita luamus supplicia convicti ; ceterum obiecta si non inprobabiliter cassaverimus, oro ut indultu clementiae tuae praeter iuris iniuriam in accusatorem meum quae volo scribam." 14. ad haec ipse Paeonium conspicatus nutu coepit consulere nutantem, placeretne condicio. sed cum ille confusus reticuisset princepsque consuleret erubescenti, ait : " annuo postulatis, si hoc ipsum e vestigio versibus petas." " fiat," inquam ; retrorsumque conversus, tamquam aquam manibus poscerem, tantumque remoratus, quantum stibadii circulum celerantia ministeria percurrunt, cubitum toro reddidi. et imperator : " spoponderas te licentiam scribendae satirae versibus subitis postulaturum." et ego :

" scribere me satiram qui culpat, maxime princeps, hanc rogo decernas aut probet aut timeat."

---

[1] In the case of Sidonius this title is commonly thought to have been purely honorary, not due to the holding of any public office. The view of Savaron that he was *comes civitatis Arvernorum* has recently been revived, but has no evidence to support it ; and the existence of an official with this title in the reign of Majorian would certainly be surprising.

precedence, when he does not blush to usurp your right to speak." 13. Then said the Illustrious Gratianensis, " This wrangle opens a wide door for satirists." Thereupon the Emperor turned his head to me and said, " I hear, Count [1] Sidonius, that you write satire." I replied, " Sovereign Lord, I hear it too." Then he said, but with a smile, " Anyhow, spare poor me." I said, " In keeping off forbidden ground it is myself that I spare." " And what," he said, " shall we do with those who attack you?" I replied, "Whoever does so, my Lord Emperor, ought to accuse me openly; if I am found guilty, let me pay the proper penalty as a proved offender; if, on the other hand, I can make out a good case against the charge, I beg that by the indulgence of your gracious clemency I may be allowed to write what I please against my accuser, short of offending the law." 14. At this he looked Paeonius in the face and by a nod propounded to the confounded courtier the question whether he approved of the terms. When the abashed Paeonius said nothing, the Prince showed consideration for his blushes and said, " I approve the proposal, on condition that you make the request on the spot in verse." " Very good," I said; then I turned round as if asking for water for my hands, and after waiting just the time that the hurrying servants take to make the round of the couch, I again reposed my arm on the cushion. Then the Emperor said, " You undertook to ask in impromptu verse for permission to write a satire." I said:

" Who taxes me with satire—mighty prince,
    Say he must prove it or be made to wince."

15. secutus est fragor, nisi quod dico iactantia est,
par Camillano, quem quidem non tam carminis
dignitas quam temporis brevitas meruit. et
princeps: " deum testor et statum publicum me de
cetero numquam prohibiturum quin quae velis
scribas, quippe cum tibi crimen impactum probari
nullo modo possit; simul et periniurium est sententiam purpurati tribuere privatis hoc simultatibus,
ut innocens ac secura nobilitas propter odia certa
crimine incerto periclitetur." ad hanc ipse sententiam cum verecunde capite demisso gratias
agerem, contionatoris mei coeperunt ora pallere, in
quae paulo ante post iram tristitia successerat; nec
satis defuit quin gelarent tamquam ad exsertum
praebere cervices iussa mucronem. 16. vix post
haec alia pauca: surreximus. paululum ab aspectu
imperatoris processeramus atque etiamnunc chlamy-
dibus induebamur, cum mihi consul ad pectus,
praefectorii ad manus cadere, ipse ille reus amicus
crebro et abiecte miserantibus cunctis humiliari, ita
ut timerem ne mihi invidiam supplicando moveret,
quam criminando non concitaverat. dixi ad extremum pressus oratu procerum conglobatorum,
sciret conatibus suis versu nil reponendum, derogare
actibus meis in posterum tamen si pepercisset;

15. At once there was an outburst of applause (if it is not boasting to say so) like that which followed the sally of Camillus; however, it was earned not so much by the quality of the verse as by its quick production. Then the Prince said, "I declare before God and the State that for the future I will never forbid your writing anything that you please, for the charge that has been fastened upon you can in no way be substantiated. Moreover, it would be an outrageous thing if the authority of the wearer of the purple should so favour private animosities as to endanger an inoffensive and unsuspecting nobleman by a doubtful charge prompted by undoubted ill-will." At this utterance I modestly bowed my head and expressed my thanks, and the face of my demagogue, in which gloom had so recently taken the place of anger, began to pale; indeed it almost froze, as if the order had been given him to stretch out his neck to the drawn sword of the executioner. 16. After this there was very little further conversation; then we rose. We had only proceeded a little way from the Emperor's presence, and we were just putting on our cloaks, when the consul flung himself on my breast and the ex-prefects grasped my hands, while my friend the offender, of all people, abased himself before me again and again, rousing the whole company to compassion, so that I was afraid that by his humiliation he might stir up against me the ill-will which he had failed to excite by his accusation. In the end, urged by a massed appeal from the dignitaries present, I told him that he might be sure that no revenge in verse would be taken for his machinations, always provided that in the future he did not vilify my actions; for

etenim sufficere debere, quod satirae obiectio famam
mihi parasset, sed sibi infamiam. 17. in summa
perculi [1] quidem, domine maior, non assertorem
calumniae tantum quantum murmuratorem; sed
cum mihi sic satisfactum est ut pectori meo pro
reatu eius tot potestatum dignitatumque culmina
et iura summitterentur, fateor exordium contumeliae
talis tanti fuisse, cui finis gloria fuit.   vale.

LIBER SECVNDVS

I

SIDONIVS ECDICIO SVO
SALVTEM

1. Duo nunc pariter mala sustinent Arverni tui.
" quaenam? " inquis. praesentiam Seronati et
absentiam tuam. Seronati, inquam : de cuius ut
primum etiam nomine loquar, sic mihi videtur
quasi praescia futurorum lusisse fortuna, sicuti ex
adverso maiores nostri proelia, quibus nihil est
foedius, bella dixerunt; quique etiam pari contrarie-
tate fata, quia non parcerent, Parcas vocitavere.

[1] perculi *Wilamowitz* : pertuli.

---

* For Ecdicius see Introd., pp. xlvi ff.
[1] Seronatus is generally said to have been Praetorian
Prefect of Gaul, but it is quite possible that he was either
Vicarius of the Seven Provinces (see p. 347, n. 2) or governor of

there was good reason, as I told him, for me to be content, inasmuch as his charge of satire-writing had brought me repute and him disrepute. 17. The upshot of it all is, my honoured lord, that I crushed one who had whispered rather than proclaimed a false accusation against me; but now that I have got such ample satisfaction, having had all those high and mighty dignitaries bowing their majesty and authority before me because of his guilt, I must confess that the insult which formed the preamble was worth while, seeing that the conclusion has been glory. Farewell.

BOOK II

I

SIDONIUS TO HIS DEAR ECDICIUS, GREETING *

1. Your countrymen the Arverni have now to bear two troubles at once. " What can they be? " you ask. Seronatus's[1] presence and your absence. Seronatus's, I say, whose very name, I may remark at the outset, makes me feel that chance, foreseeing the future, must have played a joke, just as our ancestors, going by contraries, called wars, which are the foulest of all things, *bella* (" beautiful "), and with like contradiction called the Fates *Parcae*, because

---

the province of Aquitanica Prima (perhaps in A.D. 469). He was in league with Euric, and tried to deliver the Roman territories into the hands of the Goths, until he was brought to justice by the Arvernians (VII. 7. 2). See also V. 13.

rediit ipse Catilina saeculi nostri nuper Aturribus, ut
sanguinem fortunasque miserorum, quas ibi ex parte
propinaverat, hic ex asse misceret. 2. scitote in
eo per dies spiritum diu dissimulati furoris aperiri:
aperte invidet, abiecte fingit, serviliter superbit,
indicit ut dominus, exigit ut tyrannus, addicit ut
iudex, calumniatur ut barbarus; toto die a metu
armatus, ab avaritia ieiunus, a cupiditate terribilis,
a vanitate crudelis non cessat simul furta vel punire
vel facere; palam et ridentibus convocatis ructat
inter cives pugnas, inter barbaros litteras; epistulas,
ne primis quidem apicibus sufficienter initiatus,
publice a iactantia dictat, ab impudentia emendat;
3. totum quod concupiscit quasi comparat nec dat
pretia contemnens nec accipit instrumenta desperans;
in concilio iubet in consilio tacet, in ecclesia iocatur
in convivio praedicat, in cubiculo damnat in quaes-
tione dormitat; implet cotidie silvas fugientibus
villas hospitibus,[1] altaria reis carceres clericis;

[1] hostibus *LC.*

---

[1] Whether the form *Aturribus* is correct or not, the reference
is to the town of the Aturenses (Civitas Aturensium, modern
Aire, in Gascony). It was in Novempopulana, which now
belonged to the Goths, and the Gothic court occasionally resided
there.

[2] The reference seems to be to *instrumenta emptionis* (see
Justinian, *Inst.* III. 23. 1), written contracts between vendor
and intending purchaser.

[3] The Concilium Septem Provinciarum (Introd., p. xii).

[4] Referring to the usual system of occupation by the Goths
and others, whereby the Roman landowner had to surrender
a certain portion of his estate to a " barbarian." See Introd.,
p. x, n. 2. The word *hospes* was euphemistically applied

they spared not. This very Catiline of our age returned lately from Aire [1] to make here one big draught of the blood and the fortunes of the wretched inhabitants, after a good taste of such refreshment in the other place. 2. Be it known to all of you that in his case a long-concealed spirit of brutality is being revealed more fully every day. He is openly malignant and basely deceitful; he swaggers like a slave and gives his orders like a master; exacts like a despot, condemns like a judge, accuses falsely like a barbarian; all day long he goes armed through fear and he goes hungry through avarice; his greed makes him terrible, his presumption makes him cruel; he is ceaselessly busy either in punishing thefts or in committing them; in public and amidst the laughter of those he has assembled he belches forth talk of fighting amongst peaceful citizens and of letters amongst barbarians: as for his written instructions, not having had a real schooling even in his ABC, he dictates them in public through boastfulness and corrects them through sheer effrontery. 3. Everything that he lusts to possess he makes a pretence of purchasing; he is too arrogant to pay the price and too diffident to agree to a contract of sale.[2] In the Common Council [3] he gives orders, among his counsellors he is mute; in the church he jests, at the banquet he preaches; in his chamber he convicts, in the court he dozes; each day he crowds the woods with fugitives, the farms with barbarian occupants,[4] the altars with accused persons, the prisons with priests; he brags to the

both to the owner and to his unwelcome "guest." The meaning is that Seronatus allows the Goths to encroach freely on Roman territory.

415

exsultans Gothis insultansque Romanis, inludens praefectis conludensque numerariis, leges Theodosianas calcans Theudoricianasque proponens veteres culpas, nova tributa perquirit. 4. proinde moras tuas citus explica et quidquid illud est quod te retentat incide. te exspectat palpitantium civium extrema libertas. quidquid sperandum, quidquid desperandum est, fieri te medio, te praesule placet. si nullae a republica vires, nulla praesidia, si nullae, quantum rumor est, Anthemii principis opes, statuit te auctore nobilitas seu patriam dimittere seu capillos.[1] vale.

II

SIDONIVS DOMITIO SVO SALVTEM

1. Ruri me esse causaris, cum mihi potius queri suppetat te nunc urbe retineri. iam ver decedit aestati et per lineas sol altatus extremas in axem Scythicum radio peregrinante porrigitur. hic quid de regionis nostrae climate loquar? cuius spatia

---

[1] *i.e.* assume the tonsure.

* On Domitius see *Carm.* 24. 10 n. Some of the " fine writing " in this letter is rather obscure, and the description does not supply adequate material for a plausible plan of the buildings. For the baths of Avitacum see *Carm.* 18. There have been several attempts to identify the site of the " villa." The favourite theory places it on the shores of the Lac d'Aydat, about 12 miles S.W. of Clermont-Ferrand. The very name of Aydat (Aidacum in mediaeval documents) seems to confirm the identification, and in the village church there is a mysterious

Goths and insults the Romans, mocks the magistrates and plays tricks along with the public cashiers; he tramples on the laws of Theodosius and issues laws of Theodoric, searching out ancient offences and brand-new taxes. 4. Be quick then and clear away your impediments and break off whatever is detaining you. Your countrymen in the last throes of the struggle for liberty are waiting for you. Every counsel of hope or of despair we are prepared to risk with you in our midst, with you as our leader. If the state has neither strength nor soldiers, if (as report has it) the Emperor Anthemius has no resources, then our nobility has resolved under your guidance to give up either its country or its hair.[1] Farewell.

II

SIDONIUS TO HIS FRIEND DOMITIUS, GREETING *

1. You grumble at my staying in the country, whereas I have better reason to complain of your being detained in town. Spring is now giving place to summer, and the sun, travelling upward through its highest latitudes, is obtruding an alien ray upon the region of the North Pole. No need to speak here of the climate of this district. The

inscription, possibly of the 12th century, but now thought to be a copy of a much older one: HIC ST (= *sunt*) DVO INNOCENTES ET S (= *sanctus*) SIDONIVS. But it is not very easy to accept this tempting identification, even if we make allowance for considerable changes in the physical features of the district. The question is discussed at length by Stevens, Appendix B, pp. 185–195, with the aid of a map, a plan, and an aerial photograph.

divinum sic tetendit opificium ut magis vaporibus
orbis occidui subiceremur. quid plura? mundus
incanduit: glacies Alpina deletur et hiulcis arentium
rimarum flexibus terra perscribitur; squalet glarea
in vadis, limus in ripis, pulvis in campis; aqua ipsa
quaecumque perpetuo labens tractu cunctante
languescit; iam non solum calet unda sed coquitur.
2. et nunc, dum in carbaso sudat unus, alter in
bombyce, tu endromidatus exterius, intrinsecus
fasceatus, insuper et concava municipis Amerini sede
compressus discipulis non aestu minus quam timore
pallentibus exponere oscitabundus ordiris: "Samia
mihi mater fuit." quin tu mage, si quid tibi salubre
cordi, raptim subduceris anhelantibus angustiis
civitatis et contubernio nostro aventer insertus fallis
clementissimo recessu inclementiam canicularem?
3. sane si placitum, quis sit agri in quem vocaris
situs accipe. Avitaci sumus: nomen hoc praedio,
quod, quia uxorium, patrio mihi dulcius: haec mihi
cum meis praesule deo, nisi quid tu fascinum verere,
concordia. mons ab occasu, quamquam terrenus,
arduus tamen inferiores sibi colles tamquam gemino
fomite effundit, quattuor a se circiter iugerum

---

[1] *i.e.* of withies, for which Ameria was famous. This expression has been ludicrously misunderstood; Domitius has
actually been represented as "teaching in the schools of
Ameria"! See Housman in *Class. Rev.* XIV (1900), p. 54.

[2] Terence, *Eunuchus*, 107.

[3] Settlements of considerable size, consisting largely of
tenant-farmers, slaves, and other persons attached in various
ways to the estate or to its owner, grew up in the neighbourhood of important "villas." Thus *Avitacum* is here treated
grammatically as a township, and used in the locative case.

[4] *i.e.* not rocky.

divine workmanship has so fixed its borders that we
are chiefly exposed to the heats of the west. Why
say more? The earth has grown hot; the ice of
the Alps is disappearing; the land is being scored
with irregular curved cracks gaping in the heat;
gravel lies untidily in the fords, mud on the banks,
dust in the fields; even streams that flow all the
year round have languidly slowed down; the water
is not merely hot, it boils. 2. And at this time of year,
while one man sweats in linen and another in silk,
you with your woollen gown outside and your
swathings underneath, and, as if that were not
enough, squeezed into a deep chair made of
Ameria's population,[1] begin yawningly to expound
to your pupils, whose pale faces are due quite as
much to the heat as to fear of you: "A Samian
was my mother."[2] Why not rather, if you have
any thought of your health, promptly withdraw from
the panting oppression of the town and eagerly join
our house-party, and so beguile the fierceness of
the dog-days by retiring to the coolest of retreats?
3. Just let me tell you, if you don't mind, how this
country place you are invited to is situated. We
are at Avitacum;[3] this is the name of the farm,
which is dearer to me than the property I inherited
from my father, because it came to me with my
wife: such is the harmony in which, under God's
guidance, I live with my family (I hope you are
not afraid of the evil eye!). On the western side is
a mountain, earthy in substance[4] but stiff to climb,
which pushes out lower hills from itself like offshoots
from a double stem; and these hills diverge so
as to leave a breadth of about four *iugera*[5] between

[5] The *iugerum* was about five-eighths of an acre.

latitudine abductos. sed donec domicilio competens
vestibuli campus aperitur, mediam vallem rectis
tractibus prosequuntur latera clivorum usque in
marginem villae, quae in Borean Austrumque con-
versis frontibus tenditur. 4. balineum ab Africo
radicibus nemorosae rupis adhaerescit, et si caedua
per iugum silva truncetur, in ora fornacis lapsu
velut spontaneo deciduis struibus impingitur. hinc
aquarum surgit cella coctilium, quae consequenti
unguentariae spatii parilitate conquadrat excepto
solii capacis hemicyclio, ubi et vis undae ferventis
per parietem foraminatum flexilis plumbi meatibus
implicita singultat. intra conclave succensum solidus
dies et haec abundantia lucis inclusae ut verecundos
quosque compellat aliquid se plus putare quam
nudos. 5. hinc frigidaria dilatatur, quae piscinas
publicis operibus exstructas non impudenter aemul-
aretur. primum tecti apice in conum cacuminato,
cum ab angulis quadrifariam concurrentia dorsa
cristarum tegulis interiacentibus imbricarentur (ipsa
vero convenientibus mensuris exactissima spatiosi-
tate quadratur, ita ut ministeriorum sese non im-
pediente famulatu tot possit recipere sellas quot solet
sigma personas), fenestras e regione conditor binas
confinio camerae pendentis admovit, ut suspicientum
visui fabrefactum lacunar aperiret. interior parietum

them. But before spreading out so as to allow a sufficiently large frontage for a dwelling, the hill-sides escort the intervening valley in straight lines, right up to the outskirts of the mansion, which has its fronts facing north and south. 4. On the south-west side are the baths, hugging the base of a wooded cliff, and when along the ridge the branches of light wood are lopped, they slide almost of themselves in falling heaps into the mouth of the furnace. At this point there stands the hot bath, and this is of the same size as the anointing-room which adjoins it, except that it has a semicircular end with a roomy bathing-tub, in which part a supply of hot water meanders sobbingly through a labyrinth of leaden pipes that pierce the wall. Within the heated chamber there is full day and such an abundance of enclosed light as forces all modest persons to feel themselves something more than naked. 5. Next to this the cold room spreads out; it might without impertinence challenge comparison with baths built as public undertakings. First of all the architect has given it a peaked roof of conical shape; the four faces of this erection are covered at the corners where they join by hollow tiles, between which rows of flat tiles are set, and the bath-chamber itself has its area perfectly adjusted by the nicest measurements so as to find room for as many chairs as the semicircular bath usually admits bathers, without causing the servants to get in one another's way. The architect has also set a pair of windows, one opposite the other, where the vaulting joins the wall, so as to disclose to the view of guests as they look up the cunningly-wrought coffered ceiling. The inner face of the walls is content with the plain

facies solo levigati caementi candore contenta est.
6. non hic per nudam pictorum corporum pulchri-
tudinem turpis prostat historia, quae sicut ornat
artem, sic devenustat artificem. absunt ridiculi
vestitu et vultibus histriones pigmentis multi-
coloribus Philistionis supellectilem mentientes.
absunt lubrici tortuosique pugilatu et nexibus
palaestritae, quorum etiam viventum luctas, si
involvantur obscenius, casta confestim gymnasiarcho-
rum virga dissolvit. 7. quid plura? nihil illis paginis
impressum reperietur quod non vidisse sit sanctius.
pauci tamen versiculi lectorem adventicium remora-
buntur minime improbo temperamento, quia eos
nec relegisse desiderio est nec perlegisse fastidio. iam
si marmora inquiras, non illic quidem Paros Carystos
Proconnesos, Phryges Numidae Spartiatae rupium
variatarum posuere crustas, neque per scopulos
Aethiopicos et abrupta purpurea genuino fucata
conchylio sparsum mihi saxa furfurem mentiuntur.
sed etsi nullo peregrinarum cautium rigore ditamur,
habent tamen tuguria seu mapalia mea civicum
frigus. quin potius quid habeamus quam quid
non habeamus ausculta. 8. huic basilicae appendix
piscina forinsecus seu, si graecari mavis, baptisterium ab oriente conectitur, quod viginti circiter
modiorum milia capit. huc elutis e calore venientibus
triplex medii parietis aditus per arcuata intervalla

---

[1] A writer of mimes in Greek, who had a considerable vogue
in Rome in the age of Augustus.
[2] See *Carm.* 5. 34–36 n. *Lapis Syenites* was a coarse stone,
sprinkled with numerous reddish crystals.
[3] A *modius* was approximately two gallons.

whiteness of polished concrete. 6. Here no disgraceful tale is exposed by the nude beauty of painted figures, for though such a tale may be a glory to art it dishonours the artist. There are no mummers absurd in features and dress counterfeiting Philistion's [1] outfit in paints of many colours. There are no athletes slipping and twisting in their blows and grips. Why, even in real life the chaste rod of the gymnasiarch promptly breaks off the bouts of such people if they get mixed up in an unseemly way! 7. In short, there will not be found traced on those spaces anything which it would be more proper not to look at; only a few lines of verse will cause the new-comer to stop and read: these strike the happy mean, for although they inspire no longing to read them again, they can be read through without boredom. If you ask what I have to show in the way of marble, it is true that Paros, Carystos and Proconnesos, Phrygians, Numidians and Spartans have not deposited here slabs from hill-faces in many colours, nor do any stone surfaces, stained with a natural tinge among the Ethiopian crags with their purple precipices, furnish a counterfeit imitation of sprinkled bran. [2] But although I am not enriched by the chill starkness of foreign rocks, still my buildings—call them cottages or huts as you please—have their native coolness. However, I want you to hear what we have rather than what we have not. 8. Attached to this hall is an external appendage on the east side, a *piscina* (swimming-pool), or, if you prefer the Greek word, a *baptisterium*, which holds about 20,000 *modii*. [3] Those who come out of the heat after the bath find a triple entrance thrown open to them in

reseratur. nec pilae sunt mediae sed columnae, quas architecti peritiores aedificiorum purpuras nuncupavere. in hanc ergo piscinam fluvium de supercilio montis elicitum canalibusque circumactis per exteriora natatoriae latera curvatum sex fistulae prominentes leonum simulatis capitibus effundunt, quae temere ingressis veras dentium crates, meros oculorum furores, certas cervicum iubas imaginabuntur. 9. hic si dominum seu domestica seu hospitalis turba circumstet, quia prae strepitu caduci fluminis mutuae vocum vices minus intelleguntur, in aurem sibi populus confabulatur; ita sonitu pressus alieno ridiculum adfectat publicus sermo secretum. hinc egressis frons triclinii matronalis offertur, cui continuatur vicinante textrino cella penaria discriminata tantum pariete castrensi. 10. ab ortu lacum porticus intuetur, magis rotundatis fulta coluriis [1] quam columnis invidiosa monobilibus. a parte vestibuli longitudo tecta intrinsecus patet mediis non interpellata parietibus, quae, quia nihil ipsa prospectat, etsi non hypodromus, saltim cryptoporticus meo mihi iure vocitabitur. haec tamen

[1] coluriis *Sirmond* : collyriis.

---

[1] It seems almost certain that *purpurae* means columns of porphyry (*purpureus lapis*, Lucan X. 116). *Columnae* are cylindrical, *pilae* may be pilasters or half-cylindrical pillars. These two words are contrasted by Seneca (*N.Q.* VI. 20. 6) and Petronius (c. 79), and twice in the scholia on Horace, *Sat.* I. 4. 71. *Mediae* is difficult. I take it to mean that only the middle one of the three entrances had " purple " columns.

the centre of the wall, with separate archways. The middle supports are not pillars but columns, of the kind that high-class architects have called "purples."[1] A stream is "enticed from the brow"[2] of the mountain, and diverted through conduits which are carried round the outer sides of the swimming-bath; it pours its waters into the pool from six projecting pipes with representations of lions' heads: to those who enter unprepared they will give the impression of real rows of teeth, genuine wildness in the eyes and unmistakable manes upon the neck. 9. If the owner is surrounded here by a crowd of his own people or of visitors, so difficult is it to exchange words intelligibly, owing to the roar of the falling stream, that the company talk right into each other's ears; and so a perfectly open conversation, overpowered by this din from without, takes on an absurd air of secrecy. On leaving this place one comes across the front of the ladies' dining-room; joined on to this, with only a barrack partition[3] between them, is the household store-room, next to which is the weaving-room. 10. On the east a portico overlooks the lake; it is supported on round composite pillars rather than by a pretentious array of monolithic columns. On the side of the vestibule extends inward a length of covered passage —covered but open, being unbroken by partitions; this corridor has no view of its own, so, although it cannot claim to be a hypodrome,[4] at any rate I am entitled to call it a crypt-portico. At the end of

---

[2] Verg. *Georg.* I. 108 sq.

[3] Presumably a flimsy partition, or one which does not extend all the way from floor to roof; but the expression does not seem to be found elsewhere.

[4] Underground passage.

aliquid spatio suo in extimo deambulacri capite
defrudans efficit membrum bene frigidum, ubi
publico lectisternio exstructo clientularum sive
nutricum loquacissimus chorus receptui canit
cum ego meique dormitorium cubiculum petierimus.
11. a cryptoporticu in hiemale triclinium venitur,
quod arcuatili camino saepe ignis animatus pulla
fuligine infecit. sed quid haec tibi, quem nunc ad
focum minime invito? quin potius ad te tempusque
pertinentia loquar. ex hoc triclinio fit in diaetam
sive cenatiunculam transitus, cui fere totus lacus
quaeque tota lacui patet. in hac stibadium et
nitens abacus, in quorum aream sive suggestum a
subiecta porticu sensim non [1] breviatis angusta-
tisque gradibus ascenditur. quo loci recumbens, si
quid inter edendum vacas, prospiciendi voluptatibus
occuparis. 12. iam si tibi ex illo conclamatissimo
fontium decocta referatur, videbis in calicibus
repente perfusis nivalium maculas et frusta nebularum
et illam lucem lubricam poculorum quadam quasi
pinguedine subiti algoris hebetatam. tum re-
spondentes poculis potiones, quarum rigentes cyathi
siticuloso cuique, ne dicam tibi granditer abstemio,

[1] non *om.* LVM[1].

---

[1] A *lectisternium publicum* was a sacred feast to appease the
gods, at which their images were placed on couches with food
set before them. Sidonius playfully uses this expression of the
midday meal of female slaves and dependents, with a glance
at the literal meaning of *lectisternium*, "spreading of a (dining-)
couch," combined with the other meaning of *publicum*,
"general"; one might say in English "a general spread."
In those troublous times many humble or distressed people put
themselves under the protection of the great landowners; the
wives or daughters of such men, and possibly those of some

this passage, however, a part is stolen from it to form a very cool chamber, where a chattering crowd of female dependents and nursemaids spread a feast for the gods,[1] but sound the retreat when I and my family have set out for our bedrooms.[2] 11. From the crypt-portico we come to the winter dining-room, which the fire often called into life within the vaulted fireplace has stained with black soot. But why should I speak of this to you, when the last thing in my mind at this time is to bid you to the fireside? Rather let me speak of what better suits you and the time of year. From this dining-room we pass to a living-room or small dining-room, all of which lies open to the lake and to which almost the whole lake lies open. In this room are a semicircular dining-couch and a glittering sideboard, and on to the floor or platform on which they stand there is a gentle ascent from the portico by steps which are not made either short or narrow. Reclining in this place, you are engrossed by the pleasures of the view whenever you are not busy with the meal. 12. Then if a chilled drink is brought you from that most celebrated of springs, you will see in the cups, when they are suddenly filled to the brim, spots and crumbs of snowy mist, and the glossy glitter which cups have is dimmed by the greasy-looking film produced by sudden cold. Then there are the drinks that are suited to the cups, icy ladlefuls of them, which might be dreaded by the most thirsty of men, to say nothing of you, who are supremely abstemious. From this place

---

coloni (tenant-farmers) and other workers on the estate, might be included under the term *clientulae.*

[2] *i.e.* for the siesta.

metuerentur. hinc iam spectabis ut promoveat alnum piscator in pelagus, ut stataria retia suberinis corticibus extendat aut signis per certa intervalla dispositis tractus funium librentur hamati, scilicet ut nocturnis per lacum excursibus rapacissimi salares in consanguineas agantur insidias : quid enim hinc congruentius dixerim, cum piscis pisce decipitur ? 13. edulibus terminatis excipiet te deversorium, quia minime aestuosum, maxime aestivum; nam per hoc, quod in Aquilonem solum patescit, habet diem, non habet solem, interiecto consistorio perangusto, ubi somnulentiae cubiculariorum dormitandi potius quam dormiendi locus est. 14. hic iam quam volupe auribus insonare cicadas meridie concrepantes, ranas crepusculo incumbente blaterantes, cygnos atque anseres concubia nocte clangentes, intempesta gallos gallinacios concinentes, oscines corvos voce triplicata puniceam surgentis Aurorae facem consalutantes, diluculo autem Philomelam inter frutices sibilantem, Prognen inter asseres minurrientem ! cui concentui licebit adiungas fistulae septiforis armentalem Camenam, quam saepe nocturnis carminum certaminibus insomnes nostrorum montium Tityri exercent, inter greges tinnibulatos per depasta buceta reboantes. quae tamen varia vocum cantuumque modulamina profundius confovendo sopori tuo lenocinabuntur. 15. porticibus egresso, si portum litoris petas, in area virenti

you will see how the fisherman propels his boat into
the deep water, how he spreads his stationary nets
on cork floats, and how lengths of rope with hooks
attached are poised there, with marks arranged at
regular intervals, so that the greedy trout, in
their nightly forays through the lake, may be
lured to kindred bait: for what more suitable
phrase could I find in this case, when fish is caught
by fish? 13. When you have finished your meal,
a drawing-room will offer you welcome, one which is
truly a summer room because it is not in the least
sun-baked, for, as it is open to the north only, it
admits daylight but not sunshine; before you
reach it there is a narrow ante-chamber, where
the somnolence of the ushers has room to doze
rather than to sleep. 14. How charming it is here
to have echoing in one's ears the midday chirp of
cicalas, the croaking of the frogs as evening comes
on, the honking of swans and geese in the early
hours of slumber, the crowing of cocks in the
small hours; to hear the prophetic rooks greeting
with thrice-repeated cry the red torch of rising
dawn, Philomela piping in the bushes in the half-
light, and Procne twittering amid the rafters! To
this concert you may add if you please the pastoral
muse with seven-holed flute, which often many a
Tityrus of our mountains, forgoing sleep, keeps
sounding in a nocturnal competition of song, among
the belled sheep whose cries echo through the
pastures as they crop the grass. Yet all these
changeful tones of music and cries will but fondle
and coax your slumber and make it all the deeper.
15. Issuing from the shelter of the colonnades, if
you make for the lakeside harbour, you find your-

THE LETTERS OF SIDONIUS

vulgare iubar,[1] quamquam non procul nemus:
ingentes tiliae duae conexis frondibus, fomitibus
abiunctis unam umbram non una radice conficiunt.
in cuius opacitate, cum me meus Ecdicius inlustrat,
pilae vacamus, sed hoc eo usque, donec arborum
imago contractior intra spatium ramorum recussa
cohibeatur atque illic aleatorium lassis consumpto
sphaeristerio faciat. 16. sed quia tibi, sicut aedi-
ficium solvi, sic lacum debeo, quod restat agnosce.
lacus in Eurum defluus meat, eiusque harenis
fundamenta impressa domicilii ventis motantibus
aestuans umectat alluvio. is quidem sane circa
principia sui solo palustri voraginosus et vestigio
inspectoris inadibilis: ita limi bibuli pinguedo
coalescit ambientibus sese fontibus algidis, litoribus
algosis. attamen pelagi mobilis campus cumbulis
late secatur pervagabilibus, si flabra posuere; si
turbo austrinus insorduit, immane turgescit, ita ut
arborum comis quae margini insistunt superiectae
asperginis fragor impluat. 17. ipse autem secundum mensuras quas ferunt nauticas in decem
et septem stadia procedit, fluvio intratus, qui

---

[1] iubar *add. ego.*

---

[1] Lucan V. 220, where darkness shuts off from the Delphic
prophetess the vision she has just had, and she emerges from
it into the ordinary daylight: *refertur ad volgare iubar.* In
the present passage I have inserted *iubar,* which might easily
have dropped out after *vulgare.* If the reading in the text be
not adopted, it seems best to read *egressus* for *egresso* and to
take *vulgare* as a verb: " you are made public," *i.e.* " you are
exposed to view "; but the meanings of this verb when
applied to persons do not favour such a use, even in jest.
Sidonius has several references to and reminiscences of Lucan,
and quotes him in I. 11. 7, above.

[2] There is a play on words here; the lustre shed by the

430

self exposed to " the light of common day "[1] on a
stretch of green; but there is a wooded patch not
far off, where two enormous limes link the foliage of
their separate stocks to produce a single shade from
a twofold root. In that dark shelter, when my dear
Ecdicius sheds his lustre upon me,[2] we find recreation
at ball, but only until the diminishing shadow of the
trees is driven backward and confined within the
range of the branches[3] and makes there a dicing-
space for people tired after their ball-game. 16. Now
that I have duly presented the building to you I
must still give you the lake; so listen to what
remains. The lake flows downwards towards the
east, and its wash, which surges as the wind drives
it, moistens the foundations of the house, which are
sunk in its sandy bottom. At its beginning it has
an expanse of marshy soil with deep pools, and no
would-be sight-seer can get near, thanks to the
greasy mixture of oozing slime amid an intertwining
labyrinth of cold streams and weed-grown banks.
But the moving plain of open water is cut in all
directions by small boats flitting about everywhere,
if the wind has fallen; but if a gale from the south
brings dirty weather, it forms stupendous waves, so
that the breaking of the overcast spray comes down
like rain on the foliage of the trees which stand on
the bank. 17. The lake itself, according to what is
called nautical measurement, has a length of seventeen stadia,[4] and is entered by a stream which is

glorious Ecdicius is contrasted with the dark shade (*opacitas*)
of the woodland.   [3] *i.e.* until the sun is overhead.
    [4] The stadium, a Greek measure, was used by the Romans
for nautical and astronomical measurements. Seventeen
stadia would be equal to 2⅛ Roman miles, *i.e.* almost exactly
two English miles.

salebratim saxorum obicibus adfractus spumoso
canescit impulsu et nec longum scopulis praecipitibus exemptus lacu conditur; quem fors fuat
an incurrat an faciat, praeterit certe, coactus per
cola subterranea deliquari, non ut fluctibus, sed
ut piscibus pauperetur;[1] qui repulsi in gurgitem
pigriorem carnes rubras albis abdominibus extendunt:
ita illis nec redire valentibus nec exire permissis
quendam vivum et circumlaticium carcerem cor-
pulentia facit. 18. lacus ipse, qua dexter, incisus
flexuosus nemorosusque, qua laevus, patens herbosus
aequalis. aequor ab Africo viride per litus, quia
in undam fronde porrecta ut glareas aqua, sic aquas
umbra perfundit. huiusmodi colorem ab oriente
par silvarum corona continuat. per Arctoum latus
ut pelago natura, sic species. a Zephyro plebeius
et tumultuarius frutex frequenterque lemborum
superlabentum ponderibus inflexus; hunc circa
lubrici scirporum cirri plicantur simulque pingues
ulvarum paginae natant salicumque glaucarum fota

---

[1] pauperetur *ego* : pauperaretur.

---

[1] This is a literal translation. The drains are likened to
sieves or strainers because the apertures are covered by some
kind of fine network or grating through which the water can
filter but the fishes cannot pass. Apparently there was at this
end of the lake a creek or inlet, which, since the current flowed
in that direction, Sidonius regards as a continuation of the
stream which flows into the lake at the other end. At the far
end of this inlet there are drains to carry off the surplus water.
The fishes are carried by the current into the inlet; they cannot
get into the drains, and, of course, there is a bank or dam to
stop further progress. Here the water which does not vanish
through the drains is in constant commotion, hurled back and
whirling round, and the fishes are carried round with it till they
get back to the less agitated water, where they congregate like
salmon at the bottom of a salmon-leap and grow fat and

roughly broken by rocky barriers and so whitens
with splashes of foam, and presently frees itself from
the steep rocks and buries itself in the lake.   Whether
it so happens that this river creates the lake or
merely that it runs into it, it certainly passes beyond
it, being strained through subterranean sieves,[1] with
the result that it undergoes a deprivation, not of its
waters but of its fish.   These are thrown back into
the more sluggish water, where they increase the
bulk of red flesh in their white bellies;[2] and so
it goes on: they are not able to make their way
back or to find a way out, and their obesity creates
for them what one may call a living circulatory prison.
18. As for the lake itself, on its right bank it is
indented, winding and wooded; on the left, open,
grassy and even.   On the south-west the water is
green along the shore, because the foliage stretches
over the water, and just as the water floods the
gravel, so the shade floods the water.   On the east
a like fringe of trees spreads a tint of the same
kind.   On the northern side the water presents its
natural appearance.   On the west is a vulgar and
disorderly growth of weeds, which is often bent
under the weight of the yachts that speed over it;
round this growth slippery tufts of bulrushes wrap
themselves; thick slabs of sedge also float there,
and the bitter sap of grey willows is ever nurtured

sluggish. They have not the strength or energy to struggle
back to the lake against the current; their only motion is a
repetition of the same old gyration—up to the drains, round,
and back again. At any rate, this is the best I can make of a
very obscure passage.

[2] This reference to their corpulence may contain also a side-
reference to the appearance of the bellies, white or silvery
flecked with red. See n. on *Carm.* 18. 10.

semper dulcibus aquis amaritudo. 19. in medio profundi brevis insula, ubi supra molares naturaliter aggeratos per impactorum puncta remorum navalibus trita gyris meta protuberat, ad quam se iucunda ludentum naufragia collidunt. nam moris istic fuit senioribus nostris agonem Drepanitanum Troianae superstitionis imitari. iam vero ager ipse, quamquam hoc supra debitum, diffusus in silvis pictus in pratis, pecorosus in pascuis in pastoribus peculiosus. 20. sed non amplius moror, ne, si longior stilo terminus, relegentem te autumnus inveniat. proinde mihi tribue veniendi celeritatem (nam redeundi moram tibi ipse praestabis), daturus hinc veniam, quod brevitatem sibi debitam paulo scrupulosior epistula excessit, dum totum ruris situm sollicita rimatur; quae tamen summovendi fastidii studio nec cuncta perstrinxit. quapropter bonus arbiter et artifex lector non paginam, quae spatia describit, sed villam, quae spatiosa describitur, grandem pronuntiabunt. vale.

---

[1] The boat-race described by Virgil in *Aen.* V. 114 sqq.

by these sweet waters. 19. In the middle of the deep part is a small island. Here a turning-post sticks up on the top of a natural accumulation of boulders; it is worn by the dents of oars dashed against it in the course of the circling evolutions of the ships, and it is the scene of the jolly wrecks of vessels which collide at the sports. For here it was the traditional custom of our elders to imitate the contest of Drepanum in the mythical tale of Troy.[1] Further, let me say of the land around (though this is going beyond my obligation) that it is extensive in its woodland and nicely coloured in its flowers, with plenty of sheep in its pastures and plenteous savings in the shepherds' purses. 20. But I will detain you no longer, for if I let my pen run on further, the autumn may find you still reading. So grant me only the favour of a speedy arrival (for you will allow yourself a prolonged stay as a favour to yourself), and find excuses for me inasmuch as my letter by its rather excessive precision has outrun its proper limit of length whilst anxiously scrutinizing the whole lay-out of this country estate—though even so, it has left some points untouched, in order to avoid tedium. And so the fair-minded judge and the reader of expert taste will decide that the bigness is not in the letter which has an estate of so much size to describe, but in the estate which has so much size to need description. Farewell.

III

SIDONIVS FELICI SVO
SALVTEM

1. Gaudeo te, domine maior, amplissimae digni-
tatis infulas consecutum. sed id mihi ob hoc solum
destinato tabellario nuntiatum non minus gaudeo;
nam licet in praesentiarum sis potissimus magistratus
et in lares Philagrianos patricius apex tantis post
saeculis tua tantum felicitate remeaverit, invenis
tamen, vir amicitiarum servantissime, qualiter
honorum tuorum crescat communione fastigium,
raroque genere exempli altitudinem tuam humi-
litate sublimas. 2. sic quondam Quintum Fabium
magistrum cquitum dictatorio rigori ct Papirianac
superbiae favor publicus praetulit; sic et Gnaeum
Pompeium super aemulos extulit numquam fastidita
popularitas; sic invidiam Tiberianam pressit univer-
sitatis amore Germanicus. quocirca nolo sibi de
successibus tuis principalia beneficia plurimum
blandiantur, quae nihil tibi amplius conferre potu-
erunt quam ut, si id noluissemus, transiremur inviti.
illud peculiare tuum est, illud gratiae singularis,
quod tam qui te aemulentur non habes quam non
invenis qui sequantur. vale.

---

* On Felix see *Carm.* 9. 1 n. This letter congratulates him
on his elevation to the patriciate, which he apparently received
when Praetorian Prefect of Gaul. He may have succeeded
Arvandus in this office in A.D. 469; Sundwall can scarcely be
right in suggesting 474–475 as the date of his prefectship.

¹ See *Carm.* 7. 156 n.

² Q. Fabius Maximus, Master of the Horse to L. Papirius
Cursor, fought against the Samnites in 325 B.C. in defiance of the
dictator's orders, and was with difficulty saved from execu-

III

SIDONIUS TO HIS DEAR FELIX, GREETING *

1. I am delighted, my honoured lord, that you have gained the insignia of the most exalted dignity; and I am no less delighted that the news has been sent me by a special messenger; for though you are at present a magistrate of the highest rank and through your success alone the patrician honour has found its way back after so many generations to the house of the Philagrii,[1] yet you, with your characteristic regard for the claims of friendship, find ways of enhancing the greatness of your lofty dignities by geniality, and in a fashion far from common you raise your elevation still higher by a lowly spirit. 2. So in old days the approval of the public raised Quintus Fabius, the Master of the Horse, above the stern dictator, above the haughty Papirius;[2] so Pompey, who never disdained to be the people's man, was exalted above his rivals; so Germanicus, through the affection of the whole world, rose superior to the jealousy of Tiberius. Therefore I don't want the bounty of the Emperor to flatter itself by taking the chief credit for your success. The most it could have done for you would have been to make us reluctantly let you get ahead of us, supposing we had been unwilling; but the special feature of your case, a feature of peculiar charm, is that you never find people jealous of you any more than you find them rivalling you. Farewell.

tion by the intercession of the senate and the people and his aged father. He became the mainstay of Rome in the Second Samnite War.

IV

SIDONIVS SAGITTARIO SVO
SALVTEM

1. Vir clarissimus Proiectus, domi nobilis et patre
patruoque spectabilibus, avo etiam praestantissimo
sacerdote conspicuus, amicitiarum tuarum, nisi
respuis, avidissime sinibus infertur, et cum illi
familiae splendor probitas morum, patrimonii
facultas iuventutis alacritas in omne decus pari
lance conquadrent, ita demum sibi tamen videbitur
ad arcem fastigatissimae felicitatis evectus, si
gratiae tuae sodalitate potiatur. 2. Optantii clarissimi viri nuper vita functi filiam, quod deo pro-
sperante succedat, licet a matre pupillae in coniugium
petierit obtinueritque, parum tamen votorum
suorum promotum censet effectum, nisi assensum
tuum super his omnibus seu sedulitate sua seu
precatu nostrae intercessionis adipiscatur. namque
ipse, quantum ad institutionem spectat puellae, in
locum mortui patris curarum participatione succedis,
conferendo virgini parentis adfectum, patroni
auctoritatem, tutoris officium. 3. quocirca, quia
dignus es ut domus tuae celeberrimam disciplinam
etiam procul positorum petat ambitus, sicut decet

---

* Sagittarius is not mentioned elsewhere.
[1] On the significance of the titles *clarissimus* and *spectabilis*
see Bury I. 19 sqq., Hodgkin I. 603, 620.

438

IV

SIDONIUS TO HIS FRIEND SAGITTARIUS, GREETING *

1. The honourable [1] Proiectus, a man of noble birth, who can claim the distinction of having a father and an uncle among the " Eminents " and also a grandfather who held an exalted position in the priesthood, is very eager to be received into the bosom of your friendship, if you are not averse. The lustre of his family, the uprightness of his character, the amplitude of his estate and the ardour of youth combine in equal measure to form a complete and well-balanced excellence, but he will not feel that he has reached the pinnacle of supreme happiness until he secures a share in your favour. 2. He has sought in marriage from her mother the daughter of the honourable Optantius, lately deceased; but although he has been successful in his suit—and may God bless the union!—still he considers that the fruition of his hopes is imperfectly accomplished unless in addition to all this felicity he obtains your approval either by his own assiduity or through my supplication as intercessor. For as regards the girl's upbringing you are yourself stepping into the dead father's place as a sharer in the responsibilities, bringing to the maiden at once a parent's love, a protector's support and a guardian's service. 3. So since it is no more than you deserve if the aspirations even of total strangers should seek a place in a family so famous for its good government as yours is, please act as befits a statesman of the honest party, and reward the modest appeal of your

439

bonarum partium viros, benignitate responsi proci
supplicis verecundiam munerare et, qui ita expetitus
deberes illi expetere pollicendam, securus permitte [1]
promissam, quia sic te condicioni huic meritorum
ratio praefecit, ut nec superstiti Optantio in liberos
suos decuerit plus licere.   vale.

V

SIDONIVS PETRONIO SVO
SALVTEM

1. Iohannes familiaris meus inextricabilem laby-
rinthum negotii multiplicis incurrit et donec suarum
merita chartarum vel vestra scientia vel si qua est
vestrae (si tamen est ulla) similis inspexerit, quid
respuat, quid optet ignorat.   ita se quodammodo
bipertitae litis forma confundit, ut propositio sua quem
actionis ordinem propugnatura, quem sit impug-
natura, non noverit.   2. pro quo precem sedulam
fundo, ut perspectis chartulis suis si quid iure
competit instruatis, quae qualiterve sint obicienda,
quae refellenda monstrantes.   non enim verebimur
quod causae istius cursus, si de vestri manaverit
fonte consilii, ulla contrastantum derivatione tenu-
etur.   vale.

[1] permitte M^2T^2 :   promitte.

---

* For Petronius see n. on I. 7. 4.

suppliant suitor by the kindness of your answer.
Had you yourself been so approached you would
have been right in approaching her mother in turn
and pressing for her approval of the match; but as
it is, I ask you to sanction without hesitation an
approval already given. Your kindness to the
family has conferred upon you such a position of
authority in the matter of this betrothal that even
had Optantius been living he would have had no
right to exercise a fuller control over his own children.
Farewell.

V

SIDONIUS TO HIS FRIEND PETRONIUS, GREETING *

1. My friend Iohannes is rushing into the hopeless
labyrinth of a complicated litigation, and until the
merits of his documents are examined by your
learning or by some learning like yours (if there is
any such), he does not know what to choose and what
to reject. His suit is a sort of two-sided one, and its
form is so perplexing that he does not know what
line of procedure his pleading should be ready to
advocate or to dispute. 2. On his behalf I pour
forth an earnest petition that you will go through
his papers and get ready any plea that is legally
competent, instructing him what contentions to put
forward and how, also what ones to refute. For if
the current of his case starts from the head-waters
of your advice, I have no fear of its being weakened
through any diversion of the stream by his opponents.
Farewell.

VI

SIDONIVS PEGASIO SVO
SALVTEM

1. Proverbialiter celebre est saepe moram esse meliorem, sicuti et nunc experti sumus. Menstruanus amicus tuus longo istic tempore inspectus meruit inter personas nobis quoque caras devinctasque censeri, opportunus elegans, verecundus sobrius, parcus religiosus et his morum dotibus praeditus ut, quotiens in boni cuiusque adscitur amicitias, non amplius consequatur beneficii ipse quam tribuat. 2. haec tibi non ut ignoranti, sed ut iudicio meo satisfacerem, scripsi. quam ob rem triplex causa laetandi : tibi prima, cui amicos sic aut instituere aut eligere contingit; Arvernis secunda, quibus hoc in eo placuisse confirmo, quod te probasse non ambigo; illi tertia, de quo boni quique bona quaeque iudicaverunt. vale.

VII

SIDONIVS EXPLICIO SVO
SALVTEM

1. Quia iustitia vestra iure fit universitati per complura recti experimenta venerabilis, idcirco singulas quasque personas id ipsum efflagitantes

---

* Pegasius and Menstruanus are otherwise unknown.
† Nothing further is known of Explicius.

VI

SIDONIUS TO HIS FRIEND PEGASIUS, GREETING *

1. It is a proverbial platitude that delay is often the better course, and now I have found it so. Your friend Menstruanus, having been here for a long time under my eye, has won the right to be counted also amongst *my* dear and devoted friends. He is a congenial companion, with refined manners; he is modest and temperate, thrifty and religious, and endowed with so excellent a character that when he is invited to share the friendship of any of the best people he contributes no less benefit than he gains. 2. This I write, not because it is news to you, but to do justice to my good opinion of him. There are thus three grounds for rejoicing: you have one, in having the good fortune to train up or to choose friends so successfully; the Arverni have another, for I can state with confidence that they have found in him the merit which I am clear that you recognised; and he has the third, in that the best people have formed the best possible opinion of him. Farewell.

VII

SIDONIUS TO HIS FRIEND EXPLICIUS, GREETING †

1. Since your impartiality is rightly respected by the world at large as a result of many experiences of your rectitude, I gladly and eagerly dispatch all and sundry (as indeed they themselves urgently

in examen vestrum libens et avidus emitto, quam primum ambiens me discussionis, illos simultatis onere laxari; quod demum ita sequetur, si non ex solido querimonias partium verecundus censor excludas; quamquam et hoc ipsum, quod copiam tui iurgantibus difficile concedis, indicium sit bene iudicaturi : quis enim se non ambiat arbitrum legi aut pretio aliquid indulturus aut gratiae ? 2. igitur ignosce ad tam sanctae conscientiae praerogativam raptim perniciterque properantibus, quandoquidem sententiam tuam nec victus ut stolidus accusat nec victor ut argutus inridet, veritatisque respectu dependunt tibi addicti reverentiam, gratiam liberati. proinde impense obsecro ut inter Alethium et Paulum quae veniunt in disceptationem, mox ut utrimque fuerint opposita, discingas. namque, ni fallor, supra decemvirales pontificalesque sententias aegritudini huius prope interminabilis iurgii sola morum tuorum temperantia solita iudicandi salubritate medicabitur. vale.

---

[1] This interpretation of the words is due to Dr. Semple, *Quaest. Exeg.*, p. 14.

desire) to be weighed in the scales of your judgment. My design in so doing is to get myself relieved at the earliest possible moment from the burden of examining the case and them from the burden of a quarrel. This will be accomplished only if your modest reluctance to play the censor does not lead you to shut out the grievances of the parties entirely from your presence,—and yet the very fact that you are so unwilling to give a hearing to disputants is an indication that your judgment will be fair; for who would not seek to be chosen as umpire if he were ready to concede something to bribery or favour? 2. Be gentle, therefore, to those who are now hurrying with all haste and speed to seek the advantage of your strict sense of right, for when you give the verdict the defeated party never impugns it with the idea that he has been outwitted, nor does the successful party sneer at it with the idea that he has played a clever trick,[1] but in recognition of your honesty the condemned respect you and the acquitted are grateful to you. And so with the points at issue between Alethius and Paulus: I earnestly entreat you to settle them as soon as each side has stated its case; for in my opinion, better than any decisions of decemviri or pontifices, the mere moderation of your character will be able to cure the painfulness of this almost interminable dispute by virtue of your usual health-giving judgment. Farewell.

VIII

SIDONIVS DESIDERATO SVO SALVTEM

1. Maestissimus haec tibi nuntio. decessit nudius
tertius non absque iustitio matrona Philomathia,
morigera coniunx domina clemens, utilis mater
pia filia, cui debuerit domi forisque persona minor
obsequium, maior officium, aequalis adfectum. haec
cum esset unica iam diu matris amissae, facile diversis
blandimentorum generibus effecerat ne patri adhuc
iuveni subolis sexus alterius desideraretur. nunc
autem per subita suprema virum caelibatu, patrem
orbitate confodit. his additur quod quinque liberum
parens inmaturo exitu reddidit infortunatam fecundi-
tatem. qui parvuli si matre sospite perdidissent
iam diu debilem patrem, minus pupilli existimarentur.
2. hanc tamen, si quis haud incassum honor cada-
veribus impenditur, non vispillonum sandapilari-
orumque ministeria ominosa tumulavere; sed cum
libitinam ipsam flentes omnes, externi quoque,
prensitarent remorarentur exoscularentur, sacerdotum propinquorumque manibus excepta perpetuis
sedibus dormienti similior inlata est. post quae
precatu parentis orbati neniam funebrem non per

---

* Desideratus is otherwise unknown.

VIII

SIDONIUS TO HIS FRIEND DESIDERATUS, GREETING *

1. I write to you in the greatest grief. Three days ago there departed from us amid general mourning the Lady Philomathia, a dutiful wife and a kind mistress, a busy mother and a devoted daughter, one to whom in social and domestic life her inferiors owed respect, her superiors consideration, her equals affection. Although she was an only child and had lost her mother long before, yet by her many charming ways she easily prevented her father, who was still in the prime of life, from grieving over his lack of offspring of the other sex. Now by her sudden death she has dealt a cruel blow both to the husband whom she has left a widower and to the father whom she has left childless. Another trouble is that she was the mother of five children, and her untimely decease has made her large family a misfortune. If the little ones had kept their mother and lost their father, who has long been disabled, they would seem less orphaned. 2. But happily in her case (if there is aught but vanity in the honours paid to dead bodies) it was not by the ill-omened offices of common bearers and attendants that she was laid in the tomb; on the contrary, whilst all who attended, even those outside the family circle, clasped the very bier, held it back and kissed it, her body was lifted up by the hands of the clergy and her relatives, and she was conveyed to her everlasting home, more like one asleep. After this, at the request of her bereaved father, I com-

elegos sed per hendecasyllabos marmori incisam
planctu prope calente dictavi. quam si non satis
improbas, ceteris epigrammatum meorum voluminibus applicandam mercennarius bybliopola suscipiet; si quod secus, sufficit saxo carmen saxeum
contineri. 3. hoc enim epitaphion est :

> Occasu celeri feroque raptam
> gnatis quinque patrique coniugique
> hoc flentis patriae manus locarunt
> matronam Philomathiam sepulchro.
> o splendor generis, decus mariti,   5
> prudens casta decens severa dulcis
> atque ipsis senioribus sequenda,
> discordantia quae solent putari
> morum commoditate copulasti :
> nam vitae comites bonae fuerunt   10
> libertas gravis et pudor facetus.
> hinc est quod decimam tuae saluti
> vix actam trieteridem dolemus
> atque in temporibus vigentis aevi
> iniuste tibi iusta persoluta.   15

Placeat carmen necne : tu propera civitatemque
festinus invise; debes enim consolationis officium
duorum civium domibus adflictis. quod ita solvas
deum quaeso, ne umquam tibi redhibeatur. vale.

posed, almost before the violence of my grief had abated, a funeral dirge, not in elegiacs but in hendecasyllables, and this has been engraved on marble. If you are not seriously displeased with it, the bookseller I employ will undertake to add it to the other sheets of my epigrams;[1] but if you feel otherwise about it, it is enough that a poem which is heavy as stone should be preserved on stone. 3. This is the funeral inscription:

" Torn from her father, husband, and five children by a swift and merciless death, the Lady Philomathia has been laid in this tomb by the hands of her weeping fellow-citizens. Pride of your family, glory of your husband, wise, chaste, gracious, upright and kind, a model even to your elders, you have by your sweet reasonableness combined things that are wont to be counted opposed, for a serious frankness and a merry modesty were the constant attendants of your virtuous life. For this cause do we grieve that you have hardly fulfilled three decades of existence and that in the years of vigorous life the last dues have been paid to you unduly soon."

Whether you like this poem or not, bestir yourself and make haste to visit our town; for you owe the duty of consolation to the afflicted families of two fellow-citizens. I pray God that you may discharge that duty without ever requiring a repayment of it for yourself. Farewell.

---

[1] For a discussion of this sentence see Introd., p. lxvi, n. 2.

IX

SIDONIVS DONIDIO SVO
SALVTEM

1. Quaeris cur ipse iampridem Nemausum pro-
fectus vestra serum ob adventum desideria producam.
reddo causas reditus tardioris nec moras meas prodere
moror, quia quae mihi dulcia sunt tibi quoque.
inter agros amoenissimos, humanissimos dominos,
Ferreolum et Apollinarem, tempus voluptuosissi-
mum exegi. praediorum his iura contermina,
domicilia vicina, quibus interiecta gestatio peditem
lassat neque sufficit equitaturo. colles aedibus su-
periores exercentur vinitori et olivitori: Aracynthum
et Nysam, celebrata poetarum carminibus iuga,
censeas. uni domui in plana patentiaque, alteri
in nemora prospectus; sed nihilo minus dissimilis
situs similiter oblectat. 2. quamquam de praediorum quid nunc amplius positione, cum restat hospitalitatis ordo reserandus? iam primum saga-
cissimis in hoc exploratoribus destinatis, qui reditus
nostri iter aucuparentur, domus utraque non solum
tramites aggerum publicorum verum etiam calles
compendiis tortuosos atque pastoria deverticula
insedit, ne quo casu dispositis officiorum insidiis
elaberemur. quas incidimus, fateor, sed minime

---

* Donidius was an Arvernian (III. 5. 3) and a *vir spectabilis*
(*ib.* § 1). See also VI. 5. On Tonantius see *Carm.* 24. 34 n.;
on Apollinaris, *ib.* 52 n.

1 For Aracynthus see note on *Carm.* 15. 32. The name
Nysa was applied to various mountains and places associated
with the cultivation of the vine and the legends of Dionysus;
an enumeration of them may be found in any classical
dictionary. Cf. *Carm.* 22. 233.

IX

SIDONIUS TO HIS FRIEND DONIDIUS, GREETING *

1. You ask me why, having started long ago for Nemausus, I am causing you so long a disappointment by my tardiness in arriving. I will give you my reasons for my belated return, and I will not be slow to explain my slowness, for what is pleasurable to me is so to you also. I have spent the most delicious time in visiting two charming properties and two most sympathetic hosts, Ferreolus and Apollinaris. Their estates have a common boundary, and their residences are near, being connected by a road which is long enough to tire the pedestrian but hardly long enough for a ride. The hills which rise above the buildings are cultivated by the vine-dresser and the olive-grower: you would think them Aracynthus and Nysa,[1] those heights so greatly lauded in poetic song. One house has a view over flat and open ground, the other looks out on woods; yet though they differ in their situation they are alike in their charm. 2. But why should I say more of the lie of the farms when there remains to be disclosed the whole scheme of my entertainment? First of all, the cleverest scouts were sent out to keep watch on the route of my return journey, and the two household staffs took up positions not only on the various courses of the public highways but also on the rough tracks with their intricate short cuts and on the bypaths used by shepherds, in order to leave me no chance of eluding the traps which their kindness had arranged. I admit that I was

451

inviti, iusque iurandum confestim praebere compulsi,
ne, priusquam septem dies evolverentur, quicquam
de itineris nostri continuatione meditaremur.
3. igitur mane cotidiano partibus super hospite prima
et grata contentio, quaenam potissimum anterius
edulibus nostris culina fumaret; nec sane poterat
ex aequo divisioni lancem ponere vicissitudo, licet
uni domui mecum, alteri cum meis vinculum foret
propinquitatis, quia Ferreolo praefectorio viro praeter
necessitudinem sibi debitam dabat aetas et dignitas
primi invitatoris praerogativam. 4. ilicet a deliciis
in delicias rapiebamur. vix quodcumque vestibulum
intratum, et ecce huc [1] sphaeristarum contrastantium
paria inter rotatiles catastropharum gyros du-
plicabantur, huc inter aleatoriarum vocum com-
petitiones frequens crepitantium fritillorum tessera-
rumque strepitus audiebatur; huc libri adfatim
in promptu (videre te crederes aut grammaticales
pluteos aut Athenaei cuneos aut armaria exstructa
bybliopolarum): sic tamen quod, qui inter matro-
narum cathedras codices erant, stilus his religiosus
inveniebatur, qui vero per subsellia patrumfamilias,
hi coturno Latiaris eloquii nobilitabantur; licet
quaepiam volumina quorumpiam auctorum servarent
in causis disparibus dicendi parilitatem: nam similis

---

[1] huc def. Mohr, Praef. p. xvii.

---

[1] Ferreolus was related to Papianilla, the wife of Sidonius.
We do not know the degree of relationship between Sidonius
and Apollinaris.

[2] The meaning is uncertain. See V. 17. 7 for a longer
description of a ball-game.

[3] Possibly Hadrian's famous educational institution at
Rome (IX. 14. 2), but various provincial towns copied both
the idea and the name (IX. 9. 13).

caught, but by no means against my will, and I was at once forced to take an oath that I would not give a thought to the resumption of my journey till seven days were passed. 3. Each morning saw the start of a really charming contest between the two parties about their guest, to decide which of the two kitchens should be the earlier to steam with my meal; and it was really impossible to keep the balance even by alternation, although one house had the tie of kinship with myself, the other with my family;[1] because Ferreolus is of prefectorian rank, and his age and standing, added to the just claims of his relationship, gave him a prior right to invite me. 4. Well, I was hurried from bliss to bliss. Hardly had I entered one vestibule or the other when behold! I found on one side opposing ball-players bending low amid the whirling evolutions of the *catastrophae*;[2] in another quarter I would hear the clatter of rattling dice-boxes and of dice mingled with the rival shouts of the gamesters; in another part were books in any number ready to hand; you might have imagined yourself looking at the shelves of a professional scholar or at the tiers in the Athenaeum[3] or at the towering presses of the booksellers. The arrangement was such that the manuscripts near the ladies' seats were of a devotional type, while those among the gentlemen's benches were works distinguished by the grandeur of Latin eloquence; the latter, however, included certain writings of particular authors which preserve a similarity of style though their doctrines are different;[4] for it was a

---

[4] *i.e.* Christian as well as pagan writers came in this category. Sidonius wishes to make it clear that Christian reading was not confined to the women.

THE LETTERS OF SIDONIUS

scientiae viri, hinc Augustinus hinc Varro, hinc
Horatius hinc Prudentius lectitabantur. 5. quos
inter Adamantius Origenes [1] Turranio Rufino inter-
pretatus sedulo fidei nostrae lectoribus inspiciebatur;
pariter et, prout singulis cordi, diversa censentes
sermocinabamur, cur a quibusdam protomystarum
tamquam scaevus cavendusque tractator impro-
baretur, quamquam sic esset ad verbum sententiam-
que translatus ut nec Apuleius Phaedonem sic
Platonis neque Tullius Ctesiphontem sic Demosthenis
in usum regulamque Romani sermonis exscripserint.
6. studiis hisce dum nostrum singuli quique, prout
libuerat, occupabantur, ecce et ab archimagiro
adventans, qui tempus instare curandi corpora
moneret, quem quidem nuntium per spatia clepsydrae
horarum incrementa servantem probabat competenter
ingressum quinta digrediens. prandebamus breviter

---

[1] *an* Origenis?

---

[1] *Scientia* here means expert skill, artistic mastery, as in
the next letter, § 6; the meaning " erudition " would not suit
the mention of Horace and Prudentius, who are compared as
masters of lyric poetry, and the previous sentence shows that
Sidonius is thinking only of style, or of style and diction. It
is strange to find Varro ranked as an artist in prose with
Augustine, and almost as strange to find him classed among
those " distinguished by the grandeur of Latin eloquence."
Sidonius expresses admiration for Varro's style also in *Epist.*
VIII. 6. 18. As a matter of fact, *scientia* in the sense of
erudition was the leading characteristic of Varro, as Quintilian
says in a passage which gives the lie direct to these two
sentences of Sidonius (Varro " is more likely to enhance one's
knowledge than one's style," *plus scientiae conlaturus quam
eloquentiae, Inst. Or.* X. 1. 95); and Augustine himself says very
much the same thing (*Civ. Dei* VI. 2). Augustine drew largely
upon Varro's historical and antiquarian researches, and
frequently mentions him in the *De Civitate Dei*. It may be a

454

frequent practice to read writers whose artistry was of a similar kind [1]—here Augustine, there Varro, here Horace, there Prudentius. 5. Amongst these books, the translation of the *Adamantius* of Origen by Turranius Rufinus [2] was diligently studied by readers of our faith. We would all join in a discussion, expressing our various views just as we felt inclined. We debated why Origen was condemned by some of our chief hierophants as an inept and dangerous expositor, and yet his works had been translated into Latin with such faithfulness to the letter and the spirit that Apuleius could not be said to have turned Plato's *Phaedo* or Tully Demosthenes' *Ctesiphon* [3] into such a perfect expression of the theory and the usage of Latin speech. 6. While all and sundry occupied themselves in these pursuits according to their individual tastes, a messenger would approach from the head cook to tell us that the time for refreshment was at hand. He had his eye on the passage of the hours as marked by the water-clock, and as the fifth hour was just departing he was proved to have arrived just at the right moment. The luncheon was at once short and

vague recollection of this that makes Sidonius compare the two as literary artists.

[2] Turranius (or Tyrannius) Rufinus, a contemporary of Jerome, translated the five books of dialogues " On the true belief in God," falsely ascribed to Origen, in which Adamantius is the chief speaker. The translation was certainly not faithful; Rufinus was fond of altering or modifying his originals, often in the direction of orthodoxy.

[3] These translations by Apuleius and Cicero are no longer extant, though we still possess Cicero's *De Optimo Genere Oratorum*, which was meant as an introduction to his translations of the speeches for and against Ctesiphon by Demosthenes (*De Corona*) and Aeschines (*In Ctesiphontem*).

copiose, senatorium [1] ad morem, quo insitum in-
stitutumque multas epulas paucis parabsidibus apponi,
quamvis convivium per edulia nunc assa nunc
iurulenta varietur. inter bibendum narratiunculae,
quarum cognitu hilararemur institueremur, quia
eas bifariam orditas laetitia peritiaque comitabantur.
quid multa? sancte pulchre abundanter accipie-
bamur. 7. inde surgentes, si Vorocingi eramus (hoc
uni praedio nomen), ad sarcinas et deversorium
pedem referebamus; si Prusiani (sic fundus alter

[1] seniorum *Fertig.*

---

[1] Notable among the many attempts to restrain the
extravagance of the upper classes in their feasts was the action
of C. Fabricius Luscinus, who as censor in 275 B.C. expelled
from the Senate P. Cornelius Rufinus (an ancestor of the
dictator Sulla: Plutarch, *Sull.* 1) because he possessed ten
pounds (or, according to another account, more than ten
pounds) of silver plate. This incident is recalled again and
again by writers of later ages (see, for example, the references
given by Friedlaender on Juvenal IX. 142), and it, or the law
(if there was such a law) on which Fabricius acted, is probably
the ultimate source of the custom mentioned here. Such
sumptuary restrictions as those of Fabricius and many others
were powerless to stem the tide of luxury, but it is interesting
to find his action cited even as late as Tertullian in order to
lash the extravagance of the times. In *Apol.* c. 6, after
referring to the expulsion of P. Cornelius from the Senate, he
goes on to say that in his time "whole mines of silver" are
wrought into dishes.

The word *parabsis* (*parapsis, paropsis*) is applied to a large
square dish: see Mayor on Juvenal III. 142.

[2] The difficulty of interpreting *deversorium* is greatly
increased by the use here of the first person plural. Nearly
everywhere in this paragraph the meaning must be really
plural, but if we take it so at the end of the first sentence we
shall have to assume that Sidonius was not the only guest
staying there at the time; otherwise the words *ad sarcinas
. . . referebamus* would scarcely be intelligible. This notion,

lavish, in the style of senators, who have an inherited and established practice of having abundant viands served up on few dishes,[1] although the meal is varied by having some of the meats roasted and others stewed. As we sat over our wine there were short stories, for amusement or instruction; they were started in two sets, bringing mirth and edification respectively. To sum up, our entertainment was moral, elegant, and profuse. 7. We then rose from table, and if we were at Vorocingus (this was the name of one of the estates) we returned to our baggage and our lodging;[2] if we were at Prusianum

however, seems at first sight to be contradicted by *assecularum meorum* in § 8; if there were other guests, their servants as well as those of Sidonius must have been included in the convivial company. But Sidonius would know and recognise his own servants, and it does not really follow that there were no servants of other guests in the indiscriminate crowd. Much difficulty is removed if we assume that the plural verbs have a plural meaning throughout the paragraph; moreover, several parts of this letter seem to imply that there were other guests besides Sidonius.

Deversorium may be applied to temporary quarters of various kinds. In I. 5. 9 it means "inn" or "boarding-house"; the latter is perhaps the meaning in VII. 2. 6. Here it seems to refer to some such accommodation near the house of Apollinaris. Building was still going on at both houses (§ 8 *init.*); it was indeed going on at Vorocingus when Sidonius wrote the epilogue to his poems, and his mention of it in *Carm.* 24. 54 sq. may have been suggested by what he had recently seen on the visit described here. Thus the inferences sometimes drawn from this letter about the limited accommodation at Gallo-Roman country-houses must not be taken too seriously.

Dr. Semple makes the tempting suggestion that *deversorium* both here and in II. 2. 13 means "guest-room." We should then have to suppose that Sidonius was staying with Apollinaris at Vorocingus, and that after lunching there he simply retired to his own room for the siesta; on the other hand, when he had lunched at Prusianum, one of the sons of

457

THE LETTERS OF SIDONIUS

nuncupabatur), Tonantium cum fratribus, lectissimos
aequaevorum nobilium principes, stratis suis eicie-
bamus, quia nec facile crebro cubilium nostrorum
instrumenta circumferebantur. excusso torpore meridiano paulisper equitabamus, quo facilius pectora
marcida cibis cenatoriae fami exacueremus.
8. balneas habebat in opere uterque hospes, in usu
neuter; sed cum vel pauxillulum bibere desisset
assecularum meorum famulorumque turba com-
potrix, quorum cerebris hospitales creterrae nimium
immersae dominabantur, vicina fonti aut fluvio
raptim scrobis fodiebatur, in quam forte cum lapidum
cumulus ambustus demitteretur, antro in hemi-
sphaerii formam corylis flexibilibus [1] intexto fossa
inardescens operiebatur, sic tamen ut superiectis
Cilicum velis patentia intervalla virgarum lumine
excluso tenebrarentur, vaporem repulsura salientem,
qui undae ferventis aspergine flammatis silicibus
excuditur. 9. hic nobis trahebantur horae non
absque sermonibus salsis iocularibusque; quos inter
halitu nebulae stridentis oppletis involutisque salu-
berrimus sudor eliciebatur; quo, prout libuisset,
effuso coctilibus aquis ingerebamur, quarumque [2]
fotu cruditatem nostram tergente resoluti aut fon-
tano deinceps frigore putealique aut fluviali copia

---

[1] flexilibus *R, fortasse recte.*
[2] quarumque *LV* : harumque (h *in ras. N*).

Ferreolus gave up his own bed to him. But the use of the
plural above mentioned seems against this view. Again, as
Sidonius tells us in § 4 that whenever he entered either
vestibule he found games going on, the most natural inference
is that he was not staying in either house. In the third place,
if he were staying with either of his hosts, surely he would
have told us which of them had the pleasure of putting him
up, especially as he makes so much in § 3 of their friendly

458

(so the other property was called) we turned out of their beds Tonantius [1] and his brothers, the flower of all the young nobles of their age, because it was not easy to carry our own sleeping-kit so often from place to place. After shaking off the midday drowsiness we took short rides to whet our appetites, jaded with eating, to the keenness needful for dinner. 8. Both my entertainers had baths in course of erection; in neither case were they in working order. However, when the convivial crowd consisting of my attendants and the household servants, whose heads the hospitable bowl was wont to souse and overpower, had left off drinking, at least for the moment, a trench would be hastily dug close to the spring or the river, and a pile of heated stones poured into it. Then while the ditch was heating it was roofed over with a dome constructed of pliant hazel twigs twined into a hemispherical shape; in addition, rugs of hair-cloth were thrown over this roof, shutting out the light and darkening the open spaces between the twigs, so as to keep in the rising steam which is created by pouring boiling water on hot stones. 9. Here we whiled away the hours with no lack of witty and humorous conversation, in the course of which we became wrapped and choked in the breath of the hissing mist, which drew forth a wholesome perspiration. When this had poured out sufficiently to please us we plunged into the hot water. Its kindly warmth relaxed us and cleared our clogged digestions, and then we braced ourselves in turn with the cold water of the spring and the well or in

contest for the pleasure of feeding him. In II. 2. 13, however, Dr. Semple's interpretation of *deversorium* may be right.

[1] The young Tonantius is mentioned in *Carm.* 24. 34.

solidabamur: siquidem domibus medius it Vardo
fluvius, nisi cum deflua nive pastus impalluit, flavis
ruber glareis et per alveum perspicuus quietus
calculosusque neque ob hoc minus piscium ferax
delicatorum. 10. dicerem et cenas et quidem
unctissimas, nisi terminum nostrae loquacitati,
quem verecundia non adhibet, charta posuisset;
quarum quoque replicatio fieret amoena narratu,
nisi epistulae tergum madidis sordidare calamis
erubesceremus. sed quia et ipsi in procinctu
sumus teque sub ope Christi actutum nobis invisere
placet, expeditius tibi cenae amicorum in mea
cena tuaque commemorabuntur, modo nos quam
primum hebdomadis exactae spatia completa votivae
restituant esuritioni, quia disruptum ganea stoma-
chum nulla sarcire res melius quam parsimonia solet.
vale.

X

SIDONIVS HESPERIO SVO
SALVTEM

1. Amo in te quod litteras amas et usquequaque
praeconiis cumulatissimis excolere [1] contendo tantae
diligentiae generositatem, per quam nobis non
solum initia tua verum etiam studia nostra com-

[1] extollere *T*.

---

[1] The Gard, a name known to most people from the famous
Pont du Gard, near Nîmes. This is the only passage where
the ancient name of the river is mentioned.

* Hesperius is praised also in IV. 22. 1. He taught the
son of Ruricius, three of whose letters are addressed to him.

the full flow of the river; for I should explain that
the river Vardo[1] flows midway between the houses.
Except when it is swollen by the melting of the
snows and turns yellowish, it has a red tinge caused
by the brownish shingle, and it passes down its
channels transparent, smooth, and pebbly, but is
none the less on that account prolific in choice
fishes. 10. I should have gone on to tell you of
our dinners—sumptuous ones, I assure you—had
not my paper imposed upon my chatter a limit
which my sense of decency is failing to set. The
record of these feasts would indeed form a pleasant
tale, did I not blush to disfigure the back of my
letter with a "soaked" pen. But as I am now
approaching you in person and intend with Christ's
help to visit you immediately, the dinners of my
friends will be more expeditiously related when you
and I are dining together. I only hope that the
completion of a week's interval will see the prompt
restoration of that feeling of hunger for which I
yearn: when the stomach is upset by a debauch,
nothing repairs it so well as abstemiousness.
Farewell.

X

SIDONIUS TO HIS FRIEND HESPERIUS, GREETING *

1. What I love in you is that you are a lover of
letters, and I strive everywhere to glorify with the
most profuse acclamations the noble spirit of your
great industry, by which you make me think well
not only of your first attempts but also of my own

461

mendas. nam cum videmus in huiusmodi disciplinam iuniorum ingenia succrescere, propter quam nos
quoque subduximus ferulae manum, copiosissi-
mum fructum nostri laboris adipiscimur. illud
appone, quod tantum increbruit multitudo desi-
diosorum ut, nisi vel paucissimi quique meram
linguae Latiaris proprietatem de trivialium bar-
barismorum robigine vindicaveritis, eam brevi
abolitam defleamus interemptamque : sic omnes
nobilium sermonum purpurae per incuriam vulg[i]
decolorabuntur. 2. sed istinc alias : interea tu
quod petis accipe. petis autem ut, si qui versiculi
mihi fluxerint postquam ab alterutro discessimus,
hos tibi pro quadam morarum mercede pernumerem.
dicto pareo ; nam praeditus es quamquam iuvenis
hac animi maturitate, ut tibi etiam natu priores
gerere morem concupiscamus. ecclesia nuper exstructa Lugduni est, quae studio papae Patientis
summum coepti operis accessit, viri sancti strenui,
severi misericordis quique per uberem munificentiam
in pauperes humanitatemque non minora bonae
conscientiae culmina levet. 3. huius igitur aedis
extimis rogatu praefati antistitis tumultuarium
carmen inscripsi trochaeis triplicibus adhuc mihi

---

[1] Juvenal I. 15.
[2] This church, which replaced an older one, was dedicated
to St. Justus. It was destroyed by the Huguenots in the
year 1562. Bishop Patiens of Lyons, a very wealthy prelate,
gave freely of his means for the building and restoration of
churches and for the relief of distress. When Euric laid waste
the lands which he overran after his victory in A.D. 471
(Introd., p. xxix), Patiens rescued the inhabitants from the

studies. For when I see our young men of ability
rising in their turn to cultivate that art in pursuit of
which I too " flinched from the rod," [1] I win a most
ample harvest from my own efforts. Consider too that
the mob of the sluggards has so grown in numbers that
unless there are at least a modest few like yourself to
defend the exact use of the language of Latium from
the rust of vulgar barbarisms, we shall in a short time
be lamenting its extinction and annihilation, so sadly
will all the bright ornaments of noble expression be
dulled by the slovenliness of the mob. 2. But of
this more some other time : meanwhile let me give
you what you ask for. It is your wish that, if any
humble verses have flowed from my pen since we
separated, I should deliver them to you as a kind of
payment for the length of my absence. I obey your
command ; for though you are young you are endowed
with such ripeness of mind that even we who are your
elders are eager to meet your wishes. A church
has recently been built at Lugdunum, and the
undertaking has come to the point of completion
through the zeal of Bishop Patiens,[2] a man both
holy and active, strict and compassionate, and one
who is building up by his noble generosity to the
poor and by his kindliness the not less lofty edifice
of a guileless conscience. 3. For the far end of this
temple, at the request of the aforesaid dignitary, I
have written offhand an inscription in the three-
trochee metre,[3] with which up to this date I, and

horrors of famine, and he rendered a similar service to Clermont
at a critical time. See *Epist.* VI. 12, which is addressed to him.
   [3] In *Carm.* 23. 25 sqq. the hendecasyllabic metre is more
fully described as consisting of a spondee, a dactyl, and three
trochees, *i.e.* $- - \mid - \smile \smile \mid - \smile \mid - \smile \mid - \smile$.

iamque tibi perfamiliaribus. namque ab hexametris eminentium poetarum Constantii et Secundini
vicinantia altari basilicae latera clarescunt, quos
in hanc paginam admitti nostra quam maxume
verecundia vetat, quam suas otiositates trepidanter
edentem meliorum carminum comparatio premit.
4. nam sicuti novam nuptam nihil minus quam
pulchrior pronuba decet, sicuti, si vestiatur albo,
fuscus quisque fit nigrior, sic nostra, quantula est
cumque, tubis circumfusa potioribus stipula vilescit,
quam mediam loco, infimam merito despicabiliorem
pronuntiari non imperitia modo sed et arrogantia
facit. quapropter illorum iustius epigrammata
micant quam istaec, quae imaginarie tantum et
quodammodo umbratiliter effingimus. sed quorsum
ista? quin potius paupertinus flagitatae cantilenae
culmus immurmuret.

> Quisquis pontificis patrisque nostri
> conlaudas Patientis hic laborem,
> voti compote supplicatione
> concessum experiare quod rogabis.
> aedis celsa nitet nec in sinistrum   5
> aut dextrum trahitur, sed arce frontis
> ortum prospicit aequinoctialem.
> intus lux micat atque bratteatum
> sol sic sollicitatur ad lacunar,
> fulvo ut concolor erret in metallo.   10
> distinctum vario nitore marmor
> percurrit cameram solum fenestras,
> ac sub versicoloribus figuris

---

[1] See introd. to I. 1.
[2] His poetry is praised in V. 8.

henceforth you also, can claim intimate familiarity. For the two sides of the basilica where they adjoin the altar are glorified by the hexameters of the eminent poets Constantius [1] and Secundinus; [2] these verses my modesty absolutely debars from a place in this letter, for a comparison with better poetry is too severe for a shrinking soul who is nervously exhibiting his own casual efforts. 4. For just as nothing becomes a bride so ill as a brideswoman of greater beauty, just as a man of dark skin is made blacker if clothed in white, so my humble pipe, puny as it is, becomes still meaner when set amid superior clarions; foisted into a place in their midst when it takes the lowest place in merit, it earns a double contempt by such a combination of presumption and incompetence. So the inscriptions by the poets I have named are more justly honoured than this of mine, which is a mere creation of hollow conceits and what may be called shadowy outlines. But why all this preamble? Rather let my sorry reed murmur the notes of the doggerel you have demanded of me:

" All you who here admire the work of Patiens, our bishop and father, may you by effectual supplication obtain the boon you ask for! The lofty temple sparkles and does not incline to right or left, but with its towering front faces the sunrise of the equinox. Within it the light flashes and the sunshine is so tempted to the gilded ceiling that it travels over the tawny metal, matching its hue. Marble diversified by various shining tints pervades the vaulting, [3] the floor, the windows; forming designs of diverse colour, a verdant grass-green encrustation brings winding lines

[3] This probably refers to the semi-dome over the apse, which regularly contained mosaic decoration.

vernans herbida crusta sapphiratos
flectit per prasinum vitrum lapillos.   15
huic est porticus applicata triplex
fulmentis Aquitanicis superba,
ad cuius specimen remotiora
claudunt atria porticus secundae,
et campum medium procul locatas   20
vestit saxea silva per columnas.
hinc agger sonat, hinc Arar resultat,
hinc sese pedes atque eques reflectit
stridentum et moderator essedorum,
curvorum hinc chorus helciariorum   25
responsantibus alleluia ripis
ad Christum levat amnicum celeuma.
sic, sic psallite, nauta vel viator;
namque iste est locus omnibus petendus,
omnes quo via ducit ad salutem.   30

5. Ecce parui tamquam iunior imperatis: tu
modo fac memineris multiplicato me faenore re-
munerandum, quoque id facilius possis voluptuosi-
usque, opus est ut sine dissimulatione lectites, sine
fine lecturias; neque patiaris ut te ab hoc proposito
propediem coniunx domum feliciter ducenda de-
flectat, sisque oppido meminens quod olim Marcia
Hortensio, Terentia Tullio, Calpurnia Plinio, Pudentilla Apuleio, Rusticiana Symmacho legentibus
meditantibusque candelas et candelabra tenuerunt.
6. certe si praeter oratoriam [1] contubernio feminarum
poeticum ingenium et oris tui limam frequentium
studiorum cotibus expolitam quereris obtundi, re-

---

[1] rem oratoriam *codd. plerique*: *fortasse* artem oratoriam.

---

[1] Cloisters, in front of the atrium. A "triple colonnade" is
one with three rows of columns.

of sapphire-hued stones over the leek-green glass. Attached to this edifice is a triple colonnade rising proudly on columns of the marble of Aquitania.[1] A second colonnade on the same plan closes the atrium at the farther end, and a stone forest clothes the middle area [2] with columns standing well apart. On one side is the noisy high-road, on the other the echoing Arar; on the first the traveller on foot or on horse and the drivers of creaking carriages turn round; on the other, the company of the bargemen, their backs bent to their work, raise a boatmen's shout to Christ, and the banks echo their alleluia. Sing, traveller, thus; sing, boatman, thus; for towards this place all should make their way, since through it runs the road which leads to salvation."
5. See now, I have obeyed your command as though I were your junior; remember, however, that I have to be repaid with multiple interest. That you may do so the more easily and pleasantly, you must read constantly and without carelessness, and your thirst for reading must be without limit. You must not allow the thought that you will soon be happily married to turn you from this determination, ever remembering that in the old times of Marcia and Hortensius, Terentia and Tullius, Calpurnia and Pliny, Pudentilla and Apuleius, Rusticiana and Symmachus, the wives held candles and candlesticks for their husbands whilst they read or composed.
6. And by all means, if you lament that in addition to your oratorical skill your poetical capacity and the keen edge of your tongue, which has been sharpened on the whetstone of industrious study, are blunted by the society of ladies, remember that

[2] The nave.

miniscere quod saepe versum Corinna cum suo
Nasone complevit, Lesbia cum Catullo, Caesennia
cum Gaetulico, Argentaria cum Lucano, Cynthia
cum Propertio, Delia cum Tibullo. proinde liquido
claret studentibus discendi per nuptias occasionem
tribui, desidibus excusationem. igitur incumbe,
neque apud te litterariam curam turba depretiet
imperitorum, quia natura comparatum est ut in
omnibus artibus hoc sit scientiae pretiosior pompa,
quo rarior. vale.

XI

SIDONIVS RVSTICO SVO
SALVTEM

1. Si nobis pro situ spatiisque regionum vicinare-
mur nec a se praesentia mutua vasti itineris longin-
quitate discriminaretur, nihil apicum raritati licere
in coeptae familiaritatis officia permitterem neque
iam semel missa fundamenta certantis amicitiae
diversis honorum generibus exstruere cessarem.
sed animorum coniunctioni separata utrique porrecti-
oribus terminis obsistit habitatio, equidem semel
devinctis parum nocitura pectoribus. 2. sed tamen
ex ipsa communium municipiorum discretione procedit quod, cum amicissimi simus, raritatem collo-
quii de prolixa terrarum interiectione venientem

---

¹ See *Carm.* 23. 161 n.   ² See *Carm.* 9. 259 n.
* Rusticus is mentioned in VIII. 11. 3 *carm.* 36. He lived
in or near Bordeaux. The language of this letter is extra-
ordinarily stilted.

Corinna [1] often helped her Naso to complete a verse, and so it was with Lesbia and Catullus, Caesennia and Gaetulicus,[2] Argentaria and Lucan, Cynthia and Propertius, Delia and Tibullus. So it is clear as daylight that literary workers find in marriage an opportunity for study and idlers an excuse for shirking it. To work, then, and do not let the cultivation of literature lose its value in your eyes because of the multitude of the ignorant; for it is a law of nature that in all the arts the splendour of attainment rises in value as it becomes rarer. Farewell.

XI

SIDONIUS TO HIS FRIEND RUSTICUS, GREETING *

1. If we were neighbours in respect of domicile and distance and if our meeting face to face were not held off by the long mileage of an enormous journey, I would never allow the rarity of letters to have any effect upon the attentions proper to the intimacy we have contracted; nor would I be slow about building on the foundations (already laid once for all) of an emulously cultivated friendship by piling up various manifestations of my regard. But the union of our souls is obstructed by the extended space between our habitations, though this can certainly never injure our affections, which are joined for ever. 2. Nevertheless, it follows from the very separation of our respective townships that just because we are such close friends we are inclined to treat the rarity of our intercourse, which is due to the long stretch of country that lies between us, as a sin on each

in reatum volumus transferre communem, cum de
naturalium rerum difficultate nec culpa nos debeat
manere nec venia. domine inlustris, gerulos litterarum de disciplinae tuae institutione formatos et
morum erilium verecundiam praeferentes opportune admisi, patienter audivi, competenter explicui.
vale.

XII

SIDONIVS AGRICOLAE SVO
SALVTEM

1. Misisti tu quidem lembum mobilem solidum
lecti capacem iamque cum piscibus; tum praeterea
gubernatorem longe peritum, remiges etiam ro-
bustos expeditosque, qui scilicet ea rapiditate
praetervolant amnis adversi terga qua deflui. sed
dabis veniam quod invitanti tibi in piscationem comes
venire dissimulo; namque me multo decumbentibus
nostris validiora maeroris retia tenent, quae sunt
amicis quaeque et externis indolescenda. unde te
quoque puto, si rite germano moveris adfectu, quo
temporis puncto paginam hanc sumpseris, de reditu
potius cogitaturum. 2. Severiana, sollicitudo communis, inquietata primum lentae tussis impulsu
febribus quoque iam fatigatur, hisque per noctes
ingravescentibus; propter quod optat exire in
suburbanum; litteras tuas denique cum sumeremus,

---

* On Agricola see introductory n. to I. 2. Severiana (§ 2)
was the daughter of Sidonius. This letter was probably written
at Lyons.

other's part, although when it is a case of natural obstacles we cannot rightly be the objects either of blame or of forgiveness. Illustrious lord, the bearers of your letters, men trained according to the principles of your system and displaying the modesty characteristic of their master, were admitted by me with due promptitude; I listened to them patiently and dispatched their business suitably. Farewell.

XII

SIDONIUS TO HIS DEAR AGRICOLA, GREETING *

1. You have sent me a boat which is swift and substantial, big enough to hold a couch and a load of fish too; also a boatman of wide experience and oarsmen so strong and brisk that they fly over the surface of the water as swiftly up-stream as down-stream. But you must excuse me for not availing myself of your invitation to join you in a fishing excursion; for with illness in our family I am held here by a much stronger kind of net, a net of affliction, which must needs bring grief to friends and strangers alike: so I think that if you feel a genuine brotherly affection for me, as soon as ever you take up this sheet you will think rather of returning here. 2. Severiana, our common anxiety, was in the first instance racked by an attack of persistent coughing, and is now beginning to suffer severely from bouts of fever as well, which become more acute at night; so she is anxious to move to our home outside the town; in fact, at the very moment that I took your letter in my hand we

471

egredi ad villulam iam parabamus. quocirca tu
seu venias seu moreris, preces nostras orationibus
iuva ut ruris auram desideranti salubriter cedat
ipsa vegetatio. certe ego vel tua soror inter spem
metumque suspensi credidimus eius taedium augen-
dum si voluntati iacentis obstitissemus. 3. igitur
ardori civitatis atque torpori tam nos quam domum
totam praevio Christo pariter eximimus simulque
medicorum consilia vitamus assidentum dissidentum-
que, qui parum docti et satis seduli languidos multos
officiosissime occidunt. sane contubernio nostro
iure amicitiae Iustus adhibebitur, quem, si iocari
liberet in tristibus, facile convincerem Chironica
magis institutum arte quam Machaonica. quo
diligentius postulandus est Christus obsecrandus-
que ut valetudini, cuius curationem cura nostra
non invenit, potentia superna medeatur. vale.

XIII

SIDONIVS SERRANO SVO
SALVTEM

1. Epistulam tuam nobis Marcellinus togatus
exhibuit, homo peritus virque amicorum. quae

---

[1] Possibly veterinary medicine, with which the name of
Chiron was specially associated in late Roman times; opposed
to *Machaonica ars*, human medicine, from Machaon, physician
of the Greeks in the Trojan war; but there may be a play on
the Greek χείρων, "worse": "the art of making worse."

were making preparations to move to our little country house. Accordingly, whether you come here or stay away, support my prayers by your own petitions that as she pines for the country air even the motion of the journey may turn out for the good of her health. Anyhow, both your sister and I, though wavering between hope and fear, believed that our patient's discomfort would certainly be increased if we opposed her inclination. 3. Therefore (under Christ's guidance) we are taking ourselves and our whole household away from the heat and the oppressiveness of the city, and at the same time escaping from the counsels of the physicians, who attend and contend at the bedside; for with their scanty knowledge and immense zeal they most dutifully kill many sick folks. Justus indeed will be admitted to our household by his claim as a personal friend, though if one had been inclined to jest in sad circumstances, I should easily have proved to you that he is better trained in the art of Chiron [1] than in that of Machaon. So we must the more earnestly make our appeal to Christ and beseech Him that, as our diligence has procured no cure for the patient's malady, the power that is from above may cure it. Farewell.

XIII

SIDONIUS TO HIS FRIEND SERRANUS, GREETING *

1. Marcellinus [2] the advocate, a man of tried wisdom and of many friends, showed me your letter.

---

* Serranus is otherwise unknown.
[2] See *Carm.* 23. 465.

primoribus verbis salutatione libata reliquo sui
tractu, qui quidem grandis est, patroni tui Petronii
Maximi imperatoris laudes habebat; quem tamen
tu pertinacius aut amabilius quam rectius veriusque
felicissimum appellas, propter hoc quippe, cur per
amplissimos fascium titulos fuerit evectus usque
ad imperium. sed sententiae tali numquam ego
assentior, ut fortunatos putem qui rei publicae
praecipitibus ac lubricis culminibus insistunt.
2. nam dici nequit quantum per horas fert in hac
vita miseriarum vita felicium istorum, si tamen sic
sunt pronuntiandi qui sibi hoc nomen ut Sulla
praesumunt, nimirum qui supergressi ius fasque
commune summam beatitudinem existimant summam potestatem, hoc ipso satis miseriores, quod
parum intellegunt inquietissimo se subiacere famula-
tui. nam sicut hominibus reges, ita regibus domin-
andi desideria dominantur. 3. hic si omittamus
antecedentium principum casus vel secutorum,
solus iste peculiaris tuus Maximus maximo nobis
ad ista documento poterit esse, qui quamquam in
arcem praefectoriam patriciam consularemque in-
trepidus ascenderat eosque quos gesserat magistratus
ceu recurrentibus orbitis inexpletus iteraverat, cum
tamen venit omnibus viribus ad principalis apicis
abruptum, quandam potestatis immensae vertiginem
sub corona patiebatur nec sustinebat dominus esse,

In its opening it lightly conveys a greeting, and then for the rest of its length (which is considerable) it contains the praises of your protector, the Emperor Petronius Maximus,[1] to whom, with more persistency or kindliness than justice or truth, you give the title of Most Happy, your reason being that he made his way up through all the most distinguished magisterial offices and finally reached the Imperial throne. But I can never agree with the view that counts as prosperous those who stand on the precipitous and slippery heights of public life. 2. For it is beyond the power of words to tell of the miseries which are endured every hour, life being what it is to-day, in the lives of these so-called happy men—if indeed they have any right to be so called when they appropriate this title in the spirit of a Sulla as men who have transgressed the universal principles of law and right and who consider supreme power to be supreme bliss, when all the while they are particularly wretched just because they fail to see that they are subject to a most harassing servitude. For as kings rule over men, so does the passion for mastery rule over kings. 3. Even if we here ignore the calamities of the rulers who preceded or succeeded him, this very Maximus whom you take as your hero will prove our point with the maximum of cogency; for although he had made his way up without faltering to the eminences of prefect, patrician and consul, and although, still unsatisfied, he had repeated the magistracies he had held as if they moved in recurring orbits, yet when by straining every nerve he reached the precarious peak of Imperial majesty, he felt beneath his crown dizziness, the result of boundless power; and the very man who had found it unbearable

qui non sustinuerat esse sub domino. 4. denique
require in supradicto vitae prioris gratiam potentiam
diuturnitatem eque diverso principatus paulo amplius
quam bimenstris originem turbinem finem : profecto
invenies hominem beatiorem prius fuisse quam
beatissimus nominaretur. igitur ille, cuius anterius
epulae mores, pecuniae pompae, litterae fasces,
patrimonia patrocinia florebant, cuius ipsa sic denique spatia vitae custodiebantur ut per horarum
disposita clepsydras explicarentur, is nuncupatus
Augustus ac sub hac specie Palatinis liminibus
inclusus ante crepusculum ingemuit quod ad vota
pervenerat. cumque mole curarum pristinae quietis
tenere dimensum prohiberetur, veteris actutum
regulae legibus renuntiavit atque perspexit pariter
ire non posse negotium principis et otium senatoris.
5. nec fefellerunt futura maerentem ; namque
cum ceteros aulicos honores tranquillissime per-
currisset, ipsam aulam turbulentissime rexit inter
tumultus militum popularium foederatorum ; quod
et exitus prodidit novus celer acerbus, quem cruen-
tavit Fortunae diu lenocinantis perfidus finis, quae
virum ut scorpios ultima sui parte percussit. dicere
solebat vir litteratus atque ob ingenii merita quaes-

to be under a master could not bear to be a master himself. 4. Now go back over the record of this man again and put in one scale his early life with its popularity, its power, and its long years of enjoyment, and in the other the beginning, the tumult and the ending of a principate which lasted for little more than two months: you will assuredly find that the man was more blest before the time when men spoke of him as Most Blessed. In his earlier life his hospitalities and his character, his wealth and his display, his literary reputation and his magistracies, his estate and his roll of clients, were splendid indeed; the very division of his time was so carefully looked after that it was measured and arranged by the hourly periods of the clock. But when he received the title of Augustus and was imprisoned on this pretence behind the doors of the palace, he groaned before evening that he had reached his ambition. A mass of responsibilities pressed upon him, and he could not maintain the programme of his earlier restful life; he at once abandoned the rules by which he had long regulated his existence, and understood that the business of an emperor and the quiet life of a senator could not go together. 5. His gloomy anticipations did not go unfulfilled, for although he had passed through all the other high offices of the court in peace and quietness, he actually ruled the court with violence, amid risings of the soldiers, the citizens, and the allied peoples; and all this was revealed also by his end, which was strange, swift and bitter: after fortune had long flattered him, her treacherous last act bathed him in blood, for like a scorpion she struck her favourite down with the tail-end. A man of culture who reached the rank

torius, partium certe bonarum pars magna, Fulgentius, ore se ex eius frequenter audisse, cum
perosus pondus imperii veterem securitatem de-
sideraret: " felicem te, Damocles, qui non uno
longius prandio regni necessitatem toleravisti."
6. iste enim, ut legimus, Damocles provincia Siculus,
urbe Syracusanus, familiaris tyranno Dionysio fuit.
qui cum nimiis laudibus bona patroni ut cetera
scilicet inexpertus efferret: " vis," inquit Dionysius,
" hodie saltim in hac mensa bonis meis pariter
ac malis uti?" " libenter," inquit.[1] tunc ille confestim laetum clientem quamquam et attonitum
plebeio tegmine erepto muricis Tyrii seu Tarentini
conchyliato ditat indutu et renidentem gemmis
margaritisque aureo lecto sericatoque toreumati
imponit. 7. cumque pransuro Sardanapallicum in
morem panis daretur e Leontina segete confectus,
insuper dapes cultae ferculis cultioribus apponerentur,
spumarent Falerno gemmae capaces inque crystallis
calerent unguenta glacialibus, huc [2] suffita cinnamo
ac ture cenatio spargeret peregrinos naribus odores
et madescentes nardo capillos circumfusa florum
serta siccarent, coepit supra tergum sic recumbentis
repente vibrari mucro destrictus e lacunaribus, qui

[1] inquam *LN*[1].   [2] huc *LN*[1]: hinc.

---

[1] For the meaning of *toreuma* see n. on I. 2. 6.

of quaestor by virtue of his talents and who himself
played a leading part in the good party (his name is
Fulgentius) used to say that he had often heard
from the man's very lips, when he was disgusted with
the weight of empire and longed for the old tranquillity, the cry : "Happy you, Damocles, who had
not to submit to the obligation of kingship for more
than the duration of a single meal!" 6. Now this
Damocles, as we read, a Sicilian by country and a
Syracusan by citizenship, was an intimate of the
prince Dionysius. When he praised in effusive terms
the happy lot of his patron, having, of course, no
means of knowing the other side of the picture,
Dionysius said to him, "Would you like this very day,
just for the duration of this meal, to enjoy my blessings and my ills alike?" "Willingly," said he. Without wasting a moment Dionysius stripped the humble
robe from the back of his delighted but amazed
vassal, glorified him with a purple-dyed robe of the
mollusc of Tyre or of Tarentum, and set him, all
resplendent with jewels and pearls, on a golden
couch with a silk cover over the bedding.[1]
7. He was preparing to dine in the fashion of Sardanapallus ; bread was handed him baked from the
harvest of Leontini, and choice meats were set before
him on dishes still more choice ; large jewelled cups
foamed with Falernian wine, and warm perfume lay
in icy crystal ; the reek of cinnamon and frankincense
pervaded the dining-hall, wafting foreign scents to
the nostrils ; the encircling garlands of flowers were
drying up the guests' nard-soaked hair. But
suddenly, as he thus reposed, a naked sword which
hung from the panelled ceiling began to shake over
his shoulders, and seemed each moment about to fall

479

videbatur in iugulum purpurati iam iamque ruiturus;
nam filo equinae saetae ligatus et ita pondere minax
ut acumine gulam formidolosi Tantaleo frenabat
exemplo, ne cibi ingressi per ora per vulnera exirent.
8. unde post mixtas fletibus preces atque multimoda suspiria vix absolutus emicatimque prosiliens
illa refugit celeritate divitias deliciasque regales
qua solent appeti, reductus ad desideria mediocrium
timore summorum et satis cavens ne beatum ultra
diceret duceretque qui saeptus armis ac satellitibus
et per hoc raptis incubans opibus ferro pressus premeret aurum. quapropter ad statum huiusmodi,
domine frater, nescio an constet tendere beatos,
patet certe miseros pervenire. vale.

XIV

SIDONIVS MAVRVSIO SVO
SALVTEM

1. Audio industriae tuae votisque communibus
uberiore proventu quam minabatur sterilis annus
respondere vindemiam. unde et in pago Vialoscensi,
qui Martialis aetate citeriore vocitatus est propter
hiberna legionum Iulianarum, suspicor diuturnius

---

* Nothing further is known of Maurusius.
1 Some identify this with Marsat, a village about 12 miles
north of Clermont, others with Volvic, a little to the west of
Marsat.

upon the throat of our man in purple; for it was
fastened only with a thread of horsehair, and being
alarming equally by its weight and by its sharp point
it frustrated the appetite of the scared guest as if
he had been Tantalus, for he feared that the food
that entered by his mouth might find its exit through
a gaping wound. 8. So he mingled prayers and
tears and manifold sighs, and when at last he with
difficulty won his freedom he leapt forth like a flash
and retreated from the wealth and luxury of kingship
with the alacrity with which these are usually sought;
he was drawn back to the desire of a middle position
by his fear of the highest, and was thoroughly warned
for the future against calling or thinking happy the
man who is surrounded by arms and guards, who by
this means keeps jealous watch over the riches he
has seized, and who grips his gold whilst he is in the
grip of cold steel. And so, my lord and brother,
I am not at all clear that those who press forward
to such a position are blessed; but it is certain that
those who reach it are wretched. Farewell.

XIV

SIDONIUS TO HIS FRIEND MAURUSIUS,
GREETING *

1. I hear that the vintage is answering to your
industry and to the prayers of the community with a
richer crop than the barren year threatened; and
so I imagine that you will stay some considerable
time in the Pagus Vialoscensis,[1] which was formerly
called Martialis because it became the winter
quarters of the Julian legions; for in that district you

te moraturum; quo loci tibi cum ferax vinea est, tum praeter ipsam praedium magno non minus domino, quod te tuosque plurifaria frugum mansionumque dote remoretur. 2. ilicet si horreis apothecisque seu penu impleta destinas illic usque ad adventum hirundineum vel ciconinum Iani Numaeque ninguidos menses in otio fuliginoso sive tunicata quiete transmittere, nobis quoque parum in oppido fructuosae protinus amputabuntur causae morarum, ut, dum ipse nimirum frueris rure, nos te fruamur, quibus, ut recognoscis, non magis cordi est aut voluptati ager cum reditibus amplis quam vicinus aequalis cum bonis moribus.   vale.

have not only a fertile vineyard but also a farm which
is as great as is its great owner, to keep hold of you
and your company by its manifold endowment of grain
and dwelling-places. 2. Well then, if it is your
intention, when your barns, storehouses and household stores have been duly replenished, to spend the
snowy months of Janus and Numa[1] there in sooty
idleness or " ungowned ease,"[2] remaining until the
coming of the swallow and the stork, I too will at
once cut short my unfruitful excuses for lingering in
town, so that while you, of course, enjoy the fruits
of your land, I at the same time may enjoy the
fruits of your society; for (as you well know) an
estate making large returns is no more attractive
and delightful to me than a neighbour of my own
age and of high character.   Farewell.

[1] January and February.   [2] Martial X. 51. 6.

PRINTED IN GREAT BRITAIN BY
RICHARD CLAY AND COMPANY, LTD.,
BUNGAY, SUFFOLK.

THE LOEB CLASSICAL LIBRARY

VOLUMES ALREADY PUBLISHED

Latin Authors

AMMIANUS MARCELLINUS. Translated by J. C. Rolfe. 3 Vols.

APULEIUS: THE GOLDEN ASS (METAMORPHOSES). W. Adlington (1566). Revised by S. Gaselee.

ST. AUGUSTINE: CITY OF GOD. 7 Vols. Vol. I. G. E. McCracken. Vol. VI. W. C. Greene.

ST. AUGUSTINE, CONFESSIONS OF. W. Watts (1631). 2 Vols.

ST. AUGUSTINE, SELECT LETTERS. J. H. Baxter.

AUSONIUS. H. G. Evelyn White. 2 Vols.

BEDE. J. E. King. 2 Vols.

BOETHIUS: TRACTS and DE CONSOLATIONE PHILOSOPHIAE. Rev. H. F. Stewart and E. K. Rand.

CAESAR: ALEXANDRIAN, AFRICAN and SPANISH WARS. A. G. Way.

CAESAR: CIVIL WARS. A. G. Peskett.

CAESAR: GALLIC WAR. H. J. Edwards.

CATO: DE RE RUSTICA; VARRO: DE RE RUSTICA. H. B. Ash and W. D. Hooper.

CATULLUS. F. W. Cornish; TIBULLUS. J. B. Postgate; PERVIGILIUM VENERIS. J. W. Mackail.

CELSUS: DE MEDICINA. W. G. Spencer. 3 Vols.

CICERO: BRUTUS, and ORATOR. G. L. Hendrickson and H. M. Hubbell.

[CICERO]: AD HERENNIUM. H. Caplan.

CICERO: DE ORATORE, etc. 2 Vols. Vol. I. DE ORATORE, Books I. and II. E. W. Sutton and H. Rackham. Vol. II. DE ORATORE, Book III. De Fato; Paradoxa Stoicorum; De Partitione Oratoria. H. Rackham.

CICERO: DE FINIBUS. H. Rackham.

CICERO: DE INVENTIONE, etc. H. M. Hubbell.

CICERO: DE NATURA DEORUM and ACADEMICA. H. Rackham.

CICERO: DE OFFICIIS. Walter Miller.

CICERO: DE REPUBLICA and DE LEGIBUS; SOMNIUM SCIPIONIS. Clinton W. Keyes.

Cicero: De Senectute, De Amicitia, De Divinatione. W. A. Falconer.

Cicero: In Catilinam, Pro Flacco, Pro Murena, Pro Sulla. Louis E. Lord.

Cicero: Letters to Atticus. E. O. Winstedt. 3 Vols.

Cicero: Letters to His Friends. W. Glynn Williams. 3 Vols.

Cicero: Philippics. W. C. A. Ker.

Cicero: Pro Archia Post Reditum, De Domo, De Haruspicum Responsis, Pro Plancio. N. H. Watts.

Cicero: Pro Caecina, Pro Lege Manilia, Pro Cluentio, Pro Rabirio. H. Grose Hodge.

Cicero: Pro Caelio, De Provinciis Consularibus, Pro Balbo. R. Gardner.

Cicero: Pro Milone, In Pisonem, Pro Scauro, Pro Fonteio, Pro Rabirio Postumo, Pro Marcello, Pro Ligario, Pro Rege Deiotaro. N. H. Watts.

Cicero: Pro Quinctio, Pro Roscio Amerino, Pro Roscio Comoedo, Contra Rullum. J. H. Freese.

Cicero: Pro Sestio, In Vatinium. R. Gardner.

Cicero: Tusculan Disputations. J. E. King.

Cicero: Verrine Orations. L. H. G. Greenwood. 2 Vols.

Claudian. M. Platnauer. 2 Vols.

Columella: De Re Rustica. De Arboribus. H. B. Ash, E. S. Forster and E. Heffner. 3 Vols.

Curtius, Q.: History of Alexander. J. C. Rolfe. 2 Vols.

Florus. E. S. Forster; and Cornelius Nepos. J. C. Rolfe.

Frontinus: Stratagems and Aqueducts. C. E. Bennett and M. B. McElwain.

Fronto: Correspondence. C. R. Haines. 2 Vols.

Gellius, J. C. Rolfe. 3 Vols.

Horace: Odes and Epodes. C. E. Bennett.

Horace: Satires, Epistles, Ars Poetica. H. R. Fairclough.

Jerome: Selected Letters. F. A. Wright.

Juvenal and Persius. G. G. Ramsay.

Livy. B. O. Foster, F. G. Moore, Evan T. Sage, and A. C. Schlesinger and R. M. Geer (General Index). 14 Vols.

Lucan. J. D. Duff.

Lucretius. W. H. D. Rouse.

Martial. W. C. A. Ker. 2 Vols.

Minor Latin Poets: from Publilius Syrus to Rutilius Namatianus, including Grattius, Calpurnius Siculus, Nemesianus, Avianus, and others with " Aetna " and the " Phoenix." J. Wight Duff and Arnold M. Duff.

Ovid: The Art of Love and Other Poems. J. H. Mozley.

OVID: FASTI. Sir James G. Frazer.

OVID: HEROIDES and AMORES. Grant Showerman.

OVID: METAMORPHOSES. F. J. Miller. 2 Vols.

OVID: TRISTIA and EX PONTO. A. L. Wheeler.

PERSIUS. Cf. JUVENAL.

PETRONIUS. M. Heseltine; SENECA; APOCOLOCYNTOSIS. W. H. D. Rouse.

PLAUTUS. Paul Nixon. 5 Vols.

PLINY: LETTERS. Melmoth's Translation revised by W. M. L. Hutchinson. 2 Vols.

PLINY: NATURAL HISTORY.
10 Vols. Vols. I.–V. and IX. H. Rackham. Vols. VI.– VIII. W. H. S. Jones. Vol. X. D. E. Eichholz.

PROPERTIUS. H. E. Butler.

PRUDENTIUS. H. J. Thomson. 2 Vols.

QUINTILIAN. H. E. Butler. 4 Vols.

REMAINS OF OLD LATIN. E. H. Warmington. 4 Vols. Vol. I. (ENNIUS AND CAECILIUS.) Vol. II. (LIVIUS, NAEVIUS, PACUVIUS, ACCIUS.) Vol. III. (LUCILIUS and LAWS OF XII TABLES.) Vol. IV. (ARCHAIC INSCRIPTIONS.)

SALLUST. J. C. Rolfe.

SCRIPTORES HISTORIAE AUGUSTAE. D. Magie. 3 Vols.

SENECA: APOCOLOCYNTOSIS. Cf. PETRONIUS.

SENECA: EPISTULAE MORALES. R. M. Gummere. 3 Vols.

SENECA: MORAL ESSAYS. J. W. Basore. 3 Vols.

SENECA: TRAGEDIES. F. J. Miller. 2 Vols.

SIDONIUS: POEMS and LETTERS. W. B. ANDERSON. 2 Vols.

SILIUS ITALICUS. J. D. Duff. 2 Vols.

STATIUS. J. H. Mozley. 2 Vols.

SUETONIUS. J. C. Rolfe. 2 Vols.

TACITUS: DIALOGUES. Sir Wm. Peterson. AGRICOLA and GERMANIA. Maurice Hutton.

TACITUS: HISTORIES AND ANNALS. C. H. Moore and J. Jackson. 4 Vols.

TERENCE. John Sargeaunt. 2 Vols.

TERTULLIAN: APOLOGIA and DE SPECTACULIS. T. R. Glover. MINUCIUS FELIX. G. H. Rendall.

VALERIUS FLACCUS. J. H. Mozley.

VARRO: DE LINGUA LATINA. R. G. Kent. 2 Vols.

VELLEIUS PATERCULUS and RES GESTAE DIVI AUGUSTI. F. W. Shipley.

VIRGIL. H. R. Fairclough. 2 Vols.

VITRUVIUS: DE ARCHITECTURA. F. Granger. 2 Vols.

Greek Authors

ACHILLES TATIUS. S. Gaselee.

AELIAN: ON THE NATURE OF ANIMALS. A. F. Scholfield. 3 Vols.

AENEAS TACTICUS, ASCLEPIODOTUS and ONASANDER. The Illinois Greek Club.

AESCHINES. C. D. Adams.

AESCHYLUS. H. Weir Smyth. 2 Vols.

ALCIPHRON, AELIAN, PHILOSTRATUS: LETTERS. A. R. Benner and F. H. Fobes.

ANDOCIDES, ANTIPHON, Cf. MINOR ATTIC ORATORS.

APOLLODORUS. Sir James G. Frazer. 2 Vols.

APOLLONIUS RHODIUS. R. C. Seaton.

THE APOSTOLIC FATHERS. Kirsopp Lake. 2 Vols.

APPIAN: ROMAN HISTORY. Horace White. 4 Vols.

ARATUS. Cf. CALLIMACHUS.

ARISTOPHANES. Benjamin Bickley Rogers. 3 Vols. Verse trans.

ARISTOTLE: ART OF RHETORIC. J. H. Freese.

ARISTOTLE: ATHENIAN CONSTITUTION, EUDEMIAN ETHICS, VICES AND VIRTUES. H. Rackham.

ARISTOTLE: GENERATION OF ANIMALS. A. L. Peck.

ARISTOTLE: METAPHYSICS. H. Tredennick. 2 Vols.

ARISTOTLE: METEOROLOGICA. H. D. P. Lee.

ARISTOTLE: MINOR WORKS. W. S. Hett. On Colours, On Things Heard, On Physiognomies, On Plants, On Marvellous Things Heard, Mechanical Problems, On Indivisible Lines, On Situations and Names of Winds, On Melissus, Xenophanes, and Gorgias.

ARISTOTLE: NICOMACHEAN ETHICS. H. Rackham.

ARISTOTLE: OECONOMICA and MAGNA MORALIA. G. C. Armstrong; (with Metaphysics, Vol. II.).

ARISTOTLE: ON THE HEAVENS. W. K. C. Guthrie.

ARISTOTLE: ON THE SOUL. PARVA NATURALIA. ON BREATH. W. S. Hett.

ARISTOTLE: CATEGORIES, ON INTERPRETATION, PRIOR ANALYTICS. H. P. Cooke and H. Tredennick.

ARISTOTLE: POSTERIOR ANALYTICS, TOPICS. H. Tredennick and E. S. Forster.

ARISTOTLE: ON SOPHISTICAL REFUTATIONS.
On Coming to be and Passing Away, On the Cosmos. E. S. Forster and D. J. Furley.

ARISTOTLE: PARTS OF ANIMALS. A. L. Peck; MOTION AND PROGRESSION OF ANIMALS. E. S. Forster.

ARISTOTLE: PHYSICS. Rev. P. Wicksteed and F. M. Cornford. 2 Vols.

ARISTOTLE: POETICS and LONGINUS. W. Hamilton Fyfe; DEMETRIUS ON STYLE. W. Rhys Roberts.

ARISTOTLE: POLITICS. H. Rackham.

ARISTOTLE: PROBLEMS. W. S. Hett. 2 Vols.

ARISTOTLE: RHETORICA AD ALEXANDRUM (with PROBLEMS. Vol. II.) H. Rackham.

ARRIAN: HISTORY OF ALEXANDER and INDICA. Rev. E. Iliffe Robson. 2 Vols.

ATHENAEUS: DEIPNOSOPHISTAE. C. B. GULICK. 7 Vols.

ST. BASIL: LETTERS. R. J. Deferrari. 4 Vols.

CALLIMACHUS: FRAGMENTS. C. A. Trypanis.

CALLIMACHUS, Hymns and Epigrams, and LYCOPHRON. A. W. Mair; ARATUS. G. R. MAIR.

CLEMENT of ALEXANDRIA. Rev. G. W. Butterworth.

COLLUTHUS. Cf. OPPIAN.

DAPHNIS AND CHLOE. Thornley's Translation revised by J. M. Edmonds; and PARTHENIUS. S. Gaselee.

DEMOSTHENES I.: OLYNTHIACS, PHILIPPICS and MINOR ORATIONS. I.–XVII. AND XX. J. H. Vince.

DEMOSTHENES II.: DE CORONA and DE FALSA LEGATIONE. C. A. Vince and J. H. Vince.

DEMOSTHENES III.: MEIDIAS, ANDROTION, ARISTOCRATES, TIMOCRATES and ARISTOGEITON, I. AND II. J. H. Vince.

DEMOSTHENES IV.–VI.: PRIVATE ORATIONS and IN NEAERAM. A. T. Murray.

DEMOSTHENES VII.: FUNERAL SPEECH, EROTIC ESSAY, EXORDIA and LETTERS. N. W. and N. J. DeWitt.

DIO CASSIUS: ROMAN HISTORY. E. Cary. 9 Vols.

DIO CHRYSOSTOM. J. W. Cohoon and H. Lamar Crosby. 5 Vols.

DIODORUS SICULUS. 12 Vols. Vols. I.–VI. C. H. Oldfather. Vol. VII. C. L. Sherman. Vol. VIII. C. B. Welles. Vols. IX. and X. R. M. Geer. Vol. XI. F. Walton.

DIOGENES LAERTIUS. R. D. Hicks. 2 Vols.

DIONYSIUS OF HALICARNASSUS: ROMAN ANTIQUITIES. Spelman's translation revised by E. Cary. 7 Vols.

EPICTETUS. W. A. Oldfather. 2 Vols.

EURIPIDES. A. S. Way. 4 Vols. Verse trans.

EUSEBIUS: ECCLESIASTICAL HISTORY. Kirsopp Lake and J. E. L. Oulton. 2 Vols.

GALEN: ON THE NATURAL FACULTIES. A. J. Brock.

THE GREEK ANTHOLOGY. W. R. Paton. 5 Vols.

GREEK ELEGY AND IAMBUS with the ANACREONTEA. J. M. Edmonds. 2 Vols.

THE GREEK BUCOLIC POETS (THEOCRITUS, BION, MOSCHUS). J. M. Edmonds.

GREEK MATHEMATICAL WORKS. Ivor Thomas. 2 Vols.

HERODES. Cf. THEOPHRASTUS: CHARACTERS.

HERODOTUS. A. D. Godley. 4 Vols.

HESIOD AND THE HOMERIC HYMNS. H. G. Evelyn White.

HIPPOCRATES and the FRAGMENTS OF HERACLEITUS. W. H. S. Jones and E. T. Withington. 4 Vols.

HOMER: ILIAD. A. T. Murray. 2 Vols.

HOMER: ODYSSEY. A. T. Murray. 2 Vols.

ISAEUS. E. W. Forster.

ISOCRATES. George Norlin and LaRue Van Hook. 3 Vols.

ST. JOHN DAMASCENE: BARLAAM AND IOASAPH. Rev. G. R. Woodward and Harold Mattingly.

JOSEPHUS. 9 Vols. Vols. I.–IV.; H. Thackeray. Vol. V.; H. Thackeray and R. Marcus. Vols. VI.–VII.; R. Marcus. Vol. VIII.; R. Marcus and Allen Wikgren.

JULIAN. Wilmer Cave Wright. 3 Vols.

LUCIAN. 8 Vols. Vols. I.–V. A. M. Harmon. Vol. VI. K. Kilburn. Vol. VII. M. D. Macleod.

LYCOPHRON. Cf. CALLIMACHUS.

LYRA GRAECA. J. M. Edmonds. 3 Vols.

LYSIAS. W. R. M. Lamb.

MANETHO. W. G. Waddell: PTOLEMY: TETRABIBLOS. F. E. Robbins.

MARCUS AURELIUS. C. R. Haines.

MENANDER. F. G. Allinson.

MINOR ATTIC ORATORS (ANTIPHON, ANDOCIDES, LYCURGUS, DEMADES, DINARCHUS, HYPERIDES). K. J. Maidment and J. O. Burrt. 2 Vols.

NONNOS: DIONYSIACA. W. H. D. Rouse. 3 Vols.

OPPIAN, COLLUTHUS, TRYPHIODORUS. A. W. Mair.

PAPYRI. NON-LITERARY SELECTIONS. A. S. Hunt and C. C. Edgar. 2 Vols. LITERARY SELECTIONS (Poetry). D. L. Page.

PARTHENIUS. Cf. DAPHNIS and CHLOE.

PAUSANIAS: DESCRIPTION OF GREECE. W. H. S. Jones. 4 Vols. and Companion Vol. arranged by R. E. Wycherley.

PHILO. 10 Vols. Vols. I.–V.; F. H. Colson and Rev. G. H. Whitaker. Vols. VI.–IX.; F. H. Colson. Vol. X. F. H. Colson and the Rev. J. W. Earp.

PHILO: two supplementary Vols. (*Translation only.*) Ralph Marcus.

PHILOSTRATUS: THE LIFE OF APOLLONIUS OF TYANA. F. C. Conybeare. 2 Vols.

PHILOSTRATUS: IMAGINES; CALLISTRATUS: DESCRIPTIONS. A. Fairbanks.

PHILOSTRATUS and EUNAPIUS: LIVES OF THE SOPHISTS. Wilmer Cave Wright.

PINDAR. Sir J. E. Sandys.

PLATO: CHARMIDES, ALCIBIADES, HIPPARCHUS, THE LOVERS, THEAGES, MINOS and EPINOMIS. W. R. M. Lamb.

PLATO: CRATYLUS, PARMENIDES, GREATER HIPPIAS, LESSER HIPPIAS. H. N. Fowler.

PLATO: EUTHYPHRO, APOLOGY, CRITO, PHAEDO, PHAEDRUS. H. N. Fowler.

PLATO: LACHES, PROTAGORAS, MENO, EUTHYDEMUS. W. R. M. Lamb.

PLATO: LAWS. Rev. R. G. Bury. 2 Vols.

PLATO: LYSIS, SYMPOSIUM, GORGIAS. W. R. M. Lamb.

PLATO: REPUBLIC. Paul Shorey. 2 Vols.

PLATO: STATESMAN, PHILEBUS. H. N. Fowler; ION. W. R. M. Lamb.

PLATO: THEAETETUS and SOPHIST. H. N. Fowler.

PLATO: TIMAEUS, CRITIAS, CLITOPHO, MENEXENUS, EPISTULAE. Rev. R. G. Bury.

PLUTARCH: MORALIA. 15 Vols. Vols. I.–V. F. C. Babbitt. Vol. VI. W. C. Helmbold. Vol. VII. P. H. De Lacy and B. Einarson. Vol. IX. E. L. Minar, Jr., F. H. Sandbach, W. C. Helmbold. Vol. X. H. N. Fowler. Vol. XII. H. Cherniss and W. C. Helmbold.

PLUTARCH: THE PARALLEL LIVES. B. Perrin. 11 Vols.

POLYBIUS. W. R. Paton. 6 Vols.

PROCOPIUS: HISTORY OF THE WARS. H. B. Dewing. 7 Vols.

PTOLEMY: TETRABIBLOS. Cf. MANETHO.

QUINTUS SMYRNAEUS. A. S. Way. Verse trans.

SEXTUS EMPIRICUS. Rev. R. G. Bury. 4 Vols.

SOPHOCLES. F. Storr. 2 Vols. Verse trans.

STRABO: GEOGRAPHY. Horace L. Jones. 8 Vols.

THEOPHRASTUS: CHARACTERS. J. M. Edmonds. HERODES, etc. A. D. Knox.

THEOPHRASTUS: ENQUIRY INTO PLANTS. Sir Arthur Hort, Bart. 2 Vols.

THUCYDIDES. C. F. Smith. 4 Vols.

TRYPHIODORUS. Cf. OPPIAN.

XENOPHON: CYROPAEDIA. Walter Miller. 2 Vols.

XENOPHON: HELLENICA, ANABASIS, APOLOGY, and SYMPOSIUM. C. L. Brownson and O. J. Todd. 3 Vols.

XENOPHON: MEMORABILIA and OECONOMICUS. E. C. Marchant.

XENOPHON: SCRIPTA MINORA. E. C. Marchant.

IN PREPARATION

ARISTOTLE: HISTORIA ANIMALIUM **(Greek).** A. L. Peck.
PLOTINUS **(Greek).** A. H. Armstrong.
BABRIUS **(Greek)** AND PHAEDRUS **(Latin).** Ben E. Perry.

DESCRIPTIVE PROSPECTUS ON APPLICATION

London   WILLIAM HEINEMANN LTD
Cambridge, Mass.   HARVARD UNIVERSITY PRESS